BETWEEN HEAVEN AND
CHARING CROSS

Portrait of Francis Thompson by John Lavelle, based on the sketch by Neville Lytton

BETWEEN HEAVEN
and
CHARING CROSS

The Life of Francis Thompson

Brigid M. Boardman

Yale University Press
New Haven and London
1988

Designed by Ann Grindrod

Library of Congress CIP Data

Boardman, Brigid M., 1931–
   Between heaven and Charing Cross.

   Bibliography: p.
   Includes index.
   1. Thompson, Francis, 1859–1907.   2. Poets, English—19th century—Biography. I. Title.
PR5651.B64 1988   821'.8 [B]   87-37243
ISBN 0-300-04143-8

Set 11/12 pt Baskerville by Best-set Typesetter Limited, Hong Kong, and printed and bound in Great Britain at The University Printing House, Oxford.

This book is dedicated to

the three Elizabeths

without whom it could not have been written:

Elizabeth Cartwright Hignett
Elizabeth Hawkins
Elizabeth Countess of Longford

The angels keep their ancient places: —
Turn but a stone, and start a wing'
'Tis ye, 'tis your estranged faces,
That miss the many-splendoured thing.

But (when so sad thou canst not sadder)
Cry; — and upon thy so sore loss
Shall shine the traffic of Jacob's ladder
Pitched between Heaven and Charing Cross.

'The Kingdom of God: In No Strange Land'

Contents

Illustrations

Introduction

Almost from the start of his life as a poet, Francis Thompson saw himself as one who would be understood by a future generation rather than his own. In his later years the belief amounted to a conviction, leading him to confide in one of his private notebooks:

> For me to write or speak at all is to resign myself to the knowledge that I am, in the present, addressing very few. It would be almost impossible, because quite futile, for me to write were I not convinced that the few will one day be the many.[1]

It is one of several similar entries on the limitations of his own age in recognizing the aim behind his work, which he describes here as 'a pregnant & familiar sense of a world within the world seen of eye & touched of hand'. Elsewhere he wrote of his aim as an incarnation of the spiritual world within temporal reality and it is primarily in this context that his poetry can be appreciated today to an extent that at least partly fulfils his expectations.

But there is something else that can now be appreciated which he could not foresee. The relationship between his work and his own life is in fact more revealing than anything contained in the poetry alone. The two together can now reveal not only his aim as he saw it but in addition, the reasons for his inability to convey it in his own time and for the long delay before the truth about himself and his work could be recognized.

In both these respects there was a turning-point in his life on which his whole future and reputation were to depend. It came when at the age of twenty-nine he met Wilfrid Meynell after three years' destitution on the London Streets. It was a dramatic moment, the direct cause for the awakening of his life as a poet no less than for his physical survival.

The reason for anticipating it at the outset is that the long term effects on Thompson's life as both man and poet have continued down to the present. In the years following his death Wilfrid and Alice Meynell were responsible for the earliest observations on his life and for the preservation of his unpublished writings. Their recollections then formed the basis of the biography by their son Everard, who had known Thompson almost as well as his parents did during the poet's later years. Some mention of the part played by the Meynells in Thompson's life and their influence on his work is essential in order to account for the many references to their own writings and views on him in the chapters on his life before that first meeting.

It is equally essential in accounting for the preservation of his work and more particularly the unpublished manuscripts and notebooks. When, in his will, he left all he possessed to Wilfrid Meynell it was the final seal on a unique friendship of over twenty years. Not that it could have appeared anything of the kind when the dingy lodgings were cleared after his death. Apart from a box of old pipes, pens and pencils and a spirit lamp and stove there was only the toy theatre with which he had played as a child.

But there was something else. Before he left for the hospital where he knew he was to die, Francis stuffed all the papers lying around his room into a battered tin trunk already filled with a store of papers, the extent and nature of which no one but himself was aware. And this was a bequest that was at last to reward his benefactor for a lifetime's concern for his welfare. There was almost forty years' accumulation of manuscripts and letters along with over a hundred closely filled notebooks. Most are exercise books of cheap paper generally sold at a penny each, their blue or beige covers embellished with words such as the 'Giant' or the 'Prodigious' in swirling letters. Or they are the smaller, mainly black, shiny-covered notebooks intended for office or household use. In these Francis recorded his thoughts and ideas as well as the drafts for much of his poetry and other writings. They are as erratic and as lacking in any consistent time sequence as his attitude to the practical affairs of life. To be familiar with these papers is to be more closely in touch with the personality behind them than could ever be deduced from his published work alone.

It is clear from these notebooks that during his lifetime Francis made many alterations in the drafts of both the poetry and prose before publication and that he wrote much which he chose not to print. Subsequently, a great deal was printed, the editing shared between Meynell and his Jesuit friend Terence L. Connolly of Boston College, Massachusetts. The outcome was the handing over of the bulk of the notebooks and other manuscripts to be housed in the College Library. Materially speaking, therefore, the Francis Thompson Collection has been very well preserved. This is all the more important as many of the contents are so fragile that, without professional care, they could not remain legible for long and a few are already faded beyond reprieve.

By today's standards the editing performed by Meynell and Connolly is indefensible. They felt free to make omissions, deletions and alterations, often in order to print a poem as complete but which is clearly unfinished in the drafts. When Connolly published *The Man has Wings*, a collection of poetry taken from the Boston College manuscripts, he explained that the version printed 'appears to be the one of

Thompson's preference'.[2] But the process is generally arbitrary and in many cases it is impossible to tell which, if any, of several drafts Thompson would have chosen to complete. In addition, his decision not to complete most of them shows he did not regard them as more than poetic experiments. As printed by Connolly, very few do anything for his poetic reputation and most actually detract from it. Again, in Connolly's collections of the prose writings as in Meynell's edition in the third volume of the *Works*, there is no explanation given for omissions and deletions.

Their treatment of the manuscripts has to be seen in relation to the period. Both regarded themselves as called on to uphold the acclaim they had gained for Francis in Catholic circles. For this reason the official condemnation of Catholic Modernism by the Church at the time led them to suppress any hint of unorthodoxy in his life or writings. Alice Meynell shared their view. 'He is orthodox through and through' she asserted, and Catholic theology 'might be reconstructed from his poetry'.[3] Nor must there be any association between his reputation and the 'decadent' poets of the 'nineties — the more important since his opium addiction was already well known. So when the last major transfer of his papers to Boston College was being completed Wilfrid Meynell made the condition that anything 'unpleasant' in either sense should be burned.[4] It is impossible now to tell how much may have been destroyed. Yet there is more than enough which when taken with Thompson's life and work as a whole calls for a reappraisal of the image of the pious Catholic poet created by the Meynells and Connolly and carried on by those who followed their lead.

It has not been the only image. Inevitably, there was a reaction, strengthened by changing attitudes towards religion and poetry. By the middle of the present century Thompson was being noticed chiefly on account of his opium addiction, identified with the 'decadents' who were his contemporaries. The reaction and the image it produced are best represented by his last English biographer J. C. Reid, for whom his poetry is with few exceptions a 'substitute for opium fantasies' and so 'has already faded, and is unlikely ever to awaken interest again'.[5] Reid's conclusions are not without ambivalence. He has to admit in places to a certain power in the poetry and strength of character in the personality that do not fit in with his overall assessment. But it is the overall view that has been taken up by the reviewers and carried further since. The *Times Literary Supplement* maintained that the religious developments of the twentieth century have left Thompson far behind with 'his sentimental and somewhat invalid mystical pronouncements'.[6] According to Geoffrey Grigson, the biography by Reid has shown its subject to have been a victim

. . . of that process by which a poet of Thompson's kind is canonized for a time — among the credulous who have only a poetic criterion for poetry. Thompson required an early death and a tale of opium and rags. Both were supplied and the sales of his rubbish rocketed year by year.

But not now. For, says Grigson, today even 'The Hound of Heaven' can be seen as the 'wild half-digested gush' of a personality dominated by the 'indolence and self-delusion of the drug addict'.[7] Although a few voices were raised in protest, Grigson has since been echoed by Professor B. Ifor Evans who in his study of nineteenth-century poetry has little time and no patience for Thompson's 'trailing draperies of fustian rhetoric'.[8]

In America John Walsh has gone some way towards diminishing both images, largely through his use of the notebooks and other manuscripts. But his chief concern in with the emotional and psychological aspects of Thompson's life and he has used them mainly to this end.[9]

The aim, therefore, of the present reappraisal is to set aside the earlier views and by listening to Thompson's own voice speaking through his poetry and prose, whether published or unpublished, to recreate the real personality and the real poet. By doing so in relation to the people and events that shaped his life and his poetry, it will be evident that both the man and the poet have a fuller claim to our attention today than has so far been recognised.

The Francis Thompson Collection at Boston College now comprises 297 separate manuscripts of which 246 are poetry and 51 are prose, together with 121 notebooks. The notebooks are numbered in two distinct series, one prefixed by the letters BC. This series consists of notebooks with no number when acquired by the College, whereas the other series contains those already numbered, and these numbers have been retained. In both series the sequence bears no relation to the order in which Thompson used them. Dating has to be mainly by internal evidence as he often made entries in the same notebook at different periods of his life. The only ones that can be given more definite dates are the 'Ushaw College Notebook', the 'Notebook of Early Poems', the ones in use while he was on the London streets and those kept during his last years.

There are still some notebooks and manuscripts in the possession of the Meynell family at Greatham, Sussex, together with important letters connected with Thompson's life and work. The other main collection outside Boston College is at the Harris Library, Preston. There are smaller collections in the Ushaw College archives, the Library of the State University of New York, Buffalo, the Lilly Library, Indiana

University and the Harry Ransom Research Centre, Austin, Texas. Some manuscripts and letters connected with Thompson form part of the Francis Meynell Collection at the University Library, Cambridge. Lastly, another minor collection was recently bequeathed to the Bryn Mawr College Library, Philadelphia, by Seymour Adelman, Including his correspondence with Wilfrid Meynell. Almost all Thompson's surviving letters are now at Boston College and have been published in an excellent edition by John Walsh.

I have taken two liberties in quoting from the notebooks and other manuscripts. From his College days onwards Thompson invariably replaced 'the' with 'ye' or 'y' in his drafts for both poetry and prose and all his personal memoranda. In order to avoid undue attention being drawn to this idiosyncrasy at the expense of other more important aspects of his writing, I have kept to the customary form. Secondly, in drafts at all stages of composition in poetry and prose he hardly ever erased an alternative rendering of a word or phrase but listed them, sometimes as many as six of seven, one above another. As this can appear several times in one draft I have either used the form appearing in a published text or, where there is no such text, I have had to make a choice, when necessary adding a note on the variants. On p. 344 there is an example of his method of poetic composition but it is considerably simpler than the majority of his drafts.

Quotations from the published poetry, unless otherwise stated, are from the edition by Connolly. The two volumes of poetry in Wilfrid Meynell's edition of Thompson's *Works* contain numerous errors and deletions which have been repeated in the subsequent collections. For details of these editions see the Bibliography and List of Abbreviations.

Acknowledgements

In the first place I wish to thank the British Academy, the Leverhulme Trust and the Marc Fitch Fund for grants enabling me to make several visits to Boston College and to places in England connected with Thompson and his writings.

In my Dedication I have acknowledged my gratitude to Wilfrid Meynell's granddaughter Elizabeth Hawkins for her hospitality and personal interest and here I also wish to thank her and the Meynell family for permission to make full use of papers and manuscripts in their possession.

I have special pleasure in acknowledging the permission to use and quote from the Francis Thompson Collection at Boston College, Massachussetts. Members of the College as well as the Library staff have not only provided me with the practical help I have needed but also given their support and interest over nearly ten years. In particular I would like to thank Revd. Charles F. Donovan, S. J., the College Historian, whose initial encouragement has remained constant during these years.

Other libraries and institutions have given me much useful assistance. Here I wish to acknowledge permission to quote from papers and manuscripts in the Adelman Collection, Bryn Mawr College Library, Pennsylvania: the Poetry and Rare Books Collection in the University Library, State University of New York, Buffalo: the Lancashire Library, Preston District: the archives of the Ushaw College Library: and from the Francis Meynell papers in the possession of the Syndics of Cambridge University Library.

For assistance of a more general kind I would also like to thank the members and staff of the London Library: the Catholic Central Library: the City of Bath Reference Library: the Central Library, Bristol: the Bristol Record Office: the Medical Library, Bristol University: the Central Library and the University Library, Manchester: and the Wellcome Institute for the History of Medicine. In addition I have received generous help and advice from the Society of Authors.

The Guardian and Community of the Franciscan Friary, Pantasaph, have given valuable information: also the White Canons of the Praemonstratensian Priory, Storrington. In the course of my research I have received hospitality on several occasions from the Superior and Community of the Mount Alvernia Franciscan Convent, Chestnut Hill, Massachussetts: and from the Superior and Community of the Convent of the Holy Child, Preston.

Special thanks are due to Nicholas A. Lee for providing the index and for both reading the original manuscript and photocopying the finished one. I also wish to thank the staff of 'Imprint' for prompt and efficient photocopying carried out over the years. Grateful thanks also to Ralph Coffman for assistance in providing photographic material.

My Dedication makes clear the great debt I owe to Lady Longford and to Elizabeth Cartwright Hignett. I also owe special gratitude to Lord (Asa) Briggs for his generous support and interest in the book at all stages of its progress. The other individuals who I wish to thank are so many that I can only list them in alphabetical order, acknowledging help from each in too many different directions to describe but each with its own real value:

Mrs. Charlotte Beswick: Dr B. M. Bynam: Dr N. G. Coley: Dr John Coulson: Dr Charmazel Dudt: Professor John Ferguson: Fred Green: Mrs Joan Ham: Christopher Harte: Peter Hebblethwaite: Revd. Dr J. Derek Holmes: Tom and Marie Ingram: Gordon Kelsey: Dr Russell Kirk: Dr George Krishnamurti: Dr John V. Pickstone: Charles Praeger, S. J.: Cassian Reel, O. F. M. Cap.: Revd. Michael Richards: Christian Rodskjaer: John E. Walsh: Dr John Wilders.

I would like to thank Boston College for providing illustrations for the front and back jacket; the Burns Library, Boston College for illustrations 4, 5, 6, 7, 8, 13, 16, 17, 18, 19, 22, 23, 24 and the frontispiece; the Stalybridge Local History Library for 1 and 3; and Lancashire Library, Preston District, for 2; the British Museum for 9 and 10; Gordon Kelsey for 11; Joan Ham for 12; Rachel Tapping for 21; and the Earl of Lytton for 25. Illustrations 6, 8, 21, 22 and 25 are from the Meynell Collection in Greatham, 8, 9 and 10 from the Benjamin Stone Collection. Illustration 20 is from the Collections of the Harry Ransom Humanities Research Centre, The University of Texas at Austin.

Finally, I thank Robert Baldock and Ann Grindrod of Yale University Press for combining their professional skills with a consideration and support that I shall continue to remember and value.

1

What was hid in the seed
Childhood 1859–1870

> ... whether in grief or mirth we shower,
> We make not the thing we breed,
> For what may come of the passing Hour
> Is what was hid in the seed.
> The Song of the Hours: 92–95

Victorian Preston could claim to be Lancashire's leading industrial town, since it was here that Richard Arkwright had erected the first mechanised spinning jenny as early as 1768. By the mid-nineteenth century it lay under a depressing pall of smoke from the mills and factories, spreading over those parts that still managed to retain something of its traditional character as a trade and business centre. In those earlier days the more prosperous inhabitants had created a residential area around Winckley Square and in the adjacent streets, where their successors built themselves substantial houses in the prevailing Georgian style. It was in one of these, 7 Winckley Street, that Francis Thompson was born on 18 December, 1859 soon after his parents had moved from their first home in Saint Ignatius Square. The new arrival must have been given a special welcome, as the previous year the couple had lost their first child, also a son, at birth.

Dr Thompson and his wife were Catholics and Francis Joseph was baptized at Saint Ignatius' Church, which they continued to attend after the move had taken them from the parish. He was two when his sister Mary was born and his first experience of death came in his fourth year when a second sister, Helen, died at the age of fifteen months. In 1864 another sister, Margaret, completed the family.

The fact that Dr Thompson and his wife were Catholics brings two influences to bear on Francis's early years which were to affect his whole later career and much of his writing. First, he was a 'born Catholic' and second, his father was a doctor. Socially the family was unexceptional with roots in the midlands and north where, for several generations, the Thompsons had been small traders or had practiced medicine or the law. Then sometime in the eighteen thirties Francis's

1

uncle Edward Healy Thompson, an Anglican clergyman, joined the Catholic Church. Of his seven brothers and sisters he must have been the dominant personality for he was then instrumental in the conversion of both his parents and of his younger brother Charles, Francis's father. During the next decade three more of the family followed — another brother, John Costall, and two sisters, Anne and Charlotte, who became nuns soon afterwards.[1]

The Thompson converts were not as unusual as might appear. They were taking the same way as the hundreds of others who followed Newman's lead and whose submission to the Roman Church was a direct outcome of the Oxford Movement. These 'Oxford converts' soon led one of the three main groups among the Catholics in England which developed during the second half of the century. It is important to reconstruct the main features of this wider background for it directed the home life and training of Francis's early years and the milieu in which much of his later life was to be spent.

The fact that he was born and bred in Lancashire is also important, where the first of the three groups was the one most firmly established and its outlook therefore most pervasive. It was formed by the so-called 'old Catholics', the families surviving from the penal days of almost total ostracism from public affairs and constant petty persecution in private ones. They had become in consequence a close-knit clique, deliberately shunning the outside world and retreating into the hills and valleys of the western and northern counties. While orthodox in their essential beliefs, their religious outlook had evolved over more than two centuries with very few directives apart from their native independence and their determination to 'keep the Faith'. By choice they had retained their in-built way of life after the Catholic Emancipation Act of 1829 and the restoration of the Catholic hierarchy in 1850. Both events had the effect of widening the range of activity open to them but, being drawn mainly from the landed gentry, they still preferred their country estates where they were not much affected either by public affairs or by the industrialization transforming the northern cities. As a result they were often as opposed to the changing ideas of the time as they were to the changes in the social scene.

The same conservatism made them suspicious both of the newer attitudes spread by the converts and of the continental influences encouraged by the hierarchy under the leadership of Cardinal Wiseman. In this second group, the converts, there was a further division. They either agreed with the bishops that English Catholics needed to forget their insularity and adopt the practices prevailing in the Church as a whole — which in effect meant Italy and the countries of southern Europe. Or they looked for a Catholic ethos more in line with the

English temper and outlook. A real rift had appeared, therefore, between the 'Ultramontanes' who turned to Rome for guidance in almost all religious matters and many political and social ones, and the 'liberals' who upheld a far greater degree of independent thinking within the Church, in accordance with traditionally accepted English attitudes.

Divisions of this kind tend to be arbitrary and the rift, like the separation of the first and second groups, was by no means clearly defined at the time. To understand Thompson's religious background something of the more complex web of interconnections has to be considered. Opinions differ as to the extent to which the liberals were identifiable with the Oxford converts and how far the converts themselves were an offshoot of the Oxford Movement in the Anglican Church. What can be said is that in their views on independence they were often closer to the hereditary Catholic families than to their fellow-converts who followed Cardinal Wiseman and his supporters.

Largely due to the persisting native tradition, when the hierarchy was restored in 1850 England remained a 'mission country' under the overall jurisdiction of Rome. With some notable exceptions, therefore, the bishops were determined supporters of the Ultramontane aims. Among the converts who followed their lead, Newman's contemporary and counterpart F. W. Faber represented the drive to bring English Catholicism in line with continental forms. Brompton Oratory, Faber's creation, still bears witness to the strength of that drive.

To illustrate the contrast, the liberals by and large upheld the revival of Gothic architecture led by the Pugins and carried on by the Hansom brothers and others. They saw Gothic as the native style, now expressing openly the cool untrammelled forms of worship that for centuries had survived only in chapels hidden in the homes of the remaining Catholic families. Again, in this they had more in common with the 'old' Catholics than with many of their fellow-converts.

The similarities were more apparent in the north than the south. The northern converts were for the most part less prone to new intellectual ideas and more prepared to adopt existing traditions as they found them. In Francis's family, therefore, the background of sincere and unemotional piety had roots reaching back long before the Reformation and kept alive in the meantime as the basic form of English Catholicism. To this the northern converts brought a fresh sense of dedication and more social concern without altering its essential character. In addition, among 'old' and 'new' alike there was the natural reticence of the north-countryman towards any display of feeling, of religious 'enthusiasm'.

The third group can be more clearly defined. They comprised the thousands of immigrants, mainly Irish and Italians, who had poured into the industrial towns during the earlier part of the century and who by now were forming the largest section of the Church. Its rapid growth was in many respects due to their support and the solidarity arising from their twofold sense of isolation as foreigners and as 'papists'. Yet they were hardly less isolated from the rest of the Catholic population. The lack of any realistic meeting-ground between the immigrants and the other two groups is a reflection of the overall insularity of Victorian England. Even their poverty and often appalling living conditions had made little more impact on the social conscience of English Catholics than on the country as a whole.[2]

To the non-Catholic world it was this foreign element that showed up most, due to the sheer number of the immigrants and the way their observances naturally followed the Ultramontane policies of the hierarchy. Both together strengthened the long-established fear and suspicion of the 'Roman' Church as a threat to England's democratic way of life. Anti-Catholic feeling was still widespread and was to be given a fresh impetus after the definition of papal infallibility by the First Vatican Council in 1870. If Catholics in England must obey without question almost all the Pope said — which was the popular interpretation upheld by the victorious Ultramontanes — what of their loyalty to the English constitution? The fears were well summarized in the third 'Proposition' made by W. E. Gladstone when he listed the evil influences of the Roman Church as confirmed by the Council's ruling:

> That no one can now become her convert without renouncing his moral and mental freedom, and placing his civil loyalty and duty at the mercy of another.[3]

Gladstone also recalled the notorious 'Syllabus of Errors' issued from Rome in 1864, where it appeared that the Pope and the Church must remain opposed to almost all forms of progress and new discoveries, scientific and otherwise. A wave of publicity followed Gladstone's protest, Newman leading the way for many Catholics who aligned themselves with his view should the Council's teaching have the effect he feared. As we know, in the event it did not, but the outcry at the time shows how strong and deep the native feeling was within Catholic circles as well as beyond. It also highlights the division between a majority of the Catholics of the first two groups and the immigrants who followed the Ultramontane leadership.

The anti-Catholic feeling at the time of the Council was not entirely representative. During the second half of the century an opposing swing of feeling arose, responding to Catholicism as retaining elements of security and beauty in life and art in an increasingly insecure and ugly world. Or so it seemed to many non-Catholics, who could then often join the other converts as a result of this initial attraction. But after conversion they found a different attitude prevailing among the Catholics themselves. Apart from a handful of the newcomers, for the rest the arts were generally regarded as suspect unless placed in the direct service of the Church. Otherwise they were sources of temptation to abandon, or at least to neglect, spiritual values.[4]

So what was the effect of this wider background on Thompson's own family? Anti-Catholic prejudice served to isolate them from local society and to maintain bonds with the established Catholic families and their traditional outlook. For all its narrowness in the face of changing conditions and the demands of the time it was marked by a depth and sincerity that has too often been overshadowed by its limitations. But in addition, as converts Francis's parents were unusual in the extent of their concern for the poor who formed the majority of Dr Thompson's patients. Francis therefore grew up surrounded by two positive influences that were to be lifelong. There was the uncomplicated and sincere piety with roots in the distant past and, equally practical in its expression, a keen sense of the need to relieve the social evils of the present.

Where the arts were concerned it was another matter. Here the Thompson family converts shared in the general attitude. Any potential abilities could do not more than provide a salutary side-interest, and only if guided by religious motives. John Costall's *A Vision of Judgement and Other Poems*, privately printed in 1845, shows rather less talent than was common in most reasonably well-educated families. Not does Edward Healy's more prolific output suggest much more. After his conversion he composed some polemical pamphlets and translated various devotional works, mainly from French sources. He also edited the first four volumes in a series of saints' lives, *The Library of Religious Biography*. His one attempt at publishing his own creative work, a collection of tedious sonnets, appeared when they were thought to merit attention after his nephew's rise to poetic fame. This uncle was Francis's only relative with anything like a genuine interest in literature, just so far as it could be used in the direct service of religion and the Church.

In that service, however, he had made a sufficient name for himself by 1858 to be asked to take on the editorship of the leading Catholic journal, the *Dublin Review*. His reason for declining was that he would not be a sufficiently independent agent: his sympathies were in fact closer to the liberal Catholics' journal, the *Rambler*. In the following year, the year of his nephew's birth, he was corresponding with Newman as its proposed sub-editor. Considering the vital issues being raised through the journal and their controversial nature, Newman

must have held Edward Healy in high regard to have pressed the
matter as he did. But despite the efforts to persuade him he refused
again, this time on the grounds that he was not equipped to deal with
the opposition it met with from the hierarchy. This was the time when
the inadequacy of Catholic education was being brought forward,
largely through the *Rambler*, as a matter of serious concern among the
more intellectually-inclined converts. Newman was their chief spokesman, the bishops being in general against the spread of liberal ideas
that would result if they had their way. Edward Healy continued to
exchange letters with Newman for a few years but clearly he was
not equal to taking an active part in the affairs of Newman's circle
and, by the time Francis knew his uncle, he had withdrawn from any
publicity he once shared with them. Yet this much shows that Edward
Healy had more understanding of the problems of the Church and
the differing attitudes towards them than the rest of the family. It was
a distinction that would have its effect on his relationship with his
nephew.[5]

Given this background it is not surprising that Thompson's
immediate family remained as unresponsive to his later poetic career
as they were to the literary inclinations of his early years. A professional colleague who knew his father well was to remember Dr
Thompson as 'one who had no poetic instinct himself and discouraged
it in others'. The same writer also recalled that he 'was an ornament
to our profession, firm and kind but somewhat Spartan and austere in
discipline'.[6]

From what is known of Charles Thompson this would seem a fair
summary. He qualified in 1847 at the age of twenty-eight and from the
start of his career he specialised in homoeopathic medicine. It was a
highly unusual choice as homoeopathy had been introduced in England only very recently and he must have known it would be an addition to the prejudice he would encounter as a Catholic.

Homoeopathy was already spreading in Europe since its revival
by the German physician Samuel Hahnemann (1755–1843). The
idea behind it was first developed in the ancient world but then
virtually forgotten until the publication of Hahnemann's treatise,
Organon of Medicine, in 1810. He adopted the Latin phrase *similia
similibus curantur*, 'let likes be treated with likes', to express the basic
principle of homoeopathy where the remedies used in the treatment of
a disease contain similar properties to the disease itself. Rather than
concentrating on the symptoms of his complaint the patient must be
regarded as a whole person, with what was then an unusual emphasis
on his situation, on diet and general hygiene.[7] In England prejudice
was strong against such innovations even after results had proved
their value and Charles Thompson's decision marks him as a man of
determination and firm convictions. It also shows his sense of dedi-

cation to his profession as primarily a vocation. His patients could be treated through a form of medicine which took into account their spiritual welfare as well as their physical needs. That he was not looking for material success is clear for another reason. Long before the appearance of the present-day system, a rudimentary 'health service' existed where the doctor was expected to follow the general policy that the patient paid according to his means. As late as 1895 *The Lancet* printed an address to the prospective medical student outlining the method as part of the life ahead for him:

> It has been for generations the tradition and glory of the profession of medicine that its members have always been ready to give their services without fee or reward of any kind to those whose circumstances required it. It will rest with those who are now about to enter the profession to carry on this honourable tradition.[8]

Admittedly, there was a marked reluctance in the profession as a whole to take up practice in the places most in need of medical care, the slums of the industrial-towns where the majority of the patients would have to be treated under these conditions. Often there were good reasons, especially if a doctor lacked private means and he usually had a family to support. But Charles Thompson was among those who responded to the need. His first appointments appear to have been in the industrial areas of Bristol and Manchester and his later career shows how he deliberately chose to work among the poor — in spite of the fact that according to his will he had no other income than his earnings.

A homoeopathic dispensary was opened in Bristol in 1852 but existed for only two years. Dr Thompson may have moved north after its closure.[9] No compulsory medical registers were kept until after the Medical Act of 1858 and his name does not appear on the occasional earlier lists except for the previous year, 1857, when he is located in Leicester. What is certain is that at about this time he met his future wife while employed at the homoeopathic dispensary in Manchester and after their marriage he took up practice in Preston.

One of his colleagues, Charles Brown, has left a record of his own experiences as a doctor there at the time. His account of his background shows the kind of training Dr Thompson had also received, mainly through apprenticeship followed by the most elementary of examinations. Later, Brown improved his knowledge by taking courses in Edinburgh and elsewhere but in the meantime his chief concern was for the appalling living conditions among the poor of Preston in the 1850s and 1860s. The two doctors would have worked together at the dispensary, which like others of its kind served as a compromise between a surgery and a small hospital. Such dispensaries were invaluable where local hospital care was unobtainable and

the Royal Infirmary at Preston was not to be opened until 1870.
Brown's efforts to get the basic ideas of domestic hygiene taught to
the factory girls before marriage was in line with Dr Thompson's
homoeopathic principles. These girls, who had started work at the age
of nine or earlier, had no idea of the rudiments of housekeeping and
the success of the innovation was a notable achievement.[10]

Very little is known about Francis's mother, Mary Turner. She
came from a moderately successful business family in Manchester and
appears to have been well educated. She had more sympathy with her
son's reading habits as a child than the Thompsons and encouraged
him to draw and paint, thus laying important foundations for the
visual element in his poetic imagery. Francis also attributed his
lifelong love of music to her early influence. When Mary became a
Catholic she was forced to leave home, and having found shelter with
the Holy Child nuns she attempted to join the Order at their House in
Brighton. Finding she had no vocation for the religious life she took up
the only career open to a young woman of her background and was
employed as a governess until her marriage. Like her husband she
appears to have possessed a good share of north-country determination and independence of character. There is nothing to suggest that
the couple were not well suited, the general impression being that it
was a stable marriage with little emotional content on either side.

Francis grew up in an unspectacular, probably dull home. But
the stability was very important for a child whose first impressions of
life beyond the home were full of contrasts. Winckley Street leads off
Winckley Square where, in 1862, the Thompsons moved to No. 33.
The Square still contains many of its late eighteenth-century houses
whose grace and proportions then gave elegance to Preston's main residential area. The open ground in the centre, now public, was maintained by the inhabitants of the Square as gardens for their own use.
The unusual formation provided exciting possibilities for play for a
small child. The ground dips down to a central dell with paths leading
in all directions through trees and bushes and, at that time, borders
and beds of flowers. Beyond, to the south, there were views towards
the river Ribble and the open countryside.

Divided between the comfortably spacious rooms at home and
the pleasures of the gardens, life was happily secure for Francis and the
frequent attendances at church an extension of that same security. To
Francis's awakening consciousness the sense of mystery in the strange
words and apparel of the priests as they moved among the candles
and incense was woven into the pattern of everyday things.

But to reach Saint Ignatius' Church they must pass through
another Preston where life was very different, where factories and
chimneys rose above the close-packed alleys of gim-crack housing in a
chokingly soot-blackened world. Here the locality known as the 'Old

1. Winckley Square, Preston, in 1855 (Frank Graham, *Lancashire a Hundred Years ago* (1968))

2. 'Another Preston'. The Old Starch Houses

Starch Houses' was sufficiently shocking to merit some public alarm.
In 1861 *The Builder* reported a huge sewer which 'positively discharges
itself on the surface, and forms a wide bog', where 'the boiling greasy
water from a tripe shop at the top of the street is thrown onto the
sewerage, making the matter daily worse'.[11]

Today the factories have all but disappeared and the town has
retrieved something of its original character. It is not the Preston that
Thompson knew, the 'Coketown' of Dickens' *Hard Times*:

> It was a town of red brick, or of brick that would have been red if the
> smoke and ashes had allowed it; but as matters stood it was a town of un-
> natural red and black like the painted face of a savage. It was a town of
> machinery and tall chimneys, out of which interminable serpents of smoke
> trailed themselves for ever and ever, and never got uncoiled ... It con-
> tained several large streets all very like one another, and many small
> streets still more like one another, inhabited by people equally like one
> another, who all went in and out at the same hours, with the same sound
> upon the same pavements, to do the same work, and to whom every day
> was the same as yesterday and tomorrow, and every year the counterpart
> of the last and the next.[12]

They were also the patients with whom Dr Thompson chose that he
and his family should worship rather than with the respectable
citizens attending their parish church of Saint Wilfrid, just off the
Square. To Francis, Saint Ignatius' Church must have seemed like an
oasis in this other world. But which was the real world? This, or the
gardens where the birds sang in the trees? Or was it the Church where
the two came together and the choir of factory children sang like the
angels in heaven?

After two further moves, still in the vicinity of the Square, the
Thompsons left Preston when he was five. But he was to find similar
contrasts at Ashton-under-Lyne when the family finally settled there
in 1864. Probably the main reason for the change was to procure a
practice within Dr Thompson's limited means and where he could be
comparatively free to follow his homoeopathic principles. Ashton was
noted for its support of homoeopathy, arising from a long-established
interest in herbal remedies and medical botany. Many Lancashire
towns had shared the interest earlier in the century but it waned in
most places as advances in allopathic medicine increased. But in
Ashton there were still several societies devoted to both subjects and
surviving well past Dr Thompson's time. Manchester was only some
six miles distant, where by now there was a new and flourishing
homoeopathic hospital and dispensary. A member of its staff, William
Sharp, had recently published a series of 'Tracts on Homoeopathy'
which did much to spread its popularity. Its practice was in fact so
widespread in the city and surrounding areas that in the year in which

the Thompsons arrived in Ashton it provoked a strong reaction from the allopathic, or 'orthodox' practioners. Dr Thompson might not be in a position to aspire to Manchester itself, but Ashton was within easy reach of the stimulus and support of his colleagues.[13]

There was probably another factor in his decision to move to Ashton at that time. Between 1861 and 1865 the so-called 'cotton famine' brought acute suffering to the poor throughout the north as a result of the decline in the cotton trade with America. Ashton was one of the hardest hit of the cotton towns and, in addition, the remaining farming community was equally impoverished by the spread of a fatal cattle disease during the same period. It was by now a situation where any opposition on account of Dr Thompson's religion or his homoeopathic principles were outweighed by the extreme need for medical care.[14]

His reputation was soon established. According to a patient who had been treated by him since childhood, he was as respected and loved by the Anglican and Nonconformist families he attended as by the Catholics. This patient could 'still see the worthy physician pouring the minute wonder-working drops of "rhus", "belladonna", or "aconite" into the tumblers of water'.[15] Most of his practice was among the very poor. The surgery was held in the house and if, as often happened, his patients were more in need of food than medicine, he sent them to the kitchen where Francis and his sisters would watch their mother hand out suppplies from a special store kept for the purpose. A family relative remembered the doctor's goodness to the poor as his most notable characteristic and how they 'followed him in hundreds, when he died, to the grave'.[16]

Yet to the children the life of their father's patients must have seemed strangely separate from their own. The house itself was in Stamford Street, still the main thoroughfare of the town but far more residential then than it is now. No. 224 remains at the corner of Booth Street, solidly built of the local dark red brick and with two windows whose patterned leads suggest there may have been a family chapel on the upper floor. According to the Rate Books the Thompsons lived at No. 224 until 1872 when they moved next door to No. 226. As no other occupant is named for the first house and the premises are not listed as vacant, it appears that as the practice grew Dr Thompson took over both, although he never owned either. If that was the case the home was well in line with others in the neighbourhood, which were mainly occupied by professional or business families. It is an added tribute to the doctor's reputation that his practice came to include sufficient fee-paying patients to allow for a comfortable home background.

Ashton had a long history, having been a Roman settlement and, since Norman times, a centre for the wool trade. At the end of the

3. Stamford Street, Ashton-under-Lyne, in the late 19th century

eighteenth century it still had a population of only some fifteen thousand, while the nearby village of Stalybridge was a mere hamlet of 140 inhabitants. Then, with the installation of a machine-driven mill and the discovery of a rich supply of local coal, the whole scene had changed. Within a generation the Ashton population quadrupled and in Stalybridge it rose to over twenty-one thousand. Cottages and farmsteads disappeared and a pall of smoke covered the town. In other respects its more favoured parts were separated from the factories by a natural boundary created by the river Tame. Ashton had made more effort than most such towns in attempting to improve the conditions of its workers. The District Infirmary was opened in 1860 and there were already public baths and a park. Medically speaking these were distinct advantages to influence the choice of Aston as a permanent home.[17]

As Francis grew older the contrasts that had coloured his first years impressed themselves more clearly on his childhood mind. The protective shelter of his home acted like a bulwark against the world outside with its noise and dirt and the poverty of his father's patients who gathered in the family kitchen. And as at Preston the Church was the only meeting-ground. The congregation, formed largely from Irish immigrants, shared in the faith and the observances that he and his sisters were being taught at home. And it was in Saint Mary's, their parish church, that the ceremonies which all alike attended became the main source of nourishment for his growing imagination.

There was little to be found elsewhere in the Ashton he knew, apart from one unique feature. The custom known as 'Riding the Black Lad' or 'Knight' was re-enacted each year at Easter as it had been, some said, since pre-Christian times. An effigy made from straw and holly branches, swathed in black and mounted on the leanest horse that could be found, was led through the town to a field where a cross had once stood. Here it was destroyed and burnt amid a general display of hooliganism and the pelting of all present with lumps of mud, known as 'sodding'. By the later nineteenth century the unruliness had given place to more organised pageantry but it was still a weird spectacle and must have been at once a frightening and fascinating event for a sensitive child. Even if the Thompson children were not allowed to take part in the actual destruction of the effigy they could not fail to have watched the procession at it made its way down Stamford Street in the half-light with the shouting mob following the black-clad figure of the 'Knight'. Whatever the later legends, the custom must have originated in the pagan rite where a figure representing winter and death was ceremoniously destroyed as part of the annual spring festival. The festival had been baptized by Christianity into the celebration of Easter and these deeply rooted pagan associations, brought so vividly to life for him as a child, certainly contributed to Thompson's later sense of the underlying power of the paganism Christianity has drawn into its own rituals.[18]

Another, more recent, link with Ashton's religious past must have had a special appeal for the Thompson children, from its name as much as from its origins. Curiously enough in an area where anti-Catholic feeling remained strong, the 'Thompson Cross' still stood on the outskirts of the town since its erection in memory of William Thompson, the parish priest at the time of the Reformation. He had remained loyal to the 'old faith' and died during its brief restoration under Queen Mary. It survived until the early years of this century, in spite of increased prejudice since the arrival of the Irish workers and the rise in the Catholic population. Where before there had been only a handful of Catholics in Ashton, now there were two thriving parishes.[19]

Four years after the Thompsons' arrival, local fear and suspicion reached a climax when the notorious anti-Catholic agitator William Murphy appeared in the area. Murphy, himself an Irish Catholic, had been adopted by the 'Protestant Evangelical Mission', an extremist sect consisting chiefly of politically motivated Orangemen. His fanatical hatred of all things Catholic, bred of supposed injustices to his family, was utilized by this sect for their own ends. With their support he published a number of pamphlets on the hideous crimes, moral and social, being perpetrated in secret by the Catholics of England — lurid horror-stories of the kind that have been aptly described as 'the pornography of the Puritan'. He then travelled through the country inciting local feeling by the same means in his oratorical speeches. Owing to the fear of the 'foreign' element in contemporary Catholicism he met with considerable success. Having provoked minor riots in Manchester he came to Stalybridge early in 1868, where he delivered a series of addresses culminating in an attack by the populace on the Catholic chapel. He proceeded to Ashton during Holy Week, where a similar agitation resulted in the most serious of all the rioting for which he was responsible.

Driven on by a confusion of religious and political frenzy, a mob descended on the two little churches, first demolishing the whole interior of St. Mary's and then proceeding to St. Anne's, which they also attempted to storm. The parishioners were prepared, mounting a guard inside which the rioters attacked with stones thrown through the windows. Shots were fired from both sides and, after the reading of the Riot Act failed to have any effect and three days of continual violence, the army had to be called in to restore order.

The whole parish shared in the aftermath. Their priest wrote later:

> Our church, school and presbytery were attacked and broken into, and altars, statues, and paintings were burnt; even our lives were in danger. One hundred and eleven houses of our faithful Irish Catholics were gutted; their furniture, clothing and bedding destroyed, and their provisions carried away. No protection was afforded us by the authorities. The clergy was obliged to leave the town, and for an entire month it was not deemed safe for them to do more than to revisit the parish at certain times of the day, for the sake of the sick.[20]

Even if the Thompson family was not directly involved in the riot the doctor must have been called out and casualties brought to the house for treatment at the surgery. And afterwards, since the clergy could not be constantly present, Dr Thompson was certainly called upon at all hours for the comfort and advice they would have been unable to provide. Francis's lifelong preoccupation with warfare may well date from the Murphy Riots, leaving him with a mingled sense of fascination and horror such as a nine-year old boy of his temperament would find in the initial excitement followed by the sordid reality of the aftermath. Years later he was to look ahead to the threat of war as he saw it at the dawn of the new century, and the intensity of his vision no doubt owed much to his childhood introduction to violence and his family's share in its consequences.

The more immediate outcome was the family's increased isolation from local society. According to his sister Margaret: 'Apart from the priests there and in the neighbouring parishes, no one knew us socially as we were taboo on account of being Catholics'. To her, Ashton was in consequence a 'horrid little place'. Mary also remembered 'we did not have any friends', adding that the only guests were priests. On Sundays 'often four or five would come to dine and pass the evening'. It was a typical situation for provincial Catholics of the Thompsons' class and background. 'The general attitude of others', she says, 'was hostile and suspicious', but the effect was 'to increase the fervour and strengthen the faith' of her parents. Church affairs and medical matters must have been virtually the only subjects of conversation overheard by Francis and his sisters as they sat through the Sunday evening suppers.[21]

Mary was to become Mother Austin of the Presentation Convent in Manchester and her recollections are a valuable source of information on the Thompsons' home life and her brother's early years. Most of the details were recalled in her old age when her memory was sometimes blurred about dates. But it was lucid, as is usual with the elderly, where the family background was concerned. Her description of her brother's appearance as a child carries out the impression gained from the later photographs and portraits where his eyes are his most arresting feature. She remembered them as 'a dark grey with bluish shade in them — something like the shade one sees in a mountain lake'. His hair, she continued, was 'very dark brown, so dark as to appear almost black at first sight'. His complexion was sallow rather than pale, drawing further attention to his eyes, 'full of intelligence & light' and set off by 'good, well formed eyebrows & eyelashes also very dark, almost black'.[22]

Francis admired his father, but there was very little common ground between them, either then or later. With his mother it was different. According to Mary he was always her 'pet'. He himself was to recall an incident, 'Mother missed in street' and the 'world wide desolation and terror of for the first time, realising that the mother can lose you, or you her, and the abysmal loneliness and helplessness without her'.[23] His explicit references to his childhood are rare, making this one the more significant. The experience of separation from the mother, of realising one's individual identity apart from her, comes to all children at some stage. Generally it is absorbed into their natural development. But for Francis it remained a vivid conscious memory, concealing the complex emotional ties that would direct so much in the years ahead.

On another occasion he described his mother's reaction to his precocious reading of Shakespeare:

When I was a child of seven, standing in my nightgown before the fire, and chatting to my mother, I remember her pulling me up for using a certain word. 'That is not used nowadays' she said: 'that is one of Shakespeare's words'. 'It is, Mama?' I said, staring at her doubtfully, 'But I did not know that it was one of Shakespeare's words!' 'That is just it', she answered, 'You have read Shakespeare so much that you are beginning to talk Shakespeare without knowing it. You must take care, or people will think you odd'.[24]

The gentle reproof shows how little she appreciated Francis's unusual reading habits even if she was more prepared to be sympathetic than the rest of the family. It was obviously impossible for them to understand the role which books and reading already played in providing Francis with the kind of imaginative nourishment for which they felt no need. Nor was there the encouragement he might have found at school, as the children learned at home from a governess. Nothing is known of her or her methods apart from Mary's observation that 'we must have been well instructed', since 'we were not backward when we did go away to College and school, rather we were in advance of others of our age'.[25] That was enough for her and her sister, but not for Francis. She had a clear mental picture of him at this time sitting for hours perched on a ladder to reach and read books stored away in an old cupboard. In later years he remembered it himself when contrasting mere cramming for 'information' with the kind of genuine education an imaginative child will find on his own: 'A child who loves books needs only a decent library and a ladder'.[26]

If there was no 'decent library' to hand it meant that Francis absorbed the contents of the old cupboard very thoroughly, including Shakespeare's plays, the works of Scott and several collections of poetry from the earlier years of the century. In Mary's view 'it was good as far as it went', but there was no attempt to add to it. 'My father had very little time for reading other than books concerning his profession' and she does not mention their mother as finding any more time.[27] Yet when Thompson looked back to his early years he saw them chiefly in terms of the books stored away by the rest of his family. Here he sought the beauty and romance for which, unlike them, he craved. His introduction to Shakespeare was through Cassell's three-volume edition where the illustrations by H. C. Selous had a special importance for him, recalled in an unusually detailed notebook entry:

Those girls of floating hair I loved, and admired the long haired, beautiful youths whom I met in those pictures, & the illustrations of early English history. I once pointed out to my elder sister a picture of a fair, long-locked Saxon youth, asking whether she did not think it a pity there were no such youths now. She rejoined that he 'looked like a girl'. Such was the fashion then, I explained: but she obviously thought it a silly fashion & disdained my Saxon youth. So I lapsed sighfully into the conviction (pretty near the mark) that girls understood neither beauty nor Sh. [Shakespeare]. Sh. I had already tried to read for the benefit of my sisters and the servants; but both kicked against *Julius Caesar* as dry — though they diplomatically refrained from saying so.

Comparing the pictures of medieval women with the crinolined & chignoned girls and women of my own day, I embraced the fatal but undoubting conviction that beauty expired somewhere about the time of Henry VIII. I believe I connected that awful catastrophe with the Reformation (merely because, from the pictures & to my taste, they seemed to have taken place about the same time.) And, upon my word, I am not so sure I was wrong! Anyway, there being no beautiful girls left, it was clear I could not fall in love — as I felt I should have done at once with those lovely medieval women. Therefore I never dreamed of love as a modern sentiment at all ...[28]

The light-hearted style is deceptive. He is describing his first experience of a world created from visual and verbal imagery, one no less real and far more appealing than that going on around him. It was a past world, uncomprehended even by the sisters who were closest to him. Yet he could associate himself with it more fully than he could with theirs and the first stirrings of poetic feeling arose from its mingling of dream and reality:

I had a certain sublatent, subconcious, elementary sense of poetry as I read. But this was, for the most part, scarce [sic] explicit; and was largely confined to the atmosphere, the exhalation of the work. To give some concrete examples of what I mean: In the 'Midsummer Night's Dream' I experienced profoundly that sense of trance, of dreamlike dimness, the moonlight glimmer and sleepwalking enchantment, embodied in that wonderful fairy epilogue ... I did indeed, as I read the last word of Puck, feel as if I were waking from a dream and rub my mental eyes.

The same was true of 'the atmospheric effect' of all the plays in varying degree and however hard to define, the impact was to remain. 'Never again have I sensed so exquisitely, so virginally, the *aura* of the plays as I sensed it then'.[29]

His precocity was noticed by the rest of the family, but as they took no further interest their attitude only strengthened his awareness of his 'difference' from them. It was the same with their circle of clerical friends and the few others of their acquaintance. 'People were amazed at his knowledge of good literature', Mary remembered, 'but he never made any show of it on his own account. He was a very silent boy'.[30]

Neither she nor the rest of the family realized that the silence was not natural to him — hence his desire to share his enthusiasm for Shakespeare with the servants as well as his sisters. It was imposed by a lack of understanding such as many sensitive children will react against by withdrawal. In Thompson's case it was to have far-reaching effects. Contrary to the widely popularised view of his later life, he was not by nature a recluse. Again and again in after years he would thrive in the sympathetic companionship of others and it was during periods of such companionship that his best poetry was written.

There was just one among their friends who was an exception. John Carroll was a young priest, twenty-six years old and newly ordained, when he was introduced to the Sunday evening circle soon after the Thompsons' arrival in Ashton. His friendship with the family led to a lifelong affection for Francis which was to be an important influence at several stages of his career and a vital one when it came to its turning point. As children he and his sisters were sure of a welcome at the nearby rectory in Stalybridge where Canon Carroll gave the boy the free use of its well-stocked bookshelves. He also had the run of the garden to play cricket, his other great enthusiasm, with his sisters.

Their parents admired Carroll for his vitality and dedication to the apparently hopeless tasks with which he was faced. Apart from the demands of his own impoverished parish he soon became a leading figure in the efforts to improve the standards of Catholic education in the Salford diocese. His pioneering work was later recognised in his appointment as Vicar General for the Shrewsbury diocese. In 1893 he became its Coadjutor Bishop, and Bishop two years later. Unlike the majority of his fellow-priests his interests were wide-ranging. He brought a good education and cultivated tastes to the Sunday gatherings, enlivening them also by his strong, warm personality. And in his study at Stalybridge he was always ready to listen to Francis's excited accounts of the latest books borrowed from his shelves, encouraging the child in a direction the importance of which, for Francis, he seems to have recognised from the first.[31]

Given the religious background and the example set by Carroll it was very natural that, according to Mary, her brother 'wished to be a priest from a little boy'.[32] Natural, too, that his parents encouraged him in this wish. They shared the customary Catholic sense of an honour conferred by having a priest in the family: as one of Dr Thompson's medical colleagues remembered, the father 'seemed to account it one of the greatest privileges to devote his son to the priesthood'.[33] If they had any doubts as to their son's odd ways they probably thought these would disappear when properly directed and might even conceal hidden springs of sanctity.

At that time Francis's dreaminess and lack of application to the ordinary affairs of life were not exactly promising qualities compared with those of the hard-working, hard-pressed priests of their acquaintance. Although on occasion 'he could get into a temper when roused' Mary's clearest memories were of his absent-mindedness and of 'his habit of smiling and speaking to himself, as it were, at his own thoughts'. Talking to oneself is a mark of loneliness, of the need to communicate with others, but of course his sisters did not see this. Mary's comment that 'we were so used to him that we only laughed at him' suggests they accepted his peculiarities with no ill feeling on either side.[34] And the same traits remained so much a part of his personality that when she recalled them for Everard Meynell's biography, Everard's memories of Thompson's later years echo hers:

> His tremulous, sudden 'not ready!' jerked out at the beginning of a game of cards, is still heard in the same sister's memory, and also the leaverage of calls and knockings that was required to get him from the house for church or train; and his unrecognising progress down the street. Every detail of the boy recalls the man to one who had to get him forth from his chamber when he was a grown traveller, and has often seen him oblivious in the streets, and has heard his imperative appeals for 'ten minutes more' in all the small business of his later life.[35]

Yet there was another side to this lack of order in the 'small business' of life. Francis's childhood enthusiasm for cricket was to be lifelong, as it also was for some aspects of warfare. Neither can be said to be in line with the popular image of a poet, particularly of the kind of poet he has been said to be. In both cases it was the ritual, the pattern and the movement, that appealed to him. The planned campaign, the organized game, struck a chord in his own nature far below the surface disregard for time and place. At this deeper level his poetic instinct was already beginning to fashion an order of its own, drawn mainly from the rites of the Church and from his reading. It was not an order that would comply with the world of work and the intercourse of everyday demands. But in the world of the game it was at home, as much as in the dream world of the past with which the game had much in common. The battle, for him, constituted another kind of game and in this sense he could separate its appeal from the evils of actual warfare. Here, too, he could respond to the wider context of history as an unfolding pattern and plan forming the background for the particular battle scene. In these directions Thompson's sense of time and place was to be sensitive and sure. But from first to last it could not help him in the transaction of his day-to-day affairs.

As a child the appeal of the game could be shared at its surface level with the family. At chess and cards the plan and pattern counted for much, and chess had the added attraction of an interest shared with Canon Carroll. There were patience games when he was alone, or he would teach himself card tricks to try out on his sisters. One game of his own invention must only be played in secret with them and Mary remembered how no one was allowed into the room while it was going on.[36]

For a time he belonged to a drama group organized by the parish. The theatre had an attraction for him all his life, arising from the same source as the appeal of the game and the battle. It provided the background for similar pattern and order in the plot and action of the play. And, more clearly even than the game, it provided an escape from everyday reality into the world of that other reality, the imagination. To the end of his life Thompson regretted his lack of ability for acting and after his death one of his few personal possessions was the toy theatre he made for himself as a child.

In keeping with his acting instincts, he was keen to take part in the ceremonies at church as an altar server. One of his companions had some distinctly uncomplementary memories of Francis in this capacity. At one time he was determined to wear a red or purple cassock rather than the black one required by his junior position. When told he could not, he got his own back by appropriating the lighting of the altar candles, a duty assigned to a senior, and nearly set the church on fire in the process. On another occasion, aggravated by some small annoyance, he seized the thurible, the container in which the incense was burned, and swung it by its chains with such vehemence that the glowing charcoal was scattered over the sacristy floor amid general panic.[37]

These incidents could be seen as not mere childish pranks but as indications of a need to assert himself due to more deep-seated frustrations. But much of the general picture is refreshingly normal, an aspect of his early years as important as any other. It was helping to create the healthy mental structure against which Thompson would so often measure the vagaries of his later experiences, his own and those of his fellows.

Each summer the family went to Wales for their holiday, exploring the countryside on foot. 'We were all good walkers' Mary remembered, and the habit remained Francis's first choice for recreation throughout his life. Then there were regular visits to the seaside with his sisters when he would collect different kinds of seaweed and search the rock pools for starfish, crabs and jellyfish. The sea itself cast a spell he never outgrew and was instrumental in arousing a wish to know more about the natural world. It was not so easy at home in Ashton but in this his parents were able and willing to co-operate. Contrary to the widely held view that he had no special knowledge of nature he was given a good grounding in childhood which emerges clearly in much of his poetic imagery. His mother took a special pride in her house plants and the children went with her each year to the flower show at Old Trafford. Dr Thompson occasionally made time to take his son on long country walks, glad to find they shared a common interest in birds and wild flowers. He gave Francis a microscope which opened up a new world and awoke a sense of the mysteries of

4. Francis, aged five, with his sisters Mary and Margaret

nature and science as one of the most important legacies from these early years.[38]

The picture as a whole is far from unhappy. Nor did Thompson himself regard his childhood as anything but an outwardly happy one. Yet he sensed his 'difference' from his first memories and however close the relationship with his sisters, as the three grew older he felt more and more isolated in a world which they could not enter with him. So writing had to become his substitute for other communication: 'My tongue was tenaciously disciplined to silence'.[39]

He was to celebrate the wonder of childhood in some of his best poetry. But it is not the essentially objective poetry of a Wordsworth or a Blake. When he writes of its innocence and joys and sorrows the child who never grew up in himself is almost always present to remind him of the complex mystery of a child's development. And the consequences of an arrested development could be tragic:

Yes, childhood is tragic to me. And then critics complain that I do not
write 'simply' about it. O fools! as if there were anything more complex,
held closer to the heart of mystery, than its contemplation.[40]

So he was to write years afterwards, of the 'mystery' arising from the
paradox in his own experience. An element of genuine childlikeness
remained an often attractive characteristic of his adult years. But it
was because the child he had once been eluded the normal processes
by which maturity is reached and was constantly present to him as a
humiliating negation of his adult self. Full maturity depends on being
first fully a child. 'There is a sense in which I have always been a
child' he admitted, recognising how it arose from the abnormality of
his childhood isolation which had imposed a false maturity in the
escape to his dream world:

> But in another sense I never was a child, never shared children's thoughts,
> ways, tastes, manner of life & outlook on life. I played — I never have
> ceased to play — but my sport was solitary sport; even when I played with
> my sisters . . . my side of the game was part of a dream-scheme invisible to
> them. And from boys, with their hard objectivity of play, I was tenfold
> wider apart than from girls with their partial capacity and habit of make
> believe.[41]

The exclusive association with his sisters left him with a preference for
the companionship of women but there was nothing to suggest then or
later that it resulted in any unnatural effeminacy. Compared with
many poets Thompson's masculine traits remained markedly strong.
Nor was there any sign of sexual abnormality when he shared in his
sisters' play with their dolls:

> How many a doll have I seen, which at first peered bashfully from the
> clefts of its paper; and being deceased of those envious swathings, it shone
> like a rose of prime, and was lovely in the eyes of all childhood, and the
> heart of its mistress was glad because of it: but presently some boistrous
> hand dissevered its tender limbs, and it grew meagre with ebbing sawdust;
> and at length, having lost some of its nose and all of its tresses, it fell into
> the portion of pincushions and outworn teacups.

With masculine pithiness he described how on one occasion he was
himself the cause of such a disillusioning process, due to a boy's desire
to find out 'how things work':

> With another doll, of much personal attraction, I was on terms of intimate
> affection, till a murderous impulse of scientific curiosity incited me to open
> her head, that I might investigate what her brains were like. The shock
> which I then sustained has been a fruitful warning to me, I have never
> since looked for a beautiful girl's brains.[42]

He often used a light-hearted 'cover' when he wrote of matters that
were close to his own situation. In this essay on dolls he was also

exploring his childhood escape from the real world to that of the dream and the game. But in the privacy of his notebooks he could be open in admitting the negative side:

> I did not want to grow up; I did not want emancipation from parental control ... I did not want responsibility, did not want to be a man ...

Instead, he wanted nothing more than to 'make my delight of play and the exercise of the imagination'.[43]

In his best-known essay, on Shelley, his description of the poet's childhood is based on the positive elements of this play within the imagination when it follows a natural course in the child's development. 'What is it to be a child?' he asks:

> It is to have a spirit yet streaming from the waters of baptism; it is to be so little that the elves can reach to whisper in your ear; it is to turn pumpkins into coaches and mice into horses, lowness into loftiness, and nothing into everything, for each child has a fairy godmother in its own soul; it is to live in a nutshell and to count yourself the king of infinite space ...[44]

But if, due to unnatural causes, the play becomes an escape that persists beyond childhood, then this child will fail to pass through the hard passage that leads to maturity. Thompson was to identify his own failure with his inability to achieve that ease in companionship for which he always craved and seldom found. As such it remained a constant source for mental and spiritual pain. Yet the pain would in turn form an essential part of those creative pangs without which true poetry is rarely, if ever, brought to birth.

2

The still-born Day
Ushaw and Owens 1870–1885

... what hard task abstracts me from delight,
Filling with hopeless hope and dear despair
The still-born day and parchéd fields of night.
'From the Night of Forebeing': 252–254

The decision leading to Francis's departure for Ushaw College in 1870 was primarily due to Canon Carroll, who knew the boy's literary leanings would find more scope at his own *alma mater* than at the other Catholic colleges of the time.

Francis was not yet eleven, but there was nothing unusual in starting an education designed for the priesthood at his age. In the years when higher education for English Catholics had been banned by the penal laws the colleges they founded abroad were mainly intended to supply priests for the 'home mission'. So it was that all Catholic secondary education became directed by studies best suited to this end, although those who could afford it sent their sons, at about Francis's age, to be educated abroad whatever their future career. When in the early nineteenth century religious persecution in Europe and the slackening of the penal laws at home led to the establishment of the colleges in England, the custom was continued. These colleges were still mainly intended for training priests for the dioceses they served, while continuing to provide the only higher education for Catholics in general. The Church forbade attendance at the secular universities owing to a supposed danger to faith and morals and, until the ban was lifted in 1895, the old-established custom prevailed, the main colleges being Oscot, Stoneyhurst and Ushaw.

From its opening in 1808 Ushaw assumed its own identity, which arose from its origins at Douai in the first English college abroad, founded there by Cardinal Allen in 1568. Allen himself was of solid Lancashire stock. The training he initiated was to inculcate the firm unquestioning faith needed by priests who, destined to serve the remaining English Catholic families, might have to face torture and even death. After the more extreme conditions at home had been eased the same principles were continued in a course of studies extending over some eleven years. Also in line with Allen's educational ideas, the subjects remained more wide-ranging then elsewhere. During the eighteenth century the English College at Douai took the unprecedented step of introducing English literature and arithmetic into its curriculum.

The religious upheavals following the French Revolution led to a long-desired removal to England and the College eventually made its new home in the Durham hills. Staff and students were drawn largely from the hereditary Catholic families of the north and after the restoration of the hierarchy in 1850 its chief purpose was to train priests for the northern dioceses. It did not cease to be a school as well as a seminary until 1972 and the boys who came for their secondary education did so, like Francis, at the age of eleven or twelve.[1]

In the early years at Ushaw one of the College's leading members had been the historian John Lingard. His independent, essentially native brand of English Catholicism was more firmly established by Robert Tate, one of the College's most outstanding Presidents whose appointment in 1863 lasted until his death during Francis's final year at Ushaw. In his younger days Tate had corresponded regularly with Lingard for some twenty years. They agreed on many issues, notably the use of English in the liturgy and the suppression of the more extreme forms of 'continental Catholicism'. By the time of Tate's election he was unable to develop his own views as far as he wished but he succeeded in carrying on the tradition at the College largely created by Lingard himself. He was an educationalist in a wider sense. He encouraged a liberal basis for the general courses, which in the Junior College included mathematics, history, geography, French and, most important for Francis, a special emphasis on 'English Composition'. A lover of the countryside and a keen reader himself, his cultivated tastes helped to create an atmosphere where learning was respected for its own sake and where the practical and pleasurable aspects of the boys' life were seen as part of their general education.[2]

Although Tate's influence was felt throughout the College it had more scope where the Juniors were concerned. In the Senior College the theological field and its related subject of philosophy was dominated by a much more conservative outlook. Henry Gillow, Professor of Theology before and during Thompson's years at Ushaw, was a determined upholder of the Scholastic basis for both subjects. Since the Counter-Reformation the writings of the medieval Scholastics had been constantly re-interpreted, to become by now the norm for all orthodox Catholic teaching. Gillow had no patience with those who were beginning to question the validity of the later interpretations and advocating a return to the primary sources. In later years Thompson was to see the limitations of his education in this respect very clearly.

Nor would he have agreed with either Tate or Gillow about the dangers they saw in opening the secular universities to Catholics. The alternative, the taking of London University degrees, was only a poor second best, and only then for students with a secular career ahead. There was little or no effect on the academic training of those who, like himself, were from the first intended for the priesthood.[3]

Yet over and above these considerations there remained that particular brand of native Catholicism arising from the College's origins and carried on now in an age when established values were being challenged by changing ideas and conditions. One of its best-known sons, Wilfrid Ward, was to recall this influence as he knew it in the years just before Thompson's arrival:

> In Ushaw more than elsewhere now much of its distinctive character survived, including a certain undemonstrative English staying power and piety. There was seen as perhaps no where else the 'new people' as the descendants of the old.[4]

Like many others, Thompson must have been awed on his arrival by the imposing appearance of the College, emphasized by the sweep of the open Durham hills on all sides. But for him it was also a constant reminder of his own medieval dream world. The design of most of the buildings followed the Gothic style of the Chapel of Saint Cuthbert, the patron of the College, for which the elder Pugin had been the architect. The Chapel was erected at one end of the main block, balanced at the other by the Library for which the Hansom brothers were responsible. Inside, the Library's fan vaulting and painted ceiling still witness to the best in Victorian Gothic decoration.

The same applies to several of the surviving buildings, notably the Junior College designed by Edward Pugin. It was a self-contained entity in Francis's day with its own chapel, refectory, dormitory and study rooms. Here the younger boys were allowed a greater freedom of activity to match their more broadly based studies. Francis spent his earlier and happier College years in this open yet intimate atmosphere. Owing to the limited space in the main chapel most of their services took place in their own Chapel of Saint Aloysius where the design was on a much smaller scale. Outside each boy had his own garden, resulting in a colourful and varied assortment of plots and flowers according to the tastes and skills of the gardeners. Beyond were the playing fields and beyond them the College farmlands and the open countryside.[5]

The overall design had a deliberate purpose, at once representing and protecting a life remote from the outside world. For all its forward-looking reputation compared with the rest of the Catholic colleges Ushaw still looked to the Middle Ages as the chief source for religious faith and practice. The purpose was strengthened by the choice of its

5. Ushaw, the Junior College

site, all of six miles outside Durham and even now comparatively isolated. In Thompson's day the hills and moors stretched all round, forming an appropriate setting and adding, for him, to the 'romantic' associations with a past world.

But there were to be other and more important associations. At the heart of the College life, of its buildings and surroundings, the liturgy of the Church was given a prominence for which Ushaw was by now well known. The changing seasons of the countryside beyond its walls found their formal counterpart in the rhythmic harmonies of the liturgical cycle of birth, death and resurrection as it had evolved over the centuries. The boy who at home had demanded to wear a red or purple cassock now responded more fully than he knew at the time to the greater beauties of the Ushaw ceremonial. Here was poetry of the highest order complemented and completed by the movement and colour of the rites themselves. And here, therefore, was nourishment for the poetry to come, drawing on his own inborn sense of pattern and order in arousing his awareness of the ordered pattern uniting the visual and verbal symbolism of the liturgy — which in turn is the formal expression of the cyclic rhythm uniting natural with human life in accordance with a supernatural pattern.

This rich legacy from Francis's Ushaw years lay in the future. The first impact of the College life was very different. Francis made the railway journey to Durham in the care of a senior student who remembered him as 'a timid shrinking little boy', teased by the other boys in the carriage, 'and how the bag of jam tarts in his pocket got hopelessly squashed in the process'.[6] It was more than the tarts, precious relics of home as they were, that was damaged by his introduction to school life. The early days after his arrival revealed a side to human nature of which he was totally unaware. Years later the memory of what he called 'the Malignity of my tormentors' was still vivid:

> It seemed to me — virginal to the world's ferocity a hideous thing that strangers should dislike me . . . that malice should be without provocative malice. That seemed to me dreadful, and a veritable demoniac revelation.[7]

This was something entirely different to his only other experience of violence in the rioters' attack on the Church and its consequences. Here were boys of his own age, religion and background, prepared to treat one of their kind with an unaccountable personal vindictiveness. To be liked already meant so much to him and it could only be that they disliked him — yet why? Elsewhere he was to recall the 'sick dread–yes, even despair' of these first encounters between innocence and experience. But Thompson had a tendency towards self-dramatization — perhaps it was the frustrated actor in him — and in any case such comments were only occasional jottings for a projected autobiographical essay. In another he made it clear that the miseries did not last beyond his first year:

> Denounce convention of boyhood 'happiest time of life'. Include first year at Ushaw for sake of contrast and its *refugium* or *sanctuary* of fairy tales and dream of flying to the fairies for shelter.[8]

No doubt his companions would have been as mystified on their side by such a flight, as he was by their 'testing' of his masculinity. They were doing no more than implementing those primitive initiation rites which, in one form or another, boyhood generally imposes on childhood. And at Ushaw, whatever their effects on a sensitive child, they were not allowed to degenerate into downright cruelty as happened at too many of the public schools of the time.

To outward appearances, Thompson passed the test. Before long he was joining in the other boys' pastimes, including the illicit ones. There are memories among his companions of a 'piratical band' he himself organized and of a subsequent 'battle' with an opposing troup for the recovery of stolen goods. At least on one occasion he had his share of corporal punishment for infringing the College rules by such escapades. Then there were the regular country walks when the botanical knowledge gained from his father stood him in good stead. And in all these features of College life its general atmosphere encouraged his companions to accept him with little more than a tolerant shrug at his being somehow 'different'. According to one of his schoolmates 'he was very well liked by the other boys', and despite his shyness and preference for reading rather than sport, 'was a very good handball player and by no means unathletic'.[9]

Sport was to some extent a common ground, especially the game known as 'Cat'. It was Ushaw's own game, having originated many years before at Douai. Francis's proficiency was mainly due to its similarity to cricket, for which another of his friends remembered he had the knowledge of 'a connoisseur'. But it was his other tastes that were most clearly remembered, along with the oddities of his appearance and manner that marked him out from the rest:

> At this period he was a frail looking lad, with high cheek bones and a nose if anything a trifle retroussé. We thought him 'mooney' (our euphemism for 'abstracted') ... but not melancholy, for he always had the saving sense of humour. Oft and for quite a protracted period would he stand with back to the fire and hold forth to all and sundry, till forcibly told to desist ...
>
> His mode of procedure along the ambulacrum was quite his own ... He sidled along the wall, and every now and then he would hitch up the collar of his coat as though it were slipping off his none too thickly covered shoulder blades. He early evinced a love of books, and many an hour, when his schoolfellows were far afield, would he spend in the well stocked junior library. His tastes were not as ours, for one of his masters about that time says of him that he always had two books on hand — one a tale-book, the other of a more serious complexion, e.g. biography, travel, history. Of history he was very fond, and particularly of war and battles.[10]

The boy as he appears here is very much the 'father to the man', from the coat-hitching habit to the holding forth on any subject to a sympathetic audience — at sometimes tedious length. More important, there is the sense of humour, one of nature's most precious gifts and one he would also never lose.

To his masters he was less of a personality than to his schoolmates. But they often remembered him clearly:

> I was his master in lower figures and remember him very well as a delicate looking boy with a somewhat pinched expression of face, very quiet and unobstrusive, and perhaps a little melancholy. He always showed himself a good boy and, I think, gave no one any trouble.[11]

The pranks and high spirits were kept for recreation. In class his energies went into his work because, apart from the mathematical subjects, he enjoyed it. About two years after his arrival a friend of the family who was on the College staff wrote to Dr Thompson of

Francis's progress. He was consistently top of his class in English and generally second in Latin, with other subjects well above average. Already there was some doubt that a curious 'abstractedness' might 'prove a great obstacle' to his intended future, but at present there was every hope of 'its entire disappearance'.[12]

Thompson's early biographers assumed that when he wrote of the physical miseries of school life in his essay on Shelley he was drawing on his own experiences. But except for the first months the evidence all points away from a self-identification with Shelley in this respect and his schoolfellows were vehement in denying anything of the kind. Bullying among the boys such as went on in other public schools was not allowed at Ushaw and even corporal punishment occupied a comparatively minor place in the College discipline.[13] Yet in another sense the essay is autobiographical. In it he describes a more subtle form of misery than that resulting from physical violence. Against this 'petty malignant annoyance' which over the years can amount to 'an agony' the boy at school has no defence. It is simply the fact that he has no privacy. In describing its effect on Shelley he is recalling how it affected himself:

> So beset the child fled into the tower of his own soul and raised the draw-bridge. He threw out a reserve, encysted in which he grew into maturity unaffected by the intercourses that modify the maturity of others into the thing we call a man.[14]

School life was strengthening the barrier set up in childhood and its inhibiting effect on the growth towards maturity. The medieval image here derives from his own means of escape into the dream world he had brought from home. He was learning the first real lessons of loneliness as he became conscious of his 'difference' outside his family and their limited social circle. The lessons were to bear rich poetic fruit later and it is not surprising that in one of the first poems of his poetic awakening he looked back to Ushaw to explore the isolation of the human spirit.

The original College buildings were constructed round an ancient yew tree, from which the name Ushaw was taken — 'yew' combined with 'shaw', the Anglo Saxon word for shade or enclosure. In 1891 it had to be cut down and Thompson wrote 'A Fallen Yew' in commemoration of the event. The news aroused memories of how the boys would climb its great branches or, like himself, seek a brief solitude among them. The poem is a deeply felt reminder that, for him, the Ushaw Yew would remain a symbol for the inner loneliness that can persist whatever the outward circumstances:

> Its breast was hollowed as the tooth of eld;
> And boys, there creeping unbeheld,
> A laughing moment dwelled.

Yet they, within its very heart so crept,
   Reached not the heart that courage kept
     With winds and years beswept.

And in its boughs did close and kindly nest
   The birds, as they within its breast,
     By all its leaves caressed.

But bird nor child might touch by any art
   Each other's or the tree's hid heart,
     A whole God's breath apart.

34–45

In the earliest completed text the second line of this stanza reads:

   Its or each other's isolate heart

— so making the theme even clearer.[15] Further on, Thompson makes use of a medieval image suggesting a connection between the refuge of the yew and the escape to his secret dream world:

Yourself are with yourself the sole consortress
   In that unleagurable fortress;
     It knows you not for portress.

64–66

Such were the lasting lessons learned, however unconsciously, during these years.

At the surface level his literary gifts contributed to his respectable position in his classes and could gain him special notice at other times. On the annual Speech (or 'Exhibition') Day it was customary for the boys who had done best to recite the compositions they had written for the examination, which could be on a subject of their own choice. While still a Junior, Francis 'electrified the whole College' with one on the French Revolution, when 'he recited ... with such spirit and the action of his hands was so full of life, added to the masterly English of his Essay, that his hearers were spellbound'.[16] The shyness retreated then as always when the power of words took over, releasing also his latent sense of drama in the gestures that suggested his whole body was given to the expression of his meaning. He kept this reputation throughout his time at Ushaw and in the Senior College the 'clear, rich, vigorous prose' of his recitations was a regular feature on the Exhibition Days.[17] Nor were his poetic gifts unknown and could be called on for other special occasions. The boys were most familiar with the humourous verse he was ready to compose to order. One that has survived, 'Lamente forre Stephanon', is a light-hearted and affectionate portrayal in mock medieval style of a popular prefect, confined at the time in the College infirmary.

As a Senior he shared his interests at a more serious level with at least one other boy. There exists at Ushaw a Commonplace Book owned by a contemporary, Alfred McDonagh, which dates from 1875. The entries show that he shared Francis's enthusiasm for battles as well as for general literary subjects. Francis himself contributed a typical schoolboy exercise written in Latin, 'Anthem in Die Vacationes', and dated 1876. More important, with the page where it appears a single sheet has been inserted from elsewhere with some fragmentary lines in Francis's hand on the love of Christ for the most depraved human heart. It may have been this friendship which led him to adopt his lifelong habit of substituting 'ye' or 'y' for 'the' in all his notebook and manuscript writing. McDonagh's Commonplace Book displays the same idiosyncrasy throughout.[18]

But the writing that really mattered to him was reserved for the privacy of the notebooks he began to keep while at Ushaw. From now on he was to use them for his poetry at all stages of composition and for thoughts and ideas from brief jottings to finished essays. Although none of the later kind survive from his College years the one that does, known as the 'Ushaw College Notebook', contains nine poems as well as final copies of several of his prose compositions. Whereas the prose, with one exception, was for his exercises in 'English Composition' the poems were for no eyes but his own.[19]

His preoccupation with battles and their historical setting appears in his choice of subjects for the essays. 'The Battle of Varna' examines the background with meticulous attention to the motives behind the action, their plan and pattern in relation to the historical events giving rise to the battle itself. There is a foreshadowing here of the conscientious reviewer Thompson was to become, when every facet of a book's subject and of a writer's approach to it would be considered before he formed an opinion. Another essay, 'The Storming of the Bridge of Lodi', was chosen for recital on an Exhibition Day. There is a more vivid account of the action in this piece, which reads almost like an expanded rendering of still-clear memories about the Murphy riot. The vivid description of the onslaught and resulting panic on all sides suggests some personal experience of the kind behind it.

The longest and most important piece never left the privacy of the notebook pages. Francis was obviously at a loss in giving it a title. 'An Exercise in Low Figures' simply uses the College term to denote the Junior School as distinct from 'High Figures' for the Seniors. It is in effect an uncertain mixture of fairy tale and allegory attempting to reconcile the dream world of childhood with the reality of awakening experience. Its central figure, Antoine de Bonneval, is one of those golden-haired youths Francis still secretly idealized, who watches his early years pass before him in a series of pictures appearing through a magic mirror. The mirror is a universal symbol for revealing hidden truths about the self and, in his use of it, Thompson's unconscious aim is increasingly clear as the pictures follow one another. Antoine sees himself first at the age of five, standing at his mother's knee in a tapestried castle chamber — much as Francis had stood beside his mother when she admonished him on his use of Shakespeare's words. But this mother, like her son, belongs to a world of dream-like perfection:

> ... her long fair hair surrounds him with a golden halo whilst she breathes into his ear lessons of love and piety, which takes deep root in his heart, and will bear fruit in after days (She) looks, rises, and points to the old crucifix which hangs on the wall, they kneel down, she joins his little hands, and together they pour forth an earnest prayer to the agonized Redeemer. Full well does Antoine recognise the scene, full well he remembers that first prayer which his young and innocent heart offered to God.

Then follows a scene from his tenth birthday:

> ... well he remembers the tall old castle with its moss-eaten battlements, the great door with its huge iron bars and bolts, and the lofty towers with their loopholes and embrasures. In the courtyard is assembled a goodly company. There is his father, attired for the hunt, while his favourite groom holds his grey charger, which none but himself can manage ...

The boy desires to join his father for the hunt, but

> ... the request is refused, and the gay company rides out of the castle gate, and the gay shouts and songs soon die away into the distance. The boy stands alone upon the castle steps gazing after them with a disappointed countenance, while the autumn wind plays with his golden tresses, and scatters them in wild disorder.

Then, when images from his fifteenth year begin to take shape on the mirror, the dream-experience takes on the threat of nightmare. As the shadows come together in some indescribable scene of horror 'he turned away his face, and hid it in his hands, that he might not behold the picture'. The symbolic function of the mirror causes its final message to become unbearable to the viewer — who is, of course, Francis himself.

The style is adolescent and unremarkable, except perhaps for a latent power in the contrasted imagery. It is the theme that matters, hardly needing the proof of Thompson's note that it was completed 'aetat 14'. His own childhood is called up in Antoine's first mirror 'vision' where the child is enfolded by maternal love and the protective piety of his Catholic background. The madonna-like figure is at once an idealization of his mother and the 'Mother Church', loving guides for the child in his first innocence. Then follows the break with this ideal state as the ten-year-old boy leaves the shelter of his inner castle to take the initial step forwards maturity in attempting to follow

his father to the hunt. But the attempt fails and the boy is left isolated
alike from the castle chamber of his childhood and from the adult
world. The hunt here adopts its symbolic link with primitive initiation
rites and is therefore linked with his introduction to school life as his
farewell to childhood, also at the age of ten. The departure from home
is further identified with an adult world which for Francis was known
mainly through his father and his father's calling. The grey charger
'which none but himself can manage' warns of a future to which the
son will be unequal and, unequipped for the demands of this adult
world, the boy is forced back to the castle chamber of childhood. But
being no longer a child the chamber is now his means of escape into
the dream world of the past. The girlish 'golden tresses', called up
from the picture books Francis had so admired, are now thrown into
'wild disorder' by a challenge he cannot meet.

What then of the future? As his fifteenth year approaches in the
form of the nightmare the youth hides his face, unable to leave the
dream world for the realities ahead. And here, inevitably for its
author, the story ends. The element of the fairy tale that runs through
the whole piece has broken down, the dream has betrayed him by becoming the nightmare. For the fairy tale follows a course of initiation
into the world of adult experience where testing and trials lead to the
happy ending. But this fairy tale fails in its function. It was a matter
of expediency for Francis to accept the initiation process at the level
imposed by his schoolfellows and so be accepted, 'liked', by them. The
true underlying process had been arrested at its most crucial stage
and now the past could not be retrieved except as a dream and the
future could not be faced. The mirror foretells a rejection he already
sensed in his 'difference' at both home and school, accompanied now
by other fears presented in images too horrible to define.

The poetry copied into the Ushaw College Notebook is unin-
spiring, showing little more than the ability that might be expected
from his literary preferences. There are occasional flashes of promise
in the imagery — as in 'Finchale' when he draws on his observations
during the walks around the College:

> Full in a spot which the glad sunlight laves,
> There spreads a wood, whose undulating waves
> Of foliage thick shine in the moving light
> Which shifts from tree to tree along their height.

In 'The Song of the Neglected Poet' he looks back in a forced
Shelleyan strain to the days 'When upon the golden mountains we
saw enthroned the mighty Sun'. Derivative as they are, the constant
appearance of the sun in these poems foretells the time when the sun
would be the focus for his poetic imagery. In the longest, a lyric for an
unwritten poem to be called 'Helias', it becomes a symbol for fulfilled

love. One wonders what the College authorities would have made of
the distinctly erotic mood of the lyric and its sensuous setting:

> And so my casement is wide,
>   And there comes into my room
> From the copse by the casement's side
>   The lilac's sweet perfume,
>   The rich geranium scent,
> And the breath of the rose in bloom;
> 'Tis the spirit of love from heaven lent
>   That floats into my room,
> 'Tis the spirit of love from the heaven above
>   Floats in on the wings of that soft perfume.

This is not the spirit of love such as they expected their students to call
down from heaven. Nor would they have approved what Thompson
later described as the background to his first attempts at poetic expression: the opening of the inner perception to beauty which is 'the
puberty of poetry in a youth' and which takes place in the same way
'as the sudden perception of wonder in a woman's beauty signalises
his sexual puberty'.[20]

For all the comparatively broad-minded outlook at Ushaw the
time had not yet come when adolescent instincts would be allowed to
develop independently of the direction dictated by the celibate life
ahead for the majority. When a boy passed into the Senior College his
character was watched carefully in this respect. So was his general
conduct, and the more so when he was known to be intended for the
priesthood. The range of his legitimate interests became much more
limited. 'English Composition' gave a necessary grounding in grammar and correct expression but was not envisaged as having future
uses other than the writing of sermons and the ability to compose a
well-phrased letter. Throughout Thompson's years at Ushaw it was
his aptitude for producing set pieces that won him approval. His
knowledge and love of literature itself was seen as no more than a
pastime that must not be allowed to interfere with his serious studies.
He was to look back on his literary education as typical of the low
standard then prevailing in the Catholic colleges: 'I have been asked
by a schoolmate, with no more than the natural healthy British lack of
brains, whether Tennyson was one of those fellows who lived in the
time of Queen Elizabeth'.[21] And in an undated letter he recalled how,
'being cut off from all but the most classically virtuous of the virtuous
classics', he would hunt the library for the 'stale and blue moulded
volumes' of poetry and devour whatever he could find.[22]

The contents of the Junior Library may have been well enough
stocked compared with the bookshelves at home. But as a Senior there
was nothing adequate to satisfy the need which was his real concern

— not matched, it was now feared, by his attitude to the studies preparing him for his future. Nor did he display any special outward
signs of piety by way of compensation. Particularly unfortunate, in
this respect, were his frequent excuses for absence from chapel — that
he had been reading and failed to hear the bell.[23]

So was he a suitable candidate, after all, for ordination? Early in 1877
his parents received a warning from Robert Tate:

> I spoke to Frank the other day and he tells me he is quite well and that his
> own inclinations in regard to the priesthood are not altered, but that his
> confessor has doubts as to his vocation. He is as he has always been a very
> good boy; and I still hope that he will become a good priest. In the mean-
> time I hope you will not be uneasy about him, as I am sure that his voca-
> tion will not be decided precipitately.[24]

He was certainly undergoing a serious inner conflict at this time. The
impression made on his companions was that he had 'entered into a
strange mental struggle' which they saw causing 'much anxiety to his
superiors'.[25] It was the first confrontation between his religious and
literary loyalties and the choice was by no means straightforward. For
it was a confrontation with his own personality, where both loyalties
coexisted in such a way that it was beyond his confessor's ability to
either understand or analyse.

Was the decision he was directed towards the right one? To a
close friend of his later years the answer seemed clear: 'Francis
Thompson was not built for any career that needed long systematic
and industrious study'.[26] Everard Meynell knew him even better.
Although he modified his opinion in the published biography, in his
personal view 'the disappointment was not Francis's: he knew himself
too well to wish to put on the cassock'.[27]

Neither is entirely correct. Thompson could show a marked aptitude for 'industrious study' when a subject really mattered to him
and, in his later years as critic and reviewer, often when it did not.
And according to Tate's letter at the start of his last year he was still
sincere in his hopes of proceeding to ordination. It was his confessor
who had doubts about his inner struggle. In spite of the consideration
shown by the authorities in coming to the decision to advise Francis to
leave, his departure was accompanied by acute disappointment and a
sense of failure affecting his family no less than himself.

Tate's death that same summer of 1877 was a cause of grief to the
whole College and greatly added to Francis's distress. The President
had always shown a special liking for the boy whose enthusiasm for
literature reminded him of his own earlier aspirations. His successor,
Dr Wilkinson, wrote to Francis's father soon afterwards. He also had

6. Thompson at Ushaw, aged about sixteen

a regard for 'Frank' and did all he could to ease the feelings of the parents in giving the reasons for the decision:

> He has always been a remarkably good and obedient boy and certainly one of the cleverest in his class. Still, his strong nervous timidity has increased to such an extent that I have been most reluctantly compelled to concur in the opinion of his Director and others that it is not the Holy Will of God that he should go on for the Priesthood. It is only after much thought, and after some long and confidential conversations with Frank himself, that I have come to this conclusion: and most unwillingly, for I feel, as I said, a very strong regard and affection for your boy. I earnestly pray God to bless him, and to enable you to bear for His sake the disappointment this has caused ... If he can shake off a natural *indolence* which has always been an obstacle with him, he has ability to succeed in any career.[28]

'Nervous timidity' and 'natural indolence' were the only tangible reasons, the only interpretations the authorities could give for habits and interests they saw as incompatible with those of a future priest. In a later age both might well have been recognized as signs of a nervous condition that would respond to the right kind of counselling and still allow for a vocation in a more specialised direction. Dr Wilkinson himself betrayed some uncertainty and possibly, in his view, Thompson could have had a genuine vocation. But not in the manner required of the priests trained at Ushaw, who he knew were expected to tackle the social evils of the northern parishes with an application to practical affairs such as 'Frank' would never achieve. The increasing 'nervous timidity' can be seen as a reaction to the crisis of his last months at College but the 'natural indolence' can only be interpreted in terms of the future as the President foresaw it if he were accepted for ordination.

The appointment of Herbert Vaughan to the Salford diocese in 1872 brought about a number of reforms and innovations, among them the opening of a training centre where newly-ordained priests were given a period of instruction in the problems ahead, for which their academic background gave them very little preparation. As Vaughan had been for some years a regular visitor to the Thompson family these aspects of his future must have impressed Francis during the vacations when he shared the Sunday evening suppers. He would also have heard of the Mission held in all the churches of Salford and Manchester in 1875, when services began at dawn each day and confessions heard late into the night. Unsparing with himself, Vaughan expected — and received — devoted and unremitting service from his priests.

Confronted by this challenge, Francis had failed. There must have been many times during the last year or two at Ushaw when his dream world opened up to let in an image of himself as such a 'devoted' priest — with, no doubt, the attributes he still so much admired in Canon Carroll. Before this image, too, he had failed. And now the mirror of the future held more dark shadows from which he would continue to hide his face, forced behind the drawbridge, back into his secret 'castle chamber'.

There was no realistic alternative but for Francis to follow his father into the medical profession. If Dr Thompson entertained any doubts about his son's suitability they must be silenced. The boy showed no special leaning towards the law, the only other practical alternative open to him as a Catholic and suited to his social background. On the other hand he did still show a genuine interest in science and, when time allowed, father and son continued their botanical expeditions together. Scientific studies now embraced some of the most exciting areas of modern life and medicine was changing rapidly under the influence of its discoveries. Added to this, for Dr Thompson his calling combined a care for the soul with the cure of the body and surely the years at Ushaw would bear fruit in this direction? So he reasoned and

7. Owens College, Manchester, in 1873 (from an engraving in the *Illustrated London News*, 18 October 1873)

so, too, tried to console Francis's mother in her own disappointment. He had the right contacts to initiate an application for the four-year course at Manchester's Owens College and it was a hopeful sign to both parents when Francis passed the entrance examination with honours, even if he only scraped through in the mathematical subjects.

Ashton was a short train ride from Manchester, where in 1851 Owens College had been founded by a wealthy local merchant of that name. From the first it aimed to include the subjects taught in the universities and in 1880 it was to become the basis for the new Victoria University. Since 1874 the various private medical schools by then existing in Manchester were amalgamated to form part of the College; the resulting School was now gaining a reputation as a leading centre for both research and training. Francis was one of some two hundred students who were enrolled annually, a bare fifty years after the first systematic teaching of medicine in Manchester began with a physician named Joseph Jordan instructing a handful of students in his own home.

The growth at Owens College reflected the changes taking place throughout the country. It was only since the Apothecaries' Act of 1815 that organized teaching of medicine and surgery became a requirement for qualification as a general practioner, and then it was usually a matter of apprenticeship to a doctor along with some hospital experience. But the progress in science created continual demands for improved methods and, by 1858, the facilities that before were confined to London were spreading to nine of the major industrial cities, where the opportunities for up-to-date research were most readily available.[29]

Manchester had a well-established record for scientific research. In particular the study of chemistry was of special importance for local industry and much of the College's reputation was due to the impact of its brilliant Professor of Chemistry, Henry Enfield Roscoe. His lectures ranged from geology to astronomy, demonstrating how the secrets of nature could be penetrated now as never before and how the same secrets bore direct relation to medical science. This aspect of science and of medicine as part of science would never cease in its appeal for Francis — when the laboratory and the library took precedence over the dissecting room and the operating table.[30]

In Manchester as elsewhere the laboratory was increasing in importance but at the same time the introduction of antiseptics was resulting in a trend away from the clinical methods of the past to surgery and anatomical analysis. Anatomy had always occupied a central place in training and now the dissecting of cadavers was accompanied by far more practical experience in assisting at operations. So, a year after his enrolment at the College, Thompson also entered his name in the registers of the Manchester Royal Infirmary in the autumn of 1878. From then on his time was almost equally divided between the College and the Hospital.

The Infirmary as he knew it was an imposing Georgian building in the area of central Manchester known as Piccadilly. It was well built for its purposes, with above-average standards of hygiene in the large airy wards. Outside there was a constant flow of traffic with patients arriving on stretchers or in carriage-like ambulances drawn by police horses, and with staff and patients on foot coming and going all day. In the main hall a huge bell was continually clanging, twice for medical aid and three times when surgery was needed. In the Accident Room staff and students waiting to be called for their services gathered round the fire to gossip with the nurses and patients.

There were two operating theatres with wooden tables, to which were attached leather straps for controlling those whose fear led to violent protest: the struggles reported as taking place with some of the rougher workers must have been decidedly alarming. Sawdust covered the floors and in each theatre a fire was kept burning at all seasons for sterilizing and cauterizing the instruments. Caps and gowns were beginning to be introduced for the surgeons and nurses, a cause for much joking and cynicism among the older members of staff. It was a rough and tumble world very similar to the world outside, but with a radical difference as well. However rough the life of most of the patients might be in the ordinary way, it had its compensations and pleasures. Here there was no compensation, and the coarse humour with which the staff tried to relieve the pressure only added to the sordidity of the general atmosphere.[31]

The Infirmary was within easy walking distance of the Medical School, which still exists within the vast complex that the Victoria University is today but not as part of the new School of Medicine. Its severe black and grey stonework and Gothic-style design has nothing of the grace Pugin had given to Ushaw. Here, the object was to give an impression of weight and substance similar to the municipal buildings in the city centre that date from the same period. The design must have succeeded in its practical aims, for it is still in partial use. In the main lecture room the tiers of wooden seats are patterned with hundreds of names and initials of past students. It is easy to imagine the young men of Thompson's day employing their time with their penknives as students have always done and no doubt as Thompson did himself, if the names and initials could be deciphered.

Life at the College was more orderly and the studies more varied than at the Infirmary. But from the first session anatomy occupied a central place, with practical classes in dissection accompanying almost all the theoretical work. Before the discovery of X-rays it was the only adequate means for students to gain the knowledge they needed, and they were deliberately discouraged from using the library in preference to the dissecting rooms.

For a young man with the right temperament and intellectual abilities, medicine was probably the most rewarding career he could choose. With the training offered at Owens, there were openings for achievement in an increasing number of related fields. But it was another matter for one lacking these basic requirements. The methods remained generally primitive and could be horrific, while the effects of concentrating exclusively on abnormalities in the treatment of disease was not yet recognized as the chief danger to which a student of any sensitivity was exposed.[32]

Thompson often spoke of his respect for science and referred to it explicitly in several of his prose writings. But his personal response to his experiences at Owens went too deep to communicate except through the images of disease and corruption that recur throughout his poetry. Only at the end of his life did he reveal something of the misery he had endured, and then it was to exonerate his father from accusations of harshness that could be made if the real situation were not known. His confidant, Wilfrid Scawen Blunt, recorded the account in his diary. Thompson insisted that he had only to tell his father how repugnant he found the training, and he would not have been made to persevere. But he could not bring himself to admit to another failure in his horror at the dissecting of bodies and the sight of flowing blood. The diary continues:

> 'As a boy of 17', he told me, 'I was incredibly vain. It makes me blush now to remember what I thought of myself. Neither my father nor my mother . . . had the least appreciation of literary things, or the least suspicion that

I had any talent of that kind. But I was devoured by the ambition to be a
great writer. All my medical studies were wasted, because I would not
work, but ran off from my classes to the libraries. If my father had known
it, he would not have forced me to go on . . . I was in every way an unsatisfactory son'.[33]

The escape from the College to the libraries was a development of the
earlier escape to the dream world. The difference now was that it
amounted to a fight for emotional survival. The challenge of the real
world was so much more threatening than it had been either in childhood or at Ushaw; thus the urgency of the present need bore no resemblance to anything in the past. Childhood innocence and its
pleasures, the spiritual and aesthetic graces of Ushaw, began to form
part of the dream world of romance and fairy tale. From it, he could
weave a future pattern where his hidden talents would appear,
gaining for him the praise and approval of his family which was
inseparable from the ambition itself.

The discipline at Owens was such that Thompson must have
kept the minimum requirements for attendance. It was more likely at
other times, when he was expected to study on his own, that he sought
the only means to make life bearable. Directly behind the Infirmary
the small Portico Library was available to bona fide readers and the
Central Library had been open for public use since its foundation in
1852. During Thompson's first years at the College it had grown to
the extent that it was moved to the old Town Hall and a reference
division added soon after. In 1882 the Art Gallery in Mosely Street
was opened, which he then frequented nearly as often. The visual
counterpart to the verbal image was taking hold of his imagination
and he would remain for hours contemplating the statuary in the
Gallery of Sculptured Casts. From the cadavers of the dissecting
rooms to the sculptures of classical art — the contrast was in itself
even more penetrating than the revulsion from the one or the appeal
of the other.[34]

The time spent in the libraries or shut into his room at home on
the pretext of studying was divided between both reading and writing
poetry. Very little of the poetry was allowed to survive, and what did
suggests he was right to destroy or forget the rest. Some ten years later
he wrote down a few, mainly from memory — the semi-erotic day-
dreams of any poetically-minded youth such as he had begun to compose at Ushaw.[35] Yet here and there some lines stand out, as in the
verses he called 'Lui et Moi':

> The sign that sends me out from men,
> > The sign that seals my life apart,
> > That sign is written in my heart,
> And on my brow for all may ken.

They cannot read it, one in ten,
>Know but this is not one of them;
>And look askance, as beasts contemn
Their fellow-beast that breaks the pen.

Just some few women may you call,
>Who say, 'This boy is strange, and thus
>He cannot be as one of us;
Wherefore we should be pitiful'.

O women! though you asked the skull
>Of Death to speak a bitter truth
>It could say naught more full of sooth
Than that- 'Ye should be pitiful'.

This skull teaches no anatomical lesson. Instead, from its vantage
point beyond the limits of human intercourse it pleads for pity for one
who likewise cannot share in the normal intimacies of life. The
attitude to women is worth noting, recalling the mother and the sister
who alone might show some understanding. In a few fragmentary
lines memorized from 'An Ode to the Delian Artemis' an idealized
woman first appears in his poetry, inspired no doubt by the female
forms among the sculptures at the Art Gallery. She is a goddess whose
beauty dispels the darkness of the wood and the fear from 'the savage
tenants of the lurking shades'. But she is a vision from the past
impressed upon present reality and as swiftly vanishing:

O bursting forth of queenly purity
Smiting the flying beasts of appetite
With wingéd shafts, till laired obscurity
Receive them in its fit ancestral night!

. . . .

So passes she, gone by for evermore!
One spotless myth 'mong many myths impure
Gone, as the heart of youth when eyes mature,
Gone, as 'mid earthly din a quiet tune,
Gone, all save yonder fair, attainless moon!

The beasts lurking in the dark wood of his semi-conscious fears are
driven to deeper hiding places by the momentary vision of a beauty
that can have no part in the present. The beasts return, the forms of
the dissecting room and the operating table that are the visible counterpart to fears within himself which he is as unable to define as the
shadows in the mirror of his schoolboy essay.

The lines are followed by a note: 'I am glad I remember no more
pre-Rossetti verses', which means they were written before the poem

'On the Anniversary of Rossetti's Death'. If this refers to the first anniversary, which is most likely, the poem in question was written in 1883 and the others before that date. It is clearly modelled on Rossetti. But if Thompson came to regret the dominance of Rossetti in his early efforts, one verse here stands out to mark a more positive influence:

> He taught our English art to burn
>   With colours from diviner skies,
> He taught our English art to gaze
>   On nature with a learner's eyes;
> That hills which look into the heaven
>   Have their firm bases on the earth;
> God paints his most angelic hues
>   On vapours of a terrene birth.

Rossetti has shown him how art and poetry, the visual and the verbal image, can complement and complete one another, and how both can express the beauties of the spirit through imagery 'of a terrene birth'. At the same time, in the library and the art gallery, he was learning from his own experience the truth he ascribes to Rossetti's example. The real, the physical world, was not confined to the dissecting room and the operating theatre but contained beauties that could reflect those of heaven itself.

At home during the vacations there was a temporary respite from the routine at Owens and the Infirmary. When he was not shut into his room he was walking for miles in the open countryside beyond Stalybridge. From now on walking was to be a lifelong and truly re-creational habit, always with the swift smooth stride and sudden pauses that were remembered years later by the townspeople and which earned for him the family nickname of 'Elasticlegs'. He still shared his enthusiasm for cricket with Mary. Since decorum now forbade her to make up a two-man game as in childhood, she would watch as he played alone, bowling the ball into the net and retrieving it himself. She accompanied him as often as he went to the Old Trafford ground and in her old age, after many years as a nun, she had vivid memories of the famous games they watched together in the days of the great cricketers such as Hornby and Barlow. Then, too, there were the times when he went with his mother to concerts in Manchester given by the now well-established and renowned Hallé Orchestra. With her he still shared his love of music, although he did not tell her how often his late return home during the term was due to other concerts he attended and not to the demands of his College work.[36]

Their outings did not last for long. About two years after Francis started at Owens his mother began to show signs of failing health and

8. Thompson at Owens College

within a few months was confined first to the house and then to her bed. It was a terrible shock for Francis. The one member of the family to whom he could turn for some degree of understanding and a love that never criticized or questioned was to be taken from him. He had enough medical knowledge — and his father kept nothing of the details from him — to know that the liver disease from which she suffered was fatal. The misery of those months of anticipated loss, in some ways worse than bereavement itself, can only be appreciated by having experienced it. And for Francis there was the added grief that when death came it was on the day following his twenty-first birthday. His mother died on 19 December, 1880.

During those first two years at Owens she had given him a birthday present, apparently at his request, of a copy of De Quincey's *Confessions of an Opium Eater*. Largely because of a misleading reference by Everard Meynell to its being 'a last gift', chosen 'without any known cause or purpose', she has been generally regarded as the unwitting agent in the start of Francis's own addiction to opium. This in turn is too easily associated with De Quincey's influence. Everard quotes

Uncle Edward Healy's remark as made at the time, how the book was his nephew's favourite and how the family feared 'his experiences would surpass those of De Quincey'.[37]

Everard is often vague regarding the precise order of events, and the observation must refer to a later period when the family had become aware of Francis's addiction. His request for a copy of the *Confessions* for his birthday was remembered later by another relative as due to his having read the book in the library, and this is the obvious explanation.[38] It is equally improbable that this was 'a last gift' for his twenty-first birthday. By then his mother was far too ill to have carried out such a request. To suggest that Mrs Thompson was in any way responsible for her son's addiction is grossly unfair. The fact that she gave it to him either for his nineteenth or twentieth birthday shows, rather, that no idea of its having an influence of this kind had occurred to her. For his part, Francis would not have shown his interest if doing so might arouse suspicions as to his own vulnerability. At first, like thousands of De Quincey's readers, he responded to its splendid prose and the human drama it portrays through the adventures of the spirit. Only later, when his own addiction had arisen from other causes, 'the joys of opium' as described in the *Confessions* began to dominate 'the pains' of its long-term effects. Many besides Thompson have been deceived by De Quincey's intentions in his treatment of the subject, a danger he had not foreseen when the book first appeared and one he did his best to correct in later editions.[39]

In Thompson's case his addiction seems to have started gradually, probably some time after he took his first medical exams. Owens College was not to become part of the Victoria University for another year and the power of conferring medical degrees was not granted until 1883. So in June 1879 Francis went to London to take the examinations, an ordeal greatly compensated for by visits to the opera and to museums and art galleries. He stayed with relatives in Fulham who were glad to show him the sights of the capital. But when the results came through there was no compensation for his failure. Nor was there any alternative to the prospect of another two years of added study in order to sit the exams again.

At the same time his mother was beginning to show the symptoms of her illness. Opium was still the only effective reliever for both physical pain and mental strain. As Francis saw the physical relief it gave her, so the temptation to use it to relieve his own anxious misery increased. Opium was permitted in homoeopathic practice and was easily available from his father's surgery. There was also the College dispensary and most general stores sold the tinctures of the drug known as laudanam.

Once Thompson discovered how a small dose could so transform present and future prospects, the relief soon overcame any other considerations. For an hour or two the impossible dreams of the future seemed realizable and the miserable reality of the present receded before them. His poetic gifts would bring him fame — how, it did not matter — such as his family would be proud to acknowledge. He would be free to pursue a life dedicated to the same gifts, and his mother would somehow be restored to health in the process. Then when the euphoria faded there was, inevitably, the need to repeat the experience since the contrast with reality made it harder, not easier, to bear.

Any attempt at understanding his feelings about his addiction, and those of the family later on, has to be made with the contemporary outlook in mind. It was by no means the same as today. Attitudes in general were only just beginning to harden into definite opposition to addiction and for many more years it was still often to be regarded as a lesser evil than alcoholism. De Quincey left an indelible portrayal of the effects and discerning readers admitted the dominance of the long-term 'pains of opium' over its emphemeral 'joys'. But his analysis was the product of an exceptional mind and very far from representative. He himself cited examples of many who had succeeded in controlling the use of the drug and for whom, he was therefore prepared to allow, it had few if any harmful effects. Everything depended on the extent of the control and the make-up of the individual. His list includes the poet George Crabbe, the popular preacher Robert Hall, Dean Milner and Lord Mackintosh. To these can be added the names of Elizabeth Browning, Robert Southey and William Wilberforce — and there were many others. Coleridge's self-torturing guilt towards his addiction has been so constantly studied that there is a tendency to regard his attitude as typical. But for him his addiction acted as a catalyst, arousing reactions of guilt whose origins lay elsewhere.

Opium could be obtained more easily than aspirin is today. A penny could buy either a pint of beer or an ounce of laudanum, a mixture of varying amounts of the drug with spices and distilled water. After the Pharmacy Act of 1868 all opium and opium products such as laudanam had to be labelled 'Poison', but there was no restriction on the quantity sold to any one purchaser. Nor was its sale limited to pharmacists: it could be stocked by a grocery or general store. Addiction in mild forms was so widespread as to be seldom regarded as a social evil. Only the more far-seeing recognized and feared its potential for more serious effects. Apart from its use as a pain reliever, mothers gave it to their babies to stop them crying and among the industrial workers it rivalled alcohol as an escape from their hardships.

This situation persisted until the end of the century and, in some respects, even beyond. But from the mid-century there was a swing in public opinion as another viewpoint began to gain ground. Concern had been growing as to the proper use of the drug since the so-called 'opium wars' of 1839 and 1857, arising from accusations made by China that Britain was trading illegally in opium through the Indian market. The economic issues were highly complex and never fully resolved. But the wars aroused strong feeling in England at a time when the rapid increase in addiction in the industrial cities first gave cause for alarm. Since then the Society for the Suppression of the Opium Trade had been agitating for legislation to confine its use to medical purposes, a campaign strongly upheld by churches of all denominations and particularly by the Catholics on account of the vulnerability of the Irish and Italian workers. Manchester became a major centre for the spread of addiction among the immigrants. It was the chief example used in the campaign for restrictions and a mass meeting held there in 1882 gained nationwide notice.[40]

This, then, was the background to the start of Thompson's lifelong problem. On the one hand the taking of opium outside its medical use was still accepted by a large sector of the public as permissible if kept within proper limits. On the other, the dangers of serious addiction resulting from such use were beginning to give rise to strong reactions — where it was viewed as an evil for which the individual was the responsible agent. Francis would have heard this attitude expressed often enough at home as a topic of conversation between his father and the priests in their mutual concern for the poor of the area. And at College the conflicting views were being debated among the students on medical grounds, a number of whom may well have experimented in its use on themselves.

Francis was in no doubt as to the moral issue in his own case. Later, when other factors were involved, it would be different. But at present the excuses for continuing the habit could not counteract the guilt at yet another deception to add to the shirking of his studies and the dreams of a future totally at variance with his family's expectations. His father's dedicated service to his patients and his forbearance over the failure at Ushaw, followed by the failure of the medical exams, made matters worse.

It was the deception towards his dying mother that went deepest. Significantly, his grief at her death provoked the first extant poem that reveals more than a passing glimpse of the future poet. The nature of his grief gave rise to something of the theme in much of the poetry to come, where love and guilt appear as the fundamentally conflicting elements in the human soul. The title and theme here are derived from the New Testament, but with a twist of bitter irony that also looks towards the future. 'This is my beloved son', the words that conveyed the true nature of Christ to John the Baptist, now uncover the true nature of another son:

Son of the womb of her,
Loved till doom of her,
Thought of the brain of her,
        Heart of her side:
Joyed in him, grieved in him
Hoped, believed in him —
God grew fain of her
        And she died

Died: and horribly
Saw the mystery,
Saw the grime of it,
        That hid soul;
Saw the seer of it
Saw the fear of it,
Saw it whole!

O mother! mother! for all the sweet John saith,
O mother, was not *this* the Second Death?   41

The 'Second Death' refers to the words ascribed to the Apostle John:
'Happy and blessed are those who share in the first resurrection. The
second death cannot affect them' (*Revelations*, 20:vi). Now she knows
all and all deception is over, must she not therefore have suffered an
agony on his account such as the Apostle has said is spared the souls
of the redeemed? And since she is clearly one of the redeemed, is he
not as guilty for the agony of the revelation as he must be for the condition revealed?

    The poem was first published by Wilfrid Meynell after Thomp-
son's own death, to illustrate Cardinal Newman's observation that
'we are two or three selves at once'. Meynell elaborated on the words
to suggest how Thompson here portrayed only one side of his nature,
'and he a saint of sorts'. But the truth presented in the poem is much
more complex, as also the 'half doubt', as Meynell puts it, of Saint
John's words. Thompson is unequivocal in his horror at realizing that
now his mother sees him as he really is, and it seems there can be no
doubt as to how he sees that real self. Yet there is a subtle variation
between the second verse as Thompson wrote it and as Meynell saw
fit to print it. Instead of the lines:

Saw the seer of it,
Saw the fear of it,
Saw it whole;

— the published text, for no apparent reason, substitutes:

Saw the slime of it   42
        Saw it whole

The reference to the fear she has also seen modifies the underlying mood of the poem. He is conscious of the 'mystery' in the shame and guilt and of causes for them he does not understand. She now does understand for she has seen the 'whole'. The agony remains, but has it been lessened by that full vision in which he cannot share? The idea of the ultimate mystery of the human soul to itself is so central to his later thought that the poem depends on the deleted line for its significance at this stage in his development.

In his present state of guilt-ridden grief it is not surprising that when he sat his exams for the second time Thompson failed them again — if indeed he took them at all. But Mary's accusation that he spent the fees on cricket balls and music books is hard to believe, for his absence would have been reported to the College and so to his parents. Setting this aside for lack of adequate proof, the disappointment at home over his failure was greater than ever. For Francis, the need to keep up the pretence at perseverence increased with his guilt, to the extent that he took one of the commonest means of escape from an otherwise unbearable situation: he became ill.

The Owens College registers show that he was absent for a year from the start of the summer session in May 1882. What was the reason? Was it a physical illness or a mental breakdown with comparatively minor physcial symptoms? Everard Meynell's assertion that an illness during the years at Owens marked the beginning of Thompson's reputed tubercular condition has been generally accepted without question. In the two latest biographies J. C. Reid agrees with Meynell and also agrees that the condition confirmed, if it did not give rise to, the addiction — since opium was often used in the treatment of chest ailments. In the other, John Walsh dismisses the illness on the grounds that Meynell gives the date as 1879, for which there is no mention in the Registers, and sees no special importance in the year's absence which they do show, following his mother's death.[43] If Thompson had suffered from a lung disease severe enough to cause him to be away for so long it is very doubtful if he would have been accepted back to complete the course, and especially considering his poor record. A sound physique was one of the first requirements for the medical profession. The address to prospective students to which reference has been made stresses elsewhere the physical endurance it often demanded. In addition there is no record of any after-effects and Thompson himself never spoke of such an illness.

Much more convincing is the reference to a mental breakdown made by James Thomson, whose biography was written (but not published) before Everard's appeared, and who therefore obtained information direct from one or other of the Meynell family. He was given a number of facts and details that do not appear elsewhere, including the nature of the illness. Thompson 'had been afflicted with a nervous breakdown before leaving Manchester, from the effects of which he never fully recovered'.[44] Mary remembered the illness but said nothing of its cause — only that Francis was not given opium as a medicine then or at any other time.[45] She would have known, for after their mother's death she took over the care of her brother and younger sister. Another indication that this is the correct and important explanation is the fact that at the same time Dr Thompson requested Canon Carroll's help on behalf of his son's future. It was not the first or last occasion when he recognized the Canon's understanding and by now he may well have suspected the addiction if he did not know it for certain. If Francis was taking opium secretly during the year at home the signs could not have escaped the doctor, but there is no way of knowing if anything was said on the subject at the time. His father probably hoped the habit would be broken by his absence from College and Francis may have still been able to give it up with the lessening of his need for it.

He owed the year's respite to Carroll's enquiries, which resulted in the discovery of his evasion of his classes and generally unsatisfactory behaviour. This in turn led to a family confrontation, one of the occasions Mary had in mind later when answering a question as to whether she was not proud of her brother's poetic fame. Any feeling of the kind, she had to admit, 'is duly kept under control by the great pain which such talent caused both to him and to us'.[46] The only immediate solution was to remove Francis from College for a time on medical grounds with the hope that time itself would do the rest.

He occupied himself mainly by secretly submitting poems to literary and other journals, but recurring disappointments only added to his sense of failure and to his guilt at yet another deception towards his family. At twenty-four his dependence on his home background had become unnatural, the outward sign of the vicious circle tightening around him. Temperamentally isolated from them since his first years, the feeling of 'difference' was now identified with guilt at the repeated failures to meet their expectations. And as with so many emotional disturbances of this kind the failure and the guilt bound him to their cause in the home situation. He could not know this at the time, desiring only to remain a child left free to range the dream world that is the legitimate realm of childhood. But he was not a child, and for the adult the desire fed the guilt as a constant reminder of his fundamental failure to meet the challenges of maturity.

Nor did the rest of the family know anything of the deeper reasons for his dependence. Mary did her best to cope with the practical side. After their mother's death she recalled simply that 'he required looking after like a child, although he was the eldest of the family'.[47] It was long before the days of any systematic psychological treatment for such conditions and by the following summer Francis was back at

Owens to make a last attempt at passing the exams after another two
years' study. There had been no recovery, only a respite.

His companions on the daily train journey to Manchester remembered him for his odd silent manner and how the schoolchildren
made fun of him for it. Mary vehemently denied that he ever left home
other than clean and well dressed, but he made sure that on his return
after a tortured day at the Infirmary or the College and a bout of
opium that she did not see how he looked. He crept into the house and
up to his room — and if Dr Thompson had his suspicions he still
seems to have kept them to himself. The cruellest account of Thompson as a student describes him as loose-limbed and untidy-looking
with 'a vacant stare, weak lips, and a usually half-open mouth, the
saliva often trickling over his chin'. But it was repeated at second
hand and compared with others sounds exaggerated. He was generally recalled as 'a frail, asthetic looking young man with a dark,
quiet, spiritual face', whose withdrawn ways gave no one a sign of the
'consuming fires' of his poetic ambitions.[48]

It was arranged that he should make a third attempt at the
exams in Glasgow as the standard there was thought to be less
exacting. When the results were no different than before there was no
alternative but to give up hope that Francis would ever become a
doctor. Soon afterwards, in June 1884, he finally left Owens College.

In spite of all outward appearances it was not the failure it has
always been taken to be. For six years he had persisted, however erra-
tically, in a career for which he seemed to himself, and to all later
critics and biographers, to be totally unfitted. Yet what made him
persist? Certainly not fear of his father's reactions. He knew, as he
later told Wilfrid Blunt, that he would not have been forced to carry
on against his will. Nor could the more complicated emotional ties at
home have been enough to account for his perseverance in the face of
such odds. There must, therefore, have been some deep-seated attraction for him that was as strong, perhaps stronger, than the revulsion.
Like so much else in his life the answer has to be looked for in his
writing, prose as well as poetry, but especially the poetry. The world
of the future lay in embryo, as it were, in the laboratories at Owens
and in the words of the lecturers who could inspire their listeners with
the promises held out by science. He had absorbed the world of the
past in the religious formation and liturgical beauties of Ushaw. But
the poet in him, the particular poetic gift that would be his true vocation, also needed this world of the future. The two would have to
merge in a grim confrontation with the present before they could germinate. But thereafter, the legacy from Owens would be far more
enduring than the apparent failure as he said goodbye to the lecture

rooms and laboratories and left the operating theatre for the last time.

For the next sixteen months he complied without enthusiasm with his father's efforts to settle him in some kind of employment. Apprenticeship to a surgical instrument maker in Manchester ended after only two weeks. It was an unfortunate choice, showing that Dr Thompson was still unaware of his son's aversion to the whole idea of surgery and that Francis was still unable to express it. Next he was appointed to assist with the sale of a new encyclopaedia and for two months he read the volumes — but got no further. At one stage he took some initiative himself and enlisted in the army. It was a desperate bid to throw over his family's plans for him as well as his own poetic fantasies. Perhaps he dreamed instead of achieving the fame of his childhood heroes in battles bravely won. The idea of Francis as a soldier in any realistic sense may be incongruous, yet he maintained later that he might have progressed further if his chest had met the required measurement. As it was, he returned home with another failure to report.

The effort at taking his own line of action was more significant than might appear from an incident that has gone almost unnoticed. Whatever intentions the family might have for him he knew by now that future changes for them must affect himself. Mary had made known her desire to join the Presentation nuns in Manchester, an enclosed Order where any intimacy, even with near relatives, must cease. And Margaret had accepted a proposal of marriage that meant she must leave England for good — after her wedding the following year she departed for Canada where she was to spend the rest of her life. Vital as these changes at home must be for Francis, there was another even more so. His father was to marry again. Dr Thompson and his first wife had known Anne Richardson, the sister of one of the local clergy, for many years. He would need someone to care for himself and the home when his daughters left and in his early sixties he was still vigorous and personable. The arrangement was highly satisfactory to all concerned — all except Francis, for whom it meant a crisis comparable to that of his own mother's death and which was inseparable from it.

According to Everard Meynell, whose view has, again, since been adopted, the final denouement arose when his father, noticing his flushed appearance — apparently for the first time — accused him of drinking and so the truth about the opium came out. But Mary made a significant comment on the early chapters of Everard's biography when she received a copy after its publication. They seemed to her, she said, 'a bit constrained, as if the writer had not said freely all he would like to say'.[49] The 'discovery' of Francis's condition seems to be an example, as was Everard's use of it as his reason for leaving home soon afterwards. On several occasions she herself hinted at an alternative, one that would have caused distress in the lifetime of the second Mrs Thompson if she were more explicit. It appears that Anne Richardson strongly objected to Francis remaining at home after her marriage. Apart from his lack of employment, she must have been as aware as the rest of the family by this time of his addiction. Mary's reference to her objecting to the anxiety he was causing only needs this obvious expansion to clarify the whole situation. Francis himself told Blunt years afterwards 'that it was his stepmother rather than his father who had been hard on him' at the time, although, Blunt added, 'he blamed no-one but himself'.[50]

No one, in fact, was to blame. To the future Mrs Thompson, Francis was a ne'er do well who had not only taken to opium but had failed in everything his family planned for him, and who at twenty-six should pull himself together and cease to be a financial and emotional strain on his father. Otherwise she saw him as a threat to her own prospects and the stability of her position in the Thompson home. For his part, when Dr Thompson had to face his son with the arrangements for the future he probably felt that nothing but a drastic change in circumstances such as they must bring about would be of any lasting help for him.

For Francis the shock precipitated the change. His feeling for his mother meant that the home as he knew it would cease to exist for him if her place was to be taken by another. She alone had understood something of his love of literature and given him his appreciation of art and music. And Mary, who had taken her place in the practical affairs of the home, was now leaving. Since Mrs Thompson's death she was closer to him than the rest, and was able to look back with some idea of the true situation. She knew how Francis had been regarded by their mother as 'her darling and the pride of her heart up to her death' and went so far as to say that had she lived he 'never would have left home'.[51]

As it was, early on 8 November 1885 he left a note in his sister's room and set off on foot for Manchester. Within a few days he was again in touch with his father, appealing for the rail fare to London. The money was sent, together with a promise of a small weekly allowance to help him with decent lodgings — but not enough to enable him to keep himself without finding work.

This was not a dramatic 'running away' to seek fame and fortune. There might be some expectation that he would earn sufficient to be free, as he later put it, to delight in 'the exercise of the imagination'. But Thompson still entertained the idea that it would then be possible to return to 'happy parental supervision' in a home he now transferred to his dream world. The physical break would not affect the far more vital emotional ties, and he still saw himself as the child who had pulled up the drawbridge against the adult world. As he boarded the London train a week later, with no other possessions from home apart from two books — Blake's poetry and the plays of Aeschylus — it was 'without hope, and with the gloomiest forebodings, in the desperate spirit of an *enfant perdue*'.[52]

3

The Gutters of Humanity
The London Streets 1885–1888

Death, that doth flush
The cumbered gutters of humanity.
                         'An Anthem of Earth': 338–339

Thompson's arrival in London in the grey November dusk did nothing to raise his spirits. The city he knew from visits to sit his exams was closed to him by his deliberate choice. On each occasion he had stayed with a Thompson cousin, the son of his uncle John Costall, who would have helped out this time. But he was determined to have no contact of that kind. At first there was probably a sense of shame at the repeated failures that had so far marked his career, but he did not go back on his resolve through all the miseries of the next three years; nor did he attempt to get in touch with other members of the family living in London. There were also Ushaw schoolmates who he knew had come to London in pursuit of their various professions. Years later one of them spoke with genuine regret of the way he would have welcomed Francis, whatever his condition, and given him any help he needed. Yet Francis knew he could no more fit himself into his family's lifestyle in London than in Ashton, while the ambitions and successes of his schoolfriends, reported in their intermittent letters before he left home, brought back the old sense of his difference from them — the difference that now seemed synonymous with failure.[1]

Then there was the resolve to give up the opium habit which he believed could be done by cutting himself off for a time from all contact with the past. Here, however, his determination stopped short. Like thousands of others he soon found that will-power and a change of scene were no answer and that the strangeness and stress of a new way of life meant he needed more, not less, of the drug. For the first time he was faced with the fact that he could not give it up by any unaided effort of his own. This was the worst failure yet. He had failed his family and now he was failing the God who would surely provide the strength if he were not already beyond the reach of God's mercy. His only relief was to turn again to the drug and so, for a few hours,

56

enter that state of uncaring peace which not even a reminder of the ugly awakening could disturb.

The weekly allowance from home seems to have varied but Mary remembered it was usually about seven shillings. It enabled him to find respectable lodgings near the Strand and would have done more if the first priority had not been his daily supply of opium. As most of the lodging houses only charged for the preparation of food provided by the boarders themselves he could do without a meal when it was a matter of choice — one calculated to add to the apathy and depression which are opium's first side effects.

Obviously work had to be found and at first there was no problem. 'Collectors' were always wanted by the many bookstores in the area, to transport books to and from other suppliers or deliver them to customers. Uncongenial as he found the work at least it was among books and with his educated speech and manner he might have progressed to a better position. But if the jobs were numereous, so were the applicants. He soon showed himself not only physically inadequate for the heavy tasks involved but dilatory in their performance. It was too tempting to find a seat and start examining the books he carried, rather than ensuring they arrived at the correct time and place.

So he would fit his employment to meet his main need, which this latest failure showed him was for the books themselves. On his errands as collector he was often greeted by the odd-job men who swept the crossings or cleared the streets of horse dung or, more respectably, set up their boot-blacking stands near the larger stores. Or he could be drawn into the friendly easy-going groups of the more successful when they gathered in Dane's coffee house off the Strand, over which at this time he had his lodgings. Listening to their tall tales of sudden luck and finding he could relax in their company, accepted as no more different than the next man, he decided to join their number. Surely he could earn enough to meet the necessities the allowance did not cover: increasing quantities of opium, usually in the form of laudanam, and the barest minimum of food and clothes. Then the rest of the working day would be his own, to spend in one or other of the public reading rooms in the Strand or, better still, the free Library at the City Guildhall.

In joining the ranks of the men of the streets Thompson entered another world with its own territories and firmly maintained hierarchy. At its head stood the owners of the coffee stalls, their urns protected by a portable shelter hung around with an array of jugs and mugs. On winter nights or when the theatres closed they could boast of clients from all classes of the society with which they otherwise had no connection. On cold evenings, society might also patronise the other more senior members of the hierarchy with their hot-potato

ovens or roasted-chestnut braziers. At other times, the worse the
weather, the more the boot-blacks could claim a share in the respect-
ability they might restore to the highest in the land — even if it was at
the lowest sartorial level. But the rank and file had no such preten-
sions. They were the crossing-sweepers and the cabmens' touts, who
watered the horses and ran errands for the drivers; the collectors of
horse dung for the market gardeners and the dustbin and sewer
'hunters'; and, lower still, those who extracted tobacco from half-
smoked cigars picked up in the gutters to sell to members of the
hierarchy a few grades higher up the scale.[2]

As a boot-black, Thompson thought he could augment the allowance and still retain the degree of self-respect he found among the
higher ranks of the order of the streets. He was soon disappointed. He
had none of their quick wit for self-preservation against either the
official street regulations or the much more strictly enforced laws of
the underworld itself. Ousted from his chosen pitch and not knowing
how to obtain another, within a few weeks he was reduced to earning
the required pennies by calling cabs and selling matches.

He was now one of an amorphous crowd whose position in the
hierarchy depended on their wares — from the craftsmen and women
who could still take pride in handmade goods to the lowest grades
which included the sellers of matches and bootlaces. They were only
slightly removed from the really destitute, making some attempt at
earning their livelihood rather than descend to outright begging or
scrounging. The Scots poet John Davidson brought a native realism
to his descriptions of London life unlike the self-regarding sentimentality of most similar poetry of the time. To him these 'gutter
merchants' still possessed a strange dignity born of the individual
tragedies that must have brought them to share the same degrading
plight:

> At the kerb
> Fifty and five, a ghastly row,
> With faces hell could not perturb
> So rigid were they in their woe,
> Self-centred stood. Life's undertow
> Had dragged them down: a few were old,
> A few were young, though fallen so low;
> But most were in their prime: they sold
> Unnecessary trifles manifold.
>
> A while he watched them wonderstruck;
> And scornfully they watched again.
> Not these the undistinguished ruck
> and ordinary run of men!
> Their mystery seemed beyond his ken:

What brought such mortals there, so strong,
So resolute? How, where and when
Had fortune thrust them forth among
The sufferers unsalvable of wrong?[3]

For Francis there was at first another side. By choosing to earn his
pennies in the evening he could divide the daytime between the
Strand reading rooms or walk the short distance through the City to
the Guildhall Library, which for ten years now had been open for
public use.

The Library he knew was destroyed in the last war and has been
rebuilt in line with the requirements of modern scholarship. It bears
no resemblance to the earlier building, where three great aisles
reached up to a carved roof emblazoned with the arms of the City's
leading Livery Companies. Bays led off from the central passageways
with books covering almost every known subject. Windows down each
side of the building gave ample light and it was well warmed from its
three great open fireplaces. Here Francis could be himself, shedding
his present privations and the frustrations of the past. He could range
through classical writers he had not known at Ushaw and explore
fields of modern literature that there had been even more firmly closed
to him. The reading begun at Manchester prepared the way, but was
of necessity limited by the comparatively recent opening of such
provincial libraries and the selective policies of the authorities. But
the Guildhall Library, founded by Richard ('Dick') Whittington in
the fourteenth century, has never lost its wide-ranging and liberal
reputation.

From his earlier reading Thompson was familiar with Rossetti's
poetic ideals and their sources in Walter Pater's view of the poet as
one who stood apart from other men. The idea of the poet as put forward by the generation of Wordsworth and Shelley had become
greatly exaggerated. He was now a priviledged being whose vocation
was to experience and express emotional ecstacies not allowed to
ordinary mortals and unconfined by the moralities of normal society.
Francis had favoured this image of freedom and exaltation of the
spirit, giving it a place in the dream world of his future greatness, but
now he began to recognize some serious implications. How could it
be brought in line with the kind of reality he shared in the life of the
streets? Were not the experiences of society's outcasts just as valid in
their intensity of suffering as the high-flown sentiments of the poets
who saw themselves as superior to the society they therefore chose to
flout? Now Baudelaire and his followers were opening up another
form of creative expression. The French writers had found and revealed their genius through their real-life experiences in the slums and

brothels of Paris. A few months ago Francis would have recoiled from
Flaubert and Verlaine as he recoiled from the dissecting room and the
operating theatre. Now he found parallels between what he read and
what he witnessed on the streets that gave shape to the shadows he
had been unable to face in the mirror of his schoolboy essay.

Yet did they portray the full truth? When he turned to the books
in his own pockets he recognised in both Aeschylus and Blake a wider
and deeper vision than any held out by the disciples of Pater or by the
realist French poets and writers and their English imitators. For
Aeschylus the discords of tragedy were essential to the ultimate
harmony in human destiny, raising man to a dignity beyond the limits
of his mortal life. For Blake, too, there was a comparable harmony to
be revealed when the 'dark satanic mills' give way to another order in
the coming of the New Jerusalem. Where, among the writers of his
own time, was the inherent harmony in human destiny as it came to
him from classical tragedy and Christian prophecy? Or the dignity in
human nature arising from a source outside any material circum-
stance of birth and good or ill fortune? The aesthetes were content to
ignore, like Dives, the Lazarus outside the gates of their emotional
feastings. But were not the realists also at fault, portraying the side of
life to which society had reduced its victims to the exclusion of another
dimension where Dives must atone for the suffering imposed on
Lazarus?

On the other hand, and most important of all, could one continue
to believe in that dimension when the self-styled followers of Christ
seemed content to leave Lazarus to his crumbs? And when Lazarus
in turn was too often a brutalized creature with no idea beyond
grabbing whatever satisfaction might compensate, in passing, for his
miseries? What place could the remote beauties of the Ushaw liturgy
have in the London of Charles Dickens? Or in the conditions in which
Thompson actually shared, rather than viewing them from the outside — as one eye witness among many was to do:

> I can never forget the sights I saw. Hundreds of men and some scores
> of women homeless, hungry, dirty and despairing, huddled on the steps
> of buildings, beneath arches, in stables, in vans, and even dustbins.
> Wherever there was the slightest shelter from the wind, rain and sleet
> they eagerly sought it. Others apparently beyond caring for body or soul
> sprawled in a sullen stupor on the seats of the Embankment.[4]

Thompson already knew what it was like to have to find shelter in the
cheapest lodging houses where the squalor was hardly less than in the
dosshouses. Andrew Mearns, one of the handful of social reformers
who were trying to bring the conditions to public notice, described a
typical scene:

These are often the resorts of thieves and vagabonds of the lowest type, and some are kept by receivers of stolen goods. In the kitchen men and women may be seen cooking their food, washing their clothes, or lolling about smoking and gambling. In the sleeping room are rows of beds on each side, sometimes 60 or 80 in one room. In many cases both sexes are allowed to herd together without any attempt to preserve the common decency. But there is a lower depth still. Hundreds cannot even scrape together the two pence required to secure them the priviledge of resting in those sweltering common sleeping rooms, and so they huddle together upon stairs and landings, where it is no uncommon thing to find six or eight in the early morning.[5]

While he was still receiving his weekly allowance Thompson could manage, on most days, to avoid the extremes of destitution. But his general appearance was deteriorating and within a few months he was forbidden the use of the reading room where he had arranged to collect his money, and the same soon applied to the others. His presence, he was told, caused offence among their members. According to Mary the allowance was returned to the family and until they knew of another address it could not be sent. But Francis was unable to bring himself to renew his contact with home and so risk his father finding out how he was failing yet again. Better to forego the money even if it meant foregoing the last link with a modicum of security.

A worse blow followed. To the staff at the Guildhall Library, he was just another of the increasing number of unsavoury characters who came with no object beyond availing themselves of free shelter and warmth. Many years later the Head Librarian remembered how, as a young assistant, he had been deployed to keep them out and how he saw no reason, then, for making an exception of the one who always carried a copy of 'Sophocles' in his coat pocket. The coat itself was too ragged:

> He however got into such bad straits and was so poorly clad that it fell to my lot to have to perform the painful duty of having to ask him to forgo his visits here. He always came with two books in his pocket. One, I think, was Sophocles; and had I known that I was entertaining an 'angel unaware' I should perhaps have been much more reluctant to eject him.[6]

Only 'perhaps'. Neither Aeschylus nor Sophocles could provide a passport over the frontier between those readers who met society's approved standards and those who did not.

Thompson's frequenting of the Manchester Art Gallery led him, from his first months in London, to spend hours at a time in the National Gallery. He continued to visit to Gallery until the shock of realizing how he appeared to its patrons, here no less than at the Library, put an end to his last refuge. There was one painting to which he returned again and again, 'The Procession to Calvary' by Ghirlandaio. It was the only one of the subject then hanging in the Gallery to portray Christ's meeting with Veronica. According to tradition Veronica was a woman in the crowd accompanying Christ to Calvary who in her pity for him wiped his face with her veil. The blood and sweat left the imprint of his features, an image that has been an object of pious devotion for many centuries.

Why was Thompson so attracted to this particular painting? It is notable for the contrast the artist has created between the calm, almost smiling image on the veil and the agony of Christ's own expression. Did Thompson recognise the further subtler contrast between the attractive legend and the sordid facts of the crucifixion? If so, did he make a connection between his own religious training and its remoteness from the reality of human suffering as he was now coming to understand it? And did he, perhaps, yearn for some Veronica to ease his own *via dolorosa*?

On the occasion of his last visit he was standing before the picture when he heard two women behind him discussing its subject. Obviously they were ignorant of the tradition and on an impulse he turned to explain it to them. They recoiled as if in disgust and made their way hastily to another part of the Gallery. Their reaction was the worst shock of all. These women were members of the general public, not officials at the reading rooms and the Guildhall Library. It was the final proof that his condition had cut him off from any society other than that of the streets. He never returned. Later he would meet his own Veronica, but not among the patrons of either the Library or the Gallery.[7]

There was another painting in the National Gallery at that time before which he had stood as long and as often. Rossetti's interpretation of the Annunciation, 'Ecce Ancilla Domine', captures visually the remoteness of an idealised scene such as he conveys in his poetry. As earlier in the poetry so now in the painting, Thompson found an escape from present sordid reality. It inspired the one poem of promise surviving from these months:

> This angel's feet, winged with aspiring light,
>   That kindles its own image in the floor;
> His gravely noble face, serene in might
>   From gazing on the Godhead evermore;
> This lily shining from the lilied land,
>   Making a breath of heaven in the room;
> Yon Dove, whose presence tells how near at hand
>   The mystical conception of her womb:
> Were *these* the things that roused from holy dreams
>   To holier waking the elected maid?

> Absorbed in all the great to-be she seems,
> > With pensive eyes that yet are not afraid.
> > Soon her low voice shall ratify heaven's will,
> > And hell's gate groan, and death's stern heart stand
> > > still.[8]

Surely there is a contrast here, giving the poem much of its grave sincerity, between the Blessed Virgin's awakening from her 'holy dreams' and his own from his opium-ridden dream world. There is certainly a hint of the future poetry in the angelic form 'that kindles its own image in the floor', a distinct reminder of the union about to take place between the spiritual and material worlds when Mary makes her assent. The sonnet recreates Rossetti's painting through its intensely visual imagery but the voice is Thompson's, not Rossetti's.

Apart from their foreshadowing of Thompson's future poetry, the sureness of expression in the lines shows how, given the right conditions and surroundings such as he had sought in the Library and Gallery, it was ready for utterance. But they were now closed to him and the poem remains a single witness to what might otherwise have been.

Thompson wrote poetry during the next months for his note-books are filled with it. But it was of a very different kind. Their damp-stained tattered leaves date these notebooks, for which he always contrived to find the required penny, more surely than any others. But their contents are sufficient evidence. Never again would he write the kind of verse forced from him then by the nightmares that are the price opium demands for its dreams. The only relief was to turn their horrific content into verse, externalizing the images of fear and guilt the drug was dredging up from the past and to which his revulsion for the present gave their hideous forms. They are as terrible as any described by Coleridge or De Quincey. There are the monster figures of Coleridge's 'Pains of Sleep' and recalled in his own note-books, while De Quincey's 'unutterable abortions of miscreated gigantic vermin' are paralleled in Thompson's images of agonized self-revelation.[9] They are proof of the dominance of the drug at this period of his life as never again. But they also show the nature of his mental state, for the nightmares induced by opium take their forms from the psychological condition behind the addiction itself. Among the many fragments, often incoherent, a few come together as finished poems. In 'The Owl', the bird that is traditionally the messenger of death stirs the cauldron of his dreams to confront him again with their terrifying content:

> The owl is the witch of the cauldron of sleep:
> And she stirs it and seeths it whooping deep;
> And she thrusts the witch-bits into it deep,

Gendering ghosts for the smoke of sleep.
She flings in toads from the money-dust,
And feeds it thick with the dead fat of lust;
Corpse-limbs of love, yet quivering new;
And blood of the thoughts that are writhing too,
Drawn from the place where the pang went through:
Adders of longing and fanged regrets;
Winged lizards of terror and monstrous threats!
Ah, horrible terrors, the withering threats!
And she sees with her eyes which the fires look through
Her deep sleep cauldron, reeking new;
And she laughs at sleep, tu-whit, tu-whoo!
And so murk is the sleep smoke of despair,
And so awful the spectres rising there,
And so fearful they throng on the calm night air,
That were not sleep as brief as deep,
It were better almost to die than sleep![10]

Only almost better — for if guilt provokes such punishment in this life, what of the punishment to come? The spiritual world as he had been taught to believe in it can do nothing for him now since it can have no place in his present state. It, too, has rejected him and will reject him again when the present state ends in death. The preternatural world of witches and monsters alone remains, with the images of nightmare as aberations of the visionary dream world of the past. And by recalling the witches' scenes in *Macbeth* the lines are an evocation of fear and guilt which the play as a whole exposes so mercilessly.

The most painful of these poems was 'The Nightmare of the Witch Babies', never revived in a fair copy. But in the last of the notebook drafts he added a reminder, rare for him, of the date of its completion: 'Finished before October 1886' — that is, within a year of his departure from home. It is a dreadful parody of the earlier escape to the realm of chivalry and fair medieval ladies:

A lusty knight,
    Ha! Ha!
On a swart steed,
    Ho! Ho!
Rode upon the land
    Where the silence feels alone,
Rode upon the Land
    Of the Bare Shank — Bone,
Rode upon the Strand
    Of the Dead Mens Groan,
Where the Evil goes to and fro.
    Two witch babies, Ho! Ho! Ho!
. . .

What is it sees he?
        Ha! Ha!
There in the frightfulness?
        Ho! Ho!
There he saw a maiden
        Fairest fair:
Sad were her dusk eyes,
        Long was her hair;
Sad were her dreaming eyes,
        Misty her hair;
And strange was her garment's flow.
        Two witch babies, Ho! Ho! Ho!

. . .

Swiftly he followed her
        Ha! Ha!
Eagerly he followed her,
        Ho! Ho!
From the rank, the greasy soil,
        Red bubbles oozed and stood;
Till it grew a putrid slime,
        And where his horse had trod,
The ground plash plashes,
        With a wet like blood;
And chill terrors like fungus grow.
        Two witch babies, Ho! Ho! Ho!

. . .

Into the fogginess,
        Ha! Ha!
Lo, she corrupted!
        Ho! Ho!
Comes there a Death
        With the looks of a witch,
And joins that creak
        Like a night-bird's scritch,
And a breath that smokes
        Like a smoking pitch,
And eyeless sockets a glow.
        Two witch babies, Ho! Ho! Ho![11]

The imagery is a tortured confusion from the now-shattered dreams of childhood and the years at Owens, mingling with the moral and physical corruption of the London streets. But it goes much deeper, uniting personal with universal experience. The imagery in each stanza draws together to form the 'witch babies' that give the poem its title and ultimate meaning. For they are the product of one of the fundamental archetypes whence nightmare experiences of this kind find their origin. Corresponding to the creative 'Great Mother', the positive feminine principle, is the 'Terrible Mother', devouring and destructive. She is the witch, the harpie, or any other of the many manifestations of female evil in myth and fairy tale. And as in so many myths and fairy tales, she must be confronted and overcome in a process of rebirth into maturity where the creative feminine element is free to complement and complete the energetic life-force of the masculine. Unless the process is achieved the psychic energy will be dominated, 'devoured', by the destructive counterpart. The individual then remains in a state of guilt towards a past he cannot discard and fear of a future he cannot accept. The experience lies beyond the reach of logical analysis and can only be formulated in symbolic terms — hence the profound appeal of the myth and fairy tale. But the artist, whether poet or painter, can create a symbolic interpretation arising from his particular circumstances even if he is usually unaware of the real sources of his inspiration.[12]

'The Ballad of the Witch Babies' is an interpretation of this kind, looking back to the escape to the dream world and the inability to confront the challenge of maturity. It takes up Thompson's early ideals and ambitions in the forms of the maiden and the mounted knight to choke them in the degradation of present brutal reality. Its hideous images are in effect the shadows in the mirror of Thompson's schoolboy essay as he is now forced to confront them. And the poetry within him struggling to free itself is imprisoned within the fear and guilt they represent. Seemingly, it is doomed to the death of the still-born, the monster offspring of the 'Terrible Mother' in the later stanzas:

> Its paunch a-swollen,
> Ha! Ha!
> Its life a-swollen
> Ho! Ho!
> Like the . . . . days drowned   (illegible)
> And its paunch was rent
> Like a brasted drum;
> And the blubbered fat
> From its belly doth come
> With a sickening ooze — Hell made it so!
> Two witch babies, HO! Ho! Ho!

Years later Thompson came across a version of a once-popular ballad, 'Tom o' Bedlam's Song', and recognised its resemblance to the poetry of the London streets notebooks. His own rendering of the ballad shows how indelible his memories from the streets were to be. The figure of the madman who haunts the lanes and alleys of the city had appealed to the public imagination since the sixteenth century or earlier, the scape-goat for that fear of madness which comedy rarely manages to conceal. Shakespeare was probably drawing on an early version for the 'Poor Tom' of *King Lear*, but Thompson is most likely to have known the text printed in 1682 in a collection of ballads and songs of the time. Two verses must have stood out as almost echoing his own ballad:

From the Hag and hungry Goblin
    That into Rags would rend ye
    All the Spirits that stand
    By the Naked Man
  In the Book of Morns defend ye
That of your fine sound Senses
  You never be forsaken,
    Nor travel from
    Yourselves with Tom
Abroad to find your Bacon
  . . .

With a Heart of Furious Fancies,
  Whereof I am Commander,
    With a Burning Spear
    And a Horse of Air
  To the Wilderness I wander,
With a Knight of Ghosts and Shadows
  I summoned am to Tourney,
    Ten Leagues beyond
    The wide World's end,
Methinks it is no Journey[13]

The same archetypal symbolism surrounds the figure of Tom as it had haunted his own nightmares and expressed here as the fantasies and fears of madness. Probably Thompson's particular brand of wit saw something bitterly comic in the similarity between the madman's name and his. The implications were known only to himself, as also the significance of his own rendering of the poem. Written some twelve years on, the remembered parallel is as vivid as any of the lines in the London streets notebooks:

The shadows plot against me,
  And lie in ambush for me:
    The stars conspire,
    And a net of fire
  Have set for my faring o'er me.
I ride by ways that are not
  With a trumpet sounding to me
    From goblin lists,
    And the maws of mists
  Are opened to undo me.

Hate, Terror, Lust and Frenzy,
　　Look in on me with faces;
　　　　And monstrous haunch
　　　　And toad-blown paunch
　　Do show me loathed disgraces.
I hear on imminent cities
　　The league-long watches arméd,
　　　　Dead cities lost
　　　　Ere the moon grows a ghost,
Phantasmal, viewless, charméd.

His self-identification is with the madman as a victim, not an object, of fear — a victim whose fears take on the imagery of disease and corruption in a mental world where the tournament of romance has become the battlefield of nightmare:

As a burst and blood-blown insect
　　Cleaves to the wall it dies on,
　　　　The smearéd sun
　　　　Doth clot upon
　　A heaven without horizon.
I dare not but be dreadless,
　　Because all things to dread are;
　　　　With a trumpet blown
　　　　Through the mists alone
From a land where the lists of the dead are.[14]

The anonymous ballad aroused memories which appear nowhere else in the forms they are given in the London streets notebooks. In later years they were to be repressed too deeply for direct expression. But their presence can be felt throughout his work. Until now these poems, if known at all, have either been deliberately passed over or treated as if of marginal biographical value. Yet the opium-induced nightmares were forcing a confrontation from which the drug itself could only provide a brief respite. The shadows in the mirror had come together to reveal a world where paradise will always have its serpent and the shining armour of the knight will prove no defence against the surgeon's knife. The poems were far more than the out-pourings of a hallucinated mind. They were laying foundations for the themes and images with which Thompson was to distinguish between ideal and reality in the poetry of the years ahead.

After the Library and Gallery were closed to him, did Thompson find any compensation in the poetry and ritual of his religion? Did he turn to the Church for refuge, whether spiritual or material? There is no record that he did so. Rather, the suffering in which he shared was causing him to question the value of his religious training as he discovered its inadequacy before the challenge of the London poor. At this time he appears to have been as cut off from the outward observances of his faith as from the society to which it seemed to him too exclusively to belong.

Nor was he mistaken. There was some rapprochement between the Irish priests and their fellow-countrymen but it was seldom extended to the immigrants of other nationalities, while the division between Irish and English Catholics was hardly less distinct in the London slums than elsewhere. It was said that more was done by Catholic organizations than by other denominations, but none seemed capable of tackling the most serious needs as they existed among the homeless and destitute. There were a few isolated and courageous attempts but no systematic effort to relieve the suffering, or to eradicate the social attitudes that perpetuated the conditions. According to these attitudes, charity was only merited by those capable of making a return, who were worth helping because they were potentially useful to society. In the current view there were three categories which made up the poor. There were the genuinely unemployed who deserved attention mainly because they had capabilities of this kind and because they could become a threat through also being capable of organizing the riots that took place on several occasions during the 1880s. Then there were the 'thriftless' who drifted in and out of casual labour, for whom the conditions of the workhouse might eventually force into the first group. But the third, those who lived as they could off the streets, were openly stated to be 'worthless', best eradicated by means of the 'natural law' of starvation or, if that failed, through compulsory sterilization.[15]

Later, when Thompson came to know more about these attitudes, he was to give vent to his anger and bitterness in a number of prose writings. Yet what distressed him most remained the personal degradation which he saw and shared in at this time, resulting as much from the prevailing religious outlook as from the so-called social reformers. In 'Degraded Poor', a poem he left unpublished, he attacked the hypocrisy of an ideal of 'holy poverty' that glosses over its sordid reality, showing how the conventional ideal is undermined when society denies its least members the basic right of self respect. So unconventional a protest would not, Thompson realized, be understood by his generation:

Lo, at the first, Lord, Satan took from Thee
Wealth, Beauty, Honour, World's Felicity.
Then didst Thou say: 'Let be;
For with his leavings and neglects will I

Please Me, which he sets by —
Of all disvalued, thence which all will leave Me,
And fair to none by Me, will not deceive Me'.
My simple Lord! So deeming erringly,
Thou tookest Poverty;
Who, beautified with Thy kiss, laved by Thy streams,
'Gan then to cast forth gleams,
That all men did admire
Her modest looks, her ragged sweet attire
In which the ribboned shoe could not compete
With her clear simple feet.
But Satan, envying Thee Thy one ewe lamb,
With Wealth, World's Beauty and Felicity
Was not content, till last unthought-of-she
Was his to damn.
Thine ingrate, ignorant lamb
He won from Thee; kissed, spurned, and made of her
This thing which qualms the air —
Vile, terrible, old,
Whereat the red blood of the day runs cold.[16]

Here again is a confrontation between ideal and reality, only here the
ideal possesses a validity of its own. The conflict is between two views
of the same reality — of poverty as a dedication to God and as driven
into the service of Satan. Fundamentally, the poem asks how the
traditional religious outlook can stand up to the challenges of a changing society, can dare ascribe the term 'holy' to poverty in the forms
forced upon it by that society.

Yet as he faced his second winter on the streets he was to find
there were individuals who stood out from the rest and were prepared
to give practical proof of their concern beyond a gratuitous extra
penny for a box of matches or a packet of bootlaces. John McMaster
was a shoemaker with a flourishing business in Panton Street, near
the Strand. In his spare time his duties as churchwarden at St Martin's-in-the-Fields included the charitable activities for which the
parish was becoming known and has since become famous. But he
went further. It was his custom to seek out among the poor of the
streets young men who might benefit from regular employment and a
family atmosphere and to give them a position in his workshop. If it
was an example of help offered to those who might make a return, his
aim was genuine in trying to give his protégés a chance which they
would be unlikely to find in any other way.

McMaster also saw how their spiritual welfare could depend
initially on this practical approach. Later, he denied that his first
enquiry was usually a question as to the state of their souls — which

9. East London slums in the late 19th century: Twine Court, Shadwell

10. Slum life

when addressed to Thompson met with the unpromising reply that it
was none of his business. This is how their meeting is described by
Everard Meynell and accepted since, but whatever passed between
them then did not go far. McMaster, however, was not to be put off.
He had been observing the matchseller at the corner of the street for
some time, noting the cultivated voice and manner along with his
deplorable physical condition. After a few more attempts he persuaded the young man to return with him to his home behind the
Panton Street shop, 'a damp rag of humanity' as he recalled, whose
story he felt it necessary to confirm with the Ashton police. Thompson
was then found lodgings and given an undemanding job in the shop
as general messenger. Most of his time was spent either writing at a
corner table or entertaining his workmates with lively conversation
and getting them into arguments — mainly, McMaster remembered,
on literature or medical matters. His obvious inadequacy in tackling
even the simplest routine task was overlooked on account of 'his
dignity and gentleness' of manner and his affection for McMaster's
small niece, who he would take for walks in nearby St James's Park.[17]

From his recollections McMaster seems to have been curious as
to Francis's religious beliefs without interfering in them. He said his
prayers, 'his Mass' as McMaster put it, each night, but where church-
going was concerned, 'there was something wrong between him and
the priests'.[18] McMaster would not say more, but if it indicates
Francis's estrangement from the outward observances of Catholicism
it also shows he had not given up his own personal religious life,
that it was surviving from the past into the very different present.

Another reason for his forbearance towards Thompson's shortcomings as an employee was that McMaster's family respected his
literary leanings. McMaster had hopes that by giving Thompson time
for them they might help in his future prospects. McMaster's father,
who lived with the family, had received some university education
and had given his son an interest in literature and history. On their
bookshelves Francis found the works of several classical writers and
collections of poetry. These, with the still best-loved Blake and
Aeschylus, were the main sources for the ideas he now began to put
together to form the basis for the essay 'Paganism Old and New'. The
essay was to change his life in a way the Panton Street background
alone could not have done, but it would not have been written without
that background. In the comparative peace and the encouraging
atmosphere of his new surroundings he was able to bring together
the ideas and impressions gained from his reading in the Guildhall
Library, building on origins going back beyond Manchester and
Ushaw to the religious training of his childhood.

In carefully chosen words and a measured style, he compares the
paganism of the ancient world with the forms that have survived
through the succeeding ages. The surface beauties of paganism have

been perfected through the influence of Christianity, where beauty becomes the expression of love. For true beauty, he argues, is born of the union of beauty and love purified of their counterparts in sensuality and eroticism. He speaks with increasing confidence when he comes to the dangers of a revival of paganism devoid of this Christian heritage:

> ... the paganism of the days of Pliny and Statius, and Juvenal; of much philosophy and little belief; of superb villas and superb taste; of banquets for the palate in the shape of cookery, and banquets for the eye in the shape of art; of poetry singing dead songs on dead themes with the most polished and artistic vocalization; of everything most polished, from the manners to the marble floors; of Vice carefully drained out of sight, and large fountains of Virtue springing in the open air: — in one word, a most shining Paganism indeed — as putrescence also shines.[19]

The culminating simile, drawn from the bitter associations of the last months, condemns the cult of beauty and of 'art for art's sake' as he had understood it from his reading and as it was to reach its climax in the next decade.

As a whole, the essay does more than set traditional Christian values against the neo-paganism of Walter Pater and his successors. It looks towards the time when Thompson would see Christianity as enhanced and enriched by the paganism it perfects and even now he does not find the Christianity of his own day achieving the integration of love and beauty which he says is the source of true art. Historically speaking, the essay cannot stand up to serious criticism. There is no attempt at differentiation in the view taken of the 'Christian centuries' or how the medieval outlook changed with the Renaissance. Again, the neo-classicism of the eighteenth century is not given any separate treatment, a revival of classical art and philosophy as a continuing structure at a time when Christianity had ceased to represent such a structure. Yet, having said this much, it remains true that under the conditions in which it was written the essay is a fine effort and within its own limits, successful.

The theme is supported with quotations, mostly direct, from fourteen different classical sources and eleven taken from later poets and writers — far more than Thompson could have found on McMaster's bookshelves. As he was to tell Wilfrid Meynell, the rest were drawn from memories going back to Ushaw as well as to the libraries in Manchester and London. Even if nothing more, the essay would still be a fine testimony to the memory which was one of Thompson's special gifts and one he was to use to the full throughout his life as both poet and critic. Nor was the essay finished until several months later, when he was back on the streets with no books in his possession other than Blake and Aeschylus.

The interlude at McMaster's also resulted in a group of poems he drafted in the notebooks he had used before and from which he later copied three ballads into the 'Notebook of Early Poems'. At first they appear very different from the agonized verses on previous pages of these notebooks, but their comparative shape and coherence are deceptive. The first and shortest describes the death of a knight as he rides through the woods to meet his lady and then her death from a broken heart. Feeble as the lines are, they carry on the theme of the violation of romantic love that had recurred in many of his nightmare poems and fragments. The wood as the scene of the knight's initiation instead brings him death, again identified with revulsion from flowing blood:

> It was a stream ran bloodily
>> Under the wall
> O Stream, you cannot run too red
>> To tell a maid her widowhead!
> It was a stream ran bloodily
>> Under the wall.

The oblique method of telling a story is of course part of the ballad *genre*. But it enabled Thompson to voice the fears and obsessions of his opium poems, contained now within a consciously acceptable framework. There is no way of knowing for certain, but the poetry suggests he was probably continuing with the drug at a greatly reduced rate. It does not seem to have been noticed at McMaster's at this time and the 'Paganism' essay could not have been conceived or begun if he was taking more than the amount needed to ward off the effects of actual withdrawal. This is also suggested by the second ballad, much longer and better sustained, and directly modelled on Coleridge's 'Rime of the Ancient Mariner' — where, too, Coleridge shows only residual signs of his addiction. There could be a connection here with the appeal the poem obviously had for Thompson when he was writing his own ballad. In addition, for both poets the tendency to incantation in the ballad form and to evoking the preternatural fitted with the imagery and ideas deriving from their addiction.

The tale of a band of knights seeking the Isles of the Blest was widespread in the Middle Ages and had been revived by William Morris in *The Earthly Paradise*. There is nothing notably original in the subject-matter and the treatment can be dismissed as a clever pastiche of Coleridge's great poem. Yet the imagery points towards the later poetry and is in several instances already Thompson's own. As where he describes the outset of the voyage of discovery:

> Lightly, lightly flew the ship,
>> Lightly the hours were flown;
> Until the spreading blossom of day
>> Was richly overblown

As a blown rose its crimson leaves
    Showers on the fleckéd ground,
So with a roseal dapple of clouds
    The heaven was strewn around

The way to the Isles lies along the path of the setting sun, the dominant image through the twenty-seven stanzas to follow. There are
deeply felt associations between the medieval legend and pagan myth,
for which the 'Paganism' essay had partly prepared the way and
which would become great poetry in the 'Ode to the Setting Sun'. The
sun's golden path at length appears through a noonday mist:

We saw a sunshine on the sea,
    And in the sunshine there
Were gardens, as who sees a mist
    With sunset stainéd fair

These gardens of the Isles of the Blest, inhabited by fair maidens who
lure the band towards the shores, are decidedly pagan, and no Christian paradise. The contrast implied here is the poetic counterpart to
the contrast drawn in the essay where the classical Garden of Love is
fulfilled in the paradise of Christian love and beauty.

The three knights who leave the ship in response to the maidens'
call find the Isles are only a delusion, a 'wish-fulfilment', and are lost
in the mist. And now the sunset that has guided the ship as the source
of hope gives place to the darkness of night and death:

Through him alone we knew that day
    Drew to an awful close;
For darkness was round us on the wave
And we saw no further than whom the grave
    Doth living yet enclose

The sun as a source of hope is now the precurser of fear. The contrast
will return at the conclusion of the 'Ode to the Setting Sun', to be
carried over into a final affirmation of the union of darkness and light
beyond space and time. The ballad contains no such assurance, but is
left incomplete where the verses cease with the abrupt words *cetera
desunt*.

There are definite signs, in the essay theme and the poetry, that
the congenial surroundings were causing the seeds of his poetic gifts to
germinate — until the proposal that he should spend Christmas with
his family led to an exchange of letters and news from home. They
were followed by a visit from Dr Thompson who, accompanied by
Mary, seems to have made the journey to London with the express
purpose of seeing his son with the hope of building up a better relationship. McMaster only referred later to the meeting and nothing is
known of what passed between them. The doctor's impending mar-

riage and Mary's departure for the convent must have been discussed
and Francis, unable to overcome his usual reserve towards his father,
probably said little at the time.[20] But the intensity of his reactions,
now that he knew both events were imminent and unavoidable, is
clear from the third ballad. In the notebook draft it follows other
poems and fragments written during these months and is accompanied by a note, 'all at present written above Dec. 1886'. In other
words, the 'Ballad of Fair Weather' was finished, like the others,
before his return to Ashton for Christmas.[21]

This Ballad is unmistakeably the product of the changes about to
take place at home and the fear aroused when he first heard of them,
which had been the immediate cause for his leaving and for the
miseries of the months before he met McMaster. Now they were
actually upon him, a loss made even worse by the contrast with the
Panton Street background. In future his own home was to be closed to
him for good by the presence of his stepmother and if he ever saw his
sister again after this visit the convent grill would be more than a
physical barrier between them. The visit had to be made if only for
this reason, but the prospect forced him to increase the opium if he
was to go through with it. And then, along with the euphoric intervals
of seeming confidence, the nightmares returned. The resulting 'Ballad
of Fair Weather' has to be understood in terms of these conditions
and of the profound emotional upheaval Francis was undergoing in
consequence:

> They went by the greenwood
>   The sunny-built forest,
> They went by the water
>   With hearts of the sorest;
> They sought through the branches
>   Entangled together.
> The fern and the bracken
>   A-flush in full feather
> For death in fair weather
>
> They looked in the deep grass
>   Where it was deepest;
> They looked down the steep bank
>   Where it was steepest;
> But under the bruised fern
>   Crushed in its feather
> The head and the body
>   Were lying together, —
> Ah, death of fair weather!
>
> Tell me, thou perished head,
>   What hand could sever thee?

Was it thy cruel sire
  Menacing ever thee?
Was it thy stepmother
  (Bird of ill feather!)
Snapping the stem and flower
  Hid them together,
To soil thus fair weather?

My evil stepmother,
  So witch-like in wish,
She caught all my pretty blood
  Up in a dish:
She took out my heart
  For a ghoul-meal together;
But peaceful my body lies
  In the fern-feather,
For now is fair weather.

At the outset the sunlit greenwood and the refrain suggest the hopes revived by the oasis of a 'second home' at Panton Street. But the respite is over. Fair weather is a well-recognised image for deceptive security and there can be no substitute for the loss of the real home. Then, too, the greenwood, traditionally an enchanted place of entry into the otherworld, is also potentially the dark forest where initiation must take place at the cost of all that has gone before. It is where, in countless myths and legends, the hero confronts monster forms that he must overcome or be destroyed by them — as such it had made a tentative appearance in the first ballad where it brought death to the knight in search of his lady. The initiation process is often represented by the severing of the head from the body, the higher from the lower faculties, since maturity depends on the union of the two in a restored personality existing in its own right. If the process is not completed and the individual remains bound to the child's idea of the mother, she becomes the 'Terrible Mother' because she is identified with the failure.

The severed corpse, therefore, is Francis himself as he sees the promise of his mental and physical integration destroyed by the father and stepmother, archetypal figures of menace and rejection now possessed of more than symbolic power to move him. The stepmother has become the witch of the earlier poems, while father and stepmother together arouse memories of the dissecting room and the operating theatre in the corpse's flowing blood. Here, as in so many other instances, personal experience can only find expression through the symbolic experience of mankind. The mother-figure is again transformed, as in the 'witch' poems, from a lifegiving source to one that consumes the child who cannot face maturity. And he cannot face it because maturity has come to mean the loss of all that the sunlit greenwood of childhood innocence once held for him. It has been briefly revived in the Panton Street household but can have no place in the dark forest of experience closing around him.

The significance of these lines is carried into the later stanzas through the identity of the companion in the greenwood. For in the myths the symbolism of the severed head is often allied to a parting of brother and sister, representing the separation of the sexes at puberty:

> My father, too cruel,
>> Would scorn me and beat me;
> My wicked stepmother
>> Would take me and eat me;
> My sweet little sister
>> Will weep through the heather,
> Not knowing, down there
>> Mid your clouds of dull feather,
> That death brings fair weather.
>
> But I joy me most wishful,
>> Desireless to range else
> Up here in the beautiful
>> Land of the angels,
> The beautiful angels,
>> All laughing together,
> Fan me to sleep
>> With a gale of gold feather:
> Ah, death brings fair weather!
>
> They have planted two willows
>> To kiss one another
> Where the sweet sister
>> Kisses her brother:
> The silver drooped willows
>> They mingle their feather
> Where they are lying
>> In sunshine together,
> Asleep in fair weather, —
>> Dead, in fair weather.

It does not matter that the father here bears no relation to what is known of Francis's own father. The figure is the product of his long-term sense of guilt at failing his father's expectations which, as in the Ushaw essay, had been identified at the unconscious level with the adult world. The child who cannot grow up is at the mercy of the punishing father and the devouring mother who, at this level, Francis identifies all too readily with the stepmother of fairy tale and myth.

Only the sister remains. But she must leave him to follow her own call to adult life, where the loss is the greater since her vocation means a deliberate rejection of his own sex. Once the dull 'clouds' of her nun's veil descend she will weep for him but she will not understand. So the greenwood scene shifts its meaning to the only escape left from the monsters of the forest, the delusions induced by opium. The 'land of the angels' is as deceptive as the fair weather. It heralds death, not sleep, and can only be entered by the 'death' that is the opium sleep of 'wishful' dreams that will turn into nightmares. The past lies buried with the brother and sister of childhood memories of willows and moorland fern and streams. But the child haunting the grown man will still be found lying bleeding before the parent figures in the corpse of his severed hopes.

Yet the severed head has other associations. Is there a sense of an eventual transformation here, deriving from the ancient fertility rites where the sacrificial victim must be beheaded and consumed to ensure the renewal of life? Or from the equally ancient myths where the head takes on a life of its own as an oracle, a singer or a poet? If so, there is nothing inconsistent in finding elements from each interpretation coming together at the level from which the inspiration for the poem has arisen. Rather, they vacillate throughout, conveying a sense that a turning-point is being reached beyond which the future may contain either psychic life or death — or an uneasy mixture of the two, never to be fully resolved.

The 'Ballad of Fair Weather' has not as yet received any serious comment, but apart from its biographical value it reaches beyond the poet's personal pain through the universal application of its symbolism. Like other poems from these preparatory years, it is working towards the symbolism of Thompson's greater poetry. Yet the signs of the personal predicament would remain. The narcissism of Thompson's poetry has often been commented upon, usually as one of its chief weaknesses. The reason, however, has been overlooked — self-preoccupation resulting from an incomplete break from the mother-image of childhood, the break on which mature relationships outside the self very largely depend.[22]

On the other hand it had the not uncommon effect of making him notably reticent where his actual home and family were concerned and his attitudes towards them. The self he so constantly regarded and analyzed through his poetry was the self he must live with. The events and the reactions to them which had moulded that self were too painful to be recalled except on rare occasions, and then either within the confines of his notebooks or when asked a direct question by one of the Meynells or by one who, like Wilfrid Blunt, had likewise gained his cautious trust.

As a result, he made no later comment on what must have been a highly distressing visit which was made worse by the festivities of the

Christmas season. All Mary could remember was that he seemed quieter and sadder than before.[33] It was a busy time and plans for the future must have occupied much of the family's attention in their celebration of the feast that year. There seems to have been a deliberate reluctance on all sides to discuss Francis's own future, for which he may have been grateful as well as hurt, since it let him out of awkward explanations of his activities in London before his contact with McMaster.

In any case, he found he still had a good friend in Canon Carroll, to whom he probably confided the full story of the past months. The Canon persuaded him to continue to try for success with his poetry and, with this encouragement, he wrote two poems which show that his gifts were still only waiting the right kind of stimulus to find their true voice. Both were, understandably, about bereavement. In 'Dream Tryst' he turned the memory of a childhood meeting with one of Mary's friends, Lucy Keogh, into a lament for the past rather than an address to the woman Lucy had become:

> The breaths of kissing night and day
>   Were mingled in the eastern Heaven:
> Throbbing with unheard melody
>   Shook Lyra all its star-chord seven.
> When dusk shrunk cold, and light trod shy
>   And dawn's grey eyes were troubled grey:
>   And souls went palely up the sky,
>   And mine to Lucidé.

There is still something of Rossetti here, and of Shelley, but the voice is Thompson's own. When the poem was eventually published Uncle Edward Healy complained of its 'eroticism', to which Thompson commented that the lines were addressed 'to the memory only of a child known but once when I was eleven years old'.[24] He had seen her on this visit but not spoken with her and the poem is, significantly, about the memory of the child, not the woman who aroused the memory.

The second poem, 'The Passion of Mary', was begun before he left home and probably completed because he found the draft on his return — there are none for it in the notebooks from this time. Apart from some debt to Crashaw the originality of the deceptively simple lines depends on the identification of his own state, of a son bereft of his mother, with that of Christ's Mother after the death of her Son:

> Thy Son went up the angels' ways,
>   His passion ended; but, ah me!
> *Thou* found'st the road of further days
>   A longer way of Calvary.

On the hard cross of hope deferred
   Thou hungst in loving agony,
Until the mortal-dreaded word
   Which chills *our* mirth spake mirth to thee

The unconventional twist of irony distinguishes the lines from a mere pious conceit. They also show that whatever his doubts as to outward observances and attitudes, the inbred faith of Francis's early years remained unaltered in essentials.

While at McMaster's he had sent poems to several journals and been rejected by each. Canon Carroll's encouragement only led to further disappointment, made much worse by the rejection which he was aware must follow his father's marriage when the home, as he knew it, would cease to exist for him. By the time he left for London in early January, his final protest took the form of a violent reversion to opium, for which he stopped off in Manchester before he returned to Panton Street. But the effect, and the continued need for the drug, could not be thrown off and within a few weeks McMaster found there was no alternative to a dismissal from both his home and his shop.

On McMaster's side there were good reasons. His high hopes of his intelligent protegé had met with no constructive response and did not look like so doing. He expected that the visit to Ashton would result in a reconciliation between Francis and his family such as his father appeared to desire when they met in London. Presumably it was Francis who was at fault — and now the addiction, possibly suspected earlier, was obvious and causing distress to McMaster's own family as well as to his other employees. He sincerely regretted the decision, wanting Francis 'put in a home' rather than seeing him return to the streets. But to Francis himself it was yet another rejection coming at a time when he most needed the kind of help McMaster could offer. He never spoke of the shoemaker or of the months at Panton Street. Everard Meynell tried to explain away the apparent ingratitude, but the fact remains. It was the rejection he remembered and which caused his later silence.

According to McMaster, soon after Dr Thompson's marriage the following April he visited the shop again to enquire after Francis. When Mary was asked about the incident she denied that it took place, but she had left home by then and it may have been deliberately kept from her since the result was so unsatisfactory. Francis had disappeared back into the London underworld and, if his father did try to trace him in this way, the shoemaker could tell him nothing. It is possible that McMaster confused this visit with the earlier one, but whether Dr Thompson made an attempt of the kind or not the outcome was the same. Francis had no further contact with his home

during the rest of his time on the streets. His father may have 'rejected' him because, in words attributed to him by Meynell, he 'had
finally failed to retain any permanent employment' and 'would never
come to any good'.[25] As he kept his contact with Canon Carroll
through a poste restante address Dr Thompson could have obtained
information but apparently did not do so. This sounds like rejection,
yet from what is known of him it also sounds as if it was due to his
second marriage and Anne Richardson's influence. It would fit with
Francis's own words to Blunt when he maintained that it was his
stepmother, not his father, who had really hurt him.

One fact is known. Soon after Francis left McMaster's shop, Canon
Carroll wrote to him enclosing some money and urged him to send the
poems he had just completed to a Catholic literary journal, *Merry
England*, to which the Canon introduced him when they met at Christmas time. Carroll's persistent patience and practical help, apart
from his confidence in Francis's gifts, in the face of recurring failures
and the family's attitude, is a fine tribute to his insight as well as to his
genuine Christian spirit. And on this particular letter Thompson's
whole future was to depend.

Back on the streets and in a worse state than before, Thompson
could still feel bound to make a final effort. Despite the Canon's
encouragement, his poetry had met with no success, but perhaps his
prose would fare better. So he struggled to achieve a finished text for
his 'Paganism' essay. In his own much later words:

> With a few shillings to give me breathing space, I began to
> decipher and put together the half obliterated manuscript of
> 'Paganism'. I came simultaneously to my last page and my last
> half-penny . . . Next day I spent the half-penny on two boxes of
> matches and began the struggle for life.[26]

It was late February when he left the now bedraggled manuscript of
the essay and some poems, including the two written at home, at the
journal's office in Essex Street. He gave his poste restante address at
the Charing Cross Post Office. No answer came and as the weeks went
by the last hopes faded, until he ceased to enquire for one.

For over a year, his way of life and how he survived are almost
submerged in the dingy streets around the Strand and among the
anonymous, helpless figures of the truly destitute. His usual reticence
was not the only reason for his silence about these months. There was
another, given by himself in a notebook jotting with a distinct personal application: 'It would be an executioner's trick of God if He
made the poet-nature not only capable of a pang where others feel a
prick, but of hell where others feel purgatory'.[27] In other words, there

comes a point beyond which the sensitive nature ceases to register the extent of its suffering. It was to be nearly twenty years before Thompson started to make jottings and notes for an autobiographical essay which was afterwards destroyed.* Following such an interval his words show how intense the impact had been and how closely his experiences then were still allied in his mind with earlier ones remembered from the years at Owens College:

> Only the vocabulary of the hospital, images of corruption and fleshly ruin, can fitly express the objects offered to eye and ear in these loathsome streets. The air is fulsome with its redolence of tainted humanity. We lament the smoke of London: it were nothing, without the fumes of congregated evil, effluent from congregated millions of festering souls.[28]

Or again, in a brief flash from the past:

> Seamed & fissured with Scarred streets under the heat of the vaporous London Sun, the whole blackened organism Corrupts into foul humanity, Seething & rustling through its tissues[29]

The nights were even worse. With only a few pence for his earnings and the craving for opium more urgent as his suffering increased, he was forced to join the queues for the dosshouses. The running of these places was not even yet a matter for serious public concern. So far neither official reports nor horrific descriptions had resulted in any realistic effort to improve the conditions, apart from the outstanding exception in the work of the Salvation Army. If improvement was considered at all, it was then generally dismissed as hopeless since the state of the hostels was largely due to that of the inmates. Even the best-run among them such as those supervised by the Salvation Army, could not remain free from filth and vermin and they were mostly kept by wardens who only took up the position because they were unfit for any other kind of work themselves.

Among the 'realist' novelists were some trying to call attention to the situation by their lurid descriptions, but on the whole there was more persuasion behind the reports of the few social reformers who were determined that something should be attempted. In these the bare facts spoke the truth with a force calculated to arouse the public conscience with no need for further imaginative stimulus. As in Mayhew's account of the inmates of 'The Asylum for the Houseless' as their 'last dwelling, indeed, on the road to ruin':

> It is a terrible thing, indeed, to look down upon that squalid crowd from one of the upper windows of the institution. There they stand shivering in the snow, with their thin, cobwebby garments hanging in tatters about them. Many are without shirts; with their bare skin showing through the

* See Chapter Nine, pp. 292–293

rents and gaps of their clothes, like the hide of a dog with the mange. Some have their greasy coats and trousers tied round their wrists and ankles with string, to prevent the piercing wind from blowing up them. A few are without shoes; and these keep one foot only on the ground, while the bare flesh that has to tramp through the snow is blue and livid-looking as half-cooked meat . . .

The sleeping wards of the Asylum are utterly unlike all preconceived notions of a dormitory. There is not a bedstead to be seen, nor even so much as a sheet or blanket visible . . . Along the floor are ranged what appears at first sight to be endless rows of large empty orange chests, packed closely side by side, so that the boards are divided off into some two hundred shallow tanpit-like compartments. These are the berths, or, to speak technically, the 'bunks', of the institution. In each of them is a black mattress, made of some shiny waterproof material, like tarpauling stuffed with straw. At the head of every bunk, hanging against the wall, is a leather — a big 'basil' covering — that looks more like a wine-cooper's apron than a counterpane. These 'basils' are used as coverlids, not only because they are strong and durable, but for a more cogent reason — they do not retain vermin.

Around the fierce stove, in the centre of the ward, there is generally gathered a group of the houseless wanderers, the crimson rays tinting the cluster of haggard faces with a bright lurid light that colours the skin as red as wine. One and all are stretching forth their hands, as if to let the delicious heat soak into their half-numbed limbs . . . Not a laugh nor sound is heard, but the men stand still, munching their bread, their teeth champing like horses in a manger.

In an hour after the opening the men have quitted the warm fire and crept one after another into their berths, where they lie rolled round in their leathers-the rows of tightly-bound figures, brown and stiff as mummies, suggesting the idea of some large catacomb.[30]

It is worth pausing over this scene, hard as it is to understand what anyone with Thompson's background and temperament had to endure, not for a few weeks or months but for nearly two more years. He was not exaggerating when he recalled the dosshouse inmates as

. . . these brutalized men, these lads who have lost the faculty of human speech, who howl and growl like animals or use a tongue which is itself a cancerous disintegration of speech.[31]

The medical imagery is joined by that of the farmyard — as also in a few lines of poetry on their eating habits, echoing Mayhew:

. . . as beasts at feed
With a grudging, sidelong eye
Disallow interruption — so these,
With a slant and sullen eye
Mark and not reck,
Munching . . .[32]

These were his only companions, unmistakeably the men described by Mayhew. Yet there could be another side, flickering sparks of kindness and consideration such as can still exist in the worst degradation. The notebooks speak of a 'policeman who aided me' and how 'only once anyone tried to cheat me.' He was not as they were, yet he had to share their lot and their reaction was kindly rather than hostile. Occasionally he was given useful tips, such as how to make a penny buy several mugs of tea instead of one if you bought the tea and used the dosshouse kettle. There are jottings such as 'Various queer companions. actor. D.J. possible murderer, Child in snow — grt. Queen Street'.[33] And on one occasion at least he was able, perhaps even at the time, to see a comic side:

> I have no talent for oakum-picking. Though I enjoyed the distinguished tuition of a burglar who had gone through many trials — & houses — in the pursuit of this little-known art, I showed such mediocre capacity that the master held out little encouragement to persevere. And when the profession is so overcrowded, it would be a pity for me to take the oakum out of other men's fingers[34]

But this was exceptional. When he did recount some of his memories to Everard Meynell, his hysterical manner betrayed a lasting depth of feeling — his 'rising voice and trembling laughter', as Everard says of his description of finding two golden sovereigns in the gutter.[35]

Once there was a chance meeting with an old Ushaw schoolfellow and his wife, who had themselves fallen on hard times. They shared a meal with him: but Francis would not add his distress to theirs and a possibly hopeful contact faded before it was given a chance.[36] It has been said that W. H. Davies met him in a London dosshouse without knowing the identity of the withdrawn figure who, like himself, was bent over a book and trying to shut out his surroundings. Only much later Davies was supposed to have recognized him at a reading given by the notable poets of the day. The story is attractive but without foundation for Davies was not frequenting the London dosshouses until 1899 at the earliest. In 1913 when thanking the Meynells for a copy of Thompson's *Works* he wrote that he only knew one fact about the poet before 'and it was that he had a few nights on the Embankment'.[37]

Even this is incorrect. There were very many nights when the Embankment was the better alternative. Thompson's silence about his nights of exposure was only broken when he came to write one of his last and best-known poems. 'The Kingdom of God', or to give it its alternative title, 'In No Strange Land', is a late but unmistakeable flowering from seeds sown during those nights under the arches at Charing Cross. For the present, he sometimes scribbled odd lines when the nights were too cold for sleep:

Yon stellar lights, with all the dark between
To me are as a symbol infinite
Wherein the image of my fate is seen.
Stars, & between me and my stars, the night
Present, past & future hopes doth intervene
A waste of darkness weary to the sight.
How much more weary to the wandering feet,
These stars pursuing ...[38]

And, like another symbol of the denial of his hopes, the notebook page
is torn here.

It is not surprising that he came close to suicide. In spite of later
efforts to refute it, the incident appears true in essentials even if it has
become confused and somewhat exaggerated in the telling. The original source for the information was Wilfrid Meynell. In 1894 he
took part in a weekend gathering at Blunt's home when he recounted
the story, which Blunt afterwards wrote into his diary as part of the
general description of Thompson's background and years on the
streets provided by Meynell:

> ... he once attempted suicide, spending what remained to him on a large
> dose of laudanam enough to kill two men. He divided it into two portions
> and retired to I forget what cemetery in the city and took the first half —
> whereupon he had a vision in which he saw Chatterton, who took him by
> the hand and comforted him, and reminded him how the very morning
> after his suicide a letter had come from a publisher which would have
> relieved him. So he did not take the second dose.[39]

In view of the Church's attitude towards suicide at the time Meynell's
action was unexpected, particularly as Thompson was just then becoming known among the literary circle that made up most of Blunt's
party. According to the official view, not confined to Catholic teaching, suicide was a wilful denial of divine grace by which the victim
condemned himself to eternal punishment. Meynell must have
regarded the incident as fully explained and excused by its circumstances. Apparently he still did so in 1907 when he repeated the story
to Blunt shortly before Thompson's death.[40] Blunt's *Diaries* were not
published until 1919 and the first printed version of the suicide
attempt formed part of the obituary notice on Thompson which he
wrote for the *Academy*.[41] He attributed it to the poet's 'own narrative'
but there is no record that Thompson ever told it to him personally or
to anyone apart from Meynell. Everard may have heard it direct from
him rather than from Wilfrid, for although it does not appear in the
published biography there is a note about it in the manuscript as
'a curtain to his drama'. Everard adds the question the incident so
obviously raises: 'What kept him alive, what stirred the shadow of
Chatterton — shade of Francis's shadowed mind — to help him?'[42]
Equally obviously, no definite answer is possible.

11. 'Under the Arches', from an engraving by Gustave Doré, in *London: A Pilgrimage* by Gustave Doré and Blanchard Jerrold

In each account there are discrepancies and inaccuracies and there is good reason to regard the various dates given by Blunt and the Meynells as mistaken. But the fact itself remains, confirming the depths Thompson had reached since leaving the manuscripts at the *Merry England* office. According to Wilfrid Meynell's version of the story, as retold by Blunt, he heard of their acceptance 'the very next morning' after his vision of Chatterton. This was certainly not so, but Blunt was no more correct in the obituary notice, which places the episode after he had seen his poem printed in the journal — not only a highly improbable reaction but wide of the truth for as will be seen, Thompson did not see the printed poem himself. Everard's comment implies, from its placing in his notes, that the attempt followed on from leaving the manuscripts at the office. This again is highly unlikely as Thompson was then comparatively hopeful.

The reason for the confusion is explained by each writer's preoccupation with the figure of Chatterton, whose pathetic suicide as an outcast in London was followed the next day by the promise of money and recognition. Thompson himself may well have been inadvertently responsible in drawing a parallel that in his case was valid but not so instantaneous. In addition, he may have wished to gloss over the form his more immediate relief did take. If the alternative placing of the suicide attempt is the right one it would have occurred during the summer of 1887, at about the time when he gave up looking for a letter

at the Charing Cross Post Office and when he had reached the nadir
of his distress. Shortly afterwards, perhaps 'the very next day', he
received aid as strange in its own way as the Chatterton 'vision' and
far more lasting in its influence on him.

Among the hundreds of nameless prostitutes who haunted the streets
around the Strand and Soho, one now emerged from the shadows to
show how compassion and the higher forms of human feeling could
still exist in the underworld. This particular girl had also maintained
a quality of innocence to which Thompson was to pay a moving
tribute in the poem he wrote for two of the Meynell children. It contains the only direct references to the London streets years that appear
in the poetry he chose to publish: and he did not have publication in
mind when he wrote the poem. The lines on the street girl, inspired by
his response to a child's kiss, speak for themselves of the first encounter and what it meant for him:

> Once — in that nightmare-time which still doth haunt
> My dreams, a grim, unbidden visitant-
>   Forlorn, and faint, and stark,
> I had endured through watches of the dark
>   The abashless inquisition of each star,
> Yea, was the outcast mark
>   Of all these heavenly passers' scrutiny;
>   Stood bound and helplessly
> For Time to shoot his barbéd minutes at me;
> Suffered the trampling hoof of every hour
>   In night's slow-wheeled car;
>   Until the tardy dawn dragged me at length
> From under those dread wheels; and, bled of strength,
>   I waited the inevitable last.
>   Then came there past
> A child; like thee, a spring-flower; but a flower
> Fallen from the budded coronal of spring,
> And through the city-streets blown withering.
> She passed, — O brave, sad, lovingest, tender thing!-
> And of her own scant pittance did she give,
>   That I might eat and live:
> Then fled, a swift and trackless fugitive.[43]

There is a distinct suggestion that the street girl rescued him from
an extremity such as the aftermath of the attempted suicide. But the
meeting was not a single occurrence such as the lines imply. Rather,
they express the underlying nature of a relationship of some seven or
eight months, whatever other character it took as well.

Like many others among the London prostitutes, this girl seems to have lived a double existence, not allowing her profession to interfere with her private life at her lodgings in Brompton.[44] Her name is not known nor any details of her first meetings with Thompson but as the weather grew colder with the approach of his third winter on the streets, a regular arrangement developed. When her assignments were over she took him back to Brompton with her in her cab, where, according to Everard Meynell, she 'cherished him with an affection maidenly and motherly, and passionate in both these capacities'.[45] His words are deliberately vague, as are the references in Wilfrid Meynell's obituary notice to 'a few things left that cannot be uttered' about Thompson's life at this time.[46] But much earlier, when he told the story of the suicide attempt at Blunt's house party, Meynell told this one as well. In reply to a question from Blunt as to the nature of the relationship, he repeated the answer he said Thompson had given to his own enquiry, 'that in his condition there could have been no question of physical love: he was too constantly starved'. In the later conversation between Meynell and Blunt on the poet's career, Meynell added the significant detail. 'She liked his poetry, not any of it then published, and they were friends in this way'.[47]

She was probably one of the many girls of good family and education who ended up on the streets after a single and often minor moral lapse. She certainly understood something of what Thompson's poetry meant to him and could mean in the future with a change in his circumstances. And when the opportunity did come for a change, she proved her feeling for him and for his poetry by her disappearance. She left her Brompton lodgings, and all Thompson's efforts at finding her failed. She had played her part and it ended in a perfect exit at a turning-point in his life when she knew her presence could have done him harm. But she never knew how much she gave him during those months before the change came, or how much of the future depended on what she alone had given. Unlike the McMaster episode, Francis's gratitude was such that he never forgot her. Years later he still longed to see her again:

> Often, since, have I longed to encounter her: to thank her for that graciously delicate whisper which brought such healing to my hurt, indignant heart. But I never shall, till the Day which evens all debts. It is not like (that) these lines will [sic] ever have meeting with her sweet, sad eyes. Could that be, I would desire she might read in them a gratitude which passes speech & the accumulated silences of many intervening years.[48]

He was writing in the privacy of a notebook and the lines to which he refers, the sonnet 'Sad Semele', were not written for publication:

> Who clasp lost spirits, also clasp their hell;
> You have clasped, and burn, sad child, sad Semele!

One half of my cup have you drunk too well,
        And that's the death; the immortality
Girt in the fiery spirit flies your lip.
        That to my deathless progeny of pain
You should be mother, bear your fellowship
        I' the mortal grief, without the immortal gain!
Not only I, that these poor verses live,
        A heavy vigil keep of parchéd nights;
But you for unborn men your pangs must give,
        And wake in tears, that they may dream delights.
                What poems be, Sweet, you did never know;
                And yet are poems suckled by your woe![49]

Thompson is applying the myth of the birth of Dionysus, the god of
poetic inspiration, with the birth of his own poetry. Dionysus bestowed semi-divine creative energies on his devotees originating from
the union of human and divine powers when his mother Semele, a
mortal, allowed herself to be seduced by Zeus. As a result she was
consigned to the flames of a divine punishment. So in Thompson's
poem the unnamed street girl has brought upon herself the consequences of sharing in the birth of his poetry, and still nourishes it un-
knowingly through the sacrifice of her life of pain. Yet the analogy
goes further, implied in his 'parchéd nights', her 'clasp' of his 'lost
spirit' leading to the 'hell' to which she was condemned when he left
her. The overall impression is that his 'deathless progeny' owes its
existence to the experience of physical union no less than to a union of
spirits.

All commentators on this relationship draw a parallel with De
Quincey's well-known description of the motherly care he received
from 'Ann', the London prostitute who disappeared from his life when
it promised better things. There are, however, differences that make
the comparison invidious, and more especially in any suggestion that
the story of the street girl was an invention based on De Quincey.
Apart from any other consideration, if this were so she would certainly
have been given a name. De Quincey was still nominally a schoolboy
at the time in question and he was only on the streets for some six
months, several years before he started taking opium. A 'mother-
child' relationship between the seventeen-year-old De Quincey and
his Ann is not improbable. But it is very unlikely in Thompson's case.
Everard Meynell may be right, and on her side the girl was perhaps
thankful for a friendship where her maternal and sisterly instincts
could take over from the degraded sexual side of her life. And Francis
may be right, as reported by Wilfrid, that he was 'too starved' for a
lover's role. He had found the kind of love he needed, that of a mother
and sister, to ease his 'hurt indignant heart'. Yet in an unpublished

poem written the following year, 'After Love's End', he described the relationship differently:

> We lay in sleep, I think, in sleep
>   Together, she and I,
> And each were conscious in our sleep
>   O' the other's breathing nigh.
> What came of it? the touch of lip
>   (In dream), the twine of arms, the lock
> Of wills? These things are dim, and slip
>   Our memories since we awoke:
>   None knows, nor she nor I.[50]

His weakened condition and her experienced tact may have meant that he remembered their physical union more as a dream than a reality and it may not have reached a full consummation. But it seems there were occasions when the child in each of them knew, as children also know, the stirrings of sexual love, and responded as man and woman. Perhaps the title of the poem suggests the fleeting nature of these moments and the pain that followed their poignant joy.

Thompson's assurance that she shared in bringing his poetry to its final birth is supported by the power and feeling in a poem he completed soon after her disappearance back to the London underworld which he had just left. In it she becomes the figure for all those others who are condemned to a 'hell' that has more than one meaning. Here is no 'Fille de Joie', a title chosen in deliberate protest against a society that dares to use the term for a way of life for which society itself must bear the guilt:

> Hell's gates revolve around her yet alive;
>   To her no Christ the beautiful is nigh:
>   The stony world has daffed his teaching by;
> 'Go!' saith it! 'Sin on still that you may thrive,
> Let one sin be as queen for all the hive
>   Of sins to swarm around: while I, chaste I,
>   In chill immaculateness avert mine eye:-
> 'Poor galley-slave of lust, rot in your gyve!'
> This is her doom! The ways are barriered which
>   Should lead to the All-merciful's abode;
>   The house of penitence which Mary trod
> Long since is grown an appenage of the rich;
>   And though she strive, yea, strive and strive, *how*
>   Strive!
>   The gates of hell have shut her in alive.[51]

Apart from the overall theme perhaps the most significant detail here is the 'house of penitence', the Christian community which trans-

formed Mary of Magdala from sinner to saint and which has no counterpart in the Church now become the 'appendage of the rich'. For his
part, Thompson had looked into the gates of hell, within himself no
less than as they opened to him on the London streets. He never forgot
what he saw and learned then, or the girl who was drawn within them
when she left him.

She went when she was no longer needed. But the notebooks
from this time contain lines revealing another reason for his certainty
that their relationship played a vital part in his later poetic development. At no other stage during his years on the streets could he
have begun to formulate the first hesitant ideas for 'The Hound of
Heaven'. It was after he had known what human love could mean
that he sensed how its fulfilment in the normal course of human life
was not to be for him:

> I said, 'when comest thou, O Love? I wait.
> Or art thou far or near, for thou art late:
> Out of the caverned future come to me'.
> Oh, Love came out, & sat, & laughed at me.
>
> He said, 'Behold, I have thee in my net!
> Me dost thou love, & canst not me forget;
> And thou shalt have no other love than me!
>
> Thou shalt behold the glitter of my wings,
> And groan thee for the yearnings that it brings;
> But thou shalt have no other love than me!
>
> And Love sits there, & claps his shining hands,
> Oh, Love sits there, & laughs upon the sands
> And all my heart is hungered within me.[52]

His first encounter with love in this sense had left him fearing that
however he might express its extent and depth as a poet he was not to
experience it again as a reality for himself. And in another fragment,
aware now of what it could mean to give his heart in this human context, he fears and resists the sacrifice to another demand:

> Then last God came to me
> And said: 'Thou art of everything bereft,
> Save one thing only left:
> With this thou must of thine own free will part'.
> And I with smiles said: 'Lord, what may it be?'
> Then answered He:
> 'My child, give Me thy heart'.
> And I thereat
> Cried out with tears, 'Oh Lord, not that, not that!'[53]

He was a long way yet from the final surrender to a love that, in accepting the bared self, can prove stronger than the fear of the commitment. But the resistence and the flight, the essential preparation, were to be taken up into the poem that in making the surrender would also prove him to be a true poet. It is comparatively unimportant here whether the love he had known found expression in a sexual union. What matters most is that for the first time he experienced love as spontaneous, unquestioning. At the lowest ebb of failure he had been accepted for what he was, not for what he could or should be. And without that experience 'The Hound of Heaven' could not have been written.

4
Between a Joy and Fear
The Meynells 1888–1889

Like one who sweats before a despot's gate,
Summoned by some presaging will of fate,
And knows not whether kiss or dagger wait,
And all so sickened is his countenance
The courtiers buzz, 'Lo, doomed!' and look on him askance: —

    At fate's dread portals, then
    Even so stood I, I ken,
Even so stood I, between a joy and fear,
And said to mine own heart, 'Now, if the end be here!'

                  'Sister Songs' II, 169–177

So Thompson was to describe the first moments of what he came to see as the most dramatic event in his own life and the most important for his poetic career.

The encounter was hardly less memorable for the 'despot' who awaited him. Wilfrid Meynell never forgot the half-opened door and the way his guest backed from it twice before mustering the courage to enter, 'his feet without stockings, showing through his boots, his coat torn and no shirt'. Apart from his clothes he looked so thin and haggard 'he seemed in the last stage of physical collapse'.[1] Meynell's warm hospitable nature went out to him at once. There was no embarrassment, only an instant determination that something must be done to help beyond the explanation and apology he already owed his visitor. As editor of the journal *Merry England* he had printed a poem by Thompson without the poet's knowledge.

How had Thompson heard of it, so bringing about this moment-ous meeting? Throughout his years on the streets one link with life beyond the underworld remained. He never told how much Canon Carroll knew of his affairs through the poste restante address. And on his side, as with all else where Francis was concerned, Carroll understood and respected such reticence. Neither ever said whether they met in London or whether the news was sent by letter. But towards the end of March it was from the Canon that Thompson first heard how a poem of his had at last appeared in print. 'The Passion of

94

Mary' was included in the April issue of *Merry England*, one of the poems he had left at the journal's office in Essex Street over a year ago.

A few days later Meynell received one of the two letters which now lay before him on his desk. It started with a reminder of the circumstances, how the manuscripts were delivered by hand with the written request for a reply to be addressed to the Charing Cross Post Office. It continued:

> To be brief, from that day to this, no answer has ever come into my hands. And yet, more than a twelvemonth since the forwarding of the manuscript I am now informed that one of the copies of verse which I submitted to you (i.e. 'The Passion of Mary') is appearing in this month's issue of 'Merry England'. Such an occurrence I can only explain to myself in one way; viz. that some untoward accident cut off your means of communicating with me. To suppose otherwise, — to suppose it intentional — would be to wrong your known honour and courtesy. I have no doubt that your explanation, when I receive it, will be entirely satisfactory to me. I therefore enclose a stamped and addressed envelope for an answer, hoping you will recompense me for my long delay by the favour of an early reply. In any case, however long circumstances may possibly delay your reply, it will be sure of reaching me at the address I have now given.

The whole letter was a masterly piece of tactful reproof for a situation Thompson well knew was largely due to his own unusual circumstances. Equally tactfully the postscript gave more than a hint that this was the case:

> P. S. Doubtless, when I received no answer, I ought to have written again. My excuse must be that a flood-tide of misfortune rolled over me, leaving me no leisure to occupy myself with what I regarded as an attempt that had hopelessly failed. Hence my entire subsequent silence.[2]

It was what Meynell hoped would happen: that by printing the poem he would be able to trace the poet. The nondescript envelope containing Thompson's manuscripts and accompanying letter had been mislaid before he read them and only turned up about six weeks since during one of the office's rare spring cleanings. The style of the letter and its erudite references, contrasted with its shabby presentation, aroused Meynell's curiosity as much as the quality of the manuscripts themselves — which, he was quick to recognise, were far above the ordinary. The letter lay before him now, written in a neat and necessarily tiny hand on each side of a sheet of torn paper not five inches square:

> In enclosing the accompanying article for your inspection, I must ask pardon for the soiled state of the manuscript. It is due, not to slovenliness, but to the strange places and circumstances under which it has been written. For me, no less than Parolles, the dirty nurse Experience has

something fouled. I enclose a stamped envelope for a reply; since I do not desire the return of the manuscript, regarding your judgement of its worthlessness as quite final. I can hardly expect that where my prose fails my verse will succeed. Nevertheless, on the principle of 'yet will I try the last', I have added a few specimens of it, with the off-chance that one may be less poor than the rest. Apologising very sincerely for my intrusion on your valuable time, I remain,

Yours with very little hope,
Francis Thompson

Kindly address your rejection to the Charing Cross Post Office[3]

The letter was dated 23 February, 1887. Realizing that it was now over a year since the arrival of the manuscripts Meynell had written at once to the Post Office, long after Thompson ceased to call for a reply.[4] After several weeks he decided to go ahead and print one of the poems, selecting 'The Passion of Mary' as most suited to the Easter season. The poet would surely either see or hear of it and make contact: and when Thompson's second letter told him his plan had succeeded he sent a message immediately to the new address it gave, in Drury Lane. After a few days, having heard nothing, he went himself to the address with a view to explaining the situation in person.

He found it to be a chemist's shop where the proprietor, supposing him to be a relative of his client, requested the payment of a debt of four and sixpence for laudanam. Meynell complied, on condition that a message be given to Thompson to visit him at his office.

The incident of the laudanum bill, the cryptic reference in the first letter to Parolles and to the 'strange places and circumstances', followed by the 'floodtide of misfortune' in the second, prepared Meynell for an unusual visitor. But not for the meeting as it now took place. Thompson, must have been aware that some explanation was due on his side and that questions as to his background and expectations would be asked. Knowing himself unable to give any adequate answers he allowed his appearance to speak for him. Canon Carroll had the forsight to provide him with money towards making himself presentable for this possible meeting but it was needed for more urgent purposes. The debt to the Drury Lane chemist was not the only one and an extra purchase of the drug was no doubt essential in preparation for this encounter.

With a tact native to him Meynell showed no sign of surprise when his visitor eventually entered. After the explanation and the apology were made Thompson remained silent. Sensing he needed a few minutes to adjust to the situation and what it might mean to him, Meynell looked over the papers on his desk. The originality and delicacy of at least two poems, 'The Passion of Mary' and 'Dream Tryst' were in strong contrast to others where he had earlier detected signs of the opium dream and nightmare. And the essay was unmistakeably the product of a balanced and widely educated mind as well read in the classics as in English literature. How could its measured and finely turned phrases have been composed against the kind of background from which his visitor must have come? After several minutes he decided to be quite open and asked how, in his obviously destitute condition, Thompson had found access to the books he would have needed for the quotations included in the essay.

On his side Thompson was aware of the genuine concern behind the question but he was immediately on his guard. He was not going to be patronized. What could this successful journalist understand about the life he was leading or of the anguished concentration in recalling those quotations during the weeks after he had left McMaster's? His answer was swift, spoken with the touch of acerbity that Meynell was to come to know well. 'That is precisely where the essay fails: I had no books by me but Blake and Aeschylus'.[5]

It was a crucial moment. A bond was beginning to form between them, based on the priority each was giving to the content of the manuscript and leaving other matters to be dealt with later. At this stage it could easily have been broken by an ill-advised word from Meynell. After accepting the payment for the printed poem Thompson refused both the offer of further money and an invitation to dinner. Meynell did exactly the right thing. He made no attempt to persuade Thompson to do either, asking instead if he could expect another contribution for his journal. By this means he succeeded in gaining a promise from Thompson of a second visit within a few days.

The promise was kept. This time the dinner invitation was accepted — the exchange of ideas on both sides was too exciting to be halted when the time came for the office to close. On arriving at Wilfrid's home in Phillimore Place Alice Meynell's easy greeting showed no surprise at their guest's strange appearance, having heard already about him and his work from her husband. The welcome and the surroundings, the warmth and comfort of a real home and a good meal, so worked on him that neither Wilfrid nor Alice would ever forget their astonishment at his eloquence when speaking of poetry and literature, ranging from the classical writers to the present day with equal ease. Then, at about ten o'clock, his manner changed and he became restless, saying he must be going. Asked the reason he admitted that he must earn at least ten pence each night in order to live, by selling matches and calling cabs in the neighbourhood of Soho and Charing Cross. If he did not leave now he would be too late to catch the theatre-goers who were his most likely clients.

It was all very matter-of-fact. His simple statement was accepted by Wilfrid and Alice in such a way that he knew he was not diminished in their eyes. By keeping to subjects he found mattered to them

as much as to himself and avoiding the kind of questions he feared so
greatly, they had won his present confidence and a lifetime's devotion
ahead.

Gradually, over a period of some two months, the whole story
came out. Neither Wilfrid nor Alice cared about the outward appearance of their guests and Francis became a regular one at their Kensington home. Yet for all their tactful persuasion he continued to
refuse to abandon his way of life — until, having missed the street girl
for several days at their usual meeting place he went to her lodgings
and was told she had left with no trace of where she had gone. For two
weeks he followed up every possible clue: only then, when the search
must be given up, he was persuaded to accept the offer of regular employment on the staff of *Merry England* and the hospitality, at first, of
the Meynells' own home. In addition and as an essential preparation,
he agreed to a period in hospital for treatment for his addiction and
generally weakened physical condition.

The Meynells knew they were acting in the face of much doubt as
to the outcome. Wilfrid arranged for Francis to see a doctor who pro-
nounced his case as a hopeless one of opium poisoning intensified by
his debilitated state. In May a letter arrived from Edward Healy
Thompson, who by then had seen the poem in *Merry England* and who
knew — presumably through Canon Carroll — something of the outcome. He hoped Meynell would give his nephew some good advice
such as he had tried to give in the past and failed. His summary of
Francis's character was decidedly unpromising: 'He has been a great
trouble and sorrow to his father from his utter want of ballast. He
started with every advantage, but has stuck to nothing'.[6] Meynell's
reaction was typical. He invited the uncle to write an article for the
journal, which duly appeared in the September issue that year.

There are no records to show which hospital treated Thompson
but after about six weeks he was over the withdrawal symptoms and
seemed well on the way to full physical recovery. Lodgings were found
for him but the days were passed either at the journal's office or, more
often, at the Meynells' home where most of the editorial work for
Merry England was done. It was a happy-go-lucky, cheerful household.
Visitors came and went and hardly a day passed without some crisis
either in domestic or business matters. Gradually Francis found himself absorbed into it, carried along for the present by the enthusiasm of
the Meynells and their *Merry England* staff and by the casual acceptance of their growing young family. It was all so entirely different
from anything he had known. It appealed to him but it also frightened
him. Almost from the first he sensed that his independence could be
threatened by the vitality and even by the affection on which he was
already beginning to rely for emotional as well as for material support.

Not that either Wilfrid of Alice had any conscious intention of taking over his private life. For different reasons both possessed an outstanding respect for the individuality of others. It was in fact the basis for their accepting and tolerant outlook — which at the same time was often expressed in a whirl of activities and varied concerns that tended to dominate the less confident among their circle.

Yet the bond begun at that first meeting was growing steadily stronger. Common literary interests began to show up common elements in seemingly very different temperaments and backgrounds. Both Wilfrid and Francis were north-countrymen with the northerner's respect for honest dealing and direct speech. With this went the personal reserve which, marked in Francis, also underlay Wilfrid's outward geniality. There were areas of his life that remained essentially private. No one knew, for example, what it had cost him to accept the fact that he could never aspire to the literary fame of his early ambitions. Or what he felt towards the admirers who surrounded and could monopolise the attention of his wife, who was achieving the kind of fame denied to himself. Nor did anyone know the nature of their own mutual relationship or how far Alice's withdrawn, fastidious temperament depended on his for cover and support.

Wilfrid's reserve was partly due to his Quaker origins. His home had been in Newcastle but the family was descended from the Tukes of York, founders of the first institution in England for the humane treatment of lunatics. Another more recent ancestor was a collaborator with William Wilberforce in the campaign against the slave trade. In 1868, at the age of sixteen, Wilfrid came to London. He had begun to realise the futility of his high literary hopes and with characteristic good sense decided that what abilities he possessed were more suited to the level of journalism. Shortly afterwards he joined the Catholic Church. He was received by William Lockhart, a friend and convert of Cardinal Newman, from whom he learned a brand of English Catholicism with which his Quaker background could be readily assimilated. According to Viola Meynell, the daughter who knew him best in his mature years:

> As a Catholic he had never quite shed his Quakerism. He had a Quaker's flair for business and a Quaker's industry; was for lost causes, lame dogs and forlorn friends, and for individual interpretation of dogmas, and generous adjustments of errancies in others. He brought with him into Catholicism his Quaker experience of a strong sense of the reality and presence of God ... the Church that he joined was for him the Church of the Scriptures, and he was apt to see all problems in scriptural terms; mysteries of religion did not arise ...[7]

In these respects Meynell was nearer to the English Catholic outlook than to that of many of his more 'progressive' friends. A long-established understanding had grown up between the Quakers and the Catholics of the northern counties, dating from the years when both suffered from the penal laws. Quakers, like Catholics, then tended to settle in the remoter areas where they were less likely to be molested. This led to bonds of a deeper kind in the priorities assigned by each to the Scriptures and to personal devotion. Here, too, Wilfrid and Francis were to find a fundamental accord. For all their different circumstances the roots of their religious background went back to a common source in their north-country origins.[8]

It was due to these same origins that, although Meynell shared many of his friends' more advanced ideas, he never went to extremes. His tolerant good humour towards different or even opposing ideas lay behind much of his genius as both personal friend and professional journalist. In his middle years he made a rare essay into imaginative writing in a short novel, *The Cousins*, where he set out to satirize the conservatism of the hereditary Catholics along with the radicalism of the converts. To him the two sectors were 'cousins' within the same family of the Church: as such each could be caricatured with a humour that criticized without bitterness.[9] Equally typical was his regard for both Newman and Manning, whereas most of their respective followers were as much at variance as were the personalities of the two Cardinals themselves. Meynell could respect Manning's qualities of leadership and Newman's intellectual powers, and he wrote with equal appreciation of both.[10]

During his first years in London Meynell combined work on Father Lockhart's journal *The Lamp* with parochial activities. From his base at Saint Etheldreda's in Ely Place he visited slum areas where the conditions gave him an insight into the life of the poor that was to encourage Francis to confide details of his own experiences to him as to no one else. Due to these two concerns for Catholic journalism and the needs of the poor, he won the favour and friendship of Cardinal Manning who, in 1881, handed over to him the editorship of the *Weekly Register*. Described as 'A Catholic Family Newspaper' it was run in friendly rivalry with the more intellectually inclined *Tablet*.

The extra revenue was badly needed. In 1877 he had married Alice Thompson (no relation to Francis), another of Father Lockhart's converts whose first volume of poetry, *Preludes*, was being welcomed with enthusiasm in Catholic circles. It was in fact through reading her poems that Wilfrid first desired the meeting with her arranged by Lockhart.

In the eyes of their friends Wilfrid came to represent the ideal journalist while Alice filled the expected role of a poet. Her delicate appearance and withdrawn manners complemented his robust energy and outgoing hospitality. They were in many ways foils for one another. Where his background had been plodding and uneventful hers was varied and even exotic. Her father, a close friend of Charles Dickens, inherited a fortune early in life that meant he could indulge her eccentric mother in constant prolonged holidays abroad. She and her older sister Elizabeth spent their childhood in a series of strange lodging-houses and grand semi-deserted mansions, mainly in Italy, where they were left free to develop their natural gifts with a lack of supervision highly unusual for the time. As a painter Elizabeth achieved a short-lived fame that for a few years surpassed Alice's more lasting reputation as writer and poet. Even their father's attempt at an orthodox objection to Alice's marriage to a penniless journalist did not go far and she was provided for generously at his death in 1887.[11]

Before this the early years of the marriage were a hard struggle. Their first experiment at independent journalism, *The Pen*, failed after only seven weekly issues. By the time they took over the *Weekly Register* a son and daughter had been born and during the next decade Sebastian and Monica were followed by Everard, Olivia, Viola and Madeleine. But it also saw the successful launching, in 1883, of the type of journal they had attempted earlier. As a monthly, *Merry England* was soon achieving its two main aims — as a mouthpiece for liberal Catholic ideas and the first serious effort at spreading an intelligent appreciation of literature among English Catholics in general. The title was taken from Wordsworth's sonnet:

They called thee Merry England in old time;
A happy people won for thee that name,
With envy heard in many a distant clime;
And, spite of change, for me thou keepst the same
Endearing title, a responsive chime
To the heart's strong belief . . .

     . . . Can, I ask,
This face of rural beauty be a mask
For discontent, and poverty, and crime?
These spreading towns a cloak for lawless will?
Forbid it, Heaven! — that Merry England still
   May be thy rightful name, in prose and rhyme.

Interpreting Wordsworth's lines the 'Manifesto' proclaimed that 'Frankly accepting the conditions of Modern England, we would have it Merry England too'. The means, it asserted, would be found through the contributions appearing in the journal each month on social and other reforms — but first and foremost on literature and art.

Much of the inspiration for the journal was drawn from the ideas of William Morris and the aims of the Young England Movement. The contents of the first issue were headed by an article on the Movement, following Meynell's 'Manifesto'. The distinctly paternalistic

character of the Young Englanders came through in the notion that
a past ideal could be revived and imposed on present conditions by
those whose superior position in society made it their duty to spread
the ideal throughout the rest. Enthusiasm for all things medieval was
at its height: there may have been another influence of the choice of
the title, from George Daniel's *Merrie England in the Olden Time*. As a
collection of past manners and customs the first edition, published in
1842, had recently been revised with illustrations by Cruikshank.
Where the literary aims were concerned there was a genuine opening
out of interests new to the general reader for whom the journal was
mainly intended. Above all, the sincerity behind both aims carried its
success on over more than ten years — not a bad record when publications of its kind could come and go almost overnight.

Since *Merry England* was soon to occupy an important place in
Thompson's career and already did so in his new way of life, it is as
well to look at it as it appeared at the time. Ideas on literature and
many other topics were expressed with which Francis was in full
sympathy, and freely discussed by the staff as they sifted through the
material for the next issue. In many of the articles submitted the de-
plorably low standard proved the urgency of the need the journal set
out to meet. At times there was no alternative but for the staff themselves to write most of the contents under a variety of pen-names.[12]

These occasions were lessening by now. Contributions were not
confined to Catholics, a departure from the normal practice in the
contemporary Catholic press, and articles were being submitted by
many whose names were already well known, or were soon to become
so, outside Catholic circles. W. H. Hudson, J. L. Garvin, St. John
Adcock, Hilaire Belloc and Lionel Johnson were only a few of those
who made some of their earliest appearances in its pages. The range
of subjects was wide. Apart from literary topics there were articles
on architecture and local history and Manning provided regular features on religious and ethical topics of current concern. Controversial issues were welcomed and the problems raised by science in
relation to established religious ideas were openly discussed. And if
the level was elementary and somewhat jejune it was because this was
the one most likely to impress the majority of the readers and so best
calculated to fulfil the journal's aims.

The aims also had a wider context. From about the middle of
the century the periodical press was playing an increasing part in
spreading new views and discoveries. Those who wanted to know but
lacked the time or specialization for detailed study looked to the
periodicals for summaries supplied by leading figures in the fields of
science, politics, religion and literature. Other topics such as social
conditions, education and colonial matters were publicized in the
same way. As a result, the reviewing of books became a means for

writing essays on the subjects concerned, a tendency which by now
was causing several leading journals such as the *Fortnightly* and the
Saturday Reviews to concentrate on essays in their own right. One of the
most widely read, the *Nineteenth Century*, had led the way in making
this an avowed policy since the 1870s. Most were known to follow
specific religious and political viewpoints but a few, like the *Nineteenth
Century* itself, were known to avoid such partisanship. *Merry England*
was an attempt at a compromise, Catholic in principles and basic
attitudes but embracing non-Catholic ideas and interests. In the constrained ethos of Catholic intellectual life it was a bold breakaway, an
endeavour to create a Catholic journal equivalent to the rest in standard and subject matter. In addition, by following the trend towards
the independent essay as well as the essay-review it was to provide
Thompson with the opening for much of his best prose writing. With
poetry, too, it followed the accepted custom of including samples in
each issue. Here the standard was such that a far less gifted poet than
Thompson would have stood out from the rest.[13]

There were notable exceptions. During these months Thompson
was introduced to a bewildering variety of poets as well as other
writers. Aubrey de Vere and W. E. Henley were among the best
known, with whom the younger generation felt priviledged to mix on
equal terms as guests at Phillimore Place. Of these W. B. Yeats was to
be the most outstanding, although at the time his fellow-country-
woman Katharine Tynan was more highly regarded. Ernest Dowson
and Lionel Johnson were becoming attracted to an aesthetic appreciation of Catholicism that led both to join the Church within the
next two years. Among other writers, the eccentric reformer Wilfrid
Scawen Blunt regarded Meynell as his special confidant, calling
whenever he was up from his Sussex estate and captivating the company with tales of his adventures in the East. It made no significant
difference to either Wilfrid of Alice that he had thrown off his Catholic
allegiance many years ago. St George Mivart aired views which, for a
Catholic, were considered already of doubtful orthodoxy and well
outside his own scientific field. The Jesuit George Tyrrell appeared
occasionally, later to achieve notoriety as a leading figure in the
Modernist movement in England. At this time, too, Thompson first
met the group of young Capuchin Franciscans from Crawley with
whom he was to become intimate. But at present their radical social
concerns seemed strangely at variance with his idea of the priviledged
remoteness of the religious life they had chosen.

Thompson's contact with the new young publisher John Lane
was to be important to other directions. Lane's enthusiasm for book
collecting had led to his friendship with Elkin Matthews and so to
their founding of the Bodley Head Bookshop in Vigo Street. It was by
now on the way to its position as one of the leading publishing houses

at a period when the production of finely bound volumes was one of
the chief features of the English literary scene. Meynell shared this
view of the value of a book's presentation, influenced by William
Morris and the work of Morris's flourishing Kelmscott Press. Lane
was often accompanied by William Watson, an aspiring poet newly
arrived from Liverpool and of whose future Lane alone seemed confidant. Or he came with his chief *aide* and reviewer Richard Le
Gallienne, a poet also in his own right. Le Gallienne could not have
believed he would come to regard it as a special privilege to review
the work of the Meynells' nondescript new protégé. At the social
gatherings at Phillimore Place Francis's shyness and shabby appearance were not calculated to appeal to his dandified tastes.[14]

For all their variety, the circle of the Meynells' friends and
colleagues shared with their hosts the ability to express strong
opinions in spite of the likelihood of misunderstanding or disapproval
from the more conventionally minded. This, more than the opinions
themselves, was what led them to support the Meynells' journal.

Yet *Merry England* remained essentially the brainchild of its editor. Its
success was very largely due to Wilfrid's ability to see the best in
others and so to expect the best from them. One of his truest remarks
was made about himself when he observed in a letter: 'I always think
I have a little more capacity for appreciation than other people.
Wordsworth says we live by admiration & I literally do'.[15] He was the
'usher' into the public eye for the more gifted among his contributors
and the constant advocate of the rest. To quote again from his daughter's tribute:

> A thing he inspired in his friends was reliance, the confidence that what
> was needed would be given. Of the love which means service he had plenty
> to give, and he was fast-acting in any practical heed. He was a man
> around whom natural affections prevailed, given and received.[16]

It is a psychological fact that dominant characteristics in a personality
can conceal opposing ones at a much deeper level which sometimes
appear in after years. In Meynell's case the source for the depend-
ability, the confidence he could inspire as a 'father figure' lay in a
determination, a self-will that later could take the form of a certain in-
transigence, even despotism, towards those he regarded as his 'de-
pendents', family or otherwise. It would not become marked until
after Francis's death but Francis himself was to feel its influence, and
his own later years would be more affected by it than he or anyone else
fully realized. It has not been recognized chiefly because it could not
alter or even weaken the bond begun when he found in Wilfrid a
friend he could trust and respect and who, equally important, trusted
and respected him in turn.

He was to find a very different and in some respects a deeper relationship with Alice once the two were drawn together by the emerging of his full poetic gifts. But from the first he saw in her a representative of the ideal type of womanhood such as he had imagined from the dream world of his childhood. She possessed that elusive quality of charm where the attraction of physical grace was enhanced by an aura of remoteness from the affairs of everyday life.

For all her constant childbearing and in spite of her carefully directed flair for writing about children, there was very little of the genuine maternal element about her. True, she could romp with her own family, disrupting the nursery routine to the despair of a rapid succession of nannies and governesses. Her sudden impulses, such as dragging the younger children round the house in an old trunk, were enjoyed as such by them. But she lacked something more important — that underlying steadiness and even sameness of bearing that a child looks to in an adult and those with a real understanding of children can impart without knowing it. Alice was too much of an actress for this, a quality necessary to her defence of her privacy and not easily discarded at other times. As a result her family grew up much as she had done, left to develop in their own ways and with a freedom of intercourse with their elders as unconventional as most else in the Meynell household. Her housekeeping was haphazard and servants never stayed long. The fastidiousness, the meticulous attention to detail that characterize her writing were all directed into her poetry and the essays for which she was at this time better known. And she herself often appeared to others as an extension, an exemplar, of her writing. Katherine Tynan captured the impression she made on one who knew her better than most:

> I have a vivid picture of Alice Meynell writing one of her meticulously observant essays sitting by the table — the long green-painted table in the library at Palace Court — her hat on, just as she had come in, writing on a paper-pad in the midst of the whole household, with a few visitors added. I used to wonder at how she could abstract herself. Her look of travelling back from a long way off to answer a question and then losing herself again was wonderful.[17]

The reference to Palace Court is to the house the family was to occupy some two years ahead. But the description is not dated by this and the attraction Alice inspired through her quality of detachment had been hers from her youth. It could assume a semi-religious mystique in the eyes of her many male admirers. The description by Le Gallienne is typical:

> The touch of exquisite asceticism about her seemed but to accent the sensitive sympathy of her manner, the manner of one quite humanly and simply in this world, with all its varied interests, and yet not of it. There was the charm of a beautiful abbess about her, with the added *esprit* of in-

tellectual sophistication. However quietly she sat in her drawing room of an evening with her family and friends about her, her presence radiated a peculiarly lovely serenity, like a twilight gay with stars.[18]

Francis was already aware of this subtle appeal and her appearance of living in a world of her own, remote and inviolate, had a special attraction for him during these first months when he felt his own private world was being invaded by the impact of his new experiences.

But most of all he valued Wilfrid's forbearance. If there was any disappointment that Francis was showing very little sign of fulfilling the promise of the first essay and poems, Wilfrid kept it to himself. 'Dream Tryst', the only poem besides 'The Passion of Mary' known to have been with them, appeared in the next issue of *Merry England* and, in June, 'Paganism Old and New'. In Thompson's single effort at fresh work, a review article on Bunyan, the standard was well below the earlier essay. It was completed soon after he left hospital, the effects of opium withdrawal probably contributing to its inconsistencies and lack of proper appreciation for its subject. What is of special significance is his criticism of Bunyan's treatment of Despair and Hell as unrealistic and even 'flippant'. He had recently come too close to the reality behind both concepts not to be impatient of allegory.[19]

In a disguised attempt at encouragement, Meynell invited one of his most influential friends to dine in order that the two should meet. Bishop Vaughan owned, but did not edit, the *Dublin Review*, the leading Catholic journal of the day. Meynell, knowing his previous connections with the Thompson family, hinted beforehand that Vaughan might solicit an article from his protégé. But he did not realise the awkwardness that was to arise from the Bishop's view of Francis as a 'failed priest' and from Francis's appreciation of the delicacy of the situation. Not surprisingly the occasion was one of distinct embarrassment and the article, though duly requested, was not submitted until the following year.[20]

Nor were there any new poems — until in November or early December the sonnet 'Not even in Dream' gave Meynell an insight into the mental state causing the silence. Since he knew of the street girl and had even helped in the search for her he would have understood the references to her in this lament for a loss that has left only shadows for memories:

> This love is crueller than the other love:
>   We had the Dreams for Tryst, we other pair;
> But here there is no *we*; not anywhere
>   Returning breaths of sighs about me move.
> No wings, even of the stuff which fancy move,
>   Perturb Sleep's air with responsive flight
> When mine sweeps into dreams. My soul in fright
>   Circles as round its widowed nest the dove.

One shadow but usurps another's place:
    And, though this shadow more enthralling is,
Alas, it has no lips at all to miss!
    I have not even that former poignant bliss,
That haunting sweetness, that folorn sad trace,
    The phantom memory of a vanished kiss.[21]

The idea behind 'Dream Tryst' is taken up into what amounts to the cry of a lonely, but above all of a frightened, spirit. The love that is now a memory is no more than the shadow of what has been, yet sweeter than the shadows cast over the present and — surely — over the future. For all the hopes held out since that first meeting with Meynell and the stimulating encounters that followed, there remained a constant fear of failure, of another rejection, which was inhibiting his creative powers. There had been too many before for him to believe that there would not be another now that he was unable to meet the Meynells' expectations. The only way to face the prospect was to return to the opium, even while he knew that to do so was to anticipate the very thing he dreaded.

What he did not realize was that neither Wilfrid nor Alice, once they became aware of the situation, were prepared to admit any such failure on their side. Probably through their Franciscan connections at Crawley, they heard of a recently founded religious house in Sussex where visitors in need of rest and general rehabilitation were made welcome. This was the answer. What Francis needed was much longer than a few weeks in hospital to adjust to changes whose extent they had not at first recognized. Having brought about the change, they must now arrange the adjustment to it.

On Francis's side there was no alternative but to agree to the suggestion that he spend some weeks at the Priory of the Canons of Prémontré at Storrington. He left London in February and was to remain at the Priory for over a year. That year would see the birth of his poetic life in a process which was now made possible through the meeting with the Meynells but which, like all new life, must come to full term in its own time and according to its own nature.

5

The Brood of Immortality
Storrington 1889–1890

Let me give thanks even for those griefs in me,
The restless windward stirrings of whose feather
Prove them the brood of immortality
'Ode to the Setting Sun,'
'After Strain': 34–36

The Priory of the Canons Regular of Prémontré, or Nortbertines, was founded only eight years before Thompson's arrival. Its austere facade still rises rather incongruously at the edge of the old-world village of Storrington although now, like the Canons themselves, it is a part of the village and of village life. The fear and prejudice following their arrival are long forgotten, but had been very real when the first half-dozen White Canons — so called for the colour of their habit — appeared in the area in 1881. Expelled from their Priory at Prémontré during the religious persecution in France, the foundation in Sussex was due to a gift of land from the Duke of Norfolk with the object of establishing a retreat house. Here, Catholics could come for periods of withdrawal from secular affairs, either for directed 'retreats' or simply for rest and relaxation, physical as well as spiritual. Today there are many places of the kind but then it was a comparatively new and therefore a brave venture.

The Canons had lodged with local Catholic families until the domestic buildings could be occupied. The purpose of the foundation meant that these were given priority and the Priory Church was not begun until 1902. For Mass and other services Thompson joined the community and the handful of local Catholics in the 'Old House' adjacent to the Priory, a dilapidated farm-stead converted by the Canons into a temporary chapel. By now they had a farm of their own to feed their guests and the growing number of the community as new members came over from France.

The chapel stood on the site of the present Church, now linked with the Priory by a cloister which was then an open field. The lane to the village bordered it on one side and on the other was the newly laid out Canons' cemetery. In the centre they erected a large Calvary,

108

12. The Praemonstratensian Priory, Storrington, in Thompson's time

clearly visible from the road. The Field of the Cross, as it was called, became Thompson's favourite place for reading the books sent occasionally by the Meynells and, once he was able to work again, for writing his contributions for *Merry England*.

The Canons were still nearly all French, very much occupied with their farm and with establishing themselves in their new surroundings. As yet there was no organized retreat house and visitors were rare. Although they gave him every consideration, Thompson had little in common with the community. On the other hand the rhythm and regularity of the daily recitation of the Divine Office revived the meaning the liturgy had for him as he had been introduced to it in his Ushaw days. Now it went far deeper in the reassurance of its recurring pattern woven from divine, natural and human life.

This pattern formed the background for the daily routine of the next two or three months. Thompson's early pleasure in long rambling walks returned and, having explored the village itself, he was soon tramping the downs above it for many miles around. Storrington is still typical of all that is best in the traditional English village. The addition of newer building has hardly altered the older part as Thompson knew it with its cottages, mainly of seasoned brick, set in their flower and vegetable gardens. The sense of its age remains.

Storrington is among the oldest settlements in Sussex, one of the series
strung along the prehistoric trackway leading under the South Downs
from Ditchling Beacon to Lewes. The Parish Church adds to the impression of age, with parts dating back to the Norman period and
traces of the original Saxon building. In 1543 the Rector had bequeathed an adjacent acre of land for which the rent was designated
for the ringing of the 'Great Bell' of the Church for half an hour each
evening. The land became known as 'Curfew Acre' and until the end
of the last century the tolling of the bell was a daily occurrence, followed by strokes denoting the date of the month. The sound, spreading out over the village and surrounding countryside, was part of the
pattern of local life and, for Thompson, gave it a share in the rhythmic
pattern of the liturgy itself.[1]

Here again was a whole series of new experiences. The village
was unlike any he knew, so different was it from the harsh grey stone
of its northern counterparts. Its peace and prosperity opened up a
fresh side of life to him, for which tender simple things created a
structure as strong and abiding as the constant presence of the surrounding downs. The downs were so different, too, from the for-
bidding northern moorlands, seeming to embrace and welcome the
presence of man and to offer willingly of their resources. After his
recent experiences these things gave him a sense of reassurance, the
recurring rhythm of the natural world reflected in the traditions of
village life and both reflected in the rhythm and tradition of the
Church's liturgy. The comings and goings of the last months began
to recede into a more easily accepted background. Further back, the
horrors of the London streets and, beyond them, of the dissecting
rooms at Owens seemed at times as unreal as the nightmares they had
produced, while at another and deeper level the memories remained
as real as the physical after-effects and the pangs of opium withdrawal.

At first Thompson took his walks mainly for therapeutic reasons.
Hard physical exercise is one of the best ways to counteract the effects
of withdrawal, and during the first weeks he suffered from most of
the more unpleasant symptoms — acute pain in limbs and stomach,
swollen and ulcerated mouth and jaw accompanied by bouts of compulsive sneezing and profuse sweating. Added to these were the rest-
lessness that makes any concentration impossible, the sleeplessness
that can last for nights on end and the inability to control the often
violent ideas and images streaming through the mind. In a letter to
Meynell written soon after his arrival he said he expected to feel 'very
ill just now ... it is a mere matter of holding on', adding, with an
oblique reference to the past, 'in that kind of passive endurance I am
well practised'. His request for boots to replace a pair which, new when
he came, were now 'completely worn out' says more about his walking
activities than his brief comment, 'I keep on my legs and force myself

to go out as much as possible'. He thought he would like the place once 'the short sharp strubble' was over, 'the want of books being the only real drawback'.[2]

It was not long before the walks were a relaxation rather than a duty and by May the worst was behind him. He wrote that he had recently been able to keep to a regular daily routine and was writing again. 'If I have indeed begun to acquire the power of working in the teeth of nerves and mood and bilious melancholy, then the fight is half fought. And I think I have'.[3] It was more than half fought. He was accepting the fact that if writing was usually to be an uphill struggle he could still keep to it without the stimulus of the drug.

Meynell was delighted as the first essays began to arrive. His confidence had not been misplaced after all, and if there was as yet no sign of the poet he believed Francis to be, he was turning out to be a born journalist. He had a clear, compelling style with occasional flashes of wit and was able and willing to raise opinions calculated to provoke strong reactions — just what Meynell was looking for.

Most of Thompson's contributions were review essays based on a book or books which had either been recently published or chosen with a view to widening the literary range of the journal's readers. When he was given Zola's writings and their influence as one of his first subjects he took up the challenge along lines of which Meynell thoroughly approved. The realism of Zola and his followers was regarded, in the main, as shocking and even downright pernicious. Thompson points out the mistake of confusing Zola with his imitators and defends Zola himself on the grounds that true literature demands the honest portrayal of both good and evil. Drawing on his own recent experiences though without explicit reference, he finds that evil can often be of greater service to truth and so to the literature that in turn serves truth:

> It is impossible to read many of the rose-coloured productions which pass as portraits of existence, and then lift one's eyes to the grim reality which welters all round us, without feeling that the novels in question are about as much like the existence which they profess to portray as wax is like flesh.[4]

Yet the opposite extreme favoured by many of Zola's disciples is no less removed from the realism of true art. There is no conflict, he continues, between true art and moral values. 'For art resides, not in undiscerning comprehensiveness, but in discerning selection' and, as distinct from Zola, 'Zolaism is not artistic completeness, it is artistic excess'. The novelist has every right to portray evil 'provided he portray it *as* evil, up to a certain bound', and he who dislikes the result has 'a ready remedy. He can put it down'. The argument may be rather facile, weakened by the absence of adequate definitions of its

terms of reference. But for the purpose it was excellent, with the kind
of punch that would drive its points home best to its readers.

In these early essays Thompson was beginning to discover a
literary theory of his own. 'The Way of Imperfection' explores an idea
but forward in the 'Paganism' essay where he warned of the dangers
of direct imitation of the classical writers. They aimed at a perfection
in art which is travestied in the revival attempted by the present-day
aesthetes, 'a hot-house seclusion of beauty in a world Nature has tempered by bracing gusts of ugliness'. With his recent defence of realism
in mind he maintains that 'imperfection' is as essential to true art as it
is to the true beauty of Nature. Neither the aesthete nor the extreme
realist is a true artist in the sense that Shakespeare was, who 'would
have no perfection in his characters'. The essay ends with a telling
image:

> We say, therefore, guard yourselves against this seductive principle of per-
> fection. Order yourselves to a wise conformity with that Nature who
> cannot for the life of her create a brain without making one half of it
> weaker than the other half.

This drawing on his medical past set up a train of associations
which led him to add an appendix, an 'Apologue' as he called it, to the
essay:

> Once on a time there was a hypochondriac, who — though his diges-
> tion was excellent, believed that his delicate system required a most win-
> nowed choice of viands. His physician, in order to humour him, prescribed
> a light and carefully varied diet. But the hypochondriac was not satisfied.
> 'I want to know, Doctor', he said, 'How much of this food really con-
> tributes to the building up of my system, and how much is waste material!'
> 'That', observed the sage physician, 'I cannot possibly tell you
> without recondite analysis and nice calculation'.
> 'Then', said the hypochondriac, in a rage, 'I will not eat your food.
> You are an impostor, Sir, and a charlatan, and I believe now your friends
> who told me you were a homoeopath in disguise'.
> 'My dear Sir', replied the unmoved physician, 'if you will eat nothing
> but what is entire nutriment, you will soon need to consult, not a doctor,
> but a chameleon. To what purpose are your digestive organs, unless to
> secrete what is nutricious, and excrete what is innutricious!'
> And the moral is — no, the reader shall have a pleasure denied to
> him in his outraged childhood. He that hath understanding, let him
> understand.[5]

It seems Thompson is using some tale from his student days as the
basis for his fable. In any case he is enjoying himself, the deliberately
affected style leavened by that acerbity which Meynell noticed at their
first meeting and which could give an edge to both his conversation
and his writing when he expressed himself freely.

But there is more here. Drawing on his medical background and his knowledge of homoeopathy, Thompson is calling attention to the negative elements in Nature as no less vital to our well-being as the positive ones. To excrete is as vital as to eat. It is not a poetic image and it is used for just that reason. Poetry, he can now assert, must embrace the banal and the crude in life if it is to be true to life and so, true art.

There was no real opportunity to go further into ideas of this kind in his work for Meynell. But when a contribution on Richard Crashaw was agreed on he insisted he should treat the poetry in more than usual detail. He had known and loved it since his childhood reading and its influence was to be so absorbed into his own poetry that he would often be unaware of the origins of themes and images traceable to Crashaw as their source.

The resulting essay is marred by several blunders. He sees Donne as a lesser poet than Crashaw, who he then compares unfavourably with Shelley. Yet the core of argument is original and well supported by the choice of quotations. 'Crashaw's genius', he says, 'in spite of his often ecstatic devotion, is essentially a secular genius'. In Thompson's view his chief preoccupation is the poetical beauty of his subjects and their treatment, rather than their moral or ethical content:

> He sings the Stable of Bethlehem. But he does not sing its lessons of humility, poverty, self-abnegation; he sings of the Divine Light shining from the Child, of the snows offering their whiteness and the seraphim their roseate wings, to strew the heavenly Infant's couch. The themes are religious, the poetry is beautiful; but it is not what people are accustomed to understand by religious verse.

It is doubtful whether the implied invitation to reconsider what constitutes a 'religious' poem was heeded by his readers. Few have heeded it since. The essay raises a serious question, challenging accepted norms for such poetry that continue down to the present. Thompson is not prepared to offer his own definition of either 'religious' or 'secular' poetry. The omission weakens his argument but an attempt at this stage would have been beyond him. The issue was to become central in his future poetic development and the fact that he raises it here at the start of his poetic thinking is sufficient to give the essay its own importance.

He is at his best when he turns to the attention to detail which is easily overlooked in Crashaw. As when he selects the reference to 'curled drops' of snowflakes in the 'Hymn to the Nativity', analysing the phrase with a loving admiration to be revived later in his own lines 'To a Snowflake':

> Of all the poets who have described snow, we do not recollect one besides Crashaw who has recorded this characteristic trait of snowflakes. They *are*

curled. Pluck one of the inner petals from a rose, lay it with its concavity uppermost, and you have a sufficiently close resemblance to the general form of a snowflake when falling through the air. The pressure of the atmosphere on the lower surface of the descending flake necessarily tends to curve upwards its edges. But Crashaw alone has thought of noting the fact.[6]

He was in the mood to choose a detail of this kind for special notice. His new surroundings were reviving the interest in the workings of nature that had been dormant since the days of his botanical excursions with his father. True, the years between caused him to forget much of what he learned then, to the extent that his ignorance of the names of common trees and plants was to be regarded later by Blunt as a sign of his lack of appreciation of nature. Yet Blunt himself admitted that when, during his last months, Thompson was his guest, one of the poet's few remaining pleasures was the beauty of the Sussex countryside 'he had learned to love at Storrington'. And Alice Meynell was to comment on how the two great periods of his poetry coincided with the two periods when he was living in the country, in Sussex and then in Wales.[7]

She was right to make the connection and right, too, in stressing the elusiveness of the influence compared with the way the appeal of nature appears in poets more consciously aware of its presence. Except that she should have said more conventional in their awareness. For the scientist in Thompson meant that his appreciation of the natural world was based as much or more on its wonders as on its beauties. If he forgot the actual names of trees and flowers, his response to nature's grandeur and no less awsome minutiae was very real. In a notebook in use at Storrington he recorded with precise detail the habits of birds he was observing and their different calls.[8] In another, some spontaneous lines of verse show how alert his reactions could be to the humblest sights of the countryside:

> All things are joy, all things are light,
> The spider's feet a-labouring
> From silken tulips exquisite
> Its lacy round of argent sling.
>
> The tremulous dragonfly in wonder
> Regards his eyes' twin gleaming spheres
> Within the splendent pool, whereunder
> Spawns a mysterious universe.
>
> 'Neath the woods where but hushed noises cross
> The shy fawn keeps a-dream its games;
> In the green casket of the moss
> The live gold of the scarab flames.[9]

Spring had come to Storrington and the lines echo something of the spring he felt coming now to his winter-worn spirit. The craving for opium was gone and the fear of another failure dispelled by the Meynells' warm approval and frequent praise for his work. He was gaining a confidence as invigorating as the spring and his sense of returning health.

But there was more coming alive for him as the tulips bloomed in the gardens and the dragonflies played over the village pond. If the minutiae of nature made him aware of the stirring of new life in himself, it was the grandeur of the source of nature's life that was to bring it to birth as poetry. To what did nature owe the recurring miracle of the spring but to the daily recurring miracle of light, to the sun without whose rays the sap cannot rise or the dragonfly emerge from the chrysalis? The wonder of springtime renewal was again something he had never known as he witnessed it now, giving his innate poetic gift the voice and form it had been waiting for. The long winter of its gestation now gave way to a sudden burst of song where the analogy with birth only fails in the sense that the song was born almost fully mature.

The occasion was a perfect May evening. Thompson was in the Field of the Cross where from the Calvary there was then an uninterrupted view westwards towards the sunset. The light breeze brought the sound of music from a group of travelling players outside the village inn further down the lane.[10] He had learned to love music from his mother and music was to be a constant inspiration for the poetry that lay ahead. Now it brought past and future together in giving him the final impetus for the moment of birth:

> The wailful sweetness of the violin
>   Floats down the hushéd waters of the wind,
> The passionate strings of the throbbed harp begin
>   To long in aching music: spirit-pined,
>
> In wafts that poignant sweetness drifts, until
>   The wounded soul ooze sadness. The red sun,
> A bubble of fire, drops slowly towards the hill,
>   While one bird twitters that the day is done.
>
> Behind, a leaden-purple shadow lies,
>   And shadowed on that shadow rests the hill;
> Above, a greening-yellow tincture dies
>   Where two long reefs of kindled primrose thrill;
>
> Stretches of carmined flame hang yet more high,
>   As the wine-god had spilt his burning wine

> Upon the drenchéd woofing of the sky;
>   Beneath in semi-circled line on line
>
> Descends the gradual landscape, greyly green;
>   This windmill stands up black amid the cool:
> Nature and I scarce breathe; far down is seen
>   The ghostly shining of a shadowed pool.
>
> O setting Sun, that as in reverent days
>   Sinkest in music to thy smoothéd sleep,
> Discrowned of homage, though yet crowned with rays,
>   Hymned not at harvest more, though reapers reap;
>
> Methinks that pomp whereof thou art not shorn
>   Should strike a paeaned singing out of me;
> For Song is the true deathless babe that's born
>   When fire embraces the soul's Semele.[11]

In this Prelude to the Ode the lines stretch language to its limits in painting the sunset scene, yet without any sense of strain. There are flaws sufficient for Thompson to discard most of the descriptive verses in his revision six years ahead, but they do not alter the fact that the visual content of his poetic genius is fully developed even at this moment of birth. He himself experiences it as such a moment, comparable to the birth of poetry from the union of godlike powers and human passion in Dionysus, the offspring of Zeus and the mortal Semele. Here, therefore is the source for the sonnet 'Sad Semele', looking back over the years to this moment as one which he came to see as inseparably linked with his memories of the street girl.

But poetry is only fully born when an essentially private experience becomes universal in its application. So now the music reaches him as an echo from a past where his own memories merge with the whole movement of history. It sends him back to the 'reverent days' when the rites accompanying the sun's setting celebrated the death of a god who would rise again: and the Prelude, the private moment, gives place to the Ode itself where he will celebrate in turn the abiding power of the sun over life and death:

> Alpha and Omega, sadness and mirth,
>   The springing music, and its wasting breath —
> The fairest things in life are Death and Birth,
>   And of these two the fairer thing is Death.
> Mystical twins of Time inseparable,
>   The younger hath the holier array,
>   And hath the awfuller sway:
>   It is the falling star that trails the light,
>   It is the breaking wave that hath the might,

The passing shower that rainbows maniple.
    Is it not so, O thou down-stricken Day,
That draw'st thy splendours round thee in thy fall?

1–12

If this is so then the power of death must derive from the same source as the power of birth, in the source of life itself. So the course is set, back to the origins of life in a crescendo of allusions to the creation of the world that break the barriers of time and space — 'vast seasons gone' before the sun became the Hyperion of the Greek pantheon or compelled the poet-god Dionysus's wine-drenched exultation:

Thou twi-form deity, Foster-Nurse and Sire!
    Thou genitor that all things nourishest!
    The Earth was suckled at thy shining breast,
And in her veins is quick thy milky fire.
Who scarfed her with the morning? and who set
Upon her brow the day-fall's carcanet?

77–82

The sun as the source of life fills the immensities of space and penetrates the minutest atom. From the heavens the verse moves back to the forests of earth, to the 'furnace of the mammoth's heart' and the rose 'drunk with the must of her own odorousness' flaming in the midday heat:

    While in a moted trouble the vexed gnats
Maze, and vibrate, and tease the noontide hush.

138–139

So from the worldwide wonder of the sun's power and the ages when the power commanded worship, the movement is back from space and time to the present. Now, 'shaken from thine antique throne' no nymphs or dryads pay homage to the sun in woods and pools. They have no place in a world where man has lost the capacity either to wonder or to worship:

    Must ye fade —
O old, essential candours, ye who made
    The earth a living and a radiant thing —
    And leave her corpse in our strained, cheated arms?

181–185

The answer comes at the moment when a final blaze of light appears behind the darkening hillside, which against the glory of the sky:

Stands black as life against eternity

206

It is a timeless moment, as penetrating as it is brief. For an instant the
veil of time and place is lifted to allow a glimpse of another dimension
where past, present and future are one:

> Against eternity?
> A rifting light in me
> Burns through the leaden broodings of the mind:
> O blesséd Sun, thy state
> Uprist or derogate
> Dafts me no more with doubt; I seek and find.
>
> 205–209

Nothing has been lost either from the past or the present or will be
in the future. The wonder and the worship the sun once commanded
find their true object in Christ as the bearer of eternal life and light:

> Thou dost image, thou dost follow
>   That King-Maker of Creation,
> Who, ere Hellas hailed Apollo,
>   Gave thee, angel-god, thy station,
> Thou art of Him a type memorial.
>   Like Him thou hang'st in dreadful pomp of blood
>   Upon thy Western rood;
>   And His stained brow did vail like thine to-night,
>   Yet lift once more Its light,
> And, risen, again departed from our ball,
> But when It set on earth arose in Heaven.
>
> 210–224

The twinned contrasts of Alpha and Omega with which the Ode
began now reveal their full meaning. Death only holds the greater
sway because it is the means for the power of life to be renewed. The
sun, rising and setting in the immensities of time and space is, before
all else, the symbol of the twofold process as it has been fulfilled in
Christ:

> Till Time, the hidden root of change, updries,
> Are Birth and Death inseparable on earth;
> For they are twain yet one, and Death is Birth.
>
> 236–238

The birth of Thompson's poetic life brings a vision of eternity where
life depends on neither birth nor death. He experiences it as a realization of the presence of Christ, of the eternal, within the temporal
world. But the experience itself, of life beyond the limits of space and
time, is known universally, manifested in all the world's great religions and among those who follow no one form. The 'Ode to the
Setting Sun' is at once a revelation of intense personal emotion and of
the deepest convictions of the human race.

The After-Strain revives the immediate scene. The music still plays and nothing has changed save the deepening darkness. But the darkness brings a change of mood. The Calvary in the Field of the Cross now stands out starkly in the gloom, another potent symbol:

> Now with wan ray that other sun of Song
>   Sets in the bleakening waters of my soul:
> One step, and lo! the Cross stands gaunt and long
>   'Twixt me and yet bright skies, a presaged dole.
>
> Even so, O Cross! thine is the victory.
>   Thy roots are fast within our fairest fields;
> Brightness may emanate in Heaven from thee,
>   Here thy dread symbol only shadow yields.
>
> Of reapéd joys thou art the heavy sheaf
>   Which must be lifted, though the reaper groan;
> Yea, we may cry till Heaven's great ear be deaf,
>   But we must bear thee, and must bear alone.
>
>   After-Strain 1–12

In the Prelude the setting sun recalled the rites accompanying the harvest, celebrating its power of life over death. Now Christ, the true source of life as revealed in the Ode, warns through the cross how temporal joy cannot be separated from suffering any more than birth can be separated from death. There is no reassurance that the burden once taken up will be light or the yoke anything but harsh. The Christian symbol of the cross has aroused another universal response — the isolation of the human spirit in confronting the mystery of pain.

Yet the promise inherent in the sun-symbol remains. If death is as much a part of life as birth, so suffering and joy together are equally essential to the creative life of the spirit — in which the individual, whether Christian or not, must share by reason of his humanity:

> Oh, this Medusa-pleasure with her stings!
>   This essence of all suffering, which is joy!
> I am not thankless for the spell it brings,
>   Though tears must be told down for the charméd toy.
>
> No; while soul, sky, and music bleed together,
>   Let me give thanks even for those griefs in me,
> The restless windward stirrings of whose feather
>   Prove them the brood of immortality.
>
>   29–36

The Ode, with the Prelude and After-Strain, was completed in about a month. During those weeks Thompson must have often wondered at the surge of creative energy for which there had been no previous warning, forcing from him ideas and themes and images in poetry where he knew of no precedent — and for which there was none.

His choice of the ode is significant, and was to remain his favourite form for most of his longer poems. He adapts a traditional poetic structure to his particular needs with a disregard for convention more remarkable for its overall success than for its occasional failures. When he succeeds, allegory and myth unite with idea and reality in movements that would almost certainly break down within any more constricting structure. The muscularity of the ode can also carry the weight of his imagery with the least apparent effort and the least noticeable signs of poetic strain.

In the 'Ode to the Setting Sun' Crashaw undoubtedly provided some precedent for Thompson's use of the ode and would continue to do so. The same applies to the imagery. As in Crashaw, so in Thompson's longer poems the piling up of allusions and images in a crescendo of emotional intensity arouses a response irrespective of their precise meaning. The recently completed essay on Crashaw has a place in the more marked influences on the present Ode but there are others of which he was probably less aware at the time, from Saint Francis's 'Hymn to the Sun' to Coleridge's 'Hymn before Sunrise'. The long lament for the ancient deities recalls a similar passage in the second chorus of Shelley's 'Hellas'. Even the initial inspiration could have been partly aroused by a half-conscious recollection of the mood described by Sir Thomas Browne, in *Religio Medici*, on hearing distant 'tavern music'. Thompson already knew the book well and had a lifelong admiration for its author. Then, too, there is the wider context inherited from the English poetic tradition. There is a distinctly traceable descent from the Anglo-Saxon lament and the medieval lyric to the elegiac mood of the Prelude and After-Strain. It appears also at intervals through the Ode itself — where, too, something of the poignant mingling of joy and pain, the same tradition as handed down from 'The Dream of the Rood', finds an authentic echo.[12]

But no influences of the kind can account for the way in which they are assimilated into Thompson's own voice as a poet. No earlier poet had displayed anything comparable to the daring originality of his language and imagery — or combined the height and depth of success and failure in the handling as he does here and was to do in many later poems. Already he is making use of verbs of his own creation in 'discrowned', 'dislock', 'downstricken', where by recalling the customary form the invented negative gains a far stronger impact from the sense of surprise which it evokes. Another of his inventions with the same effect, the creation of past participles from non-existent verbs, appears in 'visioned', 'godded', 'enwarfed', 'enrondured' and 'scarfed'. Again, throughout his future poetry, the emotive power of colour frequently leads him to identify sight with other sense experiences. This synaesthesia, to use the technical term, takes hold on him in the Ode:

> I *see* the crimson blaring of thy shawms

> 19

The emphasis is Thompson's, deliberately stressing the simultaneous impact of both sight and sound.

When he uses them successfully these linguistic inventions act as the counterpart to his imagery, providing a compressed tautness to underpin the bold and often disconcerting range of his allusions. Yet it is the range that can be disconcerting. The allusions themselves are so much a part of the pattern of his thought that their subtlety can easily be lost in the overall movement of the passages where they appear. To take a single but representative example from the Ode, the reference to 'the old Tartarian line' of the Mogul emperors leads to the reminder of Marco Polo in 'the Paoli's seams', the salt mines begun by the family of the great explorer which made Venice the richest city in Christendom (184–190).

Classical allusions are even more closely woven into the texture of his thought, from the fall of the Titans in the primeval universe to the precision of an analogy such as 'lithe Circean grace': or the 'Medusa pleasure' signifying the act of poetic creation that, once embraced, brings a sting of death to the conscious self. Yet the pagan world is permeated by images and ideas drawn from Scripture. The Titans exist in a world before the Fall, 'Ere yet the snake Decay had venomed tooth' — an example of compressed language that almost fails, but not quite, to convey the meaning. Or to take one where it succeeds, in the later revised text the rites of paganism recall David's dance before the Ark of the Covenant: 'Before thy ark Earth keeps her sacred dance' (154).

In several places the Ode shows how Thompson's scientific interest will direct much of his poetic vision. As when he traces the power of light in electricity back through the coal mine to the tree that once owed its life to the sun's rays. The whole process is contained in four tightly-packed lines:

> How came the entombéd tree a light-bearer,
>   Hearing for ever in his lair
> The spasm and nightmare of hell's labouring breast
> Heaving in thick unrest?

> 111–114

The allusion is not only to the traditional hell deep below earth's surface but to the 'hell' of the mine where the tree concealed within the coal partakes in 'The spasm and nightmare' of the miner's task. Again, in the next stanza science is joined by botany:

> Who girt dissolvéd lightenings in the grape?
> Summered the opal with an irised flush?
>
> 141–142

The Church's liturgy is the source for many of the most compelling images and passages in Thompson's work. The Ode contains a notable example in an allusion showing how closely the liturgy was even now being woven into the pattern of his poetic ideas:

> It is the falling star that trails the light
> It is the breaking wave that hath the might,
> The passing shower that rainbows maniple.
>
> 8–10

The lines look back to childhood memories as an altar server when Thompson must have often overheard the words recited by the priest in preparing for Mass. Placing the cloth known as the maniple over his right arm he prays: 'May I be willing to bear the maniple of weeping and sorrow, that with exultation I may receive the reward of labour'. Then at Ushaw he would have learned that the rite originated in the early Church when the maniple was used to wipe off sweat during the service. The priest's prayer therefore links this purpose with the words of the psalmist:

> They go out, they go cut, full of tears,
> carrying seed for the sowing:
> They come back, they come back, full of song,
> Carrying their sheaves
>
> Psalm 125 (126)

The phrase 'carrying their sheaves' appears in Latin as *manipulos suos*.[13]

So a whole web of associations between labour and reward come together here, related as they are elsewhere in the poem to the harvest and its rites and the burden of its sheaves. The rainbow and the shower, readily recognized images for fleeting joys and sorrows, are given far greater impact by the more complex 'maniple'. And as if to increase the impact the noun is deliberately given the function of a verb of Thompson's own creation. As with his more successful allusions of the kind, the overall meaning does not depend on an exact knowledge of the ritualistic details. On the other hand the passage where it appears is expanded and deepened when the meaning is explored and the implications recognized.

If the 'Ode to the Setting Sun' foreshadows the future poetry in its achievements, it does so too in its comparative failures. Several passages are eliminated or altered in Thompson's own later revision, by which time he knew his main fault to be the tendency to excess which he never succeeded in bringing under full control. Throughout his poetry a potentially fine passage can deteriorate into needless obscurity or empty rhetoric. In the lines

> Who lit the furnace of the mammoth's heart?
> Who shagged him like Pilatus' ribbéd flanks?

97–98

the powerful imagery in the first is threatened by the obscurity in the second. It takes a specialised study to trace the reference to the Swiss mountain so named as the alleged scene of Pilate's suicide, where the trees on the lower slopes appear at a distance like ribs along a primeval animal's back. There is an improvement in the final revised text but there follows a passage of rhetoric, all of which Thompson later deleted:

> O vivifying Sun,
> Did not thy fervours to his blood impart
> The hum of that impulse,
> Shake the lashed arteries of the mastodon,
> Beat ope the sluices of his troubled veins,
> And turge the bondless heavings of his pulse?

Thompson's more turgid passages are often marked, as here, by his medical imagery. He is on a tightrope between success and failure in lines such as these. In this instance he came to see the failure. Often he failed, if not in seeing, then in making the necessary alteration.

There are other passages in the Ode where success is equally undeniable. As when the crescendo of rhetorical questions singing the sun's praises culminates in the reminder that no life sustained by its rays can withstand the approach of the night of mortality. It is conveyed through the death of Euridice on the night of her marriage to Orpheus, the god of Song:

> ... when Song with chorded charms
> Draws from dull death his lost Euridice,
> Lo ever thus, even at consummating,
> Even in the swooning minute that claims her his,
> Even as he trembles to the impassioned kiss
> Of reincarnate beauty, his control
> Clasps the cold body, and foregoes the soul!
> Whatso looks lovelily
> Is but the rainbow on life's weeping rain.
> Why have we longings of immortal pain,
> And all we long for mortal?

185–195

The rainbow has been identified earlier with the idea of temporary relief in the image of the maniple. Now it returns as part of the realization that no such relief can lessen for long the pain of the presence of death in all life sustained by the sun. There follows the question that forms the climax to the whole Ode, leading into the last stanza where the sun becomes the symbol for Christ. But it is only the symbol of Christ because it has also signified the most ancient of all human aspirations, the 'longings of immortal pain' for life that will not end with death.

Whereas the Ode itself ranges over the whole spectrum of human history, the Prelude and After-Strain also speak for the single isolated human spirit. In this, again, the poem as a whole is representative. In all Thompson's poetry there is a degree of self-preoccupation that can make or mar much of his work. His concern for his own feelings as both man and poet arose, as has been shown, from his need to communicate with others on a level of intimacy he would never find in real life. He often allows the need to dominate other poetic considerations. But it can also, as here, unite the universal with the personal in such a way that his own experience becomes a voice speaking for the common lot of mankind. As such it forms an essential part of his poetic awakening in the Ode. The main theme depends largely on the same unconscious sources that had given rise to the tortured lines of his London streets poetry. The Prelude recalls the sun's place in pagan worship, a worship which centred on the fertility cults where the sun-god must die and be buried to ensure the renewal of life. The ritual was based on the idea of release from the bondage of the earth-mother as a birth from the womb and, according to the most ancient rites, the bondage could only be broken by the dismemberment of the god and the severing of the head from the body.[14] Thompson's earlier poetry, most notably the 'Ballad of Fair Weather', had amounted to an agonized cry for release from the bondage to the past. Now the Ode as a whole celebrates a form of release in his birth to maturity as a poet — while the bondage of his human nature, of his own individual self, remains in the Prelude and After-Strain. The distinction was to be of greater importance for himself and for his poetry than he could have known then or would ever fully realize.

But the actual writing of the Ode was an unforgettable landmark. On three separate later occasions Thompson made a similar notebook entry: 'Ode to Setting Sun begun in field of the Cross & under shadow of the Cross at sunset: finished ascending and descending Jacob's Ladder (mid or late noon?)'.[15] 'Jacob's Ladder' is the local name for a steep path up Kithurst Hill, at the far end of the village from the Priory. Steps have been cut into the turf at the steeper parts, giving the path its name, and the view from the top is one of the finest in

13. The downs above Storrington: a view from the summit of 'Jacob's Ladder'

Sussex with the downs stretching east and west and the sea to the south.

Thompson was not, however, standing there when he finished the poem and his words 'ascending and descending' do something to set the mood in which it was completed. He was already aware that the upsurge of creative energy and the soaring hopes it aroused were accompanied by an undercurrent of fear and doubt. What was this strange birth that had come about with no conscious preparation on his part, and what would it bring him? Would the harvest field prove to be indeed a Field of the Cross and if so, would the promise of poetic immortality remain as it seemed when he came to the last line — an assurance beyond the reach of the shadow from the Calvary:

And take the kindred kisses of the stars.

Yet the assurance immediately gives rise to the doubt and the two cannot then be separated. It underlies the After-Strain and is voiced very clearly in a poem he wrote soon afterwards. In 'Daphne' the poet is identified with the river nymph who, pursued by the sun god Apollo, is transformed at her own request into a laurel tree rather than give way to his demands. The sun-god personifies the poetry that had first found expression in the Ode. Only by seeking to escape its pursuing power the poet attains the laurel, not as a wreath celebra-

ting achievement but as a prison of self-sacrifice. The poem is confused and generally weak in expression but it contains a prophetic
note. In addition there are lines that show how the idea of flight and
pursuit in such a context was beginning to crystalize to form the
theme for 'The Hound of Heaven'.[16]

Fluctuations between hope and fear also provoked a sonnet, first
dashed off as if on a sudden impulse on one of the paper pads
Thompson used for re-working the Ode — there were no 'Penny Exercise Books' to be had in Storrington. The title, 'Non Pax — Expectio',
is best translated as 'Not Peace — but a Respite'. There were
moments when the scenes of his country walks seemed to give the
assurance without the doubt. But they were only moments. Their
passing would leave him the more aware of his vulnerability in the
face of a poetic birth that like all birth — as the 'Ode' itself warned —
must surely bear the signs of death:

> Lo! at the dread,
> Thy heart's tomb yawns and renders up its dead, —
> The hopes 'gainst hope embalméd in its womb.[17]

Thompson kept his fear and doubt to himself. The poem was
noncommital enough to appear in *Merry England* with only a few
minor alterations and neither Wilfrid nor Alice suspected more behind it than a reaction to the emotional strain following the completion of the Ode.

Where the Ode was concerned they, on their part, were in no
doubt. They had found far more than an able journalist in Francis, or
even the poet Wilfrid looked for: they had discovered genius. Nothing
so far had prepared them for this, and they went straight down to
Storrington to tell him so.

Not that they were uncritical. They questioned his diction in
several places and pointed out needless obscurities. What, for example, did he mean by 'foison in her tilth', a phrase Thompson dropped
in his later revision but insisted on retaining now. Surely, he argued,
anyone would recognise the Middle English form for 'fruit of her toil'
since even Shakespeare had used it in *The Tempest*. Is there an echo
here from his rejoinder to his mother to that fireside reproof so many
years before?[18]

Meynell was well aware of the very different kind of criticism the
poem was likely to meet within Catholic circles. He decided to print
it in the September issue of *Merry England* where, as editor, he introduced it by means of a tribute to Ushaw's Exhibition Days and the
way they encouraged the students' appreciation of good literature and
writing. What better proof, he continued, than the influence of the
College on the appearance of this poem from a former student as 'nothing less than an event in the annuals of English poetry'. As such it
'must needs be hailed with delight' by Ushaw and by those to whom

the poet has 'owed his training'. It was a clever move. The Ushaw background would be a reassurance for the journal's general readers whose Catholic sensibilities were going to be shocked by the distinctly 'pagan' features of the Ode. Furthermore it would be embarrassing for the College itself to react to what had been said with accusations of the kind. So it was a safeguard against such criticism until Francis was better-known and could count on the influential supporters Meynell was confident he would soon find.

To this end he went further. He asked Francis for copies of whatever poetry he had to hand and from the resulting 'Note-book of Early Poems' he extracted a selection. These, with the 'Ode to the Setting Sun' and some samples of prose, he sent to various of his friends and literary acquaintances.

He was rather too precipitate. Apart from the Ode there was little of real worth and even within his own circle the originality of the Ode was as likely to arouse suspicion as praise at this stage. Nothing notable resulted such as Meynell hoped for but there were two significant reactions. In October he received an acknowledgement from the ageing Robert Browning. 'Both the verse and the prose are indeed remarkable' Browning wrote, with 'confident expectation' of the poet's success once he has freed himself 'from all that must now embarrass him' in the way of exaggeration and excess. Any further support from Browning was cut short by his death only two months after, but the encouragement meant a lot to Thompson. He told Meynell later how the idea that his work had been praised in this way during Browning's last days was one which he would treasure to the closing days of his own life.[19]

The other reaction of any consequence was very different but equally unexpected. Uncle Edward Healy was among those who were sent the booklet. Probably Meynell felt that here at least was proof of Francis's employment as contributor to *Merry England*. Even if the poetry was not appreciated, this fact must surely be gratifying and might encourage better relations with the Thompson family. The reply was therefore surprising:

> I have followed Francis's literary course with much interest, and I have read his Ode more than once, and on perusal have found it more intelligible — for I confess that some passages were beyond my comprehension, but probably from not understanding the allusions. He has great command of diction, and no doubt the composition is overloaded with imagery, but then how gorgeous was the subject. There are lines that live in one's memory and have a wonderful music of their own.

He selects the Ode for special comment, his reactions suggesting that his earlier literary inclinations might have gone further if they had not been smothered by other considerations. He refers to Dr Thompson having sent on to him a letter Francis wrote to Canon Carroll 'which was very consolatory'. That the Canon should have passed the letter on in this way suggests how the continued contact between Francis and himself was now having a good effect at home. Edward Healy then launched into an account of the home background very much at variance with the tone of his earlier letter to Meynell on Francis's shortcomings. There had been 'no encouragement and no sympathy with his ambitions', and as for the sisters, they

> ... have so little of the poetic element in them that they seem on principle to have eschewed all poetry as if it were a temptation and a snare. No wonder that he shut himself up in himself, as he literally did in his room. This I believe to be the key to, and so far an excuse for, his deceitful proceedings, and his apparent callousness and ingratitude. No doubt the opium had the effect on his mental and moral perceptions which he now laments.[20]

Surely Canon Carroll had been at work, persuading him to see the past so differently. But the letter from Francis was the tool, 'very consolatory' and admitting to faults 'which he now laments'. Otherwise, there is no accounting for the uncle's sudden *volte face*. Yet he was still far from confident about the future. He referred to the recent death of his brother John Costall Thompson, whose early attempts at a poetic career had 'proved an utter failure, as indeed his life may be said to have been'. So might Francis end, he implied, away from the watchful eye of the Meynells.

At Storrington Francis was still very much under their eye. There was the frequent exchange of letters and the occasional visits from both Wilfrid and Alice, but above all, by mutual arrangement he was allowed only enough money for immediate needs and that was kept to a minimum. Should the temptation to obtain opium return, it would therefore be impossible for him to do so without their knowledge. The arrangement was agreed as a necessary safeguard, even if by September he could write reassuringly that 'I have learned the advantage of being without it for mental exercise and (still more important) I have learned to bear my fits of depression without it. Personally, I no longer fear it'.[21]

The fits of depression were often due to the loneliness of his present life, accentuating as it did the sense of inner loneliness that never left him for long. So he took to joining the village children whose daily walks to and from the school led them past the Priory. They loved to hear the tales he told them, remembered or invented, accepting without question his oddities of manner and appearance. They were not embarrassed by his sudden silences any more than by the clumsy boots or the shabby overcoat he rarely discarded even on the warmest days. To them he was someone who could share in and understand their world, the world of the game and the dream which was with him still from his own childhood.

One child in particular became his special friend. Years afterwards Daisy Stanford recalled how Francis would join her in picking the wild raspberries that grew plentifully on Kithurst Hill around the foot of 'Jacob's Ladder'. 'He helped me fill my basket, and childlike, any extra fine one I got I'd give him to eat'.[22] She had no idea she was making any special impression on him by her spontaneous gesture, captured in the first of his many poems on children and childhood. In form and content 'Daisy' heralds as important a feature of Thompson's poetry as any contained in the 'Ode to the Setting Sun'. It represents the other side, the apparently childlike simplicity that can convey emotions as strong as any expressed in the complexities of his longer poems. The two together, the complexity and the simplicity, are inseparable in the formation of his poetry because they were inseparable within his own personality — formed on the one hand from a complicated web of influences and experiences and on the other from the capacity to respond to joy and sorrow with the direct emotions of the child. For this other side, then, 'Daisy' now set the direction:

> The hills look over on the South
>   And southward dreams the sea;
> And with the sea-breeze hand in hand
>   Came innocence and she.
>
> Where mid the gorse the raspberry
>   Red for the gatherer springs,
> Two children did we stray and talk
>   Wise, idle, childish things.
> . . .
> A berry red, a guileless look,
>   A still word, — strings of sand!
> And yet they made my wild, wild heart
>   Fly down to her little hand.
>
> For standing artless as the air,
>   And candid as the skies,
> She took the berries with her hand,
>   And the love with her sweet eyes.
> . . .
> She went her unremembering way,
>   She went and left in me
> The pang of all the partings gone,
>   And partings yet to be.

She left me marvelling why my soul
    Was sad that she was glad,
At all the sadness in the sweet,
    The sweetness in the sad.

5–12: 29–36
45–52

'Daisy' has been compared with Wordsworth's 'Lucy' poems and Thompson accused of writing in imitation of them. But there is a radical difference, even if he was drawing on Wordsworth's metre and rhythm as best suited to his own purposes. He was equally clearly drawing on Crashaw in 'The Weeper' for the last two lines quoted here, a derivation he was to use on several occasions. But he does so within his own poetic framework, not as an addition from outside, and the same applies to the Wordsworthian form. In Wordsworth's poems Lucy is hardly distinguishable from the landscape from which she seems almost an emanation, viewed with an objectivity impossible for Thompson. His main concern is not the child herself or her setting but his own response and what it can tell him in his loneliness about the nature of human relationships:

Nothing begins, and nothing ends,
    That is not paid with moan,
For we are born in other's pain,
    And perish in our own.

57–60

As he listened to Daisy's chatter or joined in her companions' games the pleasure it gave to the child in himself could not bridge the gulf between him and them, the gulf of the years and all they had brought for the man. So the poem ends with lines on birth and death that link it with the underlying theme of the 'Ode to the Setting Sun'. It encapsulates, as it were, the essential, individual aloneness behind the 'longings of immortal pain' that gives the Ode its powerful climax.

Incidents like the encounter with Daisy, added to his reflections on his long solitary rambles, contributed to Thompson's fears and doubts that were never far off during the summer following the completion of the Ode. The village children shared in the simplicities of the natural world, present also when he returned to the Priory in the ordered rhythm of its days. Set against this was the revival of those dreams of poetic achievement that had grown with him since his own childhood until they were overtaken by the nightmare of his years on the streets. Since then there had been too much to distract him in his new life for him to be aware of their survival, but they were reappearing now, not as impossible hopes but as realizable ambitions based on a poetic power whose demand for expression could not be denied.

Yet as in the past his dreams had persisted in opposition to his religious training, so now it deepened the shadow over the future cast by the Cross as he had sensed it even at his poetic awakening. That training remained too much a part of his religious consciousness to be gainsaid any more than the poetic power could be denied. And it told him that pride in achievement and worldly acclaim were 'tools of the devil', that those who succumbed were at least in danger of hell-fire if not already damned.

His preoccupation with ambition and its potential evils gave rise to a prose piece he began soon after the Meynells' enthusiastic reception of the Ode. Sensing that he might possess similar gifts as a writer of imaginative prose, Wilfrid suggested a short story as his next contribution to *Merry England*. The result, 'Finis Coronat Opus', shows clearly that this was not his medium. His prose would always need the constraints of journalism to contain and direct his otherwise too-feverish flights into fantasy. His first effort reads like a mixture of De Quincey and Edgar Allen Poe, with a strong added flavour from the 'gothic' novelists. Only when the story reaches its climax does the emotional intensity give it a brief life of its own.

The fate of its hero is in essence a projection of Thompson's fears for his own future. Florentian sacrifices all other considerations in his ambition to be crowned with the laurel wreath that will proclaim him his city's chief poet. The scene of the final sacrifice, where he gives his betrothed over to the Evil One, is at once a pagan temple and a Christian church. Here he seeks to stifle the last call from his conscience by breaking the crucifix above the sacrificial altar. In so doing he violates far more than his own fictitious nature: he betrays a deeply unconscious desire on the part of his creator to deny the power of the symbol from whose shadow there is felt to be no escape.

However unaware Thompson was of the implications for himself behind his hero's act of sacrilege, he must have been conscious of using his encounter with Daisy Stanford to illustrate the extent of Florentian's guilt and remorse. Florentian, too, meets a child in the countryside beyond his city. Significantly the description, like most of the passages dealing with his reactions to his sin, is in the first person:

> She knew not that hell was in my soul, she knew only that softness was in my gaze. She had been gathering wild flowers and offered them to me . . . How simple it all was; how strange, how wonderful, how sweet! And she knew not that my eyes were anhungered of her, she knew not that my ears were gluttonous of her speech . . . For all this exquisiteness is among the commonplaces of life to other men, like the raiment they indue on rising, like the bread they weary of eating, like the daisies they trample under blind feet: knowing not what raiment is to him who has felt the ravening wind, knowing not what bread is to him who has lacked all bread, knowing not what daisies are to him whose feet have wandered in grime.[23]

Thompson's real concern is with the evils resulting from ambition and the fear of its effects in himself. The fear is expressed in images from his London streets days but its source lies far back in childhood and the dream world from which the ambition had taken shape against a religious background whence it then assumed nightmare forms of guilt for an indefinable evil in himself. Seen in this light Florentian's meeting with the child and the poem on which it is based gain a much fuller meaning. Behind both is the contrast between a childhood innocence Thompson felt he had never himself known and the horrors he had known too well in adult years. And behind the contrast lies the guilt first aroused in childhood, for which the horrors of the London streets become the means of its expression.

The weaknesses in 'Finis Coronat Opus' did not affect Thompson's growing reputation, still chiefly as critic and reviewer. He eventually sent Bishop Vaughan the promised article on *Macbeth* for the *Dublin Review*, and its success now produced a request for another. The subject was left to him and he chose Shelley — 'principally', he wrote to Wilfrid, 'because I remember more of him than any other poet'. A good reason considering the lack of a library at the Priory. But when he added: 'Until I was twenty-two Shelley was more studied by me than anyone else' he was hinting at a more important motive in recalling Shelley's influence during his years of growing ambition and the guilt that went with it. He was to put more time and effort into this essay than any other of his prose writings, admitting afterwards: 'It might have been written in tears, and is proportionately dear to me'.[24]

The reason is not hard to find. In exploring the sources for Shelley's genius he raised issues that touched his own predicament at a deeper level than he would ever admit. If he could justify Shelley's flights of poetic fantasy in terms of the child who never grew up, there was much he might find to justify the aspirations revived by the cosmic world of his poetic awakening in the 'Ode to the Setting Sun'. And so, to resolve the guilt that went with them. The guilt had been built into the pattern of his early years and he knew himself still to be the child of those years.

Where the essay itself is concerned the personal need behind it provokes its strongest and most characteristic argument. He writes as Shelley might have written of the universe, as the poet's 'box of toys' bestowed by the gods as his playthings:

> He dabbles his fingers in the day fall. He is gold-dusty with tumbling amidst the stars. He makes bright mischief with the moon. The meteors nuzzle their noses in his hand. He teases into growling the kennelled thunder, and laughs at the shaking of its fiery chain. He dances in and out of the gates of heaven: its floor is littered with his golden fancies. He runs wild over the fields of ether. He chases the rolling world. He gets between the feet of the horses of the sun. He stands in the lap of patient Nature, and

twines her loosened tresses after a hundred wilful fashions, to see how she will look nicest in his song.[25]

This is not as fanciful as it seems. It leads on to explain, again with a personal application to Thompson's Ode, how the poet of 'Prometheus Unbound' is essentially a 'mythological poet' — one who therefore belongs to the 'child-like peoples' for whom myth still speaks of life's universal verities.

When he moves into a more sober discussion of Shelley's poetics Thompson presents him as the heir to the metaphysicals but surpassing them in the emotional freedom and range of his imagery. Here as elsewhere in the essay Thompson betrays his limited knowledge of literary history at the time, ignoring the radical differences in outlook and aims between the seventeenth-century poets and the Romantics. The essay is also too diffuse to carry its arguments far, except for the one that meant most to himself. On the persistence of the child in Shelley and its consequences, he concludes that however regrettable its effects on Shelley the man, its presence is essential to Shelley the poet. The summary is prophetic for his own future in both respects.

It occupies his attention to the extent that he omits another topic close to his own interests: the scientific content of Shelley's work is not mentioned. What does seriously concern him is the poet's religion, and here Thompson makes his first deliberate stand as a critic of its contemporary forms:

> Shelley desired a religion of humanity, and that meant, for him, a religion for humanity, a religion which, unlike the spectral Christianity about him, should permeate and regulate the whole organization of men. And the feeling is one with which a Catholic must sympathize, in an age where — if we may say so without irreverence — the Almighty has been made a constitutional Deity, with certain State-grants of worship, but no influence over political affairs.

He goes further. However mistaken in the details, Shelley's aims were 'generous' and his theory of free love 'repulsive, but comprehensible', even preferable to 'our present *via media* facilitation of divorce'.[26]

Thompson knew very well that the majority of Catholics would certainly not 'sympathize' with Shelley's religious principles any more than they would recognize the importance of his own emphasis on Shelley's religion 'of' and 'for' humanity. The same applies to the essay's opening passages, where he takes the term 'poetry' to cover 'the general animating spirit of the fine arts'. As such, poetry has, he maintains, been for too long regarded by the Church as 'at best superfluous, at worst pernicious, most often dangerous' and while 'the separation has been ill for poetry: it has not been well for religion'. There follows a vehement appeal to clergy and laity alike to recognise the value of the arts in the life of the Church. Saint Francis and Dante

are the examples to be revived in their 'joyous openness' to art in all
its forms, in direct opposition to the 'restricted Puritannical greeting'
offered today.[27] The appeal continues, forming a basis for the essay as
first written:

> We ask, therefore, for a larger interest, not in purely Catholic poetry, but
> in poetry generally, poetry in its widest sense. We ask for it from the aver-
> age instructed, morally hale Catholic, who is not liable to spiritual cold
> with every breath of the outside air. We ask for it specially in the case of
> verse, of poetry proper, as a mere necessity, if Catholicism is ever to make
> any impression on this branch of English art.[29]

In a passage discarded from the final text he adds an equally strong
criticism of Catholic education as the root cause of much of the prejudice. It is a disgrace, he says, that Catholic schools and colleges
make no provision for the study of English literature, many students
leaving 'hardly knowing the names of Spenser, or Dryden, or Wordsworth, or the great masters of English rhetoric & English prose'.[29]

It requires some mental adjustment today to recognize the truth
of such criticism. But it was well justified at the time and would
remain so for a good many years to come. Even Ushaw's reputedly
'advanced' ideas were, Thompson now knew from his contacts with
the Meynells and their circle, still very restricted.

The essay took some six months to complete, and then not at all
to Thompson's satisfaction. 'Seemed dreadful trash to me', he wrote
in reply to Meynell's enthusiastic acknowledgement. 'Shut my eyes
and ran to the post, or some demon might set me to work unpicking it
again'.[30] To Meynell it was as welcome in its own field as the Ode and
the other poetry sent since — he had been especially delighted with
'Daisy'. He was aware of the probable reaction from the *Dublin Review*
— but then, as he observed to Francis, a rejection would only prove
how right its views were.

After keeping him waiting for several months the *Dublin* did
reject it. Thompson preserved the manuscript with unusual care,
probably because of its personal importance to himself. He never submitted it elsewhere but after his death Meynell collaborated with a
new editor and in 1908 'Shelley' appeared in the July issue — when
for the only time in its history the journal went into a second edition.[31]

His work on the essay directed much of the poetry Thompson
was also writing that autumn. In 'Buone Notte' a message from the
spirit of the drowned Shelley to Mary Williams becomes a fanciful
and very Shelleyan identification of death with sleep. In 'The Song of
the Hours' Shelley is so much the model that in the main it is little
more than a delicately wrought *pastiche*. But a few passages show the
influence contributing to the store of Thompson's own imagery as he
develops an idea he had already made his own in the 'Ode to the
Setting Sun' with its theme of birth and death:

We are columns in Time's hall, mortals,
Wherethrough Life hurrieth;
You pass in at birth's wide portals,
And out at the postern of death.
As you chase down the vista your dream or your love
The swift pillars race you by,
And you think it is we who move, who move, —
It is you who die, who die!

127–134

Man's helpless flight from an inexorable fate contained in time — that is the theme of 'The Song of the Hours'. Wherever he flees his way is still governed by the same ultimate end, his mortality. Then Thompson recalled a line embedded in his memory years before and brought to conscious level by the present poem — Shelley's brilliant imagery for time in *Prometheus Unbound*:

Once the hungry hours were hounds

IV: 73

In turn, the line recalled the earlier appearance in the poem of 'heaven's wingéd hound' as an image of the pursuit of fate itself (I: 34). The hound pursues its prey with a purposeful unswerving sense of direction whatever course its victim takes — whereas the victim's flight has no pattern or direction save that imposed by fear. And from now onwards the image was to be Thompson's own.

So, one dark afternoon in early December, 'The Hound of Heaven' took on its skeletal form in the Christian concept of the pursuit of the soul by God as part of a process reaching back to the earliest records of human hope and fear. The process unites three levels of consciousness. Thompson's own past and present experiences becomes part of a Christian heritage with roots at least as far back as the words of the psalmist:

Whither shall I go from thy spirit?
or whither shall I flee from thy face?
If I ascend into heaven thou art there;
If I descend into hell, thou art present.
If I take my wings early in the morning,
And dwell in the uttermost parts of the sea:
Even there also shall thy hand lead me:
and thy right hand shall hold me.[32]

The Hebrew sources were taken up and expanded by the writers of the early Church and Saint Augustine speaks for countless others to follow for whom the same flight and pursuit have led to self-revelation and thence to self-acceptance:

> Late have I loved Thee, O Beauty so ancient and so new: late have I loved Thee! For behold Thou wert within me, and I outside; and I sought Thee outside and in my unloveliness fell upon those lovely things that Thou hast made. Thou wert with me and I was not with Thee. I was kept from Thee by these things, yet had they not been in Thee, they could not have been at all. Thou didst call and cry to me and break open my deafness: and Thou didst send forth Thy beams and shine upon me and chase away my blindness ... Thou didst touch me, and I have burned for Thy peace.[33]

Beyond the Christian heritage lies the level of a universal consciousness. The fear that precipitates the flight from God and the search for His substitute in the natural order stems from mankind's fear of mortality. Breaking the bounds of time and creed it is a flight from a confrontation with the divine order where man must confront the source of both life and death for himself as for all else in the created world. And so both fear and flight have been woven into the pattern of death and rebirth in the natural cycle, giving rise to the myths and rituals from which Thompson had drawn his initial inspiration in the 'Ode to the Setting Sun'.

Hours have been spent and pages written on the literary and other sources for 'The Hound of Heaven'. Yet they only illustrate what the poem itself manifests, the union of personal with universal experience. Building on its mythological undercurrent it contains echoes from the Scriptures and the Fathers of the Church: from the mystical writings, the lyrics and even the bestiaries of the Middle Ages: from Milton and Crashaw, George Herbert and Collins: from Keats, De Quincey and Rossetti: and there are many more, reaching back from the immediate influence of Shelley to the no less distinct voice of Augustine. Yet for all their pervading presence these literary sources would have no power in the poem unless they were giving shape and form to a particular experience of life which is also a message about human life. And this is, first and foremost, how 'The Hound of Heaven' has to be read.[34]

The opening lines set the scene and the pace of its cosmic world, and of a flight which is a flight from time. From sunset and sunrise in the natural order to the nights and days of fear and hope: through arches of time imprinted from the arched recesses of the Thames Embankment long before their shadowy presence in 'The Song of he Hours': from the mythical Labyrinth to the byways and dead ends of memory with hauntings of griefs and joys as ephemeral as mist and elusive as water: from impossible day-dreams to the chasm of nightmare:

> I fled Him, down the nights and down the days;
>   I fled Him, down the arches of the years;
>   I fled Him, down the labyrinthine ways
>   Of my own mind; and in the midst of tears
> I hid from Him, and under running laughter.
>   Up vistaed hopes I sped;
>   And shot, precipitated,
>   Adown Titanic glooms of chasméd fears,
>   From those strong Feet that followed, followed after.
>
>   1–9

Then from the rising and falling, twisting and turning of the soul in flight to the steady pulse at the heart of the poem:

>   But with unhurrying chase,
>   And unperturbéd pace,
> Deliberate speed, majestic instancy,
>   They beat — and a Voice beat
>   More instant than the Feet —
> 'All things betray thee, who betrayest Me'.
>
>   10–15

This recurring pulse-beat gives the poem as a whole its own 'deliberate speed, majestic instancy', without which it could easily fall apart, splintered into the fragments of its brilliant, at times too brilliant, imagery. In the long passages where the fulfilment of the 'vistaed hopes' is sought in the human and natural worlds, it can merely scintillate. What, for example, is gained by extravagance such as

>   ... fretted to dulcet jars
> And silvern chatter the pale ports o' the moon
>
>   28–29

Or when the lovely promise of 'dawning answers in the childrens' eyes' is marred by the grotesque in

> Their angel plucked them from me by the hair
>
>   60

'Azured dais', 'Hearted casement', 'Wind walled palace' — each is a reminder of Thompson's constant temptation to excess, to glory in a riot of images for their own sake and forget the end for which they must remain the means. But in 'The Hound of Heaven' there are many more occasions when they succeed, sometimes, magnificently, in conveying the perennial search for a substitute for God in the world of His creation. 'Float thy vague veil about me': 'The long savannahs of the blue': 'In vain my tears were wet on heaven's grey cheek': and, with a wealth of liturgical suggestion:

> I was heavy with the even,
> When she lit her glimmering tapers
> Round the day's dead sanctities.
>
> 84–86

Beneath its verbal galaxies the poem is held together by key lines whose rythms take up the beat of the refrain in their stressed single syllables: 'But not by that, by that, was eased my human smart': 'Naked I wait Thy love's uplifted stroke': 'The pulp so bitter, how shall taste the rind?': and, in the question to which the flight and the search must lead:

> Ah! must —
> Designer infinite! —
> Ah! must Thou char the wood ere Thou canst limn with it?
>
> 133–135

The question,[35] one of the most compelling in all Thompson's poetry, is repeated in:

> Whether man's heart or life it be which yields
> Thee harvest, must Thy harvest-fields
> Be dunged with rotten death?
>
> 152–154

The rotting garbage of the London slums joins with the Sussex harvest fields to lead into the climax of the poem:

> That Voice is round me like a bursting sea:
> 'And is thy earth so marred,
> Shattered in shard on shard?
> Lo, all things fly thee, for thou fliest Me!
>
> 157–159

Man as fragile as clay on the potter's wheel haunted the human mind long before the Preacher in *Ecclesiastes* compared man's end with the pitcher 'crushed at the fountain', or Isaiah warned that he who flees from the divine mercy will be

> ... broken small, as the potter's vessel is broken all to pieces with mighty breaking, and there shall not a sherd be found of the pieces thereof.[36]

The stripped soul is now Everyman, revealed in a line where pathos rises above the merely pathetic:

> Strange, piteous, futile thing!
>
> 161

Is he therefore an object of contempt, to be discarded on the rubbish heap where all human life must end if nothing further remains? Only now when the Pursuer has overtaken him and he knows himself to be

> Of all man's clotted clay the dingiest clot

> 166

— he receives the answer. In his naked selfhood he has become as worthy of love as the child to the parent:

> 'All which thy child's mistake
> Fancies as lost, I have stored for the at home:
> Rise, clasp My hand, and come!'

> 174–176

The answer is given to Everyman but behind it lies the intimacy Thompson had known in the love and self-giving of the street girl and the generous compassion and friendship of the Meynells. Each accepted him as he was when he reached a state which in the poem becomes that of the soul stripped of all defences against its naked self. Now their human love and acceptance are translated to the supernatural level where perfected love can cast out fear.

But the poem does not end in a mystical union between the soul and God as has so often been asserted. The invitation remains open, there is no final handclasp. Instead there follows another question. The pursuit and the flight are over, the act of self-acceptance made, but there still remains a 'gloom' and a 'shadow':

> Halts by me that footfall:
> Is my gloom after all,
> Shade of His hand, outstretched caressingly?

> 177–179

The shadow from the Calvary in the Field of the Cross still lies over the end of 'The Hound of Heaven'. The underlying promise remains, given in terms of the child in Everyman who seeks and will find a home in eternity. But within the limits of his own experience the voice from Thompson's past years, the censorship imposed on his childhood consciousness, would never leave him, never be entirely silenced by the Voice speaking at the end of the poem:

> Thou dravest love from thee, who dravest Me.

Thompson himself knew where the real strength of 'The Hound of Heaven' lies. Years later when he was making his autobiographical notes on his years on the streets he recalled how the first idea for the poem then came to him — a distinct reference to the lines where pursuing love demanded a total surrender which he could not then take further. Probably there were others for which there is no record but which remained in his own memory when he wrote:

> At this time visited me the rudimentary conception of 'The Hound of Heaven' — certainly, with all its shortcomings, the greatest of my odes: and this because it embodies a world-wide experience in an individual form of that experience: the universal becoming incarnated in the personal. It was a very rudimentary conception with nothing like the scope it later took to itself, but I felt it great in suggestion, — too great for my present powers of execution. Fortunately I shrank from executing it: and when I ultimately encountered it again I was much like the fisherman who freed the *ginn* from his vessel.[37]

He remembered the sense of release rather than the nervous tension that went with it. 'I am sometimes like a dispossessed hermit crab', he wrote to Meynell in the New Year, 'looking about everywhere for a new shell, and quivering at every touch'.[38]

The physical and psychological symptoms to which he also refers were due to the fact that he was in need of a 'new shelter' of a kind Storrington could no longer give him. 'The Hound of Heaven' was not completed there but after he returned to London in March. The past months had done much for him but, as the poem progressed through its final stages, he was aware that what he would now need was to test out his new-found role as a poet in the environment where his future lay. And it would not be Storrington. For all that he gained from the Sussex country-side Thompson was not and never would be a countryman. He was by birth and temperament better suited to take the stresses of society rather than those resulting from its absence.

This is very far from saying he was unresponsive, and the opening up of the natural world had been essential to the awakening of his poetic consciousness. The 'Ode to the Setting Sun' owes as much to the fields and hedgerows around the village as to the views from the Field of the Cross and Jacob's Ladder. In the long central passages of 'The Hound of Heaven' where the flight from God becomes a search for His substitute in the created world, the whole poetic concentration is on the wonder and beauty there revealed. Then, in one of those measured lines that hold the key to the whole, comes the moment of disillusion:

> Nature, poor stepdame, cannot slake my drouth
>
> 99

Surely the image of the stepmother is signifant here, penetrating as it does to Thompson's most deeply felt emotions of fear and guilt. It comes as the opening bar of the next movement, leading into the stripping of the aspirations for which Nature has been the poet's singing voice and now will only 'speak by silences'. This in turn is essential to the confrontation at the end of the search and to the end of the flight in the revealed self. It is therefore also essential to the restoration that follows:

> All which I took from thee I did but take,
>> Not for thy harms,
> But just that thou might'st seek it in My arms.
>
> 171–173

The words reach back over centuries of Christian teaching: that delight in the beauties of God's creation must lead to the worship of their Creator if they are not to become substitute objects of worship themselves. The attempt to reconcile the poet's vision of beauty with the Christian vision of heaven is almost as old as Christianity itself, while behind it lies the pagan delight in the senses where there is no conflict because the gods of the ancient world were incarnations of man's deepest aspirations and the fears that accompany them. The three levels of consciousness in 'The Hound of Heaven' meet here in Thompson's personal need to re-interpret the traditional teaching in terms that would open up the Christian framework as he had inherited it to admit a wider and more profound application.

While working on the poem and before he left Storrington, Thompson tried to formulate this central issue on an intellectual plane by making it the basis for an essay. 'Nature's Immortality' starts with the light touch with which he often introduces grave topics. For all our idealization of nature, Nature herself, he maintains, 'has no heart':

> You speak and you think she answers you. It is the echo of your own voice. You think you hear the throbbing of her heart, and it is the throbbing of your own. I do not believe that Nature has a heart; and I suspect that, like many another beauty, she has been credited with a heart because of her face.[39]

The words are, in effect, another rendering of the moment of disillusion in the poem. Nature, he continues, only comes to man's aid when she is understood as existing by the divine will, for then she can be said to share in the one true ideal he seeks — immortality. It is not difficult to trace here an attempt to answer the 'longings of immortal pain' in the 'Ode to the Setting Sun' by means of the ultimate 'silences' of the natural world in 'The Hound of Heaven'.

Thompson then develops the idea to show that human creativity stems from the Creator God who 'reveals his conception to man in the material forms of nature'. But there is a radical difference. In all human art there are three stages: the initial idea, the mental image it arouses and the reproduction of the image. For God there is no middle stage; no mental image is needed between the divine idea and its manifestation. 'Earthly beauty is but heavenly beauty taking to itself flesh'. In other words, there is a kind of sacramental union between the physical and spiritual worlds, reaching beyond the limitations and distortions of the human condition. Thompson is feeling his way towards a view of the function of poetry within that condition which will become central to his thinking and much of his writing. For the present he is content to assert that to find a meaning behind the created world it must be seen as the direct expression of the divine Mind: For 'with Him rests the great concept of creation'.[40]

In 'The Hound of Heaven' Thompson's poetic inspiration leads him to 'incarnate the universal in the personal'. Here his intellect is groping towards a parallel idea in the spiritual dimension incarnated in the particular beauties of the natural world. But the emotional experience contained in the poem is not matched by the intellectual reactions in the essay, which raises more questions than it attempts to answer in an argument that is too facile to satisfy any but the average *Merry England* reader. On the other hand the questions and the argument show how his poetic inspiration was already looking for the support of an intellectual structure. If the act of poetic creation could be proved to reflect the divine creativity, then his ambitions need no longer be feared and whatever other shadows might lie across the future its 'brood of immortality' would be assured.

As he prepared to leave the Priory, descending Jacob's Ladder for the last time and saying goodbye to Daisy and her friends, Thompson was preparing for a future that would have seemed as impossible as his childhood dreams when he arrived fourteen months before. He could not confide it to anyone, not even to the Meynells. Only his notebook knew his determination that the life he was about to take up in London was to be directed by the poetic life that had come to birth at Storrington. Both must now work towards a new ideal, a transformed ambition: 'After the Return to Nature, the Return to God. Wordsworth was the poet of the one, I would be the poet of the other'.[41]

The Laurel — or the Crucifix
London 1890–1892

From Moses and the Muses draw
The Tables of thy double Law!
. . .
Teach how the crucifix may be
Carven from the laurel-tree

'To a Poet Breaking Silence': 9–10
21–22

Soon after his return to London Francis settled into lodgings near Queens Park. Third Avenue lies between Kilburn Lane and the Harrow Road and here, at Number 25, he was to pass the next sixteen months.

The high ideals with which he left Storrington now faced the challenge of reality. The area is very little changed, a nondescript repetition of streets of terraced artizans' dwellings, 'respectable' with the dreariness the term can imply. Apart from the traffic, the main difference is the absence of the smoke and soot which turned any attempt at domestic or even personal cleanliness into a major effort. Francis learned not to notice the dust accumulating on the piles of papers and manuscripts which his landlady was told, to her constant annoyance, not to disturb: while neither he nor she cared any more about the state of the dingy lace curtains than for the view beyond the rain-smeared window.

It was different on the Harrow Road with its sleazy shops and peeling paintwork and its jostling bustle of cockney life. Buying his pork pie supper in the evening market or his beer at his favourite pub, the 'Skiddaw', Thompson was often more at ease than when the Meynells persuaded him to join other guests for dinner. Here his shabby overcoat and shabbier boots fitted in and no one thought the less of him if he forgot to shave or get his hair cut.

All the same he was lonely. Back in his lodgings he compared the cheerful Meynell household with the depressing room he had to call home. It made him homesick for the many happy memories of the Ashton of his childhood and even for whatever remnants might still remain of the home that it once was, or as he now fancied it to have been. That spring he began a letter to Canon Carroll starting with a greeting to 'everybody' at Stamford Street and ending, several months later, with messages for his sisters and 'best love to my father'.[1] It was written intermittantly between March and August and was itself intended only for Carroll. To him he confided that his reason for leaving Storrington was largely due to the 'acute mental misery' of his last months there, the rejection of the opium habit having 'quite destroyed my power of bearing the almost unbroken solitude in which I found myself'. It was his only explicit comment on the strain accompanying the composition of 'The Hound of Heaven', when the need for the relief of companionship seems to have revived temptations which, he had assured Meynell a few months before, he no longer feared.

He was, he told Carroll, 'immensely relieved' since his return to London. The letter was written over a period when he was becoming increasingly involved in the interests of the Meynells and their literary activities. Yet already there were problems, such as when he had to review a book by one of their friends which he considered badly written. 'You don't know how hampered one is in these ways'. Meynell, he admitted, had problems as well. According to some influential *Merry England* readers the 'Ode to the Setting Sun' was 'not a thing that should have appeared in a Catholic magazine' and an anonymous letter warned 'against publishing anything of mine, since it would be found that paganism was at the bottom of it'. There were no problems, however, where Meynell's own views were concerned. They had both been equally amused at the suggestion that 'Buone Notte' was not suitable for Catholic ears, and at 'good Uncle Edward's' complaint that 'Dream Tryst' was a 'dangerously erotic' love poem. Thompson's comment that this could not be so 'for I never in my life was in love' in the way his uncle meant is not as naïve as it sounds. It shows that he regarded his relationship with the street girl as one of a different order.

Taking up the letter a few weeks later Thompson wrote that the only poem of his which so far met with approval outside the immediate Meynell circle had been some lines on the death of Stephen Perry, a Jesuit priest whose astronomical studies were much admired. 'A Dead Astronomer' is a cleverly worked out tribute, dismissed by himself as a 'gracefully turned fancy'. He was anxious to point out that the favourable criticisms he received were from the Meynells' friends and colleagues. If 'Buone Notté' was to them 'a little masterpiece', 'Daisy' regarded as 'a lovely little lyric' and 'Daphne' considered 'very fine', these were not his own views. 'I am given to exuberance, long sentences, sentiment, philanthropy, (in the form of believing goodness to exist even in outcasts), and sometimes to preaching'.

Throughout the letter Wilfrid's ideas and opinions dominate in all other directions:

> I admire more highly than ever the courage and resource which Mr Meynell holds on his course through the dense sea of Catholic literary ignorance. He has, in my opinion — an opinion of long standing-done more than any man in these latter days to educate Catholic literary opinion ... He conciliates, and insinuates soothingly his opinions; while I, with my vehement manner of writing, drive a furrow straight ahead, ploughing up prejudice on every side.

He was thinking partly of the rejected 'Shelley' essay and partly of another, 'Our Literary Life', rejected this time by the *Tablet*. Rejected, he told Carroll, because 'I had said that Cardinal Wiseman too often wrote like a brilliant schoolboy'.

As the proprietor of the journal, Bishop Vaughan may well have taken exception to the remark. But it shows how Thompson was beginning to understand more about the affairs of the Church and its leaders than he could have gained from his earlier background. He was not to know that his view of Wiseman would be repeated, without the conciliatory 'brilliant', in later comments from the Cardinal's associates, for many of whom Wiseman's immature judgements amounted to just such a 'schoolboy' outlook.

There were probably other reasons as well. Thompson had accused the English Catholics of narrow-mindedness in refusing to allow that there was any merit in the literature of the present day. He then went further, pointing out how moral values need not be confined within 'the comparatively narrow medium of professedly religious writing'. The assertion was too new not to be unpalatable to the average reader of either *Merry England* or the *Tablet*. Nor would they yet accept that literary excellence appreciated for its own sake will not 'thereby do less, but rather more homage to Him who still writes with His finger in the dust of our minds'.[2]

His comments on individual writers in the essay are often penetrating. As when he says of Manning: 'A style macerated of all succulance. A mortified style; you can feel the hair shirt behind it'. He pays a daring tribute to Mivart's scientific integrity and is confident that Newman is the only great English Catholic writer of the day.

Newman's death in early August brought a request from Meynell for an obituary poem, and the letter to Carroll ends with a comment on his reluctance at having to write verse to order and in such haste. For all that 'the three little stanzas' he told the Canon he had just 'knocked off' are worth more notice than he implies:

When our high Church's builders planned
To re-erect within the land

The ruined edifice,
What was the building's price?

Stern was the toil, the profit slow
The struggling wall would scantly grow:
What way to expidite?
Men had of old a rite!

Into the wall that would not thrive
He gave him to be built alive,
A human sacrifice.
And lo! the walls uprise.

Thompson was using the term 'high' Church here as Catholics first applied it among themselves before it was taken over into the better known Anglican distinction. It denoted the enthusiasm of the converts in contrast to the self-effacing tendencies of the 'old' Catholics, whose outlook was correspondigly 'low'. It could also sometimes include the Ultramontane faction and Thompson probably had both in mind when he wrote the poem. The sentiments were too plain for the lines to be found in any collection of his poetry. Yet they meant more to him than his comment to Carroll suggests, staying in his mind to reappear several years later in the context of his own poetic career.[3]

If he saw Cardinal Newman's life as a sacrifice to the future life of the Church he was soon to find something unexpectedly similar, despite its very different manifestations, in the life of Newman's great opposite, Cardinal Manning. He was already in full agreement with Meynell as to Newman's place in the Catholic literary world: now he was gaining an equal regard for Manning in other directions. In his old age the Cardinal was better known for his work on behalf of the poor than he was remembered for the controversies and animosities of his earlier career. Wilfrid often spoke of his lively interest in Catholic journalism and involvement in social matters, disregarding convention in joining with other denominations in the effort to deal with the conditions of the poor and the problems created by unemployment. Then, like everyone else in England, he knew how last year Manning had resolved the weeks' long strike of London dockers, single handed and with none of the resulting violence that seemed inevitable. The achievement, it was generally recognised, was due to the understanding existing between the London poor of all creeds or none and the prelate who, for all his Ultramontane principles, held the work of the Salvation Army in higher regard than the charitable efforts of his fellow-Churchmen. By now the activities of William Booth's 'Salvationists' were well-known, but the idea of a mission to the poor based on military lines had been anticipated, since 1872, by Manning's own 'League of the Cross', a Catholic temperance society with pageantry

and discipline borrowed from army traditions. It proved outstand-
ingly successful even before Booth carried the idea further, for which
Manning gave wholehearted support.[4]

Then in 1890 Booth published a full length account of the present
work of the Salvation Army and its aims for the future, *In Darkest
England and the Way Out*. Beneath its idealized portrayal of their under-
takings and over-optimism for the future the basic ideas were sound.
'What is the use', Booth demanded, 'of preaching the Gospel to men
whose whole attention is concentrated upon a mad, desperate struggle to keep themselves alive?' And along with the martial discipline
governing the Army as a corporate body, in their work among the
poor the question must always be asked: 'What does it make of the
individual?'

Booth was also ahead of his time in seeing self-help as the only
long term solution for those capable of responding. 'Labour Colonies'
had been put forward before as an answer to unemployment, lack of
work-opportunities being too often mistaken for refusal to work. The
able-bodied were to be virtually forced, by offering no alternative, into
severely disciplined centres for training in manual labour. The main
objects were to improve the economy while ridding society of a potential menace in hundreds of disaffected poor living at a level of near, if
not actual starvation. Booth's proposals, on the other hand, for 'self
helping and self sustaining communities' were humane in concept and
primarily concerned with the welfare of individual members. In addition, the advocates of the Labour Colonies offered no alternative to
the workhouse for those who had fallen below the category of 'em-
ployable'. But Booth saw the totally destitute as souls to be saved no
less than the rest, towards whom the Christian had an obligation to
provide whatever might be possible in the way of food and shelter that
would be neither penal nor repressive.[5]

Thompson read the book and also some of the pamphlets and
articles it provoked from its many critics. In their view Booth's
innovations must result in religious despotism, forcing the acceptance
of the Salvation Army tenets as a pre-requisite for receiving their
charity. A few, like T. H. Huxley, held that poor relief was a subject
for political, not religious, concern. But the majority were not worried
on this account, seeing it as a moral duty for the Churches to take responsibility along the socially acceptable lines that would not seriously disturb their peace of mind or the view that poverty was, like the
charity they chose to bestow on it, a 'means of grace'.[6]

Thompson's own ideas were not changed since his heated lines
on 'holy poverty' provoked by his experiences of the London streets.
He knew that much of what Booth said about the Salvation Army
shelters was very different in practice. Cleanliness and orderliness
were not the rule, as Booth claimed, nor could they be in the face of

the grim realities. Booth maintained that none was compelled to join the Salvationists' gatherings but Thompson knew how impossible it could be to avoid the crudely rousing services that were part of the nightly routine. Yet he was also aware of the effort to confront the actual conditions rather than disguising them in the trappings of piety. Again, if there were many who could never respond to Booth's self help projects the principle itself was surely the only constructive basis for the way ahead. Above all, Booth recognized and respected the needs of those incapable of responding and this, for Thompson, was what stood out most clearly in the book as a whole. And when Meynell, knowing his views and the extent of his personal knowledge, asked him for a review they agreed he should take the opportunity to draw attention to the wider issues it raised.

Apart from the rejected 'Shelley' essay the result was the longest piece of prose writing Thompson had yet attempted. As printed in *Merry England* it is too diffuse and too long to be a literary success. But it is even less successful in the version put together for the *Collected Works* where deleted passages and arbitrary additions from elsewhere make for patchiness and a far more marked lack of structure. In its original form the value of the essay lies in its content. He bases his criticisms of Booth's achievements and ambitions on his own knowledge of conditions which in the book are too easily shaped to fit the argument. At one point he makes a guarded reference to the personal element in the essay, which otherwise he keeps carefully veiled:

> I have knowledge, not indeed great or wide, but within certain narrow limits more intimate than most men's, of this life which is not a life; to which food is as the fuel of hunger; sleep, our common sleep, precious, costly, and fallible, as water in a wilderness; in which men rob and women vend themselves — for fourpence ... [7]

His main point, however, is that when the 'trimmings' of the Salvationists' 'military symbolism' are removed, the principles uncovered are essentially those of the Gospels, never better put forward than through the 'chivalrous militarism' of Saint Francis and his Order. From here on the essay becomes an urgent appeal to Catholics to learn from Booth's example rather than criticize the details. For there are immense resources within the Church, above all in the special vocation of the three Franciscan Orders, the friars and sisters and those laymen of the Third Order, who now number over thirteen thousand. Surely here is the means for aid as valuable as any provided by the Salvationists, whereas at present the only tribute he can offer to Catholics is for the work undertaken by the Little Sisters of the Poor, and the single shelter for the homeless in Providence Row. Thompson's description of the shelter draws on still vividly painful memories:

> What such an institution does, and how much remains to do, may be impressively realised by one who watches the nightly crowd of haggered men

outside this Refuge; the anxious waiting while the ticket-holders are slowly admitted, the thrill — the almost shudder — through the crowd when the manager emerges to pick out men for the vacant beds left over after the ticket-holders' admission, the sickening suspense and fear in all eyes as — choosing a man here and there — he passes along the huddled ranks, the cold clang with which the gates of mercy shut in those fortunate few, but out the rest; and then the hopeless, helpless drifting off of the dreary crowd . . .

Memories of this kind set off passages where the rhetoric serves genuine feeling. Below the surface of proselytising and vulgarity he admits in many of the Army's tactics is the far more vital challenge:

Before me stretched an immense, soundless, bitter ocean. On its shore stood a string of benevolent children equipped with sugar-basins. What were they doing? They were throwing lumps of sugar into the waves, to sweeten the sea. Here was this vast putrescence strangling the air at our very doors, and what scavengers of charity might endeavour its removal? Now comes by a man, and offers to take on himself the responsibility of that removal: in God's name, give him the contract!.

Yet it will be an admittance of failure. The Catholics of England possess the means to outstrip the Salvation Army in its present work and future aims. The appeal is to the Franciscans in particular, but the message must be heeded by all: 'The most disastrous daring is better in such a matter than but too certainly disastrous quiescence'.

The essay was welcomed by Meynell as calculated to disturb the lethargy he too deplored. He also knew that in the event of serious criticism both he and Thompson could be sure of Manning's support. Only recently Manning had asked him to accompany Bishop Vaughan on a tour of the Salvation Army shelters in an attempt to bring the Cardinal's appointed successor to a better understanding of the conditions he had so much at heart himself. Vaughan was of a different calibre. At each shelter his main concern was the protection of Catholic inmates from the dangers of proselytism and on their return he could only labour this point to the Cardinal. For him, he admitted, any undertaking on behalf of the depraved characters he encountered must be from a sense of Christian duty: 'The natural man in me has no love for the world'. To which Manning's answer was typical, of a kind to appeal to Thompson no less than it did to Meynell: 'God so loved the world that he sent his only begotten son — but that is a detail'.[8]

On the publication of *In Darkest England* Manning wrote to Booth to assure him 'how completely my heart is in your book'.[9] Meynell now saw to it that he also read Thompson's review-essay, with the result that Manning sent the author an invitation to a private interview. It took place in the bleak barrack-like building Manning had taken over from the Horseguards on his appointment to Westminster.

His 'office' consisted of a screened off portion of the first floor, untidy and with no pretence at the appearances due to his position. Their conversation is not recorded except that little was said on either side and the Cardinal urged his guest to come again. It was a not uncommon habit for Manning to encourage visitors during his last lonely months, but in Thompson's case there was more reason. Here was one who knew what it was to be among society's outcasts and who, it seemed, possessed something of his own burning anger against the society that persisted in turning its back upon them. Perhaps he sensed a deeper affinity which he desired to take further. There was a strangely common ground between the lonely prelate and the lonely poet in the austerities the one had chosen and which the other was constrained to accept. It is therefore regrettable that the onset of Manning's final illness shortly afterwards meant that there were no more visits.

Thompson's essay was read by a wider public than any he had so far written. His criticisms of the Salvation Army went comparatively unheeded. What were noticed were his proposals, 'a bugle blast' which should be heard 'throughout Christendom' according to W. T. Stead in the *Review of Reviews*. As editor of the influential *Pall Mall Gazette*, Stead had earlier collaborated with Booth in revealing to the public the horrors of the traffic in child prostitutes in London. He remained on intimate terms with Booth and informed Thompson by letter how his essay 'delighted the Salvation Army people at headquarters more than anything that has happened for a long time'.[10]

The sudden publicity meant that Thompson was the centre of more attention than before from the Meynells' friends and associates, many of whom also regarded him now as a rising star among the poets. It gave him a new confidence, such as he would show from now on when the company was more concerned with his ideas and interests than with his oddities of manner and appearance. The circle that gathered in the Meynells' drawing room each Sunday evening varied, but in the main the conversation centred on literary topics. At times Thompson became a lively contributor. The poet and critic Alfred Hayes remembered the glowing light in his eyes if the subject in hand held a special appeal for him and 'the inexhaustible well of literary allusion which was a revelation to those who knew him'. Those, that is, who knew his everyday manner of self-effacing reserve. W. E. Henley was another who was taken by surprise at his fund of knowledge, describing his conversation as 'brilliant' on occasions. To Katherine Tynan he appeared 'a rich, abundant, intemperate talker'; too intemperate at times, striding about the room and clutching his evil-smelling pipe while pursuing his 'flood of argument'. When in the mood he could hold forth on almost any subject, however trivial — a habit the busy *Merry England* staff could find tedious and irritating. On one well remembered occasion he was deployed to 'entertain' the critic J. L. Garvin, notorious as one of the most fluent talkers of the day and whose arrival coincided with a particularly full morning's work. Garvin reported later to the Meynells that he had been 'overwhelmed' by Thompson's eloquence on the respective merits of Lyons and ABC teashops.[11]

There were many times when he was neither an inspired nor a garrulous talker, but would be enclosed in his usual reserve. If he sensed a lack of fellow-feeling from others he would appear as Le Gallienne remembered him, 'a rather ineffective personality, sitting silent and shrunken within himself'.[12] This must have been the impression he made on the members of the Rhymers' Club when Meynell took him to one of their meetings, hoping to widen his contacts with poets of the day outside the Meynells' own circle. The experiment was a distinct failure. Francis sat silent throughout the evening, forming an opinion of the proceedings which he voiced afterwards 'with some scorn'. He was impatient of the self-conscious poses adopted by most of the 'Rhymers', the group of younger poets who had formed their 'club' the year before. They met either in each other's houses or, as on this occasion, at the Cheshire Cheese in Fleet Street. Francis must have passed the seventeenth-century inn, well known for its associations with literary men, very often during his London streets years. Perhaps that was partly the reason for his silence when he found himself in the upper room where the poets were reading their, to him, affected and mainly trivial verse. There were too many contrasts between the effete ideals of these young men and the sordid truths in life of which they seemed so unaware. Also they took themselves much too seriously. 'I never heard a Rhymer laugh' reported another of their guests, 'and all of them, except Yeats, read their verses with hushed voices'.[13] Francis would never lose his ability to laugh and especially at foibles of this kind. He might have qualified his reaction if Yeats had been present that evening, for he was to be one of the first to welcome Yeats as a true poet, distinct from the rest of the group. Some years later when his own poetry was well known, he was invited as guest of the evening to one of the Rhymers' houses. After much persuasion he agreed, only to embarrass all present by remaining as silent as on the first occasion.[14]

If the Meynells could be irritated by his lapses into garrulity and sometimes awkward silences, they always found him courteous towards themselves and their guests and willing to give the children the attention for which they often had little time to spare. Above all there was the conscientious care that went into everything he submitted for *Merry England* and occasionally for the *Weekly Register*. Both journals,

in fact, were showing a marked increase in circulation since his contributions began to appear. Between 1888 and the last issue of *Merry
England* in 1895 he contributed some thirty essays and reviews. There
were only about half a dozen he regarded as more than hack work but
almost all stand out from the general run of such writing. And some of
his best poetry, together with the 'Ode to the Setting Sun' and 'The
Hound of Heaven', is to be found among the thirty-seven pieces that
first appeared in its pages.

The practical side was another matter. Time and again Francis
would arrive panting on the night before a contribution was due. He
was not so much forgetful as incapable of living according to any but
his own time scale and to do otherwise, as his work with the Meynells
meant he was bound to do, cost him an enormous effort. If an idea
came to him on his way from his lodgings it was not unusual for him
to wander off in another direction and end up hours later in some
quite different part of the city. For their part Wilfrid and Alice recognized his disregard for time and absent-mindedness as so much a
part of him that they went unquestioned, along with his disreputable
clothes and constant, obnoxious pipe.

Wilfrid came to accept the fact that the chances of an appointment being kept or not were about equal. It was not always forgetfulness. If a 'fit' of inspiration came on him Francis would become
oblivious to all else. On one such occasion about this time he sent
Wilfrid an apologetic note:

> Unfortunately I fell into composition on the way; and when I became con-
> scious of matters sublunary, found myself wandering about somewhere in
> the region of Smithfield Market, and the time late in the afternoon. I am
> heartily sorry for my failure to keep my appointment, and hope you will
> forgive me. I thought I had disciplined myself out of these aberrations,
> which makes me feel all the more vexed about the matter.[15]

It may be that such 'aberrations' were partly due to an impulse to
return to the life of the streets, which in later years was to become at
times a conscious compulsion. But there is no reason to doubt that
poetic inspiration was also responsible. In any case, whatever the
excuse the apologies were always genuine and always accepted on
Wilfrid's part.

Thompson's correct destination was no longer Phillimore Place.
Soon after his departure for Storrington, Alice's father had died and
she inherited the money made over at the time of her marriage. It was
used to build the house that became the Meynells' home and the
home of their seven children for the next fifteen years. When Francis
returned to London in 1890 they were settling in at 47 Palace Court, a
wide turning off the Bayswater Road that still gives the impression of
a comparatively secluded square. Wilfrid and Alice exercised a keen

14. 47 Palace Court from a
drawing attributed
to Everard Meynell

47 PALACE COURT

interest in the planning and design of the house, choosing for the
exterior the red brick and gables of the 'Dutch' style that was fashionable at the time.

Inside there have been many alterations and the great staircase
that was the main feature has gone. It led up through the five floors,
joining the hall and dining room beyond the entrance hall with the
library and drawing room on the first floor, then continuing to the
many bedrooms needed for the family and their frequent guests. The
library was the heart of the home. At the long refectory table the work

on Wilfrid's journals was divided between his staff, while underneath,
weaving in and out of their legs, the children composed their own
family magazine. All available wall space was given over to shelves
and cupboards for the various books and papers which here achieved
some semblance of order — notably absent from the rest of the rooms
where they overflowed onto chairs and floor.[16]

The distance from Third Avenue to Palace Court was not more
than three miles and seemed less to a habitual walker like Thompson.
But from the Harrow Road, past Paddington and into the refinements
of Bayswater, he entered a different world. Different in more than
social appearances. Everything in the Meynell household was in such
contrast to the life that now seemed mapped out for him. Back in the
shabby surroundings of his lodgings there was the constant sense of
physical and mental isolation, the datelines to be kept even if he must
sit up writing all night. Then having delivered his 'copy' he would
return to sleep through the rest of the next day, disrupting whatever
attempt he made at a more orthodox routine such as he knew he
needed if he was to withstand the recurrent craving for a more
effective stimulant than the ever-present pipe.

The days he passed at Palace Court were, on the other hand, full
of a cheerful camaraderie where he was generally treated by the Meynells as one of the family. Yet there was an underlying difference, the
nature of which neither he nor they ever became fully aware. For, to
Wilfrid and Alice, he was never to grow up. To Wilfrid, for all his high
regard for Francis as both poet and prose writer, he would always be
the waif of their first meeting. It was the regard of the fond parent for
a gifted child whose success in life depended on constant fatherly
concern. Francis on his side was well aware of his material dependence, while in other respects during these early months Wilfrid took
the place of the father he had needed as a child and who the child in
him still looked for.

The home, too, was giving him something of the family life he
had craved as a child. Yet it was too late to do more than provide a
surface compensation, while below the surface it intensified the regrets and the desire to regress — a desire which the Meynells' attitude
was bound to foster. And towards Alice as the mother, his feelings
were at first very much those of the child for whom she was the centre
of the home. She was older than Francis by twelve years and, for all
her youthful appearance and manner, her long experience of marriage
and motherhood meant that she appeared to him as the counterpart
to the devouring negative mother figure of the more recent past. To
her he would always be 'my child', the term she often used when referring to him. But with the development of his poetic powers the relationship on his side began to change. The child who had invested the
ladies in his picture books with an ideal of feminine beauty now com-

peted with the poet who sought an ideal of perfect womanhood. As a poet Thompson was always insistent as to the nature of the relationship and of her role as the feminine principle in his poetic life, for which she was, as he expressed it, an 'idealization of a woman'.[17] The poet in Alice accepted the homage on these terms and neither she nor Wilfrid allowed anything in it to disturb the understanding between the three of them. Thompson's role as a poet was essential in maintaining this balance, but so also was his position as the dependent child. If it was once broken there was no knowing — and they did not choose to know — what might result.

Well before Thompson first knew her, Alice was the centre of a group of admirers among the poets and writers who frequented the Meynell home, a situation that became accepted as part of the family life. At first Francis seemed to be merely following their example, until the closer associations through their work and the more intimate conditions of their friendship as poets produced underlying reactions on each side. According to Viola, who of all the family was probably closest to her parents: 'In Thompson's love for Alice Meynell, Meynell found no reason for distress, and Thompson no cause for elation'. Yet her further observation: 'It was a relationship so simple and altogether untortured as to afford no field of investigation for the analytically minded of the present day',[18] does call for qualification. She may have been right in defending them from the kind of psychological probings she had in mind, but not for the reasons she gives. To suggest there were no painful repercussions for the Meynells is, in the light of later developments, at least doubtful: whereas in Thompson's case it is to discount much that was to appear in his letters and notebooks and above all in the poetry he wrote at this time.

During the summer of 1890 he began the series of poems 'Love in Dian's Lap' where Alice is the central subject. Significantly, when reviewing Thompson's first book of poetry Meynell chose the series as examples of the best poems in the collection.[19] Their quality justified the choice but there was perhaps another motive. No one should suspect any uneasiness on the part of himself or his wife at the sentiments contained in them, which the majority of readers would know were addressed to Alice. If there was an unease which the observation set out to conceal, it is impossible to do more than speculate. But for Thompson there was certainly another side to the relationship, the physical attraction without which the poems could not have been written. The connecting link between the seven that formed the original Sequence is the sublimation of this physical attraction into an 'affinity of souls'.

Throughout, he follows the example set by the poets of seventeenth century who from Donne to Dryden concealed powerful personal emotions within seemingly intellectual conceits. He also draws

on them to augment the rich store of his own visual imagery which is
one of the distinctive features of the Sequence — to the extent that
three of the poems in the series as first written are concerned with
portraits or portrayals of their subject. The same then applies to two
of the six poems added later.[20]

In 'Her Portrait', the poet can be allowed to delight in the 'love-
liness corporeal' of the painting since in its purity he fancies her physical beauty 'might the soul's begetter be':

> God laid His fingers on the ivories
> Of her pure members as on smoothéd keys,
> And there out-breathed her spirit's harmonies.
>
> 98–100

This concentration on a portrait, or as in 'Gilded Gold' on an assumed
appearance, is used as a safety valve throughout the Sequence. Physical attraction can be permitted at least a cautious outlet since it is
not the lady herself who is the direct object. In 'Before her Portrait
in Youth' he treasures an early painting of Alice which she has discarded:

> This drooping flower of youth thou lettest fall
> I, faring in the cockshut-light, astray,
> Find on my 'lated way,
> And stoop, and gather for memorial,
> And lay it in my bosom, and make it mine.
> To this, the all of love the stars allow me,
> I dedicate and vow me.
> I reach back through the days
> A trothed hand to the dead the last trump shall not raise.
>
> 43–51

In the same poem Thompson refers to 'the poet's iron crown' that has
crushed her early bloom along with her poetic gifts: while in 'Her
Portrait' the spirit of Poetry has rocked himself to sleep in her heart.
Since her marriage Alice had published no further poetry and apparently had written none. Now, during this summer of 1890, there
appeared the first poem of her mature years, 'Veni Creator'. It is
typical of her later verse, condensed in feeling and content and with
an idea presented 'in embryo' as it were, left to the reader to make the
interpretation for himself. Thompson was inclined to criticize the idea
behind the poem but, as poetry, it was, he assured Canon Carroll, 'a
perfect miniature example of her most lovelily tender work'.[21]

Alice was becoming more than an ideal of womanhood for him.
She began to assume the poetic ideal he had set himself on leaving
Storrington. 'To a Poet Breaking Silence' stands out from the rest of
the Sequence in addressing her in this new capacity:

Too wearily had we and song
Been left to look and left to long,
Yea, song and we to long and look,
Since thine acquainted feet forsook
The mountain where the Muses hymn
For Sinai and the Seraphim.
Now in both the mountains' shine
Dress thy countenance, twice divine!
From Moses and the Muses draw
The Tables of thy double Law!
. . . .
Ah! let the sweet birds of the Lord
With earth's waters make accord;
Teach how the crucifix may be
Carven from the laurel-tree,
Fruit of the Hesperides
Burnish take on Eden-trees,
The Muses' sacred grove be wet
With the red dew of Olivet,
And Sappho lay her burning brows
In white Cecilia's lap of snows!

1–10
19–28

Thompson was never to learn the lesson he asks of her. The thread of lyricism by which she succeeded within her own severely prescribed limits would never satisfy the craving for poetic immortality released in the 'Ode to the Setting Sun'.

For the present their exchange of poetic ideas provided a stimulus for each and gave him a pleasure he was able to keep distinct from more personal emotions. His surviving letters to her start from this time: enthusiastic but not uncritical commentaries on her writing and brief, often caustic, comments on his own. As when having been told of his 'splendid faults' he dismissed 'this correction in sugar' with the observation: 'If my Muse rouges — tell her so; though she vow and protest that it is no more than fashionable Muses be'. Alice could understand when he confided to her the effort of putting his deeper thoughts into words, when ideas could so often be inhibited by 'the mere dead weight of language, the gross actualities of speech'.[22]

Paradoxically, it is the poets and creative writers who are most aware of this barrier between thought and its adequate expression, and for Thompson it added to the reserve deriving from his background and first years. Although there were times when it could be discarded if his mood and the company were right, in the ordinary way he was increasingly most at ease when sent off to amuse the children. There had been McMaster's niece and then Daisy and her friends but his feeling towards the Meynell children went much further. His attempt at acknowledging what this meant to him resulted in his longest poem. If 'Sister Songs' is not among his best, it is the one into which he put most conscious care.[23]

The idea came to him in March or April, soon after completing 'The Hound of Heaven'. It arose from a sudden memory of a curiously shaped cup he remembered seeing years ago at the South Kensington Museum (now the Victoria and Albert) when he was in London for his first medical exams. Designed with two lips and two handles, it was thought to have been the model for the 'amphicypellon' or 'cup on either side' described in Homer as carried to the gods by the cupbearer Hephaestus. This poem should be an amphicypellon, a double offering to the two Meynell sisters he knew best.[24]

He made a start, but then began to have scruples. Finishing 'The Hound of Heaven' meant he had already been excused a good deal of work wanted for *Merry England*. 'Thought that my duty to Mr Meynell imperatively required that I should sacrifice the poem'. So he wrote to Canon Carroll, and the episode that followed was obviously of special importance to him, for he gave it more attention than anything else included in the Journal Letter. As recounted to Carroll it reveals something of what his poetry meant to him at the time and the kind of conflict it aroused:

> During a week I struggled with the impulse, which was so strong as to prevent me from writing prose, though I would not yield to it. Then at last I stifled it; and as a result I can write neither prose nor poetry, and have made myself unwell.

A few days later he took up the letter again. In his distress he said he had asked advice from Elizabeth Blackburn, the Meynells' chief collaborator on their journals as proof reader and general critic. During the first months of their acquaintance Thompson held her views on poetry in high regard, and certainly in this instance they were to the point. She had, he continued, reproved him severely for not seeing how his real duty was to use 'the special gift that God had given me'. He regarded the exchange between them that followed as worth repeating word for word:

> 'Ah! if I stood alone!' I said, but it is injustice to Mr Meynell'. She rejoined that she could quite understand that consideration making me unhappy; but that if there were loss now, it would be repaid to him ultimately. 'With regard to some of his *protégés* I think, and sometimes tell him, that he is wasting support and encouragement on worthless people; but I have no such feeling at all with regard to you'. I acknowledged that I had a strong

impression that the poem would be for mere beauty — not for power of
thought — the best that I had done. 'Then write it by all means'. 'I can't
now; the impulse is past'. 'There, you see!' she said. Then I confessed that
it was to have been addressed to two of Mr Meynell's children; and she
was downright vexed. 'Oh, I wish you had written it', she said. 'Oh, you
horrid boy! To think that those creatures should have been so near immortality. I hope it will come back to you'. I shook my head and said that
if ever it did, it would not be while this weather lasted; it would need air
and sunlight to rekindle the poem.

Mrs Blackburn was to act as go-between on several later occasions,
not always to Francis's advantage. On this first one, however, she did
the right thing. She went to the Meynells and told them the whole
story. Alice, she reported back, 'had simply wrung her hands' and
Wilfrid 'said I had acted very foolishly, and was never to do such a
thing again'. So now he was more distressed than ever — not from
Mrs Blackburn's 'good scolding' but at his own mistaken view of the
poem:

> I had no idea that it would give them any particular pleasure, or I would
> not have throttled it. I thought I should be consulting only my own selfish
> pleasure in writing the poem. Now I am miserably endeavouring to re-
> suscitate it; neither able to write it or leave it alone. And I am despondent
> and wretched.[25]

There was more behind the importance he attached to the incident
than he knew. If the poem as he first conceived it was to have been 'for
mere beauty — not for power of thought', then even if it could have
been 'the best that I have done', was it in line with the ideal he set
himself on leaving Storrington? Was it not rather a betrayal of his gift
as 'the poet of the return of God'? Given the Meynells' unstinted
praise for his poetry so far and their encouragement, this seems the
more likely motive behind his scruples, for which the reason as he
genuinenely believed it to be was the necessary cover. It is worth
adding that his account as given to Carroll shows how, in spite of their
admiration for his poetry, the Meynells and Mrs Blackburn saw him
primarily as a child to be alternately scolded and encouraged. And his
deliberately dismissive reference to the weather hints at a certain impatience on his side.

In any case, the result was that he determined to write the poem
even if he could not recapture the first flush of its inspiration. He was
in fact working on 'Sister Songs' intermittently until the following
winter — or, to give the poem its title at the time, 'Songs Wing to
Wing'. As both titles indicate, it is divided into two 'Parts', addressed
respectively to Madeleine and Monica Meynell, Madeleine being
given the name Sylvia as the one by which she was generally known in
the family. The two are very different, barely held together as a single

entity. Part the First, with its 'Proem', runs to some four hundred lines celebrating the joys of spring and of childhood in contrast to the poet's lament for the share in them which he can no longer hope for. In the main he keeps the concentration on the child and the homage offered by spring to her innocence. Even the passage where her kiss recalls the kisses of that other very different child of the streets is brought in chiefly to stress this child's spontaneous gesture. In Part the Second, more than twice as long, the sense of his own isolation intensifies to pervade the whole:

> Love and love's beauty only hold their revels
> In life's familiar, penetrable levels:
> What of its ocean floor?
> I dwell there evermore.
> From almost earliest youth
> I raised the lids o' the truth,
> And forced her bend on me her shrinking sight;
> Ever I knew me Beauty's eremite,
> In antre of this lowly body set,
> Girt with a thirsty solitude of soul.
>
> II, 49–58

At times the mood can evoke a memorable image, as when he addresses the child:

> I will not feed my unpastured heart
> On thee, green pleasaunce as thou art.
>
> II, 502–503

Of all Thompson's longer poems, 'Sister Songs' illustrates the depths of turbid obscurity to which he could descend and the heights he could reach elsewhere:

> As the innocent moon, that nothing does but shine,
> Moves all the labouring surges of the world.
>
> II, 262–263

The almost Shakespearean tone reappears in:

> . . . the yet untreacherous claws
> Of newly-whelped existence
>
> II, 665–666

The passage on the street girl is followed by one where his reflections on the encounter say more about what it has come to mean for him than the description of the encounter itself:

> . . . so long myself had strayed afar
> From child, and woman, and the boon earth's green,
> Journeying its journey bare

Five suns, except of the all-kissing sun
          Unkissed of one;
          Almost I had forgot
          The healing harms,
And whitest witchery a-lurk in that
Authentic cestus of two circling arms:
          And I remembered not
          The subtle sanctities which dart
From childish lips' unvalued precious brush,
Nor how it makes the sudden lilies push
          Between the loosening fibres of the heart.

I, 308–322

'Five suns' from the episode of the street girl lead back to the year of his illness at Owens following his mother's death, indicating it was then that the troubles of his adult life really began.

In spite of the many digressions into his adult life and its troubles, the two parts of the poem succeed in keeping their overall theme consistent. The lines which at the start celebrate the morning of youth and spring:

Mark yonder, how the long laburnam drips
Its jocund spilth of fire, its honey of wild flame'.

'Proem', 26–27

— reappear as part of the sunset scene at the end:

And, glimmering to eclipse,
The long laburnam drips
Its honey of wild flame, its jocund spilth of fire.

II, 743–745

Thompson is reverting here to his sun symbolism, enclosing the whole poem in the life of a day, the childhood day where the morning joy must contain the seed of sunset sorrow. The image also suggests some actual moment of sudden beauty flashed on his eye amid the drabness of Queen's Park. The initial impulse may have faded but there were times when it revived to give the poem lines of the kind of 'mere beauty' he had told Mrs Blackburn he first envisaged for it.

It was finished in time for him to leave it surreptitiously on the mantelpiece of the Palace Court drawing room on Christmas Eve. The delight and gratitude with which Wilfrid and Alice received it caused him to take it back again a few days later to add an 'Inscription'. Offered as the poem was to the parents rather than the children themselves, the added lines concentrate on his feeling towards his two 'guardian spirits':

One twines from finest gracious daily things,
Strong, constant, noticeless as are heart-strings,
The golden cage wherein this song-bird sings;
And the other's sun gives hue to all my flowers,
Which else pale flowers of Tartarus would grow . . .

                                   16–20

He likens his poem to the 'fond and fancied nothings' of a child's gift, offered by one who is 'their youngest nursling of the spirit's kind'. It is the gift of a gratitude expressed through the 'safety valve' of his role as the dependent child. Yet what of that 'cage' which, however, gilded, is still an image of constraint, of imprisonment?

The underlying complications in his relationship with the family did not affect the many occasions of genuine pleasure he shared in their company. That Christmas was one he never forgot for its simple spontaneous delight, the first of a long series only broken by the years he was away from London and when, towards the end of his life, illness prevented him from joining them. Midnight Mass was the solemn focal point, after which Christmas Day was given over to jollification and present giving. There was no tree, regarded as a new and 'protestant' innovation. Instead the gifts were arranged in the 'present place' assigned by long custom to a window seat in the Library. There was the traditional turkey dinner, after which came a family tradition in the competition to guess the number of leaves on a giant pineapple, the table's centrepiece. Wilfrid's home-made wine added to the general merriment, brewed in utmost secrecy some weeks earlier from a recipe known only to himself and dispatched in specially designed cases to favoured friends.[26]

That first Christmas was followed by a spell of bitter weather, when the Round Pond in Kensington Gardens froze for long enough for Francis to set about teaching the older children to skate. On one such occasion his pleasure in their company called for a note of thanks to Wilfrid. 'If the children had half so delightful an afternoon as I had with them I shall not have any doubt that they enjoyed themselves'. Having described their antics with mock serious fun he must, he says, 'thank you warmly for your kindness in trusting the children to me. Or shall I say trusting me to them? For on reflection I have a haunting suspicion that Monica managed the party with the same energy that she devotes to her skating'. She has been 'most solicitous' for his own pleasure in the sport rather than interrupting it to attend to their efforts. 'A needless anxiety, since I desired nothing better than to play with them. Indeed they could not have been better or kinder'.[27] There is nothing forced or ungenuine in the way he writes here. When alone with the children, with no disturbing challenge from the adult world, he could allow the child in himself free play.

Then, as now, Kensington Gardens was the most pleasant part of Hyde Park with its lawns and flower beds and the changing attractions of the Round Pond for the children. During the previous summer Francis had often taken them to the Gardens, as glad to escape the duties of journalism as the rest of the adults were to proceed without interruption. When not joining in their games he would seat himself on a bench with the exercise book where 'Sister Songs' was taking shape. Everard, older and more observant than his sisters, noticed how he was often 'at prayer as well as at poetry' at such times.[28]

On some days he came alone, but usually it was not for long. He was a familiar figure to the other children who frequented the Gardens and who, like the Storrington school children, made him a partner in their games in return for his ready fund of stories. Nor did their nursemaids doubt the intentions of the quiet-voiced young man who, for all his shabby appearance, was never anything but reserved and courteous towards them and their charges. One small girl in particular attached herself to him. 'The dearest child', he told Wilfrid, excusing a lapse from more serious matters on the grounds that her parents were regular readers of the *Weekly Register:*

> I rather fancy she thinks me one of the most admirable of mortals; and I firmly believe her to be one of the most daintily supernatural of fairies . . . Of course, in some way she is sure to vanish: elves always do, and my elves in particular.[29]

Sadly for him he was right. His 'elves' would vanish as they left the realm of elfland, finding him then an awkward, sometimes even an embarrassing presence in the Palace Court household, to be tolerated rather than welcomed. 'We certainly did not dislike the poet' Olivia remembered. 'But he was accepted as one of the accidents of life when we were young . . . he was just *there*'. Madeleine went further. Asked in later years if she had liked him she admitted: 'I should almost have said *no* to that', explaining how his sudden silences and untidy appearance made him seem to her in some way 'uncanny'. There was probably a special reason for her feeling towards him as she recalled it. Younger than Monica, the other sister celebrated in 'Sister Songs', the two were often subjected to attending readings of the poem before their parents' admiring friends. She could remember how she dreaded such occasions, 'utterly bored' as she was by them. Viola, more cautious and as usual more penetrating, came to see Francis's insistence on the bond between himself and them as 'perhaps the exaggeration of a man too much deprived of personal ties'. She remembered how his comings and goings went generally unnoticed, with none of the excitement natural to children towards a welcome visitor. For the younger children it was just that he was too familiar a figure to call for special attention, and Viola's tribute can be said to outweigh their criticisms as they grew older. In their earlier years 'they were never afraid or strange with him, and a child would hold his hand as naturally as hold her doll'. This confidence also led them to play tricks on him, delighted when he appeared quite unconscious of the fact. The teasing went largely unnoticed by their busy parents but Katherine Tynan, a frequent visitor, observed it; also that he was more aware of it than he let them see — and how he still took it in good part when, later, they poked fun at his 'queer, odd unworldly ways'.[30]

In the summer of 1891 he went with the family for a holiday at Friston in Suffolk. There were picnics on the Broads and pranks in the yard and barns of the farm where they were staying. Through all of this Everard recalled Francis as an indistinct figure, vaguely present as 'part of the general gentle world' only known in childhood.[31] Yet for Francis himself the pleasures and the poignancies of the holiday remained as vivid memories. They come together in the poem he wrote after an evening walk with Monica, when her sudden spontaneous gift of a wild poppy reminded him of Daisy and the wild raspberries. 'The Poppy' is among the best, if not the best, of his poems on his feeling for children and childhood as it affected his own emotional life:

> Summer set lip to earth's bosom bare,
> And left the flushed print in a poppy there:
> Like a yawn of fire from the grass it came,
> And the fanning wind puffed it to flapping flame.
>
> With burnt mouth, red like a lion's, it drank
> The blood of the sun as he slaughtered sank,
> And dipped its cup in the purpurate shine
> When the Eastern conduits ran with wine.
>
> Till it grew lethargied with fierce bliss,
> And hot as a swinkéd gipsy is,
> And drowsed in sleepy savageries,
> With mouth wide a-pout for a sultry kiss.
>
> A child and man paced side by side,
> Treading the skirts of eventide;
> But between the clasp of his hand and hers
> Lay, felt not, twenty withered years.
>
> She turned, with the rout of her dusk South hair,
> And saw the sleeping gipsy there;
> And snatched and snapped it in swift child's whim,
> With — 'keep it, long as you live!' — to him.

The sunset and its meaning for him as a poet is transferred, through
the child, to the poppy and its very personal meaning for the man
behind the poet:

> 'Was never such thing until this hour,'
> Low to his heart he said; 'the flower
> Of sleep brings wakening to me,
> And of oblivion, memory.'

> 'Was never this thing to me,' he said,
> 'Though with bruiséd poppies my feet are red!'
> And again to his own heart very low:
> 'O child! I love, for I love and know ... 31–38

He knows her affectionate gesture is no more to her than a fleeting
fancy. From the child, 'frankly fickle and fickly true' he passes to his
own pain. The harvest field of the present scene merges with further
overtones from the 'Ode to the Setting Sun' as the image of the reaper
reappears among the poppies:

> The sleep-flower sways in the wheat its head,
> Heavy with dreams, as that with bread:
> The goodly grain and the sun-flushed sleeper
> The reaper reaps, and Time the reaper.

> I hang 'mid men my needless head,
> And my fruit is dreams, as theirs is bread:
> The goodly men and the sun-hazed sleeper
> Time shall reap, but after the reaper
> The world shall glean of me, me the sleeper.
>
> 64–72

The Suffolk harvest field in the sunset light has revived the promise of
his poetic awakening and his life's gleanings, his 'brood of immortality', will be preserved from the reaper's knife. But the shadow falls
again across the promise. For all the world's esteem there may be nothing in it for him, nothing left but the legacy from the past for which
the poppy now becomes a symbol as a 'flower of withered dream':

> Love, love! your flower of withered dream
> In leavéd rhyme is safe, I deam,
> Sheltered and shut in a nook of rhyme,
> From the reaper man, and his reaper Time.

> Love! *I* fall into the claws of Time:
> But lasts within a leavéd rhyme
> All that the world of me esteems —
> My withered dreams, my withered dreams.
>
> 73–80

The flower itself he did preserve, pressed and then carefully sewn into the notebook where it still remains. Faded and transparent, it witnesses to the lines he scribbled down at the same time. The flower will bleed of its colour and fade but it will live on in the poem born from the heart's blood of his own pain:

You gave me a heart-red poppy,
And a heart-red word: —
In a book I kept the poppy,
Stained & dead;
In a book I kept the word,
Quick & red.[32]

The child's actual share in 'The Poppy' may appear slight but, as these lines show, the poem depends on it — on those 'twenty withered years' separating him from her and stained with poppies for which her innocent gift brings associations leading away from her childhood dream world to the 'withered dreams' of his own presaged future.

If he had any preference, Monica was his favourite of the sisters. His special feeling for her contributed to the complex emotions in the second part of 'Sister Songs' and it also gave rise to the most moving of his poems addressed directly to the children, 'To Monica Thought Dying'. Early the following year the whole family attended Cardinal Manning's lengthy funeral obsequies, which took place in bitter winter weather. As a result Monica developed pleurisy and for several days her life was in danger. Thompson's description of her childish gaieties, her delight in the 'shop' where she distributed sweets to all who would 'buy', is poignantly true of the way an adult reacts to the presence of death when it threatens a vivid young life. He is not speaking for himself alone as he sees Death at play now with the child's toys, at the same time forcing from her in delirium the words she had so often spoken in her own play:

Nay, never so have wrung
From eyes and speech weakness unmanned, unmeet,
As when his terrible dotage to repeat
Its little lesson learneth at your feet;
As when he sits among
His sepulchres, to play
With broken toys your hand has cast away,
With derelict trinkets of the darling young.
Why have you taught — that he might so complete
His awful panoply
From your cast playthings — why,
This dreadful childish babble to his tongue,
Dreadful and sweet?

68–80

Thompson takes the game, for him so much a part of childhood's dream world, to make it central to the theme of one of his most mature poems. His use of the ode form is mature, and he exploits its versatility to the extent that form and content are essential to one another. What the content implies, the form expands and clarifies.

The last of the Meynell children was born in May 1891. Thompson did not anticipate that he would be asked to be godfather and when the request came he was overwhelmed by gratitude and pleasure. So much so that afterwards he wrote to Meynell: 'Even now I am utterly unable to express to you what I feel regarding it. I can only hope that you may comprehend without words'. It is, he adds, an instinctive recoil from any outward show of emotion 'which I think, you share sufficiently to understand and excuse me'.[33]

With the letter he enclosed a poem written for the occasion. Perhaps because 'To my Godchild' was composed in far less time than was usual for him, it betrays something of his awareness of the 'feud' between the child and the man in himself as he desires that his godson shall be spared similar pain. He offers the poem with the hope that the child who is to be his namesake may become the kind of poet he senses he himself will never be:

> When you have compassed all weak I began,
> Diviner poet, and ah! diviner man;
> The man at feud with the perduring child,
> In you before Song's altar nobly reconciled;
> From the wise heavens I half shall smile to see
> How little a world, which owned you, needed me.

                                                    36–41

When the child, too, reaches heaven, if he seeks the poet there:

> Turn not your tread along the Uranian sod
> Among the bearded counsellors of God;
> For if in Eden as on earth are we,
> I sure shall keep a younger company

                                                    52–55

He must pass 'the roseal lightenings', 'the crystalline sea' and, with an echo from Coleridge, 'the Lampads seven' — and the poem ends with the line chosen by the Meynells to immortalize Thompson's own name in the epitaph for his tombstone:

> Look for me in the nurseries of heaven.

To Wilfrid and Alice it was a perfect reminder of the child he had always been to them and who they had protected over the years. But for Francis, the poem as a whole spoke for the pain-filled longings of his manhood, unable to free itself as he desired his namesake to do, from 'the perduring child'.

In all the recollections of Thompson's attitude to children and in all his writings on children and childhood, one fact stands out clearly. There was nothing of the unhealthy sexual attraction a man can feel for children, and especially for little girls. While they would still accept him into their games and make-believe he was at ease with them in a way he could not have been otherwise, given his hypersensitive temperament in all sexual matters. And when they left that first world behind them he accepted the change in the relationship as saddening but inevitable and made no effort to alter it.

Before the birth of Francis Meynell, Alice's pregnancy probably gave rise to the idea for the essay 'A Threnody of Birth'. Thompson was to take it up again much later in 'An Anthem of Earth' and, compared with the poem, the essay seems little more than an exercise in rhetoric. But taken on its own merit it succeeds in creating a compelling contrast between the glorious legacy of achievement from the past inherited by the newly-born child and the end at which all material achievement must arrive for the man he will become. The assertion of the 'Ode to the Setting Sun', that 'Death is Birth', is deliberately reversed in presenting the legacy only in terms of physical life and material attainment. Any other consideration is equally deliberately set aside as Thompson takes Hamlet's 'What a piece of work is man' as his theme:

> . . . his heart is builded for all heights, all deeps, all immensities, all pride, potency, infinity; it is arrassed with purple passing the palaces of kings; that it may stall the grey-rat, and the carrion-worm lodge statelily: his brain is sown with subtleties, mysteries, complexities, that for last and lowly masterwork it may conceive the simple daisy.[34]

The wonders of the physical world form part of the same heritage, and here Thompson makes a first attempt at formulating his ideas on science and its legacy for future generations. Science, he asserts, unites the past with the present and future, facing 'Janus-like' towards the great traditions laid down over centuries while also looking forward towards 'unborn cities of the new earth'. Nor will he admit any reasons for doubting the consequences:

> For she has discovered life in putridity, and vigour in decay; dissolution even and disintegration, which in the mouth of man symbolise disorder, in the works of God has discerned to be undeviating order, and the manner of our corruption no less wonderful than the manner of our health. And she is not affrighted, knowing the new things are as the old, and the ways of mutability

immutable, since the Author of all newness is Himself ancient, and of all change Himself unchangeable.

In Thompson's view of science, medical research was always to have pride of place. The laboratories at Owens held very different memories to the dissecting rooms.

The whole tone of the essay made it unsuitable for *Merry England* readers, and he wrote it with a view to striking out on his own. He sent it to the *National Observer*, the review which had recently replaced its predecessor, the *Scots Observer*. He already admired the editor. W. E. Henley, whose writing stood out against much that he despised among his contemporaries. Receiving no acknowledgement he wrote eventually to remind Henley:

> As I am now the older by some months, & the wiser by no intelligence, I conclude that you did not like it. Consequently I send you a fresh article, which is nothing that the other was. It is not imaginative, it is not over the head of the reader, if he have a head.[35]

The second essay, 'Modern Men: The Devil', was very different, being a survey of the devil at work in the modern world and carried out with a caustic and generally rather forced wit. But behind its brittle surface there is the idea that change is only relative, inseparable from the traditions out of which it arises. In this case, the devil's methods may be adapted to the contemporary scene but his trade remains unaltered:

> He is still, like his ancient adversary St Peter, a fisher of men. He deals in souls like a politician, and gets them nowadays for almost as little . . . So that whereas formerly a man might be secure of a fair price for his soul, while a clever fellow found it good business, and lived sumptuously on the proceeds of the negotiation, the days of great bargains in suchlike ware is past: and it were much, o' these days, if Faustus should sell his salvation for an Under-Secretaryship, or a mining-swindle, or a laureateship . . .[36]

The attempt at independence failed. Neither essay was accepted and Thompson did not feel justified in taking the time for further efforts of the kind. He realized he must resign himself to the confines of the Catholic press. After all, if Meynell was 'using up body and soul for the benefit of the blubber-brained Catholic public', what right had he to aspire to anything different?[37]

Yet he was not resigned. Apart from 'Sister Songs' — or 'Songs Wing to Wing' as the poem was still called — there was no opportunity to write another of any length or with the significance he felt he should give to his poetry, if only he could be allowed the time. 'A Corymbus for Autumn', composed that summer, he rightly regarded as little more than an exercise in the handling of images and sound effects.

The limitations on his prose were hardly less frustrating. All he could do was make the most of the occasions when he could expand his subject in directions he wanted to explore more than the subject itself. The whole issue of *Merry England* for April 1891 was given over to his account of the life and work of Saint John Baptist de la Salle, the pioneer of Catholic education for the poor. Having outlined the Saint's life with a marked absence of the hagiographical effulgence common at the time, he then used it to illustrate how true charity lies in recognizing the interdependence of all members of society on one another. This was what really interested him:

> He who separates his atom of humanity from its fellow-atoms thereby drops from among the agencies of Nature; since only by chemical combination with his fellows, by reciprocal exertion and acceptance of action, can he change, or modify, or produce anything ... There is one thing you can do for and by yourself; you can kill yourself. You cannot live for yourself, though you may try to live for yourself; nor can you, in any permanence, live by yourself. You may rot by yourself if you will, but that is not doing; it is ceasing.[38]

The passage, with its characteristic use of science by way of illustration, speaks for the loneliness of the room in Third Avenue — which, Thompson knew, was only one among many others.

Later that year he found a similar opportunity when reviewing a collection of letters by the Jesuit George Porter, Archbishop of Bombay. Their importance, for him, lay in the Archbishop's daringly unconventional views on penance and mortification in the commonsense attitude he brought to bear on the subject — which Thompson with his medical background to support him fully endorsed:

> We find our austerities ready-made. The east wind has replaced the discipline, dyspepsia the hair-shirt. It grows a vain thing to mortify the appetite — would we had the appetite to mortify![39]

This was well ahead of its time. For many years yet the traditional idea of the 'mortification of the flesh' continued to be one of the chief indications of holiness. Towards the end of his life Thompson was to develop the article into a much longer essay but the message would still go largely unheeded.*

Thompson's occasional ventures into fields he was unable to explore further strengthened the more serious frustration where his poetry was concerned. Together with the high ideals with which he had left Storrington, there had already been a conflict between the poetry he felt called upon to write and the principles of his religious background. The conflict was still with him, still casting its shadow

* See Chapter Ten, p. 317

over any inspiration that sometimes came to him. Was he destined, as Alice now seemed to be, to unite the laurel with the crucifix? Or was this yet another empty ambition to be set aside in meeting the demands of Wilfrid's Catholic journalism? Both Wilfrid and Alice made their view clear when it was a matter of continuing with 'Sister Songs'. But how far could he depend on their guidance when they could not know how the finished poem departed from the ideal he had set himself as the poet of the return to God? Yet what of the ideal? Was he aspiring to heights which he had not the power, after all, to attain and worse still, no right to contemplate? For over a year now, since completing 'The Hound of Heaven', there was nothing to suggest that he was not entertaining more than another empty ambition.

In this frame of mind he was ready to see the way to an answer close at hand. Before he left for Storrington he met the group of young Capuchin Franciscans who, on his return to London, he found were now regular visitors at Palace Court. They supplied him with much useful information about their Order for his essay on the Salvation Army, its call to the Franciscans having been largely due to their influence. It led them to confide their views to him on the Church in general as well as on their Order in particular. With the optimism of youth they envisaged a Church of the future relieved of the trammels of convention, reaching out to the needs of common humanity with a new awareness of the working of the Spirit through the physical world and by material means. In this they saw the Franciscans as uniquely suited to lead the way: the Friars must exchange the safe retreat of their monastic life for the streets and slums of the cities. In theory it sounded a fine ideal. The danger lay in the tendency inherent in all such ideals to overthrow the structures of the past rather than to utilize them — to destroy rather than to reconstruct. But in essentials, the friars were anticipating an outlook which in recent years has become widespread in the Church, although still without coming to terms with the danger from which it seems inseparable.

As they talked and planned and exchanged ideas, Thompson felt they were moving in a direction he had already been taking without knowing it, to which the friars now gave a recognizable purpose and aim. If on their side they were called to be 'heralds' of a new era of spiritual vitality in the Church, then, they assured him, he would be its 'prophet'. They had earlier given Coventry Patmore a similar recognition. His poetry celebrating the marriage bond as a spiritual union appeared to them to be in line with their view of the interrelationship between the spiritual and material worlds, the basis for their idea of the Church of the future. But Patmore was an old man and seldom left his home in Hampshire, whereas here was this young poet of their own generation who shared their aspirations and whose gifts seemed no less in accordance with them than Patmore's.

On his side Thompson's hopes for his poetic future revived. So
many of the friars' ideas on social and religious issues appeared to
tally with his own and their eagerness to devote themselves to the
needs of the poor appealed to him for its sincerity, even if he doubted
its practicality. Furthermore, the basis for their 'System', as they
called it, could surely be one to which he might dedicate his poetry,
arousing a new sense of the life of the spirit incarnated within material
forms. If he was to be 'the poet of the return to God' this could be the
meaning of the call and, if so, his poetic ambition need not cause him
to have qualms of conscience.

Of the four friars at Crawley who formed the nucleus of the
group, Father Cuthbert was the one with whom, at first, Thompson
had the most contact. Up to now he had never been in a position to
talk on an equal intellectual footing about topics on which there was
no comparable meeting ground with the Meynells. Not that they were
lacking in support. Both Wilfrid and Alice agreed in principle with
what they understood of this notion of change in the Church, but
neither was intellectually equipped to take it far for themselves.
Wilfrid was willing to provide the means for spreading the 'System'
further through the pages of *Merry England* and in 'A Wayside Essay'
Father Cuthbert took the so-called dangers of science and rationalism
as examples of the need for change in the Church's attitude towards
the modern world. In his view the contributors to *Lux Mundi*, the
Anglican attempt at answering the challenge, were moving in the
right direction. Catholics should not, he was careful to point out,
accept all the propositions put forward, but they should give serious
consideration to the principles behind them. From these principles
Cuthbert deduced that the real dangers ahead would not arise from
either science or materialism but from an insistence on a 'rationalistic
basis for belief overriding the moral and ethical foundations of religion
whose roots are within the heart and will of the individual'. It was a
cautious way of saying that the dangers were due to the dominance of
dogma over individual conscience.[40]

The writers for *Lux Mundi* had set out to meet the challenges of
the time. By advocating a similar outlook among Catholics, the essay
implied a warning of danger from the dogmatic pronouncements of
the Church if these continued to fail to take positive account of the
issues at stake by merely condemning them. Here, as in the veiled
reference to the individual conscience, Cuthbert was venturing a
criticism of the Church that was being spoken aloud on the Continent
and would be in England a decade ahead. It is perhaps significant
that, through the Meynells, the group came in contact with the future
leader of the Modernists in England, the Jesuit George Tyrrell, who
was also an occasional visitor at Palace Court. In naming his first
serious study of the contemporary Church *Christianity at the Crossroads*,

Tyrrell could have had the title, if not the contents, of the little heeded 'Wayside Essay' in mind.

Father Cuthbert was their chief spokesman but the nominal leader of the group was Father Alphonsus. As Guardian of the Crawley friary, he was in a position to encourage attendance at the Meynells' Sunday evenings and to give extra weight to the ideas and practical proposals under discussion. The main project, inspired by Booth's book and closely connected with Thompson's essay, was now a 'College of Priests' trained to go out to work with the people as well as minister to them. Cardinal Manning himself had wished to start a similar organization among the priests serving in London and he gave his tacit support. In fact the idea foreshadowed the 'Worker Priests' movement in Europe that lay some sixty years ahead. But as put forward by the Franciscans then, and in its later form, the movement could hardly succeed. Given the nature of the priest's vocation as understood then and now, the emotional and physical demands of such a calling could only be met by a very few.

Alphonsus had other aims, more immediate in effect and considerably more disturbing in their influence. He was widely read in the writings of the Eastern mystics and was infiltrating the methods and symbolism of Eastern thought into his addresses to the young friars who came to Crawley for the studies preceding their ordination. He was ahead of his time rather than mistaken in his view that Christianity could find much to value in these sources. But the notion of a new 'System of Philosophy' combining Eastern and Western principles was beyond the scope of any member of the group. Consequently they were unable to distinguish between the value in Eastern methods of mental training and meditation and the more fundamental divergence from the teachings of Christian theology and philosophy.

One of Father Alphonsus's students, Angelo de Bary, became an enthusiastic supporter of the 'System' soon after his ordination in 1889. Like the rest he joined the Order at an early age, in his case only fifteen, and as the group's youngest member he was to be most influenced by its ideas. When Thompson first met him he was taking the course in theology at Crawley, where the lector, Father Anselm Kenealy, was encouraging the young priests in his charge to read widely in all fields of modern thought from Nietzsche and Darwin to Newman and Wordsworth. Anselm was probably the most outstanding member and the intellectual leader, capable of retaining a firm belief in the Church's teachings while ranging over the whole spectrum of contemporary scepticism and doubt. His main shortcoming was that, like many of his kind, he failed to recognize the vulnerability of those less intellectually well-equipped than himself. He was to be Thompson's special friend and confident and he never forgot his first impressions of the poet's 'nervous energy that seemed to make him

abound in vitality', or the 'wonderful eyes' that more than compensated for his otherwise unimpressive appearance.[41]

The friars provided the kind of stimulus that enabled Thompson
to shed his usual shyness. The meetings at Palace Court led to invitations to stay at Crawley, and on several occasions during that summer
of 1891 he spent a few days at the Friary. On at least one occasion the
Meynells took a short holiday there as well. Anselm remembered the
pleasure the children gave among the community and many years
later he wrote to Alice reminding her of the visit and of an afternoon in
the buttercup fields when she entertained them with the songs that
were another of her accomplishments.[42]

It was a happy, relaxed interlude but it did not last long. When
Thompson went again in the autumn he found the Friary had no adequate heating and he already suffered from the actual cold as much as
from the colds caught in consequence. Cuthbert and Angelo were ill
with influenza and unable to see him. He could still take his long
walks but the weather was not encouraging, he wrote to Meynell
likening his present feelings to Touchstone's: 'in respect it is not the
city, it is tedious'.

There were more important reasons for the failure of this visit. In
the same letter there is a hint that he was beginning to have doubts
about some of the ideas put forward by his friends. 'I am getting a
little sick of this talk about "individualism"', and he saw a danger in
identifying the term with certain brands of 'socialism'. If this should
go further he could foresee the 'System' degenerating into an exclusively social concern, lacking the spiritual vitality that must be its
motivating power.[43]

Shortly afterwards Thompson wrote again to Wilfrid asking to be
allowed to return to London. He was still entirely dependent on the
Meynells' arrangements for him, having no money for his ticket, and
for the first time there is a note of irritation on this account. From the
letter it appears that the visit had been arranged by them at least
partly for their own reasons — of which he was well aware. 'It would
not be necessary for me to spend my time at Palace Court', he assured
them, adding that he could easily write in the Reading Room at the
British Museum instead.[44]

It was understandable if Wilfrid and Alice were instrumental in
planning the visit. For all their tolerance of his erratic ways and their
regard for his work, Thompson's constant presence could become a
strain. They had to attend to the interruptions of his discourses on this
and that when they needed to get on with their own writing and there
were the frequent minor crises in his domestic and financial affairs
which he expected them to sort out for him. In addition Wilfrid was
not well, being overworked and suffering from recurrent sore throats,
while Alice was often distracted by the accidents and illnesses of one

or other of the children. Francis sensed the strain and on his return
he kept his word and spent a good deal of his time at what is now the
Reading Room of the British Library.

Thompson, too, had his reasons for the change. When not
writing his articles for the Meynells, he was reading all he could find
on mysticism and the cults of the East, trying to test for himself the
validity of the ideas put forward by his Franciscan friends. For the
present he kept his studies to himself, as well as the general uncertainty they aroused and the cloud cast over his earlier hopes.

He knew there was a further cause for the strain at Palace Court
for which he was not responsible but which he shared. The Meynells'
friendship with the Catholic scientist St. George Mivart had grown
since 1885 when Alice wrote a warm appraisal of his contributions
to science in an article for *Merry England* entitled 'For Faith and
Science'. By then Mivart was living nearby in Seymour Street. He
attended the same church and, being twenty-five years older than
Wilfrid, began to take an almost paternal interest in the family and
their affairs. His letters to Alice date from about this time. She confided doubts and uncertainties to him which he countered with re-
assurances as to the essential goodness of the created world, its order
and purpose confirmed by science rather than otherwise. Her regard
for his views shows plainly in her article, where his interpretation of
Darwinism, based on the separate origin of differing species, is proclaimed an 'undisproved victory'. It was a victory for those Catholics
and many others who, by following his line of argument, could accept
the principle of evolution while maintaing a distinct position for
man within it.

Her article also praised the scrupulous care with which he pursued his theories as a scientist. But now he was entering the field of
theological enquiry without observing the same caution. As early as
1885 he answered a letter from Alice on her fears concerning hell and
eternal punishment with an assertion that the traditional teachings on
the subject would have to be revised, unacceptable as they were to the
majority of Christians of all denominations. He was right in thinking
that her doubts were shared by many, if not most, serious-minded
Christians. He was also right that a re-statement, at least, of the precise teaching of the Church was called for. True, for Catholics there
was the interim state of purgatorial 'cleansing' from sin after death,
circumventing the division of 'saint' from 'sinner' and 'heaven' from
'hell' which the other denominations were expected to uphold. But for
all, the concept of hell had become a central issue in the wider unrest
regarding the application of Christian principles in the modern world.
Mivart's downfall, as a Catholic, began when on entering the con-

troversy, he took his interpretation of the meaning of hell too far in public assertions that were opposed to the beliefs which were still generally understood. His view, that those condemned to hell could yet hope for ultimate redemption, cut across orthodox teachings to the extent that in a few years he was to leave the Church chiefly on account of the further issues it would then raise.[45]

Thompson shared in the discussions at Palace Court and, more than most, in the anxiety which they aroused. He felt bound to agree in principle with Mivart. In the privacy of his notebooks he could make his own assertion:

> Justice & love in God are not opposed & divided things: the justice of God is itself love. He does not punish in our sense: His punishment is a benign mitigation of the consequences which sin inevitably brings to the sinner. His condemnation is charity, & Hell itself a mercy. Yea, we could speak of a 'merciful Hell'.[46]

Yet there was a serious qualification. Because he was still the child of his religious background, for him there could be no escaping the fear of eternal punishment inculcated from his earliest years. So whereas there might be a 'merciful Hell' for the rest of mankind, he could have no such confidence for himself. Alice, he knew, shared something of his fears and he could discuss them with her. Shortly before the storm of protest following the appearance of Mivart's articles he wrote to her:

> You know that I believe eternal punishment: you know that when my dark hour is on me, this individual terror is the most monstrous of all that haunt me. But it is individual. For others — even if the darker view were true, the fewness is relative to the total mass of mankind, not absolute; while I myself refuse to found upon so doubtful a thing as a few scattered texts a tremendous forejudgement which has behind it no consentaneous voice of the Church.

In this he shows himself better informed than the majority of Catholics, both then and later. There has never been a definitive pronouncement on the nature and form of hell and eternal punishment. He has, he tells Alice, been trying to voice what he calls his 'convictions' on the subject in poetry. He directs her to a packet of his papers where she will find 'the new "Epilogue" to my "Judgement in Heaven" where I have given the spirit of them, which is better than any letter'.[47]

His observation on 'A Judgement in Heaven' here is nearer to the spirit of the poem than a later notebook entry, where he couples it with 'The Making of Viola' as an example of 'the natural temper of my Catholic training in a simple provincial home'.[48] What he means is that both poems treat heaven and its inhabitants with an intimacy that is as natural to him as the imagery drawn from the Church's liturgy. The comment is more true of the earlier poem, where Viola Meynell receives her physical form and features as gifts from the angels and saints — one of Thompson's more fanciful and less successful childhood poems. Taken in this sense it is only a very partial description of 'A Judgement in Heaven'. But if the other side to his 'Catholic training' is included, the fear and guilt expressed in his letters to Alice, the comment takes on more meaning.

By using a metre derived from Anglo-Saxon poetry, Thompson gives his theme something of the combined dignity and simplicity of his sources. But the theme itself is entirely his own. A Poet, glorious in the raiment of his achievements, arrives in heaven accompanied by an insignificant Rhymer clad only in rags. But before the Judgment Seat the Poet voluntarily strips himself to reveal the 'dim and shaméd stole' of his inadequate humanity. Thus stripped 'The Poet addresses his Maker':

> Thou gav'st the weed and wreath of song,[x] the weed and wreath
>   are solely Thine,
> And this dishonest vesture[x] is the only vesture that is mine;
> The life *I* textured, Thou the song[x] — *my* handicraft is not divine
>   44–46

Turning to the despised Rhymer he acknowledges him to be the greater, worthier of the raiment than himself, for

> Better thou wov'st thy woof of life [x] than thou didst weave thy
>   woof of song[49]

At his words the heavenly host around the Throne, fickle as their counterparts on earth, turn from the Poet to acclaim the Rhymer. Only the Magdalene, the patron of repentant sinners, directs them to the true nature of the Poet's robes — for their removal has revealed his flesh lacerated as by a hair shirt and his laurel wreath has left marks as from a crown of thorns. The limited range of the Rhymer's gifts may have caused him to lead the more virtuous life. But the Poet has atoned for the pride of his ambitions through the suffering imposed by genius. And in the final verdict, before God they are equal, 'two spirits greater than they know'.

The attempted self-justification behind the lines is clear enough. At first it is not so clear how the main poem relates to the Epilogue, which starts with the bold assertion:

> Virtue may unlock hell, or even
> A sin turn in the wards of heaven.
>   1–2

It depends on how the terms virtue and sin are interpreted. Since all men are created as separate individuals, each arrives in heaven by his own way:

> There is no expeditious road
> To pack and label men for God,
> And save them by the barrel-load.
> Some may perchance, with strange surprise,
> Have blundered into Paradise.
>
> 22–25

Therefore many so-called sinners reach heaven who, by orthodox standards, would be consigned to hell. Applying the theme to the main poem, Thompson is now concerned with the fate of the Poet rather than the Rhymer:

> The Rhymer a life uncomplex,
> With just such cares as mortals vex,
> So simply felt as all men feel,
> Lived purely out of his soul's weal.
> A double life the Poet lived,
> And with a double burthen grieved;
> The life of flesh and life of song,
> The pangs of both lives that belong;
> Immortal knew and mortal pain,
> Who in two worlds could lose and gain,
> And found immortal fruits must be
> Mortal through his mortality.
>
> 34–45

Again, the shadow of the Cross reaches from the field at Storrington. The 'deep austerities of strife' undergone by this Poet will win his salvation no less than the Rhymer whose limited gifts left him free of the evils of ambition. Yet for Thompson himself there could be no such assurance: only the fear that the fruits of his own genius, his 'brood of immortality' would leave him with nothing but the withered dreams of the Suffolk poppy field.

Thompson was still suffering from his 'dark hour' at the time of Manning's death in January the following year. It seemed to many, even among the Cardinal's critics, that the last bulwark had been removed between the certainties of the past and the changes that must lie ahead if the Church was to survive in the modern world. Thompson took a gloomy view of the immediate future under Manning's successor, Bishop Vaughan. 'We have exchanged a genius for a satisfied mediocrity' he wrote to Katharine Tynan.[49] The comment may have been unfair, but he knew he was far from alone in his reaction, while he also had in mind those dreary Sunday evenings at home when, as Bishop of Salford, Vaughan was his father's chief guest — and that other unfortunate encounter later at the Meynells' dinner table.

Thompson's regard for Manning arose mainly from the Cardinal's profound concern for human suffering. Then, during their brief meeting, Thompson sensed how aware Manning was of the suffering of the poor because he embraced it into his own asceticism as truly as it had become an enforced part of Thompson's own life-experience. All this, and the memories from the streets it evoked, came over him when soon after the funeral Meynell asked him for an obituary poem. A few days later he left a note at Palace Court, despairing at once of writing the poem and of ever fulfilling the hopes Meynell still had for his future. He was, he said, about to disappear back to where he came from, 'resigned to the ending of an experiment which even your sweetness would never have burdened yourself with, if you could have foreseen the consequences'.[50]

The already strained relationship with the family together with his reaction to the Cardinal's death produced a crisis which Meynell succeeded in easing with his usual patient tact. But the poem as it was written within the next week or two was a product of the same mood. Even after Thompson revised 'To the Dead Cardinal at Westminster' for publication in his first volume of poetry, the comparison between the Cardinal and the Poet dominates the whole. The Cardinal, now assuredly in heaven, knows the secret of the Poet's future fate:

'Can it be his alone,
To find, when all is known,
          That what
     He solely sought

'Is lost, and thereto lost
All that its seeking cost?
          That he
     Must finally,

'Through sacrificial tears,
And anchoretic years,
          Tryst
     With the sensualist?

                                        157–168

The Cardinal's self-imposed asceticism has met its reward. But what of the suffering imposed on the Poet by his doubts as to the true nature and purpose of his gifts? The poem ends with an appeal for enlightenment before it is too late:

     Tell!
Lest my feet walk hell.

It could hardly be called an obituary poem in the accepted sense. But, for Thompson in his present mood, the highest tribute he could pay to

the dead Cardinal was the power to resolve such doubts that he was
enduring as to his own final destiny.

These doubts were also part of his increasing anxiety at sharing
in the enthusiasm of the Crawley friars for their 'System' and at his
prospective role as its 'prophet'. Could he, should he, accept the
mantle with which Patmore had earlier been invested by them? In his
letter to Alice referring her to 'A Judgement in Heaven' for his reaction to Mivart's disturbing ideas, he comments on 'those Manning
verses which I do not like to read again'. He knew she would understand how both poems were connected with his 'dark hour'. Her poetic sensibility had, like his own, been deeply affected by the issues
Mivart was raising, while her high regard for Coventry Patmore gave
her an added interest in the ideas of the Crawley friars. His two most
serious doubts about their 'System', Thompson tells her in the same
letter, are due to Patmore's influence. The first is the identification
between physical and spiritual love. This, he says, he must reject as he
has understood it: 'The permanence of carnal in the Heavenly union
would make it to me un-heavenly'. Yet his own idea of heaven is basi-
cally more 'human' than Patmore's. According to Patmore only those
capable of the highest form of love in this life, uniting its spiritual and
physical manifestations, are worthy of the heavenly union. This too he
must reject:

> I do not believe in an exclusive society of Duchesses in either life. I reject
> the thought that Heaven is a select little spritual aristocracy. That is *has* its
> aristocracy, yes- but its commonalty too.

His strong vein of common sense was beginning to tell. It also underlies his second reason for doubt when he says he refuses to 'tie my life
to any system of metaphysics or mystic theology':

> If such an aid help one to realise one's life, one's aspiration; so far it is good
> for one. If it confuse and perturbate one's life, one's ideas, it is clearly ill
> for one. And one simply excretes it. I may admire: but ... I will have no
> more of it than fits my nature.

He is, he adds, going to Crawley to talk the whole matter over with
Father Cuthbert. If he finds he is expected to 'tie' himself in this way,
or to accept Patmore's ideas wholesale

> then this famous common System, though legions of Coventry Patmores
> stood behind it, and hordes of Father Cuthberts, shall not stand before the
> instincts of my own soul ... For what am I a poet, but that my soul's in-
> stincts may stand like lighthouses amidst the storms thought?[51]

Yet he knew even as he wrote that he could not trust his 'soul's instincts' where his poetry was concerned any more than he would now
trust what he saw as the friars' 'system of metaphysics'.

Through Thompson, both Wilfrid and Alice were becoming more involved with the friars and their ideas. At about this time they spent a day with Wilfrid Blunt at Crabbet Park. It was only a few miles from the Friary, which had been built at his own expense some thirty years earlier. The group came under discussion in connection with the interest Manning had taken in their practical proposals before his death. In his diary, Blunt reported Meynell's account of the 'new movement':

> A movement of the widest sort, rationalistic and mystic, which embraced all forms of religion and repudiated the finality of any doctrine of the Church, a kind of positivism and creed of humanity in which Plato, and Buddha, and Mohammed were alike canonized as saints, and Christ himself hardly more than these. He assured me that such doctrines were widely held by the younger priests, and that some of their most zealous and able exponents were to be found among our monks at Crawley.

Blunt was given to exaggeration and it is unlikely that Meynell went so far, although it was true that the 'System' was spreading beyond the Crawley group. But his interpretation indicates how easily it could be understood in such a way, one he admits to finding 'almost incredible'. The Eastern influence appealed to his own enthusiasm for the life and thought of the East, leading him to add that if this new movement should be formally approved 'I may still be loyal to all my ideas without quarrelling with the Catholic Church'.[52] Too eccentric to remain a Catholic in the orthodox sense, he was at heart closer to the Church than his intellect allowed him to admit. He retained a patron's interest in the Friary and was later to give the group important material support.

Thompson's visit to Crawley and his subsequent long talk with Father Cuthbert brought a temporary reassurance, but it did not last long after his return to London. He had recently changed his lodgings and the room at No. 1, Fernhead Road, still in the same area, was no less dismal than before. The hours spent there or at the Reading Room were lonelier than ever as the sense of a deliberate neglect at Palace Court grew, with probably no more foundation than the family's many other preoccupations. It made his correspondence with Alice all the more precious — until, during September, a series of misunderstandings arose between them. These were mainly due to overwrought nerves on both sides, but for him there was an added factor in the jealousy he began to feel towards Coventry Patmore. His attitude to Patmore's influence on the Capuchin 'System' and the way it seemed to have undermined his earlier expectations played a part in this, so that when something was said to prompt the idea that Patmore — who he had not yet actually met — was preferred by Alice to himself, the idea became an obsession.

For the past few months he had felt that they were on equal terms in their letters and occasional conversations. His role of dependent child was in fact temporarily set aside as he confided to her some of his deepest feelings, topics of concern to them both. He had never before layed open his emotional and spiritual life to another. Now the neglect he sensed from the rest of the family amounted in her case to one of rejection. Then a chance remark from Elizabeth Blackburn, harmless in itself, led to a series of confused, often distraught, letters which could only add to the demands he was making on Alice's time and patience.

The letters veer between determination to cease distressing her by his presence and pleas to see her to 'explain everything' yet again. She is 'My own dear lady and mother' and he never 'anything but your loving child, friend and sympathiser'. Or is he? In another he begs her to 'endure' his efforts to make her understand, 'for you are a friend, a mother; while I, over and above these, am a lover — spiritual as light, and unearthly as the love of one's angelic dreams, if you will — but yet a lover ...'. On several occasions Patmore's part in the whole unhappy affair is clear. He will, he says, leave off coming to Palace Court since he is causing so much distress. He sends her some kind of memento, 'in memorial of the time before this man's shadow fell across me ...'. It is only because 'it would have been the death-knell for all our souls' that he has desisted from writing to Patmore himself.[53]

The tone of these letters, so unlike Thompson's usual precise and often humorous manner, betrays his unstable condition. Wilfrid and Alice were well aware of it, and suspected opium to be the cause. And the strain on their own harrassed nerves was dangerous, as was the threat to the accepted child-image on which so much in their mutual relationship depended. It was probably Alice's unconscious reaction to the threat behind their earlier confidences that led to her change of mood, so setting up the reactions giving rise to the present situation.

Then came the crisis. Entering the Library late one evening, long after they thought he had returned to his lodgings, Wilfrid and Alice found him lying on the floor in what was unmistakeably an opium stupor. They were not deceived by his excuses of exhaustion and over-strained nerves: something urgent must now be done. Their first duty was to the children, and with this proof of their suspicions Thompson's regular visits to Palace Court must be discontinued. They tried roundabout means, apparently fearing the consequences for Francis if they faced him with the truth. But on his side he realized they had discovered his condition, and their reaction seemed to him to be the beginning of an end he so often feared. He determined on the only course he felt he could take, and left his lodgings to spend several days wandering the streets and sleeping on the benches along the Embankment.[54]

The attempt was short-lived. Wilfrid found him without much difficulty, among his old haunts in the Strand to which he had threatened to return before. The resulting showdown meant that when the Meynells suggested a solution to the present situation for all of them, he was in no position to do anything but agree. They had discussed the whole affair with Father Cuthbert, who not only showed a fine sympathy towards themselves and for Francis but also put forward a practical solution. Francis could stay for as long as seemed advisable at the Capuchin Friary in North Wales, where he himself was a frequent visitor. Father Anselm was already there, having left Crawley ostensibly for reasons of health, and had been given the task of editing the Order's journal *Franciscan Annals*, sent out each month by the community at Pantasaph. He would welcome Francis's assistance, while the work for *Merry England*, the Meynells were assured, could also be continued. The excellent air and regular hours would improve his obviously weakening health, along with the equally important companionship and support from the friars. Given this background and Francis's ready promise of co-operation, the problem of the opium relapse could surely be overcome.

It was a solution for the Meynells and as such, accepted by Francis. But he felt it to be another and even more bitter failure, written into the only verses he attempted while the preparations for his departure were under way. In 'How the Singer's Singing Wailed for the Singer' the 'Singer's Singing' is personified in the wasted immature form of his earlier promise. She who could have become the Singer's bride and lover must remain 'for ever barren' and as the vision fades:

The morn dawned weeping-grey; and weeping-grey
He saw her mist into the weeping day,
And knew her tears had washed his name away.[55]

What he could not know was that the departure for the mists of Wales heralded instead the climax of his poetic career and, at first, the happiest months of his adult life.

The Heart-perturbing Thing
Pantasaph 1892–1894

Yea, and the lowest reach of reeky Hell
Is but made possible
By foreta'en breath of Heaven's austerest clime.

These tidings from the vast to bring
Needeth nor doctor nor divine,
Too well, too well
My flesh doth know the heart-perturbing thing;
That dread theology alone
Is mine,
Most native and my own.

'The Dread of Height': 67–76

The date for the journey to Pantasaph was decided by the departure for Ireland of one of the Meynells' guests, H. A. Hinkson. He was the husband of Katherine Tynan — who retained her maiden name in the literary world — and his offer to accompany Francis as far as Chester meant leaving before Christmas. A day or two after his thirty-second birthday Francis arrived at Euston accompanied by a fellow lodger, punctual for once but clad as usual in his incongruous brown ulster, to which a bowler hat had been added as if to mark a special occasion. His luggage consisted of a single carpet bag along with a bundle of back issues of the *Sunday Sun*, provided by his landlady as entertainment for the journey and bequeathed, unread, to Hinkson at Chester.

Hinkson was a cricket enthusiast and the two found they had a good deal in common. To Hinkson's surprise the poet was 'very human' on this and other sporting topics. At Rugby, after collecting a snack from the station buffet, they found their carriage full of noisy and grubby Irishmen returning home after autumn work on the harvest. Hinkson was annoyed but Francis soon started chatting with them — also to Hinkson's surprise. He would not forget that journey. One of the men had a badly cut hand with blood oozing from a dirty bandage:

> Thompson spoke to him about the cause of the injury, which the Irishman made light of . . . However, he gently insisted on seeing the wound, and

having given the man a few words of advice as to its treatment, skilfully
bound the bandage round it so that the least soiled part of a not very clean
rag should be next to the wound. Then he turned to me, half-apologeti-
cally. 'You know', he said in explanation, 'I was a medical student, and so
I know a little about such things'.[1]

Another of the men had a birdcage wrapped in brown paper which
he placed carefully on the luggage rack. When the train stopped at
Crewe, the party made a dash for the refreshment room but several
were too late returning, among them the owner of the birdcage.
Francis was genuinely upset on their behalf until he was told they
could catch another train within an hour. He examined the cage and
found it contained a small canary, which he insisted Hinkson should
hand over to the Stationmaster at Chester with instructions to return
it to the owner on the arrival of the next train from Crewe. He himself
was hustled off by the friar from Pantasaph who was to accompany
him for the last part of the journey. Hinkson may or may not have
complied but his recollection of the incident ends with a chance
meeting with Francis at the Meynells' some years later: 'his first
words to me were an enquiry after the Irish harvester and his canary,
and he was greatly disappointed that I was unable to assure him of
their reunion'.
    On leaving Chester it was too dark to see anything of the bleak
Flintshire coastline or the hills inland where, only a few miles distant
from Pantasaph, Holywell still remains a well-known pilgrimage centre. Pantasaph itself is more a district than a village, named after both
a nearby hollow or 'pant' at the base of the hill above and the local
saint, whose own holy well further down the valley is commemorated
by the town of St. Asaph.
    Francis was to lodge at the guest house, known as Bishop's
House. It was managed for the friars by Michael Brien and his wife,
whose welcome was all the warmer on account of the few visitors who
normally stayed only a night or two on some business at the Friary.
Finding the house full of children was an unexpected pleasure for
Francis. The Briens had a boy and four girls ranging from eight-year-
old Agnes to Margaret, or Maggie, who was twenty and in charge of
the guests' personal needs.
    Bishop's House was only a few minutes' walk from the Friary and
Francis soon learned how the friars had come to Pantasaph at the
invitation of Lord and Lady Feilding. At the time of their wedding
they began to build a church in the Feilding estate to mark the occasion, and when both became Catholics before the church was completed, it took a High Court ruling to allow the church to be similarly
'converted'. Having won their case they decided to go further by
establishing a monastic community. In this they were following a

custom among the younger converts from landowning families who
on inheriting their estates considered it a privilege to invite religious
communities from abroad to re-establish themselves after some three
centuries of exile. Accordingly, when the Capuchins settled at Pantasaph in 1852 it was the first English foundation since the Reformation. As with other similar newly founded communities, there were
problems arising from their dependence on their patrons. The Franciscan Order had arisen largely as a reaction to the great religious
houses of the Middle Ages which the convert families generally
desired to reproduce. The outcome at Pantasaph was an uneasy compromise between the architecture and the internal arrangements. The
impressive exterior with its 'gothic' pinnacles and buttresses still
remains in unexpected contrast to the bare walls and simple furnish-
ings within.[2]

The Friary played a leading part in the spread of the Order after
its return to England and was now the centre for the course in philosophy preceding the final theological studies followed at Crawley. The
Capuchin journal, *Franciscan Annals*, had been sent out from Pantasaph each month since 1877. In addition to information on the
affairs of the Order it carried articles of general Franciscan interest
and Father Anselm, as its new editor, succeeded in including a wider
range of topics, his own interests giving them a greater philosophical
and literary bias. Father Cuthbert was right in expecting Anselm
would welcome the suggestion that Thompson should join the journal's staff and both were confident the poet would prove a valuable
asset.

First, however, a period must be allowed for the initial effects of
opium withdrawal. The return to the drug had been short-lived, with
nothing like the effects from the years on the streets that Thompson
experienced at Storrington. He now knew what to expect, while what
he had not expected — the sudden change in his prospects since his
arrival — did more than anything this time to lessen the symptoms.
They were painful but not agonizing. In a draft for a letter to the
Meynells, his mood was one of 'light hearted exhilaration' where he
'must laugh out or weep out'. So he would choose to laugh, since
whatever else he repented there was nothing to repent in having come
to Wales:

> ... if I were in London I would simply take a header into the Thames —
> only that's such a damnably dirty place for a poet to drown in. But I am in
> a most unconventional state at present; ready to go smash among all con-
> ventions like a bull in a china-shop ... I have half a mind, by way of final
> outrage, to make love to what I think the loveliest girl I have ever seen.
> But I have still some convention hanging about me in a tattered condition
> ...[3]

The letter was probably not sent in this hysterical form and after Christmas he could write much more calmly to Mrs Blackburn. Maggie Brien, 'the loveliest girl' was now simply 'very pretty and refined', whose charms were not rated as highly as the luxury of a fire all day in his room. He had climbed the hill behind the Friary where a Way of the Cross still leads up through the woodland to a great crucifix on the summit that can be seen for miles around. It was to become one of Thompson's favourite places for writing and reflection, with views of the mountains to the west and, to the north and east, of the estuary and the sea. On this first climb a 'glorious mixture of moonlight and sunset' brought back memories of the sunset scene at his poetic awakening — and with some hope of its revival. He had, he told Mrs Blackburn, 'Spent Xmas Eve writing verses — a poor thing but mine own'.[4]

He was referring to the draft for 'Little Jesus' which, according to a firmly held belief at Pantasaph, he composed before the Christmas crib in the Friary chapel.[5] Whether the finished poem is a 'poor thing' is a matter of opinion, but it is very much his own in more senses than the one he meant. Very probably it was at least inspired by the crib. Saint Francis himself is said to have started the custom and it has always been given an honoured place in the Christmas celebrations of the Order as a reminder of its three characteristics of simplicity, poverty and childlikeness. For Thompson it had a special meaning that Christmas. The warmth of his welcome, followed by sharing the seasonal festivities with the Briens as well as at the Friary, gave him that feeling of acceptance which he knew so rarely and valued so much. So too the Christ Child of the Christmas crib, Christ as the child in man, might now accept the child in himself in a way he had not known even in the early years of his memories of the crib at home in Ashton:

> Didst Thou kneel at night to pray,
> And didst Thou join Thy hands, this way?
> And did they tire sometimes, being young,
> And make the prayer seem very long?
> And dost Thou like it best, that we
> Should join our hands to pray to Thee?
> I used to think, before I knew,
> The prayer not said, unless we do.
> And did Thy Mother at the night
> Kiss Thee, and fold the clothes in right?
> And didst Thou feel quite good in bed,
> Kissed, and sweet, and Thy prayers said.
>
> Thou canst not have forgotten all
> That it feels like to be small:

And Thou know'st I cannot pray
To Thee in my father's way —
When Thou wast so little, say,
Couldst Thou talk Thy Father's way? —

                                                           23–40

In one sense the simplicity is deceptive. There is so much from the
past in the need for the Mother and the distance from the Father
whose example is beyond his reach. In another sense the simplicity is
very much Thompson's own, the fundamentally simple faith which
that same past had given him.

Early in the New Year he could assure Meynell '"c'en est fait"'
regarding the opium. In spite of a heavy snowfall he was ready to start
exploring the surrounding countryside where 'everything is beautiful
for the time of year'. He was, however, housebound until his boots,
already in a bad state when he left London, could be replaced. It was
again mutually agreed that he should have no money in his own keeping. As at Storrington, the arrangement would relieve him of the
temptation to obtain opium locally or through the post. But it caused
other problems besides the boots. How should he get his letters
stamped? Should he ask Father Marianus or Father Anselm, the two
friars he saw most often? Anselm had only just left him 'after a prolonged discussion of all the things "none of us know anything about"
as Marianus says — when he is getting the worst of an argument'.[6]

He need not have worried. Marianus had already written to
Wilfrid explaining the difficulty in supplying Francis's practical needs
as he seemed too shy to ask. Would Meynell direct him to ask for
whatever he required in the way of pens and ink and such like necessities? So the matter was settled for the present, although Anselm seems
to have been mainly responsible and remained his chief confidant.[7]

Marianus also told Meynell 'Thompson is ever so much better'.
Thompson's own letter shows him benefitting from the lively exchanges with the friars, who on their side began to have a regard for
his mental abilities equal to their admiration for his poetry. Anselm
was to remember him at Pantasaph chiefly as 'a brilliant talker' who
could have been 'a great orator':

> I enjoyed his splendid ideas and the diction, at once beautiful
> and virile, with which he clothed them, even in ordinary conver-
> sation. He was pleased, on his part, to take the keenest interest in
> metaphysical topics, at that time my chief delight.[8]

So Anslem recalled those first months, rather differently recorded by
Thompson himself in a notebook entry: 'I am taking a course of scholastic philosophy, as people take the waters at Baden — because,
being the staple commodity of the place, they feel bound in principle to

15. Aerial view of the Friary,
Pantasaph (above)

16. A 'station' on the Way
of the Cross at the Friary,
Pantasaph (right)

drink it'. Just now, however, he admitted finding it 'most satisfying liquor'. He could not help being flattered that he should be accepted by the others as their equal in philosophical discourse. But there is a warning in the added comment: 'You shall drown in letters. And may God have mercy on your soul'.[9]

The subject was important enough to him to be examined in another and unusually long notebook entry. Anselm had been surprised that his actual knowledge of philosophy was limited to 'a smattering of Coleridge, some superficial second hand Plato — supplemented by direct reading of the *Symposium*, into which I plunged like a duck into water'. Anselm assumed he 'had absorbed a considerable amount of scholastic philosophy', which in Thompson's view suggested that the subject was not, as was so often stated these days, an imposition on 'the free movement of human thought'. Since he had formed similar ideas with no formal training 'How could this be, were scholasticism the artificial & unnatural thing it is conceived?[10]

To re-interpret the Scholastic philosophy of the Middle Ages, from which most later Catholic theology was derived, was one of the aims of the liberal minded Catholics. In this they were anticipating a major trend in twentieth century theology in its emphasis on the principles of development in Scholasticism as distinct from the rigidity of more recent forms. Thompson had already heard the subject discussed at Crawley in connection with the friars' philosophical 'System'. Not surprisingly, his doubts at that time were temporarily taking second place to the opportunity for exchanging ideas in company where his own received gratifying attention. It would not last long but while it did, it gave him the confidence and mental stimulus he needed for the renewal of his creative powers.

The 'course' planned by Anselm was often carried out in conversations during the long country walks in which the two shared an equal pleasure. They covered many miles together on the hills round the Friary — except on the occasions when Anselm was aware of subtle differences between the poet and the philosopher, when 'it was best for me and for him that he should walk alone'. Anselm was not blind to the difference. What he failed to recognise was its extent and, later, the extent therefore of its influence on Thompson's religious and poetic development.

Anselm's portrayal of Thompson as he remembered him at Pantasaph is at once sympathetic and realistic. 'He hardly ever knew what day of the week it was', to which was added the inconvenience of turning day into night — and *vice versa*:

> His career was a lament of unpunctualities. He thought and read and wrote at night when he should have been asleep. He slept far into the day when he should have been up and doing.[11]

In spite of this he could keep to time if he felt it to be important enough. Anselm had 'no recollection of any unbroken appointment made with me' — although the further assertion: 'He was regular in his religious duties' was mainly due to the Briens' cooperation. At first his habit of constantly missing Sunday Mass caused some shocked surprise at the Friary. When Anselm tactfully mentioned the matter:

> He was greatly upset: admitted he had overslept himself and, anyhow, forgot it was Sunday, and gave strict orders that they (the Briens) were to keep banging on his door on Sundays and Holy Days till it was certain he was up and about.

His absent-mindedness caused affectionate humour among the friars. As when he would return from a walk in torrential rain with his unopened umbrella still tucked under his arm — or when, in lighting his pipe, he would use up a whole box of matches, holding each alight until he had finished a sentence. '"May I trouble you for a match, Father", he would say, in a tremulously courteous tone: "Yes, Francis, what particular brand of matches do you smoke?"'

He would laugh then, a rare laugh, although his sense of humour grew more marked as his health improved and he knew himself 'emancipated from the thralldom of opium'. And on that subject Anselm could assert: 'During Thompson's stay at Pantasaph I never saw him in any but a normal condition. And I was constantly seeing him'.

The improvement in health affected his appearance, causing his physical assets to be more noticeable than his deficiencies:

> He had a great and spacious forehead, a splendid pair of large grey eyes that seemed always changing into light blue, a small but definitely combative nose and the orator's mouth of no particular symmetry. About his whole appearance there was a suggestion of physical frailness, yet withal, of nervous energy and grace from his delicate features to the tips of his artistic fingers ... He had a springy step but with a certain shyness that clung to him through life.[12]

Like other descriptions of Thompson by those who knew him best, there is the suggestion of an elusive charm of manner and bearing that was dependent for its appeal on being entirely unselfconscious.

It was probably this, along with the unaffected courtesy that went with it, which led Maggie Brien to respond to the attraction which Thompson continued to feel towards her from their first meetings. In the early days after his arrival at Bishop's House it was natural that Maggie, isolated as she was from male companionship, should have been flattered by his shy appeals for her attention. The relationship that grew up between them as a result must not, however, be identified too closely with the poems to or about her which he later collected under the title 'A Narrow Vessel'. They were written after it

had eased off into a delicately balanced friendship. Both knew by then
that it could not go further: but for him there was certainly a nostalgic
sense of regret and for her, at least something of the same.

Although the 'Narrow Vessel' sequence elaborates their relationship beyond the facts, the main theme depends on it as it existed at the
time — the appeal and frustration aroused by the limitations of a
girl's feelings who is incapable of the deeper emotions of love. On
Thompson's side he recognizes how a display of such emotions could
harm

> her trust, her shyness free,
> Her timorous audacity.
>
> 'A Girl's Sin — In His Eyes'
> 41–42

Instead he must be content with the 'happy, alien, little things' that
make up her life (The Way of a Maid 22). Or are they all? Is there on
her side a capacity to respond which, if called upon, could crush the
narrow vessel of her experience? When she denies the advances she
has just coyly attracted, is she 'glad of the doing' or is it that she must
be

> sedulous to be glad
> Lest perhaps her foolish heart suspect that it was sad
>
> 'Beginning of the End' 23–24

Several of the poems are written in the past tense and in the last it is
clear that the episode is over for them both. On her side, in 'giving
part not whole' she then 'Took even the part back'. So for him it is
now 'Best unthought since love is over' ('Epilogue' 5–8).

There are manuscript poems almost certainly written during
their intimacy which come much nearer the truth. It was probably the
reason why Thompson chose not to include them in the published
sequence, for they say more about her limitations and his frustration
than he may have thought it fair to her to reveal:

> One thought of mine has nobler art
> Of love, than all your little heart;
> Which God made shallow, for He knew
> Your days in joy should have small part.
>
> And so I love you more than can
> You, dearest dear, love any man.
> To your straight clod-walled days, the boon
> Of love's fine sense were cruel ban.
>
> What hardest heart could wish it you?
> Nay, do, poor child as children do —

> Love me as long as the whole space
> Between two playthings leaveth you.[13]

These stanzas contain something of the tenderness and regret he knew
in the passing affection of children, carried through twenty-three
verses where his love for Maggie can never mean more to her than a
plaything to a child.

In another of these poems she herself speaks of her idea of love as
'a sunbright holiday' from the tedious round of her daily chores, to be
compared with 'the shaping of a new dress'. But the concuding verses
strike a different note:

> As if there were not trouble enough!
>   I do not think it right
> That any man should make of love
>   A thing that's half affright!
>
> Oh, the old days when love I lacked,
>   Happy to know not lack!
> And could I leave him, or he me
>   And laugh the old days back![14]

There is a distinct warning here that the fragile vessel could indeed
be easily cracked, if not broken. So he drew back: and so, later, the
published Sequence came to be written while the rest of the poems
were likewise held back.

In the Sequence one poem stands apart from the rest as being
inspired from a very different source. There must have been occasions when Thompson's feeling for Maggie reminded him of the girl of
the London streets. For all the differences between them, Maggie's
untainted innocence recalled for him the strangely preserved childlikeness of the street girl. So when, in preparing the 'Narrow Vessel'
poems for publication, he turned up a poem inspired by her he payed
her a secret tribute by giving it a place among them. Perhaps he had
a secret motive as well. 'Love Declared' is an attempt to express a
sexual union that could have no part in the love described in the rest
of the poems — compared with which it is also the best:

> ... forward like a wind-blown flame
> Came bosom and mouth to mine!
>   That falling kiss
> Touching long-laid expectance, all went up
> Suddenly into passion; yea, the night
> Caught, blazed, and wrapt us round in vibrant fire.
>   Time's beating wing subsided, and the winds
> Caught up their breathing, and the world's great pulse
> Stayed in mid-throb, and the wild train of life

Reeled by, and left us stranded on a hush.
This moment is a statue unto Love
Carved from a fair white silence.
                    Lo, he stands
Within us — are we not one now, one, one roof,
His roof, and the partition of weak flesh
Gone down before him, and no more for ever? —

5-20

After Thompson's death Elizabeth Blackburn confided to Meynell
that he had once told her the poem 'was only his imagination of "what
might have been"'.[15] She seems to have been the only one to recognise the poem's difference and to have had the temerity to face him
with it. Whether his answer satisfied her or not, what he did not tell
her was that it went much further than a 'might have been' in his
feeling for Maggie Brien. It revived an experience which he knew he
could never repeat with Maggie herself.

What Maggie did give him was a taste of life's lighter side such as
had not often come his way — as when they played with the younger
children, he 'tearing round the garden like a schoolboy', or when she
teased him out of his occasional irritations at her flightiness. To the
children he was 'our brother' and Mrs Brien, who he found 'a very
motherly kindhearted woman', also treated him as one of the family.
As a family, they accepted that Francis and Maggie should be attracted to each other by what they regarded as a natural and harmless
instinct. According to Agnes he and her sister were often together but
another sister, Emily, thought it did not go far on Maggie's side. Yet
Mrs Blackburn may have been nearer the truth when she wrote from
her more mature observations that Francis 'did love her in quite a
human way' while undoubtedly 'she did love him for all her reticence'. To which it must be added that when Maggie died, unmarried
and only a few months before his own death, his photograph was discovered preserved behind one of the pictures in her room.[16]

Francis was adjusting to another way of life, with all the casual
give and take of a large family living at close quarters. The Briens
were content with keeping poverty at bay and were then free to enjoy
whatever else was allowed them. Maggie was the product of her background, as unheeding of the deeper implications of love as the family
was unconcerned with the affairs of the world beyond their valley.
Accepted as one of the household, Thompson found in it a counterpart to the degrading effects of poverty as he had shared them on the
London streets. There was something here of the poverty and simplicity Saint Francis bequeathed to his Order, and Maggie possessed
something of that other Franciscan quality of childlikeness to which
he responded on his arrival in the poem 'Little Jesus'.

On the other hand, the limitations of the Briens' outlook were not characteristic of the true Franciscan spirit. According to a draft for an unpublished essay on 'Franciscan simplicity', it is not an ignorant simplicity — the simplicity of the peasant. It consists, mainly, of 'the contentment of every man to be and appear just what he is'. There is in this the 'spontaneous candour of the child combined with adult consciousness', which for Thompson should also be combined in the true poet. So, he concludes: 'Two things in this world *are* poetry and luckily do not know it — the child and the Franciscan'.[17]

It was the underlying spirit of the Order which Thompson had in mind here rather than some of the more specific forms adopted by the Capuchins. Since their origin soon after Saint Francis's death, the Capuchins — so called for the distinctive hood attached to their habit — concentrated on intellectual pursuits while retaining, they claimed, the principles of Franciscan simplicity and poverty as defined by the main branch of the Order. After their return to England their work was mainly among the poor, and Thompson's essay on the challenge of the Salvation Army drew on the ideals of the young friars at Crawley in their desire to bring the spirit of Saint Francis in line with the needs of the present time. But they were equally concerned with the intellectual framework of their training and its adaptation to the modern world. This had already resulted in Anselm's virtual banishment to Pantasaph and Cuthbert's prolonged periods there, where work on the *Annals* meant keeping their expressed views within more orthodox channels. But their collaborators, Marianus and Alphonsus, were sympathetic towards their 'System', and the animated discussions in the journal's office at the Friary took up the arguments and proposals they had first put forward at Crawley.

Thompson was already regarded by them as a kind of poet-prophet for their ideas. The eloquence noted by Anselm now led them to hope that he might become their spokesman on topics they were not free to take upon themselves. His first essay for the *Annals* arose from a discussion with Father Anselm on the uses and abuses of 'organized' religion. It is not easy today to see how daring Thompson's viewpoint was for the time:

> Many think in the head; but it is thinking in the heart that is most wanted. Theology and philosophy are the soul of truth; but they must be clothed with flesh, to create an organism which can come down and live among men. Therefore Christ became incarnate, to create Christianity.

Nor should truth so clothed be confined to theology and philosophy. 'A great poet' he asserts, 'who is also a great thinker, does for truth what Christ did for God, the Supreme Truth'. He clothes truth in the 'flesh', in a form by which it can be recognised:

This is a concrete example of an abstract principle — The supreme necessity under which truth is bound to give itself a definite shape. Of such immutable importance is form that without this effigy and witness of spirit,
spirit walks invisible among men.[18]

The present age, with Ruskin as its spokesman, identifies 'form' with
the 'formalism' that denies true religious feeling, the 'religion of the
heart'. Thompson does not dispute the evils of formalism in this sense
but the distinction is essential: 'To avoid formalism by denying form,
is to remedy carnality by committing suicide'. He fails to define what
is really meant by the term 'formalism' and his conclusion is weakened by promptings from the over-enthusiasm of his Capuchin supporters — where the triumph of true form will result in no less than 'a
new heaven and a new earth'. But as a whole, 'Form and Formalism'
is a bold exposition of the interplay between the inner spirit and
outward forms of religion. If the subject-matter was largely directed
for him, he made it the occasion to explore how emotion and intellect
might work together in the poetry of religious truth.

The philosophical content is even more marked in his second
essay for the *Annals*, 'The Image of God'. Taking the words 'Let us
make man to our image and likeness' from the Book of Genesis he
follows Thomas Aquinas's system of 'correspondence' as applied to
the term 'likeness'. According to Aquinas, the human body can be
said to resemble its divine model *per modem vestigii* — taken literally, as
a footprint corresponds to the form of the foot. Even if any such resemblance must now be blurred by the effects of sin, it follows that
when God created the human soul in his own image he gave the body
this vestigial likeness to himself. The human body, Thompson concludes, is therefore at once the material shape of the soul and 'the
most perfect correspondence of Himself which lay within the possibilities of matter'.[19]

It is not difficult to see Thompson continuing the argument of his
previous essay here in presenting matter as the essential complement
to spirit. There are also echoes from his much earlier and independent
speculations on the imperfection of material forms in 'The Way of
Imperfection'. Here, the idea of the material world incarnating the life
of the spirit is revived in the two *Annals* essays, giving them an importance that is independent of the influence from his Capuchin friends.

Thompson was taking what he needed from his philosophical
studies but such needs were limited. Unlike the true philosopher he
was mainly concerned with the value and significance of material
forms considered for their own sake. It was what mattered to him as a
poet, and there are occasional notebook entries suggesting he already
knew this. If Father Anselm was surprised at Thompson's grasp of
philosophical concepts he would have been even more so to find the

comment: 'Philosophy & mystical theology will not in the least enable you to get to heaven, any more than the knowledge of the sun's rays will enable you to light your fire'.[20] Yet Anselm, who said of himself that he 'found poetry no hindrance to philosophy', acknowledged it might not work the other way round for Francis — who on returning a selection of Aquinas's writings observed 'that if he allowed himself to become too interested in them he would write no more poetry'.[21]

Francis meant what he said to an extent which he may not have appreciated at the time. The thought patterns of philosophy were not for him, even if its subject matter gave rise to the kind of eloquent discourses that called up his linguistic powers. Beyond that level he sensed danger — and potential conflict. Significantly, there were no more essays for the *Annals* along the lines of the first two. Nor was he pressed for further contributions of a kind that in any case would have aroused criticism for their deliberately provocative content. Apart from a two-part essay on the writings of Saint Francis, 'Sanctity and Song', and an equally unremarkable poem, 'Franciscus Christificatus', they comprised mainly translations from Latin poetry and prose which were considered to have some special application to the Franciscan Order.[22]

Thompson remained a welcome member of the *Annals* staff even if from now on 'he suggested and inspired a good deal more than he actually wrote'. The observation was made by Father William, who occasionally helped out in the journal office. His further comments are important in the light of the discontinued essays:

> ... he was of a surety one of the most interesting, and one of the most charmingly simple, and — we must add in these days of doubt — one of the most intensively and instinctively orthodox members of our little flock.[23]

As Master of Novices, Father William was more concerned than the rest with the orthodoxy of their views — he had been the one to draw attention to Francis's recalcitrance in the matter of Mass attendance. His comment here arose from a passage in the essay 'Form and Formalism' which applies the term 'form' to the formulated teachings of the Church. In this sense the unchanging nature of the essential structure depends on its capacity to incorporate changing needs and conditions:

> Yet may not form change? Yes, insofar as the life changes, but not otherwise. The Church is like man's body, which grows to completion altering or adding a little in superficialities and details of figure, but unchanging in essential line and structures ... you may add in non-essentials, you may develop in essentials; but you shall not alter in essentials by so much as a clause of its dogmatic theology.[24]

According to Father William, the passage anticipates 'the message of the Papal Encyclical *Pascendi Dominici Gregis*, which was given to the world fourteen years later when he was on his deathbed'. Father William's own words were written less than two months afterwards and in its condemnation of Catholic Modernism the encyclical had, he knew, condemned many of the ideas circulating at Pantasaph during Thompson's time there. Any hint of unorthodoxy such as the essays could at least imply must therefore be withstood, not only in Thompson's own defence but in defence of the Capuchins as well.

He would, however, have found it more difficult to account for another observation on the subject which, like many of the kind, Thompson did not write for publication:

> We are too much given to thinking that the Almighty, getting tired of His slow ways of teaching, came down suddenly from heaven and finished off the whole of revelation in a neat and complete little compendium, with His Holiness the Pope as perpetual editor, to keep it up to date like an Encyclopaedia ... All the prophecies were wound up and fulfilled down to the last tittle; all was said and completed-needing just a little trifling definition from a Council or so; there was nothing more left but for all mankind to get to Heaven as fast as they could, now that the way was entirely surveyed and mapped out for them.[25]

Or again, in one of his brief jottings: 'Some people treat dogma as an egg collector does eggs — suck all the yolk out of them & present you with the shell'.[26]

On the other hand, Father William need not have been anxious on Thompson's behalf. The outspoken entries in the notebooks and which occasionally appeared in letters arose from the strength of his fundamental belief rather than from serious questioning of the faith of his early years. Nor did he at any time in his later life wish to become involved in theological controversy. Anselm, in a rare reference to the 'theories' circulating at Pantasaph as leading to 'what is now known as Modernism', noted how Francis refused to be drawn in when they took a theological turn. 'He instinctively disliked and distrusted them, dismissed them with an abrupt interjection and a characteristic shrug of his right shoulder'.[27]

Yet he could also afford to be critical because the essentials of Christianity he had been taught from the first were never a cause for doubt. His estrangement from the Church during his years on the streets was due to its lack of adequate concern for the poor. It did not alter his belief in those essentials any more than his later criticism of the Church's attitude to literature. His faith remained the most positive legacy from his home background and which the influence from Ushaw had greatly enriched.

In this sense, as a 'born Catholic' he differed from almost all other Catholics with whom he came into contact at Pantasaph and elsewhere. Coventry Patmore was to recognize something of the difference in an observation recalled by Viola Meynell: 'He is of all men I have known the most naturally a Catholic. My Catholicism was acquired, his inherent'. Commenting on this herself Viola remembered 'the habits of simple piety which are sometimes discarded with youth but were retained by him in maturity'. There was nothing of the philistinism which he hated nor anything 'merely ornamental' about the sign of the cross with which he would start a page of writing, or the medal of the Blessed Virgin hung around his neck or the careful grace said before each meal.[28]

If there was any need to account for the falling off of his contributions to the *Annals*, there was a reason ready to hand in a new demand on his time more exacting than any so far. Early in May came news to challenge his energies well beyond the requirements of either the *Annals* or his work for the Meynells. He knew Wilfrid had sent a selection of his poems to John Lane and now Richard Le Gallienne, as Lane's chief reader and advisor, reported:

> Lyrical poems by Francis Thompson. Would certainly publish. Rich, colourful, oriental things. Remind me very much of Crashaw. Lack concentration and form, but are marked by a fine, extremely Latinised style, a sumptuous fancy, & some splendid lines.[29]

He advised 'a rigid revision' of most of the poems, but not 'to rob them of their charm of prodigality'. Within a few days of receiving the report Francis was hard at work.

It was the stimulus he needed for a burst of creative energy for which his restored health and congenial surroundings had been preparing him. According to Le Gallienne one of the poems most in need of revision was 'To the Dead Cardinal'. As he deleted or altered the verses he now saw as too personal for the poem's intended subject, the mood in which he had written it came back to him in contrast to the way he now felt. The contrast provided the impulse to write another poem in the same distinctive metre, taking the earlier theme in a new direction. Before, he had invoked the spirit of the dead cardinal to aid one whose human weakness could otherwise lead to hell. Now the same weakness would become the means chosen by God to reunite fallen human nature with Himself. Once man accepts his dependence on his Creator he is transformed by the divine power: and since he learns to accept through recognizing the limitations of his sensible nature, sense and spirit are equally essential to the process. The poem was, in effect, expressing some of the basic ideas behind his two *Annals* essays. And as if to counteract the too-personal element in 'To the

Dead Cardinal' it concerns the state of man rather than of a man. Its title, 'Any Saint', refers to anyone who recognizes and then responds to the paradox of his actual littleness and potential greatness:

> Man! swinging-wicket set
>   Between
>   The Unseen and the Seen;
>
> Lo, God's two worlds immense,
> Of spirit and of sense,
>   Wed
>   In this narrow bed;
>
> Yea, and the midge's hymn
> Answers the seraphim
>   Athwart
>   Thy body's court!

74–84

There are echoes from an earlier source. The 'tremendous Lover' taking the soul by storm in 'The Hound of Heaven' becomes 'this too-gentle Lover' who awaits man's acceptance of the same underlying paradox that before brought about the climax of the flight and the pursuit. 'God's clay-sealed ark' must first know himself as 'Compost of Heaven and mire': again the echo comes from 'earth's dingiest clod' in 'The Hound of Heaven' who must experience 'how little worthy of any love thou art' before the response to love's call can be made. Yet there is also a subtle difference. The command 'Rise, clasp My hand and come' is phrased more boldly in the last stanza of 'Any Saint':

> Rise, for Heaven has no frown
> When thou to thee pluck down,
>   Strong clod
>   The neck of God.

This is bolder because the onus is on man's share in the twofold process of recognizing his littleness and his greatness. The dominance of spirit over sense in 'The Hound of Heaven' is replaced by an interdependence between the two which Thompson had been exploring in his recent prose writings. He knew he could not take them further without encountering intellectual barriers he was not prepared or equipped to overcome. But could he fulfil his calling as a poet by celebrating this theme in verse? It would become no less than the divine presence in the world as God's creation, an incarnation of spirit in sense that gives to creation its full meaning and purpose. If so he might indeed come to be known as 'the poet of the return to God' and in addition might still meet the expectations of the friars, whose

'System' derived so largely from a similar concept of the relationship between the natural and supernatural worlds.

That it could be the way ahead for him led to another poem, begun almost as soon as he had finished 'Any Saint'. 'Assumpta Maria' was written in August, the month when the Church commemorates the death of the Blessed Virgin as the taking up into Heaven of her physical body — the flesh that gave Christ His human form and which could not therefore itself be subject to corruption. The feast of the Assumption is marked by some of the richest symbolic language of the Church's liturgy. Having found a new poetic voice, could he use it to speak with that language? If so, his tendencies to excess could be directed to revive its vigour and significance and its resonances from pre-Christian sources. A renewal of the emasculated forms of much present-day liturgy was long overdue and Thompson's poem made a bold and intentional break with convention:

> Who is She, in candid vesture,
>   Rushing up from out the brine?
> Treading with resilient gesture
>   Air, and with that Cup divine?
> She in us and we in her are,
>   Beating Godward: all that pine,
> Lo, a wonder and a terror —
>   The Sun hath blushed the Sea to Wine!
>   He the Anteros and Eros,
>   She the Bride and Spirit; for
>   Now the days of promise near us,
>   And the Sea shall be no more.
>
>   77–88

These lines revive the ancient symbol of the Blessed Virgin as the chalice containing the wine and water of Christ's divine and human nature. It is then carried on into Thompson's favourite symbol of the sun, here the sign of Christ's transformation of human nature by uniting in himself the Anteros and Eros of divine and human love. She who, at the Annunciation became the Bride of God, shares in the continuing process of incarnation after the Assumption, the indwelling of God in man. The Assumption is also at once a prefiguring and a promise of the final act in the process. The waters of physical birth symbolized by the sea partake in the water symbolism of the Apocalypse, where the sea as the source of present life on earth is absorbed into the ultimate vision of a new heaven united with a new earth.

The poem owes more to its sources than to its treatment of them: as Thompson admits at the end, he has become a 'thief of Song'. Yet if the attempt at retaining his own voice has at least partly failed, he succeeds in drawing his images and allusions together in an overall movement where the simultaneous drive upward and downward is very much his own.

As it appears in the form published after his death the poem has been seriously mutllated, with no acknowledgement of the three stanzas deleted from Thompson's own final text. The first gives the flavour of the two that follow:

> See in highest heaven pavilioned
> > Now the maiden Heaven rest,
> The many-breasted sky out-millioned
> > By the splendour of her vest.
> Lo, the Ark this holy tide is
> > The un-handmade Temple's guest,
> And the dark Aegyptic bride is
> > Whitely to the Spouse-Heart prest!
> > > He the Eros and Anteros,
> > > > Nail me to Thee, sweetest Cross!
> > > He is fast to me, *Ischyros*,
> > > > *Agios, Athanatos!*[30]

Undoubtedly Thompson has allowed his symbolism to overrule poetic discretion. In all three stanzas the exuberance clogs and cloys the senses. But there is another reason for their removal. When included in the poem they enhance the pagan sources from which so much of the liturgy for the feast derives its theme and imagery.

In a letter to Alice Meynell enclosing the poem he referred to the sources as including 'a few images drawn from the heathen mythology' which he asserted were 'almost absurdly easy to defend. I have made some very careful deference to orthodoxy'. He was sure, he added, that Father Anselm (who was away at the time) would regard them in the same way. He probably said more but the letter has also been mutilated, apparently deliberately.[31]

Thompson must have known that in the poem's finished form as he wrote it he had made a definite break with the conventional interpretations of its subject. Why then was he so insistent on its 'orthodoxy'? This was in fact a symptom of his own concern and doubt on the subject which in turn went back to the long hours in the British Library Reading Room before he left London.

The symbolism that played such a vital part in the birth of Thompson's poetry had by this time become an absorbing study in its own right, the meaning of symbols as he found them expounded and analysed in the books from which he copied page after page of meticulous notes. The publication of Frazer's *Golden Bough* in 1890 was followed by an influx of literature on the connections between paganism and Christianity that Frazer carried well beyond symbolism alone.

Thompson knew he was treading on dangerous ground and he kept his studies to himself. They covered a wide range, apart from a notable concentration on the symbolism of the sun, the signs of the zodiac and influences from other planets. There are pages of notes on the meaning of jewels and precious stones and as many or more on nature symbolism. But they are not written down at random. There is a constant recurring theme in the connections between symbols of different races and periods, leading to detailed notes and comments on Egyptian hieroglyphics, the Dragon and the Bull as they appear in the ancient civilizations and, more often than most, the Tau or Headless Cross. Two commonplace books are filled with extracts on animal symbols, on the symbolism of the psalms and their connections with pagan tribal symbols. Several of the later notebooks show that the studies begun the year before he left London were continued intermittently for the rest of his life. But by far the greatest number of entries can be dated to that year and on through the four when he was at Pantasaph. Throughout, his main line of enquiry remains constant in tracing the connections between the original meaning of symbols and their adaptation into Christianity.[32]

The entries are often in the form of drawings, either his own sketches or, more frequently, carefully copied from his sources. The sources themselves are rarely given, excepting his detailed use of Goblet d'Alviella's *Migration of Symbols* which had appeared in French in 1891 and was available at the Reading Room before he left London. But the English translation, published in 1894, was either added to the library at Pantasaph or Thompson obtained it for himself. From this he took down some forty pages of notes and drawings, many of which are also included in an unused review of the book where he added a long excursus of his own on the symbolism of the Winged Globe.[33] D'Alviella's approach was not controversial in itself in comparing the appearance of specific symbols at different times and places, and the book seems to have been known to the friars. They certainly knew the writings of Swedenborg through Swedenborg's influence on Patmore, and Thompson made extensive notes and comments from the main works, then easily available in the cheap editions published by the Swedenborg Society.[34]

As a result, together with the friars' enthusiasm for Patmore's own writings, Thompson's attitude towards the older poet began to change as he joined in the lively discussions at the Friary following the appearance that spring of Patmore's *Religio Poetae*, a series of prose reflections based on a lifetime's study of the common sources of mystical and poetic inspiration.

There was another factor, at first hardly less auspicious than the accusation which he had made before leaving London. The unreasonable jealousy where Alice was concerned passed with the passing of

his mood at that time, but earlier this year he found Patmore's un-
acknowledged use of his own ideas called for another accusation: that
of plagiarism. Thompson had sent Meynell a draft for a 'projected
article', parts of which he was convinced Patmore had then used in an
essay on 'The language of Religion' in the April issue of *Merry England*.
The parallels between its treatment of the symbolic language of the
Church as originating in that of the ancient world and the views expressed in his own neglected draft must have looked like more than
mere coincidence. The same month he wrote to Meynell: 'If Mr
Patmore does not remember a certain parable about a rich man, a
poor man, and a ewe lamb, and feel no prick of conscience — then he
is a hardened poet. My projected article, I may observe, is the ewe
lamb'.[35]

He was in no doubt that Patmore as well as Meynell knew its
contents. He tried to treat the matter lightly, aware that Wilfrid and
Alice might regard it as a residue from his previous jealousy. But
when he detected similar borrowings in *Religio Poetae* it was a more
serious trespass and one which demanded direct action. He wrote to
Patmore, drawing attention to a passage from his article on 'poets
born with an instinctive sense of correspondencies hidden from the
multitude'. He then quoted his own words:

> The truth is that inward resemblances may be as superficial as outward
> resemblances; and it is then the product of fancy, or fantasy. When the re-
> semblance is more than a resemblance, when it is rooted in the hidden
> nature of things, its discernment is the product of the imagination. This is
> the real distinction; fancy detects resemblances, imagination identifies.

'Now', he continued in the letter, referring to *Religio Poetae*, 'you will
see of what I accuse you. Masters have privileges, I admit, but I draw
the line at looking over their shoulder various odd leagues away'.
Keeping to the same courteously light tone he concluded by assuring
Patmore of his admiration for the book as a whole, which in his view
'stands by the streams of current literature like Cleopatra's Needle by
the dirt-eating Thames'.[36]

Whether Patmore was aware of it or not, there is certainly a
marked similarity between the passage Thompson quoted and a more
detailed one from the essay in *Religio Poetae* that gave the book its title.
Patmore, too, had distinguished between the poet whose appeal is
through fancy and the true poet whose inspiration derives from the
imagination, a 'spiritual insight, which enables him to see celestial
beauty and substantial reality, where all is blank to most others'. By
the same power 'he detects in external nature, those likenesses and
echoes by which spiritual realities can alone be rendered credible and
more or less apparent'.[37]

Patmore's reply has not survived, but it satisfied Thompson who wrote a second letter, also now lost, which he referred to later as 'conciliatory' and which paved the way for the friendship that was to develop after their first meeting in the autumn.

Meanwhile, the correspondence and its outcome overcame the hesitation he had felt when Meynell asked for a review of *Religio Poetae*. He now agreed to it and was working on it intermittently between June and August, the months when his poetic inspiration returned with 'Any Saint' and 'Assumpta Maria'. Significantly, the topic he selected for special praise and comment was the essay on 'The Language of Religion' derived from Patmore's *Merry England* article and tracing the Egyptian origins for several Christian symbolic rites.[38]

From now on Thompson was to be encouraged by a number of Patmore's findings in the sense that he came to see the older poet's views on poetry, and the language of poetry could often give more credence to his own. But despite the similarities in their lines of enquiry there was no 'borrowing' on Thompson's side of the kind of which he had accused Patmore. Nor, as he now also came to admit, need Patmore have derived his views from anything he himself had written. They were working from common sources. Apart from his more recent study of pagan and Christian symbolism Patmore had read widely in the Christian mystical tradition, with which Thompson was familiar from his religious training. The other major source for Patmore's ideas, the writings of Swedenborg and the hermetic philisophers who influenced Swedenborg, were also already familiar to Thompson in his reading both before and after his arrival in Wales. He would never attain the same degree of actual knowledge of these sources that Patmore acquired over a period of at least thirty years — a fact which Thompson readily acknowledged when referring to the other as his 'Master' in age and experience.

It is as important to stress the sense in which Thompson used the term, as the whole question of the extent of Patmore's influence. Until now it has been generally asserted that he was merely following the older poet's lead in the ideas and symbolism of much of his later poetry and prose. The mistake is due to the neglect accorded to the extent and nature of the notebook entries as well as the time and circumstances when they were chiefly made.[39]

In addition to the copious extracts on symbolism, the notebooks contain several essay drafts begun soon after his arrival at Pantasaph and on similar themes as the 'projected article' sent to Meynell — which has not itself survived. He probably intended these other essays for the *Annals* until his doubts as to the contents of his first two contributions caused him to leave them unfinished. The essays as well as the 'projected article' were stimulated by a series of articles which had been appearing in *Merry England* under the pseudonym 'XYZ'. The author, Robert Francis Clark, was a Jesuit and a member of the Pontifical Biblical Commission set up to examine the uses and abuses of historical criticism when applied to the Scriptures. It was one of the most controversial issues among Catholics at the time and his position gave added weight to the series for those who, like Thompson, knew his identity. Called 'The Story of a Conversion' the articles were in effect studies of the analogies between the Scriptures and the writings of the ancient world, using the transference of symbols from one culture to another as the main line of argument. When he began to plan his essays Thompson wrote to Father Clark. The letter has disappeared, but judging by Clark's reply, it must have been on the symbolism of the points of the compass, a topic studied by Clark and closely related to one of Thompson's own projected essays.[40]

The draft for this essay identifies the Hebrew word for West with the Sea and the Mother as symbols of Sense, whereas Thompson maintains that the East has possessed similar analogies with the Spirit through its ancient associations with Fire and Light. Like the other drafts it is unfinished and, compared with the notes on symbolism, confused in expression: regrettably, several have been printed without sufficient reference to their original state. But each was obviously planned to concentrate on some aspect of the cross-currents between the symbols found in the literature of the ancient world and their appearance in the Scriptures. In places they also show the extent to which he was prepared to go in making the connections. As where the God of the Old Testament is identified with the Set of Egyptian mythology to become the Destroyer: and then, through the Hebrew meaning of the same word, the Anus or life-principle.[41]

From his other studies Thompson must have been aware that in such a revival of the primitive Father Figure as both Creator and Destroyer he was touching on one of the deepest paradoxes in human psychology, indefinable unless present in dreams and mythology. And, absorbing as these studies had become, they were also disturbing. How far could they aid him in his future role and how far might they actually divert him from it? So when he wrote to Alice insisting on the 'deference to orthodoxy' in 'Assumpta Maria' it was in effect an uneasy reassurance directed at his own growing doubts.

There is a vital clue to these developments concealed in an autobiographical note on the events of that spring and summer, written some years later:

Reach Pantasaph. Anselm. *Faust* and Hebrew, Mrs M's books running. *Religio Poetae.* Letter conciliatory to C.P. Letters to and from Md. Studies continue. Autumn or late summer Md. comes. Poetry returns. *Any Saint.*

(date uncertain, any time late winter to spring or summer) *Assumpta Maria* (just before Md's coming).[42]

The note forms part of a series he made for an autobiographical article that never reached publication and is not now extant. But when the abbreviations are clarified it becomes in itself a kind of inner 'journal' of what he remembered as most important to him during the period it covers. There was Alice Meynell's success with the appearance of her first volume of poetry after eighteen years' silence, together with her essays in *The Rhythm of Life*. It was followed by the acclaim of Patmore's *Religio Poetae*. Both were important to Thompson in view of the fact that his own poetry was under consideration and these other successes increased his desire for an even greater achievement. The 'letter conciliatory' to Coventry Patmore ('C.P.') explains and expands the existing earlier one. But over and above the rest is the entry on his continuing 'studies' and the references in connection with them.

Anselm's personal regard for literature was secondary to his philosophical training but both contributed to the course of reading begun soon after Thompson's arrival. As it progressed the subjects recalled in the note, '*Faust* and Hebrew' suggests that he confided something at least of his recent studies to Anselm, who then encouraged their continuance. The symbolic content of the language of the Old Testament was a topic Anselm was pursuing on his own account through his knowledge of Hebrew, a knowledge he imparted to a limited extent to Thompson as a kind of 'sideline' which Thompson himself came to regard as an important influence on his more private interests. Then, the selection of *Faust* for special study meant studying also the effect on the play of Goethe's reading of Paracelsus and the hermetic philosophers' writings with which Thompson was familiar, and which Anselm knew had guided so much of Patmore's philosophical ideas. By this means Anselm probably hoped to draw the two poets closer together and it was certainly a contributing factor, coming as it did at this time.

Yet even with Anselm, Thompson could not go far with his more personal and disturbing concerns. His only real confidant, with whom he shared a good deal more, was Elizabeth Blackburn: 'Letters to and from Md.' 'Madam' was his nickname for her, earned by her tendency to manage his affairs that was part of her domineering character and which she took with equally characteristic good humour. The firm line she adopted over the writing of 'Sister Songs' was typical. And if there were other times when he was irritated by her interference he tolerated it on account of her genuine affection for him. In addition he could respect her outspoken critical views while not usually agreeing with them.

Then, during those last months in London, a bond had arisen between them which by mutual consent they kept to themselves. Whether by accident or through her well-developed powers of observation, she came to know of the reason for his long hours in the Reading Room. And at a time when he felt no one cared for him or his affairs, he found in her a sympathetic as well as an enthusiastic listener to his ideas and the basis for them in his present studies. When he left for Wales she continued to copy down notes and extracts for him from the Reading Room books he had used, sending them in the letters he included in the significant memoranda for his auto-biographical note. So too he included her arrival, coinciding with the entry on the return of his poetry. She came at Father Anselm's invitation for an extended, if often interrupted, period, ostensibly to write a series of articles for the *Annals* on Franciscan history. Although he did not know the extent of her share in Thompson's interests, Anselm probably had another reason for the arrangement. She would provide companionship for his protegé when he was to be increasingly called away for temporary duties elsewhere.

One aspect of Francis's studies was known only to her. There must have been some hints in his conversations with Anselm, who remembered how Francis had at that time 'what seemed to me a morbid fear of freemasonry'. To him it was no more than a curious detail. Similarly, when Everard Meynell commented briefly on Francis's knowledge of symbolism he noted some accompanying 'suspicions of the Masons' but said nothing further on the subject.[43] But Elizabeth Blackburn knew far more of what it meant to him as it first arose from his work in the Reading Room and it was carried on by her as part of her researches on his behalf. Considering her volubility in other directions, it is the more to her credit that she kept the matter to herself until her letters and notes were found among Francis's papers after his death. Most were contained in a sealed-up packet which, when opened, led to a surprised enquiry from Wilfrid Meynell. Her reply suggests that the contents were recognizably intended to form a book:

> As to the Freemasonry notes I imagine they could be collated and disin-tangled to prove at least more than interesting. His plan, often discussed, was to begin with the Gnostics, go down through the Templars and other military orders — till, reaching the Reformation period and the Rosi-crucians, with the French Revolution, modern Masonry in its mischievous Contintental attitude stood clearly revealed. How much or how little he wrote I of course don't know. At first I took slight notice but as he went on he showed a wonderful appreciation of what lawyers call 'evidence' — and it was surprising to see how he fitted in the pieces — more puzzling than any jig-saw — to make a perfect picture — but that was in talking and I don't think I ever saw a line of his except that connected with my own re-

searches at the BM he asked me to make when he first went to Pantasaph when I had charge of it then but as I told you it was sealed up.[44]

On leaving London Thompson obviously left the bulk of his work on the subject in her care as safer than having it with him, and since even she did not know the contents of the sealed packet he was placing a trust in her which she respected. It is therefore impossible to know what the packet contained. Its destruction, however regrettable now, is understandable. Thompson himself was well aware of the risk he was incurring as a Catholic in considering such a project as Mrs Blackburn described and the risk still applied to any publicity given to it after his death. Always a controversial subject, freemasonry had become more so in recent years, and in 1884 it was condemned outright by Pope Leo XIII in the encyclical *Humanum Genus*. Catholics were forbidden to have any dealings with the Masons or their practices. On the Continent they were closely associated with occultism, Satanism and pseudo-mystical cults claiming to possess the key to the meaning of life and the future of mankind. Most English writers attempted to draw a distinction between a valid Masonic tradition and these accretions, but elsewhere there was barely a dividing line.

There was, however, no shortage of literature both in England and abroad and a spate of such publications occurred at just the time when Thompson took up the subject. The darker aspects were emphasized by J. K. Huysmans in *Là-bas*, which appeared in an England translation in 1891. His revelations of the orgiastic practices and blasphemous rites within Freemasonry were carried further the same year with the publication in England of Gabriel Jogand Pagé's *The Mystery of Freemasonry*. Earlier, writing under the name of Leo Taxil, he had been a devotee of the cult of Lucifer and since his conversion he attacked the cult in *The Brethren of the Three Points* as one of the most obnoxious forms of Freemasonry in America.[45]

These and many similar publications were easily available at the Reading Room, first to Thompson and then to Elizabeth Blackburn. Taken together with his general symbolism studies they were, from the start, warnings of the evils inherent in the evolution of symbols when the true function of symbols has been neglected. Instead of uniting the spiritual with the material worlds, symbolic rites and practices could then be the means for exalting the senses at the expense of the spirit, so opening the way for some of the darkest drives in human nature. That this was how he continued to view Freemasonry appears clearly from a notebook draft for a letter prepared after his return to London, but which was never sent. It is addressed to an unnamed member of the French hierarchy, asking for the support needed to complete his book. Its plan and purpose are described in accordance with Mrs Blackburn's account. He calls it 'a history of

hidden evil' which 'must be published abroad and anonymously for if
published here I should be detected as the author'.[46] It is in effect a
'begging letter' drafted at a time of serious financial need and it is well
for his reputation that he thought better than to take it further. But in
showing how he regarded Freemasonry its existence in the draft is of
real value.

More than the sealed packet may have been destroyed once Meynell knew the danger to Thompson's reputation if such a preoccupation should come to light. But there are notes and comments scattered
through the notebooks to show that his main concern was the survival
of pagan worship in the rituals of Freemasonry and among the sects
with which it had become associated. The purpose behind these sur-
vivals was what mattered to him. The surviving notes are mainly in
the form of extracts from obscure occult journals on the expectation of
a 'universal brotherhood of man' based on a new 'worship of mankind'. He comments in one place: 'It is impossible for anyone acquainted with the spirit and methods of Freemasonry, as it has left its
ruthless fingerprints on the wrist of history, not to recognise in these
. . .' and the rest has been deleted.[47]

What have remained apparently intact are the so-called 'Notes
on Symbolism' in Mrs Blackburn's handwriting, sent by her from
London as part of her researches.[48] Most of the contents are not on
symbolism itself but are directly related to the subject as it related to
the intended book. There are notes and extracts from Paracelsus,
Gnostic writings and the survival of pagan rites and symbols in the
worship of idols among the Knights Templars — regarded by many
as the precursors of the Freemasons. At one stage Mrs Blackburn
added a comment on what, to her, appeared 'such an awful revelation
of wickedness' that she had even found it hard to find reassurance
from her own faith.

It was well for her that her work on his behalf ended with her
departure from London. It was probably also well for him that the
subject could not then be taken further. He knew enough to add to his
doubt as to the future for his poetry and it would continue to oppress
him when the doubts increased later.

For the present, during that summer of 1892 there was much else to
occupy him. There was the recurring task of submitting contributions
for *Merry England* and the pretence, at least, of collaborating on the
Annals — over and above which was the much more demanding revision of his poetry for its publication in the autumn. He was in fact
busier than he had ever been and even made out an 'Order of the
Day' for himself in an attempt to allow time for prayer and, more successfully, for a walk of several hours each afternoon.[49]

Hard work and hard walking went well together. He was physically and mentally fitter now than he had ever been or would be again. During these months there are hardly any complaints as to his health in his letters apart from occasional bouts of depression. At times he might still 'suffer like Old Nick' inwardly, but he could hold his own and 'the blessed mountain air keeps up my body'.[50]

The improvement shows in the change in tone of the letters to Meynell, now businesslike and confident in dealing with the practical details connected with preparing his poems for the press. There are also distinct signs of frustration at having no money for stamps or personal necessities: what had before been a necessary precaution was becoming an unwelcome reminder of a dependence for which he no longer felt the need. But he was too diffident to raise the matter, knowing that in other respects the dependence was inescapable. The future for his poetry would be largely due to Meynell's backing and his continued stay at Pantasaph was only possible with Meynell's support in the arrival — often erratic — of the monthly cheques for his lodgings.

His improvement shows, too, in the occasional anecdotes he knew both Wilfrid and Alice would enjoy. He might dislike having his clothes obtained for him but in his thanks for them he could see the comic side:

> I received the clothes, which were very welcome. The trousers alone bothered me, proving ludicrously wide, and too short. After a strategical survey of them, I shut myself up and went in for three days of daring tailoring operations. As a result, they are now re-formed in a sufficiently tolerable manner, which reflects great credit on my versatile genius.[51]

Again, when the orchard fruit began to ripen he reported: 'Madam has been eating apples, like her Mother Eve, and like her Mother Eve has been very much upset by them'. Although to be fair he must admit 'I have also been a little out of sorts over the last two days'.[52]

His feelings towards Alice were also changing. It was to her rather than to Wilfrid that he wrote with painstaking attention to the texts of his poems as they were to appear on publication. For her part she took the same care with her suggestions while respecting his final decisions. They were coming together on equal terms as poets and it seemed that the emotional strain of the past year was forgotten on both sides. Yet when Wilfrid suggested, typically, that the dedication of his poetry should be addressed to Alice rather than including himself, Thompson's protest makes it clear how much he knew he owed to both:

> I should belie both the truth and my own feelings if I represented Mrs Meynell as the sole person to whom I owe what has been given me to accomplish in poetry. Suffer this — the sole thing, as unfortunate necessi-

ties of exclusion would have it, which links this first, possibly this only
volume, with your name — suffer this to stand. I should feel deeply hurt if
you refused me the gratification.[53]

The book, called simply *Poems*, appeared early in November. Its
presentation was in line with the high standards for which the Bodley
Head, Lane's publishing house, was now known. The unusual almost
square format (Pott. 4 to) gave it a subdued individuality. The poems
were well placed and spaced on thick art paper and the grey-green
covers bore, on the front, a simple design of gold circles. Only the
frontispiece marred the intended impression of high quality work
offered modestly by a hitherto barely-known poet. Laurence Houseman, Lane's chief designer and illustrator, had recently provided
frontispieces for poetry by John Davidson and Katharine Tynan. It
was an honour that he should do so for Thompson but the attempt at
a literal presentation of selected passages from 'The Hound of Heaven'
was a distinct mistake. As Thompson wrote to Meynell — who also regarded this as the book's one failure: ' "The Hound of Heaven" is just
the poem which a draughtsman who knew the limits of his craft would
have avoided'. With the rest he was fully satisfied — 'beautifully got
up' — although a reaction had set in and he found he could not share
the Meynells' expectations for it. 'Your interest in the volume is very
dear to me' he wrote to Alice, adding: 'I cannot say I myself feel any
elation about it. I am past the time when such things brought me any
elation'.[54]

He was not in fact past such feelings as his concern for the reviews of *Poems* would show. The Meynells were right in regarding the
depression as a natural after-effect of the effort he had put into preparing the book for publication. To offset it they arranged for him to
come to London to celebrate the occasion among their friends and
those who would be sure to give him their support.

The outstanding event of his visit was his first meeting with
Coventry Patmore, who afterwards wrote to his wife Harriet:

> I saw F. Thompson yesterday, and had some private talk with him. All I
> saw in him was pleasant and attractive — so I asked him to come for some
> Sunday to Lymington, which he joyfully promised to do.[55]

On his side Thompson, who only opened up in that way when he was
fully at ease, obviously responded as warmly. He probably did spend
a Sunday at the Patmores' country house outside Lymington although
there is no direct record of it. When recalling the later friendship
between the two poets Patmore's youngest son Francis, then a boy of
ten, remembered his namesake chiefly for his 'peculiar fear of dogs'.
Patmore had a retriever, Nelson, and in fairness he felt bound to add
that 'as my father delighted to feed the dog on huge quatities of raw
meat, till it became the terror of the district, Thompson may be ex-

cused'.[56] If he was referring to a visit at this time Thompson can be excused on other grounds as well. Only a few weeks before he had been badly bitten by the Friary watchdog.

Due to the Meynells' careful chaperoning the first reviews gave *Poems* the welcome that was to be expected from their own circle. Wilfrid rightly foresaw a danger if Thompson should become identified with a closed Catholic 'clique'. In his own review he asserted that all great literature, with which the work of this 'new poet' must certainly be ranked, expresses the true 'aroma of Catholicism'. And Katharine Tynan, aware of the accusations of obscurity that were no less likely, wrote of the few who would possess the poetic sensibility to recognise 'some of the finest harmonies in earth and heaven'.[57]

The initial support, following the London visit and the meeting with Patmore, raised Francis's spirits for a time. After his return to Pantasaph, at Christmas his old enthusiasm for acting was revived by attending the nativity play put on by the local convent school. He was 'very much amused at the infantile efforts of the performers', Father Alphonsus wrote to Meynell, assuring him that Francis was 'in excellent health'.[58]

He wrote in the same week that Patmore's criticism of *Poems* appeared in the *Fortnightly Review*. The article aimed at forestalling charges of plagiarism which often followed the appearance of Thompson's poetry in *Merry England*. The term could not, he argued, be applied to 'true poets' in any pejorative sense:

> The ideas, and to a certain extent the language and style, of true poets become the common property of the guild, and all that is demanded of them is, that they should improve or vary what they take from each other, so as, in some sort, to make it their own.

Was there also a private hint here that he had not forgotten the accusation leading to his first exchange of letters with Thompson and so to the growing understanding between them?

In summarizing the themes of the poems and their treatment there are, he admits, 'cheap sublimities' and archaisms to mar a 'truly splendid command of language'. But they are the defects of early work and cannot destroy an unmistakeably great gift. Here is 'a Titan among poets' who yet must remember 'that a Titan may require and obtain renovation of his strength by occasional acquaintance with the earth'. There follows a passage where he knew Thompson would understand and appreciate the symbolism:

> The tree Igdrasil, which has its head in heaven and its roots in hell (the 'lower part of the earth'), is the image of the true man, and eminently so of the poet, who is eminently man. In proportion to the bright and divine heights to which he ascends must be the obscure depths in which the tree is rooted, and from which it draws the mystic sap of its spiritual life.[59]

Igdrasil, unites heaven with earth, spirit with sense. By taking the symbolic tree as his illustration Patmore was touching the chord of Thompson's present uncertainties. The earlier poetry had soared too high, leaving its roots neglected. His symbolism studies were taking him down to the roots and the insight of the older poet seemed to him to confirm the movement as essential to his future as a poet. This, more than anything else in the review, caused Thompson to describe it as 'a landmark in my life'. As so often when his deepest feelings were aroused, he expressed them through a medical image. Whereas, he wrote to Alice, 'other critics notice the symptoms of one's poetic maladies, he diagnoses the seat of the disease'.

From this letter it is clear he was beginning to wonder if there could be a future for his poetry after all. There was nothing to reassure him since his writing of 'Any Saint' and 'Assumpta Maria' the previous summer and he was now dissatisfied with these: 'it does not seem to me that either poem comes to much'. No one at Pantasaph had seen them apart from 'Madam', whose judgement he was beginning to find 'too easily prejudiced to be reliable'. He was irritated, too, to discover she had been writing that he found Pantasaph 'dull' — an attitude much closer to her sentiments than his, he assured Alice. He admitted to having been 'out of order' recently but 'it was never anything but one of those causeless-seeming disturbances to which I am, you know, intermittently subject'.[60]

Although Elizabeth Blackburn was no doubt exaggerating, there was some truth in her observation. It was not that he found Pantasaph 'dull', but as the reviews of his book increased he did feel cut off, only hearing of them piecemeal and usually some time after they appeared. His letters barely conceal his frustration at having to depend on the friars to lend him copies of the main ones, and there were many he claimed he never saw. Those he did obtain he preserved carefully. Nor was he indifferent to the sales of the book which, as they reached the two thousand mark that spring, he found 'truly astonishing'.[61]

Largely due to Patmore's reputation and the length and detail of his review, the critics outside the range of the Meynells' contacts suddenly began to take notice. During February the well-managed start to Thompson's public career changed to a storm of praise and protest, proving to the literary world that here at last was a poet demanding serious attention. Early that month he was distressed that so prominent a critic as Arthur Symons should find his borrowings resulted in 'a splendour of rags and patches, a very masque of anarchy'. Symons took particular exception to the use of early sources mixed with much that was taken from poets of the present century. Yet the next week H. D. Traill praised the mingling of 'old world mysticism with modern thought' as 'a mark of true originality' in 'a new poet of the first rank'. Andrew Lang wrote anonymously of *Poems* as 'more pose than passion' at the same time as J. L. Garvin eulogised the volume as 'reaching the peak of Parnassus at a bound'.[62]

In general there was more praise than protest. The two together were arousing a degree of publicity that even the Meynells had not dared to hope for. They were enjoying all the excitement in which Thompson, far away in Wales, had little share. Instead the varied reactions tended to increase his doubts. What did it all amount to anyway? Apart from Patmore what did any of these critics on whom his future reputation depended know of the true sources of his inspiration or of the aim of his poetry? What did he yet know of them himself? There was no one in whom he could confide. Anselm was at present away and such matters were beyond Madam's limited acumen. Nor could he be sure what further mischief might result from her letters to the Meynells.

To her he was unquestionably a genius, and she was also genuinely fond of him. In a letter which she was careful to ensure he did not know she was writing, she told Wilfrid of her anxiety on account of his inability to feel any 'human elation' at his success:

> It is so odd to read all the well merited praises and then realise how outside the pale of humanity this great genius is — more irresponsible than any child with a child's fits of temper and want of foresight and control. And with it all he is deeper and more wonderfully learned than when he left London. Indeed his flashes of genius are astounding & when they pass, they seem to leave no trace behind.

She was sure he must be obtaining opium from somewhere, which would account for these strange moods, doing no serious work and staying in bed most of the day. When he denied this she had told Father Anselm of her fears, but his enquiries on his return to the Friary met with the same response. More may have been said — Francis suspecting her interferences — for she added: 'I am advised not to say anything more to him'. Yet she could still see no other reason for the disturbing change in Francis and ended her letter with the warning 'that to allow him any money for his own use' is 'simply to furnish him with a weapon to commit suicide'.[63]

What she did not know was that the signs she took to be symptoms of addiction arose from an intense inner struggle. For, overriding all the delay and doubts since last summer, his poetic powers were again at work as he began the first tentative drafts for a poem greater in conception than any he had attempted since he left Storrington.

The Lenten season with its twofold promise of Easter and spring, of supernatural and natural rebirth, provided at once the theme and the

initial inspiration. At Easter the Meynells visited Pantasaph —
ostensibly to celebrate Francis's success with *Poems* but also to find out
for themselves what truth there might be behind Mrs Blackburn's
fears. Although they could only stay a few days the visit was a happy
one. Wilfrid and Alice left fully satisfied that all was well and Francis,
with a sudden burst of creative energy, completed the poem the following week.

'From the Night of Forebeing' is prefaced by two quotations. The
first, from Sir Thomas Browne's *Urn Burial*, provides the title: 'In the
chaos of preordination, and night of our forebeings' (Hydriotaphia:
Urn Burial, V:17). It is followed by a line from the first chapter of Saint
John's Gospel: '*Et lux in tenebris erat, et tenebrae em non comprehenderunt*'
('And the light shone in the darkness and the darkness did not comprehend it'). In the poem the 'chaos of preordination' of man's
origins and early beliefs is gathered into the 'night of forebeing' of
the Easter liturgy. The '*lux in tenebris*' of the second quotation acts as a
reminder of the climax of the liturgy in the Paschal Vigil, when the
'uncomprehending darkness' is symbolically dispelled by the lighting
of the 'New Fire'. There follows the singing of the great Easter hymn,
the *Exultat*, and thereafter the whole complex ritual is directed by the
triumph of light over darkness, of life over death.

The ode was again the form he found best suited to the demands of his theme. In conception and treatment it stands together
with his first two Odes, with one outstanding difference. Its two distinct parts are so divided as to create a break which, in terms of its
success as a poem, flaws the whole. Yet in another sense the flaw is
valuable as a kind of imprint on the stage of Thompson's poetic development at this time.

The opening lines celebrate the spring as a rising of new light
from the East with the echoes from the 'Ode to the Setting Sun' that
recur throughout, Earth and nature share in a movement of resurrection where the pagan and Christian worlds become inseparable.
The greening larch is as true a herald of resurrected life as the graves
that gave forth their dead on the first Easter night. And the sun
remains the central symbol for all life, natural, human and supernatural:

> Hark to the *Jubilate* of the bird
> For them that found the dying way to life!
> And they have heard
> And quicken to the great precursive word;
> Green spray showers lightly down the cascade of the larch,
> The graves are riven,
> And the Sun comes with power amid the clouds of heaven!

76—82

In the language of pagan and Christian alike, the Earth has become at once the Bride and Mother of the Light which is Life:

> O Earth, unchilded, widowed Earth, so long
> Lifting in patient pine and ivy tree
> Mournful belief and steadfast prophecy,
> Behold how all things are made true!
> Behold your bridegroom cometh in to you,
> Exceeding glad and strong.
> . . . .
> Look up, O mortals and the portent heed!
> In very deed
> Washed with new fire to their irradiant birth
> Reintegrated are the heavens and earth;

> 87–92
> 97–103

The Scriptural allusions culminate in the reminder of the Paschal Vigil and the Blessing of the New Fire symbolising the light shining in the darkness of man's 'forebeing'. But the sources go deeper. The allusions carry within themselves the ancient symbolism of the Earth Mother who is also the Bride of the Sky Father who is likewise the Lover. They open the way for the central sections of the poem, a paeon of praise to Light as the great symbol of life. The command 'Let there be Light' around which the whole Paschal liturgy revolves, penetrates far beyond the darkness of earth's winter to the darkest regions of the human spirit. It reaches at once to 'the secret chambers of the brain' and the 'vine-out-quickening' sources of sensual desire:

> And round and round in bachanal rout reel the swift spheres
>   intemporably.

> 168

Until now the Ode has captured the element of turbulent joy in the liturgy of the Easter Light, penetrating the darkness within man and raising his primeval being to a height of cosmic renewal embracing at once human, natural and supernatural life. But over half is still to follow. The cosmic vision gives place to an inner vision of the poet's own winter of the spirit:

> My little-worlded self! the shadows pass
> In this thy sister-world, as in a glass,
> Of all processions that revolve in thee

> 169–171

In its celebration of resurrected life the poem has united earth with heaven in the symbolism of the Easter liturgy as a fulfilment of the rites of the pagan world. Now the corresponding stirring of new life within the poet cannot break free from the shadows in the glass:

> Shade within shade! for deeper in the glass
> Now other imaged meanings pass;
> And as the man, the poet there is read.

197–199

Was Thompson aware of that far-off image of the glass in his schoolboy essay, recording shadows too fearful to confront? It is the same symbol here, for the man and the poet whose fears are bred from those of the boy. Can the Lux in Tenebris he has identified with the sun as the primeval fire dispel the shadows? Or will it, as the New Fire of the Paschal Vigil, cast a yet deeper one — reaching back to the shadow from the Cross cast over the poem that marked his birth as a poet? In that poem the sun became the symbol uniting the rites of the ancient world with the sacrificial death and resurrection of Christ. Now, in the coming of spring of earth, it is again the symbol uniting the pagan rites of renewal with the liturgy of the Paschal Vigil. Only now he is speaking with the authority of the traditional language of the Church, giving it a new direction that draws its vitality from origins far beyond the confines of the Christian centuries. But if this is to be the poetry of 'the return to God' can the process of renewal be transferred to the inner movement? Will the sacrifice to an unknown future, on which such a renewal depends, lead to a poetic rebirth — or will the challenge to his powers prove too great?

> Stern the denial, the travail slow,
> The struggling wall will scantly grow:
> And though with that dread rite of sacrifice
> Ordained for during edifice,
> How long, how long ago!
> Into that wall which will not thrive
> I build myself alive,
> Ah, who shall tell me will the wall uprise?

253–260

If Thompson was unaware of the earlier mirror image, he was surely aware of the source for his imagery here in the lines he had written on Newman. Only there he had no doubt of Newman's self-sacrifice as an assurance of new life for the Church. How could he be sure for himself that the direction he had followed over the past months was even worthy of a similar dedication? Or if it was, that as a poet he was worthy of making it? There might be moments when he was aware of the possible future:

> the wings
> Hear I not in praevenient winnowings
> Of coming songs, that lift my hair and stir it?

269–271

— but there could be no assured answer and again the shadows return:

> Nature, enough! Within thy glass
> Too many and too stern the shadows pass.

295–296

Yet whereas the schoolboy essay ended at this stage the poem is not ended. Too much has intervened: and if it has left the man with a body 'rifted, marred', it has given the poet the 'fortitude' to wait for a full confrontation:

> And power is man's,
> With that great word of 'Wait',
> To still the sea of tears,
> And shake the iron heart of Fate.
> In that one word is strong
> An else, alas, much-mortal song

312–317

There follows an attempt to anticipate a 'vision' which will unite the renewed life of nature with the spirit of his future poetry. It is too generalised and assertive to convince, while the concluding lines merely return to the demand for an endurance of the spirit until the time for confrontation is clear:

> Firm is the man, and set beyond the cast
> Of Fortune's game, and the iniquitous hour,
> Whose falcon soul sits fast,
> And not intends her high sagacious tour
> Or ere the quarry sighted ...

362–366

Yet the game, which had always appealed to him for its pattern and ritual, is no child's play now. Within the game there is always the element of conflict and here the image is much closer to that other form of conflict which held an equal fascination for him, the battle. Then, the falcon as bird of prey represents the power of restraint demanded by the impending conflict, the capacity to await the true quarry. And the quarry will be the moment of truth when it comes to dispel the uncertainties behind the whole second part of the poem.

'From the Night of Forebeing' was finished during long days on the open hills. That same week Elizabeth Blackburn wrote to Wilfrid:

You will be glad to hear that Francis has written an Ode which I hear is longer than anything he has done yet. Also that the 'frenzy' being on him he has begun another poem yesterday. No one sees him but Fr. Anselm, to whom he comes every evening and whom he tells of his work. He told him last night that since you had left he seemed to have a return of all the old poetic power. Of course he is flying over hill and dale and never to be seen, but I am sure you will be as glad as I am at this fresh development.[64]

It was probably this letter that led Alice to describe Francis at Pantasaph in a draft for her essay 'At Monastery Gates' on which she was working at the time:

When the poet comes drifting in from his walks over the tops of the hills, his light Shelley-figure looks as though it were brought home by the sea winds.[65]

Her etherialized picture of the poet in his setting must be measured against the one gained from his own letters. The previous autumn he had written scathingly to her of those city dwellers for whom nature is a work of art 'kindly lent by the Almighty for public exhibition', while even in the country few realize 'that she is alive, has almost as many ways as a woman, and is to be lived with, not merely looked at'. He proved his point by adding how he recently 'companied Nature in her bed-chamber no less than in her presence-room', sleeping out to savour the smells and sounds of the countryside at night.[66]

Since that time he had been acquiring an intimacy with the natural world which was more akin to Wordsworth than to Shelley. When he sent the completed Ode to Alice he compared its length with Wordsworth's 'Intimations of Immortality' with the observation: 'My fear is that thought in it has strangled poetic impulse'.[67] He must have had Wordsworth in mind during those days on the hills to have made the otherwise irrelevant comparison as to the length of his poem. Wordsworth, 'the poet of the return to nature' he was once so confidently determined to equal as 'the poet of the return to God' — how far could it be said that this Ode promised any such achievement?

In her letter, Mrs Blackburn referred to 'another poem begun yesterday'. The poem, 'An Anthem to Earth', was the outcome of Thompson's conflicting feelings towards nature and natural life. He must come to terms with this other compelling power over the life of man as part of the created world. In 'From the Night of Forebeing' the symbolic forms of nature incarnated the spiritual within the temporal world. Unless he could prove that this was so, he was merely making a travesty of Wordsworth rather than moving in a new direction of his own. Worse, he was in danger of experiencing just that exaltation of the senses at the expense of the spirit he so feared in the abberations of Freemasonry. To find the answer he must follow the course of nature itself as a power over man independent of any further dimension, the temporal reality as distinct from the symbolic forms derived from it.

Whereas 'From the Night of Forebeing' was written in a few weeks, he was working on 'An Anthem to Earth' throughout the following spring and summer. His preoccupation with Wordsworth and with the Immortality Ode in particular became the guiding principle behind the poem. It may have been his reason for departing from the ode form as likely to make a comparison too intrusive. Instead he made his first attempt at blank verse, an experiment where, as he wrote later to Alice Meynell, 'I have not confined myself to the strict limits of the metre, but have laid my hand at one clash among all the licences with which the Elizabethans build up their harmonies'.[68] He was not prepared to judge the result for himself. The blank verse has the effect of creating an even greater contrast than in his other longer poems between the strength of his poetic powers and their corresponding weakness when they are overplayed.

In Wordsworth's Ode the infant enters the world 'not in entire forgetfulness' of the mysterious source of the 'one life' in man and nature. Thompson refuses man any such legacy. The child is born 'In nascientness' from the darkness of the womb with none of Wordsworth's 'clouds of glory' to cloak his vulnerability, exposed to the life force of nature as the universal Earth Mother. Yet for a few years the child plays unthinkingly among her 'silken robes', heedless of her 'grave designs'. As he grows she seems to offer him the beauties of the created world as toys for his pleasure. He is the child of the Shelley essay, for whom the make-believe of childhood leads to the aspirations of the youth. The poem is here modelled on passages from 'The Hound of Heaven' where the essay had a similar influence:

> Then, O Earth, thou rang'st beneath me,
> Rocked to Eastward, rocked to Westward,
> Even with the shifted
> Poise and footing of my thought!
> I brake through thy doors of sunset,
> Ran before the hooves of sunrise,
> Shook thy matron tresses down in fancies
> Wild and wilful
> As a poet's hand could twine them;
>
> 33–41

But the time must come when the dreams of youth can no longer sustain the illusions of the child's make-believe:

> In a little thought, in a little thought
> We stand and eye thee in a grave dismay,
> With sad and doubtful questioning, when first
> Thou speak'st to us as men: like sons who hear

Newly their mother's history, unthought
Before, and say — 'She is not as we dreamed:

69–74

Nature has shown herself to be the 'poor stepdame' of 'The Hound of
Heaven', reviving Thompson's deep-seated fear of the stepmother as
the perversion of the true life-bestowing mother. In lines that also
revive the unused essay 'A Threnody of Birth', the limits of man's
mortality, the root cause of the betrayal, act as a direct antithesis to
the 'intimations of immortality' Wordsworth found in nature:

> His heart is builded
> For pride, for potency, infinity,
> All heights, all deeps, and all immensities,
> Arrased with purple like the house of kings, —
> To stall the grey-rat, and the carrion-worm
> Statelily lodge. Mother of mysteries!
> Sayer of dark sayings in a thousand tongues,
> Who bringest forth no saying yet so dark
> As we ourselves, thy darkest! We the young,
> In a little thought, in a little thought,
> At last confront thee, and ourselves in thee,
> And wake disgarmented of glory . . .

117–128

In the Immortality Ode the fading of 'The Vision splendid' leads
Wordsworth's child and youth to a maturity that enables him to 'find/
Strength in what remains behind'. Here, too, there is a corresponding
process:

> In a little strength, in a little strength,
> We affront thy unveiled face intolerable,
> Which yet we do sustain.
> Though I the Orient never more shall feel
> Break like a clash of cymbals, and my heart
> Clang through my shaken body like a gong;
> Nor ever more with spurted feet shall tread
> I' the winepresses of song; naught's truly lost
> That moulds to sprout forth gain . . .

143–151

For Thompson, this new direction leads beyond the visible forms of
nature to embrace the wonders made known by science:

> In a little sight, in a little sight
> We learn from what in thee is credible
> The incredible . . .

198–200

Yet the 'sight' is too limited to penetrate the underlying mysteries. For all its claims, science is still, as in 'A Threnody of Birth', the blind worm within the soil of nature:

> Making it capable of the crops of God

206

If the mysterious workings of nature are beyond man's understanding, so also those within man himself remain formless shadows haunting the labyrinths and distant corridors of the human mind:

> Wherein I wander darkling of myself

239

The reminder of the mind's 'labyrinthine ways' from the Hound of Heaven' creates a deliberate contrast between the course of the soul in that poem and the course of human life as it is followed here. Instead of reaching a climax in the submission to a supernatural power stronger than life or death, man is here at the mercy only of nature as the final purveyor of both:

> Thou giv'st us life not half so willingly
> As thou undost thy giving

268–269

His decline is traced in images of the rapacity of wild beasts and in medical images underlining the ruthless course of nature through human history. The individual is no more than a worthless fragment to whom nothing remains but the 'little dust' from which she drew him. And even this she, like the wild beasts, will eventually consume:

> Much offal of a foul world comes thy way,
> And man's superfluous cloud shall soon be laid
> In a little blood.

293–295

To be true to its theme, the poem should end when as nature's offspring he receives from her no more than the ending of his troubles 'in a little peace'. But something does remain. Death, returning man to the dust of his physical origins, is at the same time a release:

> Pontifical Death, that cloth the creuisle bridge
> To the steep and trifid God — one mortal birth
> That broker is of immortality

348–350

The one reference beyond the claims of nature weakens Thompson's deliberate theme but it adds to the poem's significance in drawing attention to the motive behind its composition. He was in a sense compelled to insert the lines, written towards the end of the months

when he was working on it and which had given him part of the
answer he was seeking at the start.

By then 'An Anthem to Earth' was proving that beyond Wordsworth's 'intimations of immortality' derived from the one life in man
and nature, for him there must always be that other dimension. He
knew now that 'From the Night of Forebeing' pointed the right way
ahead through the symbolic language of poetry and the Church, the
two together incarnating spiritual realities through the material forms
of the created world. In 'An Anthem to Earth' he deprived nature of
any meaning beyond the limits of physical life and death. And nature
had shown herself to be as deceptive as the stepmother who, in accordance with Thompson's own darkest fears, devours the life over which
the inserted lines on death as release confirm she has no ultimately
valid claim.

The doubt, however, remained. Was he equal to the challenge
presented by the two poems taken together in this way? Was he
capable of sustaining its intellectual demands while retaining the
'poetic impulse' he already found threatened by the conscious intention behind 'From the Night of Forebeing'? And if retained, would
it result in a betrayal of the true function of symbolism as he had
found it betrayed in the rites of Freemasonry and those cults where
the senses were exalted at the expense of the spirit? The extent of his
self-doubt led him to add a 'Proemum' to 'An Anthem to Earth', suggesting that the poetic life revived by the two poems might after all be
stillborn and the new direction indicated by them no more than a
dead end:

> Ah!
> If not in all too late and frozen a day
> I come in rearward of the throats of song,
> Unto the deaf-sense of the agéd year
> Singing with doom upon me, yet give heed!
> One poet with sick pinion, that still feels,
> Breath through the Orient gateways closing fast,
> Fast closing t'wards the undelighted night!

34–41

The shadow cast over his future from the Cross at Storrington was
certainly being deepened by one cast from the Calvary at Pantasaph.

But in this gathering sense of doom that even the creative power
possessing him at the time could not dispel, there were other factors at
work. 'An Anthem to Earth' took five months to complete and in the
same week he began it, Father Angelo arrived at Bishop's House, to
remain there until the following December. Then when the poem was

in its final stages, Coventry Patmore made his long promised visit to the Friary. It was their presence at this crucial time which was to bring about the second great turning-point in Thompson's life as both man and poet.

The Old Icarian Way
Pantasaph 1894–1896

O dismay!
I, a wingless mortal, sporting
With the tresses of the sun?
I, that dare my hand to lay
On the thunder in its snorting?
Ere begun,
Falls my singéd song down the sky, even the old Icarian way.
'The Mistress of Vision': 100–106

The reason given for Angelo's arrival in April was the same as it had been in sending Anselm to the Friary over two years before. An undefined 'breakdown' in health was a convenient pretext for removing the more troublesome members of the Order to the comparative seclusion at Pantasaph, where lighter duties and the mountain air provided good grounds for so called 'recuperation'. For Angelo this included a temporary dispensation from following the rule of the Order and he was therefore given a room at the Guest House rather than staying at the Friary.

His 'breakdown' the previous winter coincided with Father Cuthbert's departure from Crawley, who since that time was himself being sent to Pantasaph more often than elsewhere. Neither made any secret of the real reason, or why they met with the Order's special disapproval. During the past two years Cuthbert's scheme for a 'community of priests' dedicated to social work had progressed. Support was found from outside the Order and a rudimentary plan drawn up. Then, according to Angelo's version of the affair, it was 'betrayed' by one of their number to the authorities in Rome before they were ready for its proper Canonical presentation within the rules of the Order. The previous autumn Wilfrid Blunt, whose interest in the project grew with its increasingly revolutionary flavour, provided the funds for Cuthbert and Angelo to take a petition to Rome to lay before the Father General and other Church leaders — for what he regarded as 'a good and timely undertaking which may well lead to noble things'.

17. The Welsh mountains near Pantasaph

All the same he was not surprised when, according to a later entry in his diary, they 'came back with a flea in their ears'. In Angelo's words the petition was rejected out of hand as 'altogether Utopian'.[1]

What the authorities do not seem to have realized was that by sending Angelo and Cuthbert to join Anselm at Pantasaph the original Crawley group was virtually reformed. The only difference was that Angelo was now taking the lead, with the result that largely due to his influence Francis became, as he put it, their chief 'centre of interest'.

At the Guest House he and Francis were of necessity often together. Nor was it, at first, only by necessity. Angelo was also a keen walker and they spent much of the summer days exploring further afield than Francis had been so far, along the coast and into the mountains. But it was in the evenings when they were joined by the rest of the group in Angelo's room that he remembered the poet most clearly. It only needed a deliberately provocative remark to arouse the eloquence for which, as for his philosophical insights, they shared in Anselm's admiration. Or if, as often happened, he was not in the mood for philosophy, they would begin by drawing him out on the niceties of cricket style and whatever controversial issues were raised

by the latest County Cricket scores. The difference was that whereas
to Francis these were matters worthy of attention in their own right,
for the rest they were the means for leading him on to more exalted
topics.

Angelo is still remembered at Pantasaph for his outstanding intellectual abilities. With their respective gifts he and Francis were
the natural leaders and Francis was undoubtedly flattered by the way
they would hang on his words. More important, he found much-
needed encouragement in the future they predicted for his poetry.
Most of the group, which now included several of the younger members of the Pantasaph community, could recite whole passages from
Poems. But according to Angelo it was the more recent unpublished
poetry they regarded most highly 'as heralding a new era for the
World and the Church'. In the symbolism of the 'Ode to the Setting
Sun' and 'From the Night of Forebeing' they saw the Church's liturgy
— and therefore the faith it expresses — open out into a new 'world
embrace':

> He had written Christ and His Advent into every sunrise and every sunset.
> He had invented a 'lawful' liturgical Sun-worship, dedicating to that first
> of symbols of Christ, the life and death and glory of the Worlds that drew
> their subsistence from the Sun. Thompson read into the seasonal move-
> ments of the Universe the story of a transcending liturgy of divine religion.

Here was an inspiration, a source of faith such as they could not now
find in the formal offices and prayers of the Church:

> In a sense, such poetry was a comfort and a compensation, for it incarna-
> ted Hope, as it were, in palpable form, and clothed it with such a raiment
> of natural beauty, that the God of Nature thereby, through the bow of His
> analogies from the process of the visible Creation, seemed to give new
> assurances of the truth of the promises of the God of Grace. The entire
> Creation, in this Thompsonian 'orchestra', acclaimed, in the felicity and
> appropriateness of its service, that this Hope of the World was true.

Yet in retrospect Angelo was not writing of himself so much as for
his companions. During that summer his changing outlook caused
him to have doubts above the enthusiasm he had at first shared with
them. In the ideas behind Patmore's writings he could still find the
promise 'of a really inclusive governance of God, including earth and
heaven in one'. On the other hand, by no means all of Thompson's
poetry celebrated this glorification of the material world as the hope
for the future of mankind. Patmore's world-view could accommodate
the kind of humanitarian religion he was beginning to look for.
Thompson's, he realized, could not:

> The 'Assumpta Maria', and several others, are filled with allusions to the
> approaching earthly 'days of promise'. But, in other poems, the balance of

earthly and supernal hope is delicately preserved, so that anyone can take the thought of such poetry to relate to a 'Here' or 'Hereafter' accordingly as he has the mind to do so ... For me, Francis Thompson was nine-tenths seer, whether he willed it or no, to one-tenth creator of the beauty of poetic fiction. In the end, however, my sympathies were curtailed, because the commonest of social reformers brought to me more of the only poetry I was really interested in, rather than a poet whose visions of world-atonement were chilled to death by sentences that hinted that they might permissibly relate to cloud-lands.[2]

On his side Thompson was not unaware of the trend of Angelo's ideas even from their earlier contact. Before they met again at Pantasaph he had attempted to explain his views on symbolism in a letter he probably did not send because it was too outspoken. In the notebook draft for it he doubted if he would succeed, since Angelo's 'extreme breadth & openness of mind' was so often at war with his 'materialistic prejudices'.[3]

Patmore's long-awaited visit to the Friary eventually took place towards the end of the summer. A few days after his arrival he wrote to his wife of the animated discussions arising from *Religio Poetae* that had begun already between himself, Francis and the friars. Anselm, he found, was in full agreement with his views on divine and human love. In private 'he went all the length with me in the honour of the nuptial embrace'. In company he might not be so open, but all the friars forming the group were following similar lines in their interpretations of his most recent ideas. Nor were their common interests always so exalted. 'The Fathers help me get through my cigarettes, of which I would like to have another consignment as soon as possible', he added. Francis proved to be 'a delightful companion, full of the best talk'.[4] Francis was in fact put entirely at ease by Patmore's obvious desire to take their friendship further. He wrote delightedly to Alice of how even at their first meeting on Patmore's arrival: 'He bore himself towards me with a nobility and magnanimity which are not of this age's stature'.[5]

As a member of the Capuchin Third Order Patmore had been to Pantasaph on several occasions for retreats and spiritual refreshment. He was permitted to lodge at the Friary instead of at the Guest House, although this time he came mainly for a holiday and to discuss the contents of his recent book. He was also planning a further collection of prose, to become *The Rod the Root and the Flower* and on this, too, he wanted to air his views where he was sure of support. For by now he was much too sure of them to feel the need for advice.

The discussions with the friars took place in the evenings and during the day various excursions were made into the surrounding countryside, when Francis was often a welcome and willing companion. Patmore particularly wished to visit St. Beuno, the Jesuit

House of Studies some twenty miles distant where in 1874 Gerard
Manley Hopkins came to follow the course in theology as part of his
training for the Society. When inviting Thompson to join him Patmore must have said something of his friendship with Hopkins, aware
perhaps of certain characteristics the two poets had in common.
Hopkins, he knew, had sought a new form of poetic expression to
celebrate God's presence in the created world. It was what first drew
him to the young Jesuit when they met ten years before and now he
found Thompson pursuing very similar aims. What he probably did
not recognize was the temperamental affinity between the two. The
priest in Hopkins was always at war with his aspirations as a poet.
He would have responded to Thompson's conflicting loyalties with
an understanding impossible now to Patmore, whose exalted views of
poetry and the role of the poet had advanced considerably further
since the time of their friendship. Nevertheless Patmore may well have
regretted that Hopkins' early death five years before meant the two
poets would never meet. He probably showed Thompson some of
Hopkins' poetry, which was to remain unknown until 1918. But in
1902 a short early lyric, 'Heaven haven', appeared in an anthology of
verse and was the subject of a special comment by Thompson in his
review. It is unlikely that the poem would have aroused his attention
unless he already knew others, only possible through his contact with
Patmore.[6]

Anselm accompanied them on the visit to St. Beuno. He recalled
how Patmore entertained them on the way with jokes and comic
stories that kept Francis in fits of laughter — an allusion to a side of
both poets that has so far gone unrecorded. When they arrived
they were shown round the library, their Jesuit hosts politely but persistently lamenting the lack of literary works. Still in the same mood,
and with characteristic impatience, Patmore delighted Francis and
Anselm by shocking the rest of the party with a sudden 'Oh, damn
literature', adding more restrainedly, 'we're interested in philosophy
and theology too you know'. One of their hosts, then a student with
secret literary leanings of his own, was surprised to find it was
Thompson rather than the much more renowned Patmore who most
impressed him. 'I longed to tell him how much I admired his work',
and, too shy to do so, he listened instead to Thompson's vivid account
of another recent visit to the shrine at Holywell. It was in fact Thompson who 'led the conversation' although this was not the main reason
for his impression:

> But my own mind was occupied with the man, rather than with what he
> said ... As men commonly understand the word there was no 'fascina-
> tion' about Thompson. There was something better. There was the *sancta
> simplicitas* of the true poet and the real child.[7]

Patmore could afford to give him the lead. The Jesuit student was unusual in finding Thompson the more outstanding of the two, for Patmore's prestige in Catholic circles was assured and his appearance alone impressed itself in any company as belonging to a personality confident in its capacity to dominate. At seventy-three he was still physically vigorous, fully equal to the long walks he and Francis took together that autumn. To passing observers on the hillside roads and mountain paths they must have seemed an oddly assorted couple, worthy of an extra stare. 'The real child' so quickly recognized in Thompson by the young Jesuit gave almost an appearance of one beside Patmore, his short slender frame barely reaching to the other's broad shoulders. The older man's distinguished features, the beaked nose and piercing eyes beneath eyebrows almost as bushy as the heavy moustache, were in equally marked contrast to Francis's straggly hair and vague beard. What they might not have noticed was that Patmore hardly needed to slacken his pace to match the stride that often surprised Francis's walking companions.

For the two poets their outward discrepancies were of no consequence. Patmore found in Thompson more than a ready listener. He was gaining a fresh intellectual vigour from their exchanges such as Thompson was more ready to admit on his side. According to a later notebook entry:

> What I put forth in a bud, he blew on & it blossomed. The contact of our ideas was dynamic: he reverberated my idea with such & so many echoes that it returned to me greater than I gave it forth. He opened it as you open an oyster, or placed it under a microscope, & showed me what it contained.[8]

Thompson was never to change in his estimation of Patmore as a poet of the first order and he continued to go a long way with Patmore's thought. He accepted the principle that was its central tenet. Human love was at once a manifestation of and a preparation for the divine love already existing between God and man, to be brought eventually to its perfected state in accordance with God's original intention before man chose to sin. He could also accept the place occupied by the Incarnation in this teaching as the highest form of the union between God and man for which human love was the symbolic counterpart. He was aware that much in this was not original to Patmore but derived from sources with which he was already familiar himself in the Christian mystical tradition and its application to human love as expounded by Swedenborg. The Christian mystics stressed the need for the soul's purification in preparing for the divine union when it would rise above its earthly limitations. Swedenborg countered the movement with one where God descends to inhabit and transform the physical life of man. Patmore's originality lay in his attempt to draw the two movements together within the context of traditional Catholic teaching, and his reputation in his later years rested largely on an apparent success that, to the more progressively minded, promised well for the future.

But during the evening discussions with Angelo and the others of the group, Thompson was becoming disturbed about the extent to which this promise was leading in directions which Patmore himself did not intend and with implications he failed to recognize. He was known to be an outspoken critic of the Church, but in *The Rod The Root and The Flower* he was to go much further than before. His earlier condemnations of the current Catholic outlook and its limitations now formed the basis for prophesies of the changes that must take place if Christianity itself was to survive. 'The foul, puritanical leaven of the Reformation has infected the whole of Christianity' he asserted, to the extent that it was now impossible to speak of the Incarnation in its fullest sense. As a result, 'the Catholic Church itself has been nearly killed by the infection', charging with impurity the 'human love which is the precursor and explanation and initiation into the divine'.[9]

Such were the views being aired for the benefit of the admiring circle at Pantasaph. But Thompson foresaw, as the others did not, how close they could come to the materialism he also feared behind Angelo's anticipations for the 'Church of the Future'. The extent to which he was correct is confirmed by a letter Angelo wrote to Patmore soon after the appearance of *The Rod The Root and the Flower*. Having praised the book highly, he compared its main argument with an essay he had recently completed on the Incarnation where, he told Patmore, 'I dwelt at some length on the real identity of the divine with the human and sensible', leading to a conclusion from which he quoted the key passage:

> The life of the Incarnation is never realized without that perfect content-ment in this present life which the God-man found or desired to find in His earthly surroundings. The ideal of Christianity is found in perceiving the presence of God here below, and in the attainment of beatitude and peace on this earth, which ought to be the Kingdom of God and perfectly like the Kingdom of Heaven.[10]

Accordingly, Angelo interpreted Patmore's definition of human love as coming closest to anticipating this perfected state.

From his first meeting with the friars at Crawley onwards, Thompson could never accept the notion of 'perfectibility' on these or any other terms. His preoccupation with the subject as discussed at Pantasaph resulted in another essay draft, written for his own purposes and not for publication. He gave it the significant title 'An Enemy hath done this', referring to the words spoken by the sower of good seed in the Gospel parable when he finds cockle growing in the same field. There is good seed in the hopes for the future held out by the group, where now a growth of falsehood has appeared. He agrees with Patmore 'that the fall of man was the fall of natural love', from which it can be said to follow that 'the re-establishment of man must be the re-establishment of natural love'. Yet for Thompson this is only one aspect of the Fall. In practice he sees the celibate state as the only one possessed of any degree of per-fectibility, still the surest and most direct way to unite the soul with God. For society in general to expect any such attainment through the marriage bond as defined by Patmore he finds no sign in the foresee-able future. From this he turns to the aspect that mattered most to him at the time, the role of the poet as he and Patmore had argued it out on their walks together:

> And the justification, I may add, of the Catholic poet, if God should think fit to make Poetry His servant (as since the New Law He has not done), would lie in this: that he should aid in the purification of that basis, natural love. Divine love is for higher prophets than he . . . [11]

Having denied the central tenet in Patmore's philosophy of love, he now denies the poet the vocation that, for Patmore, is inseparable from it. He was himself experiencing an opposition between two views of poetry — and all art — that has probably always existed in one form or another but not with the same urgency which it had received during the preceding century. The accepted Christian view of art as imitation of nature in order to give glory to nature's Creator was being openly challenged by those who, in the wake of the Romantic move-ment, professed art to be an expression of an individual creative in-stinct at once working on and transforming nature to meet its own ends.

For Thompson, the opposition came as a fear of the effect of 'poetic impulse' with at the same time a fear that 'thought' must strangle it. In his case the twofold fear was the product of his religious background and training. He might rebel against their limitations but the framework remained, at once constricting and sustaining his creative powers. It meant he could never be free from the constraint it imposed, the shadow first cast over the future by the Cross at Storrington. But the urge to break the constraint provided the main-spring for his inspiration, which if it could betray him into the false freedom of feverish rhetoric, could also raise him to the height of true poetic achievement. His study of symbolism and the symbolic lan-guage of the liturgy had seemed to open a higher way for further achievement — until he found it leading to a deceptive vision such as that put forward by Angelo and to which Patmore's philosophy could undoubtedly lead. It was a substitution of the symbol for the reality he first found represented by the evils inherent in Freemasonry. Then

the way was open instead for the kind of impulse, the mistaken ambition, that was a travesty of the 'poetic impulse' of Wordsworth and
Wordsworth's successors. The fear of the effect of following its lead
meant he could never follow Wordsworth's 'return to nature' with a
'return to God' that would satisfy his initial aspiration. And so, rather
than compromise, he determined to overcome the aspiration itself.
His future poetry was to show what it cost him to keep to his re-
solution.[12]

Thompson made no attempt to explain the difference in their
outlook to Patmore. He knew his friend too well and valued their
friendship too highly to risk challenging the other's authoritarian
confidence in his self-appointed role. And there still remained the
stimulus and satisfaction of their shared interests as poets.

There was more to the bond between them than this. Patmore's
infatuation — for so it must be called — for Alice Meynell went
much further in outward expression than Thompson's feeling for her,
even at its most crucial stage before he left London. As a result there
had been some cause for offense, the nature of which was never
divulged, and recently a rift had arisen between Patmore and the
Meynells causing him a pain for which he found some relief in calling
on Thompson's sympathy.

By now Thompson had worked through his relationship to an extent which Patmore could not achieve. Even in old age he remained
attractive to women as well as attracted by them. Alice felt herself on
much less secure ground with him than with Thompson, who was to
her still first and foremost 'my child'. Patmore could confide in
Thompson because he was aware that there was no rivalry such as he
felt towards Alice's other admirers. Of them he was bitterly and un-
reasonably jealous, pouring his sensitivities out in the series of letters
he wrote to Thompson after leaving Pantasaph. In his replies Thompson did his best to ease a misery he did not now share but could
understand. After all, at one time he himself had been just as unrea-
sonably jealous of Patmore.[13]

It was in fact Patmore's attitude during his visit that finally enabled him to overcome feelings which the other's more passionate
display forced him to see in a clearer light. According to an unusually
revealing notebook entry, while at Pantasaph Patmore elicited a promise from him which he later regarded as a turning point:

> I was decided. I thought I owed to him and to her whom I loved more
> than my love of her finally to uproot that love, to pluck away the last fibres
> of it, that I might be beyond treachery to my resolved duty. And at this
> second effort I finished what the first had left incomplete. The initial
> agony had really been decisive, and to complete the process needed only
> resolution . . .[14]

He called it 'a second effort', the first having been made on leaving London and apparently weakened by the Meynells' visit the previous spring. Their departure provoked the poignant sadness of 'In Her Paths', a lyric where he attempted to transfer his feeling for Alice to a sensuous appreciation of the natural beauties recently enhanced by her presence. But it was only an attempt. There had to be a direct confrontation of those feelings before the 'second effort' could succeed, and for this Patmore was undoubtedly responsible. The proof lies in a long unpublished poem, an ode of some two hundred lines which may have been written later but which refers back to a crisis point reached in the autumn of 1885. For the letters he exchanged with Patmore during the ensuing months show that by then the crisis was over. Nor would a third effort ever be needed.

'Love Divided Against Itself' follows the course of a love divided between physical attraction and the fear of its consequences to a re-conciliation, what would now be called a sublimation, on a spiritual plane:

> This labouring love is proved with child of fear;
> In strange antiphony,
> Unintermittantly,
> The love that bids 'come near',
> Is answered by the love that menaces, 'Withdraw!'

The pain of wresting such love from the heart can only be compared with the cleansing fire of Purgatory:

> Nay, and that fire, deterging and divine,
> Is but His love, which tortures more and more
> From dross the virgin ore,
> For as this lady's love yields unmeant pain,
> Through thine own integral stain,
> Though she of naught but tenderness is fain;
> So the high love where thou shalt lie immersed
> Avoidless searcheth out each smirch accursed,
> Assimilating thee with sharp constraint,
> Not of His choice, but thine,
> And thine is to thyself the cruelty,
> Since where dross is, flame may not but refine.[15]

For Thompson no other way was possible. There could be no future to a love which, for all his efforts at disguise, he now did not flinch from confronting as an 'amorous furnace' fired by lust.

An awareness of this dangerous drive behind his feelings shows in places in the 'Love in Dian's Lap' poems. But there are more distinct references in the shorter Sequence to which he gave the title 'Ultima'

and which, according to his autobiographical notes, was completed
towards the end of Patmore's visit. The poems mark a final sacrifice of
what emerges as a powerful physical desire: a sacrifice where, as in 'A
Holocaust', the pain can only be expressed through memories still
haunting him from the London streets:

> O God! Thou knowest if this heart of flesh
>   Quivers like broken entrails, when the wheel
> Rolleth some dog in middle street, or fresh
>   Fruit when ye tear it bleeding from the peel.
>
> 13–16

The second image says more about his sensibilities than almost anything else he wrote on the subject.

The sacrifice once made, there was no going back. But the pain
remained acute for some time. In a letter to Patmore referring to a
poem he was addressing to him, Thompson admitted it also brought
on 'a violant paroxysm of the A. M. malady' such as he had not
known since he determined to 'put my passion under my feet'.[16] The
poem, 'A Captain of Song', is a tribute to Patmore the poet. It pays
private homage to the man Thompson knew was still tormented by a
similar passion:

>   . . . a soul
> That hath to its own selfhood been most fell,
> And is not weak to spare:
> And lo! That hair
> Is blanchéd with the travel-heats of hell.
>
> 35–39

The letter is one of the series they exchanged after Patmore's
departure. Apart from his effusions concerning Alice Meynell, the
main topic was the interpretation of symbols they both still found was
their other chief point of contact. The following summer Thompson
wrote that he was working on a poem which 'outsiders' might regard
as derived from Patmore's views on the subject in *The Rod The Root and
The Flower*, then just published. To forestall any such reaction from
Patmore himself, he asserted what could not well be contradicted in
the light of earlier 'coincidences' of their ideas: 'To yourself such coincidence is explicable'.[17]

The poem, the 'Orient Ode', aims at reviving the theme of his
first Ode. But there is hardly a flicker of the earlier creative fire in its
consciously worked out liturgical symbolism. Thompson told Patmore
it was derived from the Easter liturgy, which a year before had inspired 'From the Night of Forebeing'. But the universal element in the
symbolism as he used it had all but disappeared, to be replaced by
an insistence on the sun symbol as confined within its conventional

Christian interpretation. Thompson was well aware of the failure and its cause. He had lost the daring that was essential to his earlier powers. 'I do not care to desecrate by weak handling the highest themes' he wrote to Patmore when sending him the completed poem.[18] There was, however, a reassurance in one sense in Patmore's reply. He was happy, he said, to find the similarities between their ideas, 'but the visions could not be true were they quite the same, and no one can really see anything but his own visions'.[19] Thompson knew better than his friend how true the words were and, beneath the surface 'coincidences', how different their visions had become.

In his letter to Patmore on the composition of the 'Orient Ode', Thompson apologised for a recent break in their correspondence due, he said, to another of his attacks of 'inertia' and 'nervous prostration'. The recurrence of symptoms similar to those described by Elizabeth Blackburn the year before coincided with the publication, against his wishes, of 'Sister Songs' in book form. At the end of the letter he wrote of the appearance of his 'ill-destined volume' as 'a bad business and something I cannot mend'.

The suggestion was first made in the full flush of the Meynells' enthusiasm for the general reception which *Poems* had received. They must keep Francis in the public eye now, and in their view 'Poems Wing to Wing', as 'Sister Songs' was still then called, would undoubtedly do so. The intimate family connections with the twin poems blinded them to the faults in structure and the linguistic excesses the critics had already selected as Thompson's main weaknesses. He knew this and strongly opposed the proposal — which until the end of the year was taken no further. Then, in November, Angelo's departure from Pantasaph was used as an opportunity for the two to travel to London together, Francis not having been at Palace Court since he met Patmore there just a year before.[20] Patmore left the Friary in October and life looked like being very dull through the winter — the more so since the Briens had given up their charge of the Guest House and their removal necessitated a change of lodgings. At Ivy Cottage, where he was to remain in the care of the village postmistress until the next summer, there was none of the easy intimacy he valued from the Brien family. So he welcomed the invitation to stay on in London over Christmas, sharing in the celebrations with the Meynells as on that first Christmas, when his gift of the 'Offering to Two Sisters' was in effect his acknowledgement of all he owed to their parents. The occasion was used to raise the subject of publication again, with the result that his persisting sense of obligation overcame his better judgement and he consented.

There were problems from the first. John Lane had his own

doubts and was only persuaded to publish when Meynell offered to print a limited edition privately, so providing Lane with type and proof sheets. These few copies were still called 'Songs Wing to Wing' and, after Thompson's return to Wales, it took a tedious exchange of letters before his alternative title of 'Sister Songs' was finally accepted for Lane's publication.[21]

A more troublesome incident arose over the proofs. It is impossible to be sure if Thompson was correct in asserting that Meynell failed to provide him with a complete set and then so delayed sending the missing sheets as to cause Lane much inconvenience. But so he believed, writing Lane an angry letter blaming 'the broken reed of Palace Court' for the delay and with the advice: 'for heaven's sake in future do not depend on Palace Court sending me anything if you wish for expedition and the avoidance of misunderstanding'.[22]

It was treated as a 'misunderstanding' and the affair patched up. But it was also the first serious instance of Francis's growing frustration at his dependence on the Meynells. Until now it had been mainly due to the need for replacements of boots and trousers and such like necessities. But the professional failure, as he saw it, to provide him with copies of his own work was another matter. His anger would have increased if he knew how Meynell took the responsibility of refusing the frontispiece prepared for *Sister Songs* by Houseman. Like the one for *Poems* it was in poor taste and Meynell was right in his decision — but not in neglecting to consult Thompson beforehand.[23]

Instead there was another 'misunderstanding' with Lane himself. An Agreement signed by Thompson in May apparently did not reach the publisher and a second one sent by Lane a month later varied in some of its details. Thompson's letter pointing out the discrepancies politely but firmly shows him well able to look after his affairs. In addition, Lane's warning of the book's doubtful reception did not surprise him even if it was the first he knew of Lane's disagreement with the Meynells on the subject:

> I am not a business man, but my own judgement was against the public printing of the poem until I had a more assured position as a writer; though the Meynells, and I understood you, thought otherwise. Consequently I had already considered the advisability of following it by a collection of new poems, which I have already commenced to revise for that purpose. I am happy to find that your opinion coincides with mine.[24]

Thompson had grounds for feeling he was being kept in the dark by such lack of communication. Whatever the future for his poetry he was still concerned for his reputation as a poet, and felt threatened by an action which he now found Lane saw in the same light. Nor is there any reason to doubt that because of this he was thinking of collecting the work done over the past two years for a further publi-

18. Creccas Cottage, Pantasaph. The wing on the left has been added in recent years

cation. But the letter was written in June 1895, the month *Sister Songs* appeared, and at the time the proposal was not much more than an attempt to offset the expected reactions from the critics. He told Lane that his health was too uncertain at present for any definite decision and although his real uncertainty was for the future of his poetry, it was more than an excuse. The symptoms he described to Patmore seem to have been connected with the stomach upsets to which he was also prone and he had to ask Wilfrid for a repeat of the homoeopathic medicine prescribed by his father for the same trouble when he was at Storrington.[25]

Towards the end of the summer, however, several occurrences led him to make up his mind. In the first place the Briens, now settled into their new home just over the hill from the Friary, asked him to rejoin them. He was delighted, and by mid-August had made the move to Creccas Cottage where, for no extra charge, he was given both a bedroom and a sitting room. Furthermore, the reviews of *Sister Songs* were no more discouraging than he expected, the general opinion being that the poems possessed an emotional and aesthetic appeal to offset their undeniable faults.[26]

The Meynells, however, were disappointed. Whatever their personal view they now realized that *Sister Songs* was still an example of Francis's early work and a publication of more recent poetry was important in the light of these reactions. In September Wilfrid made a short visit to Pantasaph to discuss the proposal he knew had been put to Lane. But Francis was not going to be persuaded this time. He remained firmly non-committal and his decision was largely due to a much more unlikely incident that took place soon afterwards.

There were plenty of local traditions of ghosts and haunted houses and that autumn a crop of strange appearances occurred around Pantasaph. Like a good many others, Thompson claimed to have had an encounter of the kind, at a derelict house on the Feilding estate with the improbable name of Pickpocket Hall. Rumours of the haunting reached the owner's younger brother Everard Feilding who, having a special interest in such matters, brought a friend with him for a week's holiday in order to investigate. There had been an early snowfall and the two spent several cold and unsuccessful nights at the Hall — after which, hearing that the poet Francis Thompson was living nearby and had actually seen the ghost, they decided to ask for his co-operation. That evening they called at Creccas Cottage, to be told the poet was still in bed. When they called later he was still not up. So they composed a letter which, according to Feilding's later account, was intended to appeal to the kind of poet they imagined the author of *Poems* to be — both were already admirers of Thompson's work. But they ended it on a different note, with an invitation to 'breakfast' at 9.30 the next evening to confer with them and their unseen companion at the Hall. This was the kind of humour at his own expense which Thompson enjoyed and at the appointed time he turned up 'and breakfasted while we supped'. Feilding's memory of that night was not of any ghost but of a very real personality, and very different from the poet as they had imagined him to be:

> We said at once to one another: 'This is not the man to whom we wrote that letter'. For, instead of parables in polysyllables and a riot of imagery, we found simplicity and modesty and a manner which would have been almost commonplace if it had not been so sincere. But the charm and interest of his talk grew with the night, and it was already dawn when, the ghost long since forgotten, we escorted him back across the snow to his untimely lunch.[27]

Thompson did, however, describe to them his own encounter with the ghost as an experience 'which had charged his body like a battery so that he felt thunderstorms in his hair'. Not that he took the matter at all seriously himself. In a later letter to Alice he referred to the night at Pickpocket Hall when the ghost had eluded them because 'as he was a racing man, he probably found our conversation too literary to put off his incognito'.[28]

The 'conversation' on that strange night was much were important than any ghost could have made it. The sudden intimacy with the two strangers as they huddled in the shadows of the ruins loosened Thompson's tongue and he confided his gathering doubts and flickering hopes about his poetry as he could not have done in any other company or surroundings. It actually helped that neither Feilding nor his friend could follow him very far. As they saw it he should carry on writing poetry because he was a poet, without looking to the outcome. Their uncomplicated encouragement opened the way ahead for him. It was in effect a challenge for which, on reflection afterwards, he could find no excuse to avoid the struggle he knew would be entailed in consequence. He owed it to those who, like his companions that night, admired and respected his work so far. And if the outcome was to be an apologia for a reputation that must end almost before it had begun, so be it.

Thompson was no longer being called upon for contributions to *Merry England* since the last issue had appeared earlier that year, mainly due to Meynell's increasing responsibilities on the Board of Directors for Burns and Oates, the leading Catholic publishing house. He needed every extra hour it allowed him during the winter that lay ahead. 'Shut up for last book about Nov.' was how he recorded the long dark months of 'night & day work'. The painstaking revision of existing poems could be as taxing as the composition of new ones. 'The whole book I look back to as a bad dream' he told Alice the following summer, 'so unexampled in my previous experience was the labour I bestowed upon it'.[29]

Much of the contents of *New Poems* was in fact drawn from poems already written, eight of which had appeared in *Merry England* or elsewhere. But apart from those written expressly for it, the title was justified by the extent of revision to which the rest was subjected. The many reworked drafts show how in each case Thompson was aiming at economy and clarity. Most of the changes suggest an advance in poetic sensibility without any significant loss of the original vitality. But there are places where the extent of the problem confronting him in this respect is clear from the comparative failure to transfer the earlier virility to the more refined version. To take a representative example from the 'Ode to the Setting Sun', the poem that received the most exhaustive revision of any, the following lines appear in the text as printed in *Merry England*:

> Thou sway'st thy sceptred beam
>   O'er all Earth's broad loins teem,
> She sweats thee through her pores to verdurous spilth.
>   Thou art light in her light,
>   Thou art might in her might,
> Fruitfulness in her fruit, and foizon in her tilth.

On their first reading of the poem, the Meynells had taken exception to the obscurity of the last line, defended then by Thompson on account of its Middle English origins. Now he replaced the whole passage with:

> Thou sway'st thy sceptred beam
> O'er all delight and dream,
> Beauty is beautiful but in thy glance:
> And like a jocund maid
> In garland-flowers arrayed,
> Before thy ark Earth keeps her sacred dance.
>
> 150–154

Despite the fine imagery of the last line there is a sultry 'earthiness' in the lines as first written which does not survive the revision. The whole revision process was aimed at modifying over-exuberance or needless obscurity, but there was a notable exception where another motive was at work in directing the change. In the Prelude to the 'Ode to the letting Sun' he deleted the lines describing the sunset scene, substituting verses where the immediate response is modified by an objectivity born of the years between then and now. Then, the Cross had first appeared as part of the gathering shadow cast over the end of the poem in the After Strain. Now, as he sought to revive the experience of that evening, the Cross rises on the scene at the very start:

> Yet, in this field where the Cross planted reigns,
> I know not what strange passion bows my head
> To thee, whose great command upon my veins
> Proves thee a god to me not dead, not dead!
>
> For worship it is too incredulous,
> For doubt — oh, too believing-passionate!
> What wild divinity makes my heart thus
> A fount of most baptismal tears? — Thy straight
>
> Long beam lies steady on the Cross. Ah me!
> What secret would thy radiant finger show?
> Of thy bright mastership is this the key?
> Is *this* thy secret, then? And is it woe?
>
> 17–28

Nor, since he had now written the sonnet 'Sad Semele', could he allow the lines to remain where at the birth of his poetry, he had then been so passionately convinced that

> ... Song is the true deathless babe that's born
> When fire embraces the soul's Semele.

— and the lines were deleted.

By far the most important section he collected together under the title 'Sight and Insight'. In his own grouping it consists of five existing poems and seven new ones written during the months of preparation. Two others were added by Meynell as editor of the *Collected Works* — and so, in all later editions — with no acknowledgement or explanation. 'Carmen Genesis' is little more than a series of commonplace reflections on the process of poetic creativity and 'Ad Castitatem' has been put together from unfinished notebook drafts. In them Thompson was exploring the idea of chastity as a form of desire and no less intense in the emotions it evokes. To print the scattered drafts as a considered whole is even less defensible than to insert the result among the 'Sight and Insight' poems where, as with 'Carmen Genesis', it detracts from the intentions behind the group as Thompson put it together.[30]

The first poem, 'The Mistress of Vision', was composed to set the pattern and overall direction of the rest. It has been subjected to two main interpretations, both equally false. The attempt to identify the 'Mistress' with the Blessed Virgin and the theme as deliberately 'mystical' is as far from Thompson's aim as the second view of the poem as being derived from esoteric sources borrowed from Patmore.[31]

The poem's twenty-six stanzas, of very unequal length, move uneasily from dream fantasy to an ideal that poetry cannot attain. The 'Lady of fair weeping' in her remote and secret garden is at first a Shelleyan creation, a fantasy woven by the child of the Shelley essay who, in so many respects, is Thompson himself. The first nine stanzas revive his childhood dream world where the medieval ideal of beauty is faintly coloured, no more, by mystical associations drawn from the 'Song of Songs'. Yet because that world gave rise to Thompson's first poetic awareness it forms part of the overall movement of his poetry which is the theme of the poem, recurring throughout as the 'dream lands' of Luthany and Elenore.

The theme becomes more explicit as the Lady takes on the attributes of the sun symbolism that had aroused his poetry to life:

> Light most heavenly-human —
> Like the unseen form of sound,
> Sensed invisibly in tune, —
> Like a sun-derivéd stole
> Did inaureole
> All her lovely body round
> Lovelily her lucid body with that light was interstrewn.
>
> 29–36

There is a distant but distinct echo here from the play of the unseen musicians on the evening the 'Ode to the Setting Sun' was begun.

The dream world then becomes one of primeval symbols where

the Lady's song is of earthquake and thunder and voices speaking of
'ancient secrets'. But the singing has another message, a warning that
now recalls the shadow cast from the Calvary in the Field of the Cross
on that same evening:

> On Golgotha there grew a thorn
> Round the long pre-figured Brows.
> Mourn, O mourn!
> For the vine have we the spine? Is this all the Heaven allows?
>
> 92–95

The vine wreath, the symbol of pagan joy, has become a crown of
thorns in the realization that the whole movement of his poetic aspirations has been a false flight of Icarus:

> From the fall precipitant
> These dim snatches of her chant
> Only have remainéd mine; —
> That from spear and thorn alone
> May be grown
> For the front of saint or singer any divinizing twine.
>
> 107–112

The Lady's song changes to short sharp lines of command based on
the principles of Christian asceticism:

> 'Pierce thy heart to find the key;
> With thee take
> Only what none else would keep;
>
> . . .
>
> Plough thou the rock until it bear;
> Know, for thou else couldst not believe;
> Lose, that the lost thou may'st receive;
> Die, for none other way canst live.
>
> 125–127:
> 134–137

No flight of imagination or display of poetic 'impulse' here. The
contrast is deliberate, the uncompromising paradoxes pointing the
only way ahead when poetic sight has brought an insight beyond his
powers to express. The way takes in the Wordsworthian vision of the
'one life' but must pass to a further region beyond the reach of that
vision:

> 'When to the new eyes of thee
> All things by immortal power
> Near or far
> To each other linkèd are,

> That thou canst not stir a flower
> Without troubling of a star;
> When thy song is shield, and mirror
> To the fair snake-curléd Pain,
> When thou dar'st affront her terror
> That on her thou may'st attain
> Perséan conquest; seek no more
> O seek no more!
> Pass the gate of Luthany, tread the region Elenore.
>
> 149–162

The vision of the one life is only a partial revelation of a sacramental union between earth and heaven, the flower inseparable from the star in the eternal vision of their Creator. This he had apprehended in his prose writings as well as through his poetry. But to partake in that vision was, as he had feared from the first, beyond the reach of his poetic powers. He knew that the only way ahead for his poetry was one of acceptance, of reflecting and absorbing the shadows in the mirror that again reappear from his schoolboy essay as the fears generated in his childhood years deepen the shadow of the Cross over the years of his life as a poet.

The Lady of the poem, who is the spirit of poetry in the message it has for him, becomes now the mistress of his vision whereas before she has been a temptress to a false paradise. But there is no promise of poetic achievement when the mists surrounding the dream lands of Luthany and Elenore are dispelled, revealing the way to a truly heavenly vision. Nor will there be any precedent among the 'holy poets' on whom he has so often drawn in the past — 'holy' as those who once dedicated their gifts to the service of Christ and His Church, and as those of recent times who have followed Wordsworth in a dedication they saw as no less sacred:

> When she shall unwind
> All those wiles she wound about me,
> Tears shall break from out me,
> That I cannot find
> Music in the holy poets to my wistful want, I doubt me!
>
> 183–187

All he can hope will remain to him will be 'the ghost of the rose' of his poetic promise, raised from the ashes of its first blooming:

> And from out its mortal ruins the purpureal phantom blows
>
> 177

Throughout the poem Thompson is more concerned with the meaning for himself than with its outward expression as he juxtaposes the many threads that had woven the pattern of his poetic life so far. But for this same reason it possesses an importance in his poetic development that merits its place at the start of the 'Sight and Insight' group — where the achieving of his new 'insight' leads to a drastic denial of what he sees as his wrongly directed poetic 'sight' so far.

'By Reason of Thy Law' takes its title from the 'De Profundis', the sixth of the seven penitential psalms and often recited as a prayer for the dead. 'By reason of thy law I have waited for thee O lord' is the cry of the repentant sinner who knows that the 'law' which punishes does so in order to release him from guilt. According to Thompson's application to his present condition:

> From food of all delight
> The heavenly Falconer my heart debars,
> And tames with fearful glooms
> The haggard to His call;
> Yet sometimes comes a hand, sometimes a voice withal,
> And she sits meek now, and expects the light.
>
> 21–26

The cost of the submission is reserved for the companion poem, 'The Dread of Height'. Here it forces him to appeal against such a denial of his past aspirations:

> How shall my mouth content it with mortality?[13]

— while at the same time he now knows that to seek further is to meet with the fate of Icarus:

> For low they fall whose fall is from the sky
>
> 56

What then can be preserved from those early expectations?

> Lower than man, for I dreamed higher,
> Thrown down, by how much I aspire
> And damned with drink of immortality?
>
> 63–65

The agonizing behind the question has to be measured against the mood of mingled fear and hope in the 'Ode to the Setting Sun' where 'the restless windward stirrings' warning of future pain also promised a 'brood of immortality' born from it. This is the starkest of all the 'Sight and Insight' poems, ending with a recurrence of the falcon imagery as the enforced submission wrings from him the cry:

> Ah, for a heart less native to high Heaven!
> A hooded eye, for jesses and restraint,
> Or for a will accipitrine to pursue! —
>
> 89–91

In the last poem of the group, 'Retrospect' speaks only the direct truth as he must accept it, stripped of imagery and with the sun now the focal point for failure:

> Alas, and I have sung
> Much song of matters vain,
> And a heaven-sweetened tongue
> Turned to unprofiting strain
> Of vacant things — which though
> Even so they be, and throughly so,
> It is no boot at all for thee to know
> But babble and false pain.
>
> What profit if the sun
> Put forth his radiant thews,
> And on his circuit run,
> Even after my device, to this and to that use;
> And the true Orient, Christ,
> Make not His cloud of thee?
> I have sung vanity,
> And nothing well devised.

                                        1–15

But at the end there comes a change. If this is where the insight over and above the poet's sight has led him it could also lead further:

> Therefore I do repent
> That with religion vain,
> And misconceivéd pain,
> I have my music bent
> To waste on bootless things its skiey-gendered strain:
> Yet shall a wiser day
> Fulfil more heavenly way,
> And with approvéd music clear this slip.

                                        35–42

There is more here than a vague hope for a compromise such as it might appear. With the sense of failure there went another much less defined sense that another age would see the failure differently: when 'A wiser day' would permit the freedom to explore beyond time and space without condemning it as a trespass into mysteries there concealed. The nearest Thompson came to expressing it was in two drafts for a long unfinished poem apparently begun during the winter he was working on *New Poems*. Both drafts were given the significant title 'Incipit Canticum Novum' and both were composed in the epic style of Old English poetry he had first used in 'A Judgement in Heaven', adapting the rhythm to that of blank verse. It was a choice well suited

to the heroic theme of a spiritual battle and to the language and
imagery borrowed from the Old Testament prophecies.

Underlying many incoherent and incomplete lines, a distinct
theme emerges for each text which, given Thompson's state of mind
when they were written, connects the one with the other. In the first
the poet doubts if a call to prophesy a coming cataclysm in the name
of God comes instead from Lucifer, the devil concealed as an angel
of light. The result is a psychomachia or battle of the soul, the text
breaking off before the outcome. The conflict is first provoked when
the symbolic tree Igdrasil is presented as the starting point for the
poet's prophecy, the validity of which for this end he cannot accept.
Bearing in mind Patmore's use of the same symbol in the review of
Poems which Thompson regarded as a 'turning point' for him, its re-
appearance in this context and at this time cannot be mere coincidence. Patmore had taken the tree, which reaches to heaven from its
roots in hell, as the model for Thompson to follow in the twofold
movement of his poetry. This, he asserted, would confirm the poetry
as possessed of the prophetic spirit of the true poet — a spirit which
Thompson's poet is driven to deny.

The second draft is based on the story of the Flood with the Ark
being given its traditional application to the 'tempest tossed' Church
in the world. The dove sent out over the waters of the world is here the
poet of the future, a divinely appointed emissary whose mission is to
proclaim a new age dawning over the waters of strife that have submerged the old. But, for the poet of this poem, the time has not come
to fulfil his role and he is driven back to the Ark, wounded and fearful
as if from some undefined conflict. Nor does he bear any olive branch
promising peace. Yet before the text breaks off he is awaiting a further commission, for which he will be endowed with the attributes of
the falcon rather than those of the dove:

> Surely not for nothing hast Thou tempered my soul,[x] in fire and
>   in running tears
> But Thou hoodest mine eyes like a falcon,[x] that I prey not till
>   Thou point me the quarry.
> Stay me, and break me, and bit me,[x] that I tremble not when
>   Thou bridle me for war.[32]

Here the image of the falcon reaches out beyond the restraint and
frustration in 'From Reason of Thy Law' and 'The Dread of Height'.
Fragmented and confused as they are, in these drafts Thompson
comes closer than ever before to giving poetic form to his sense that
another age could bring a release and a new poetic mission. And in
places there is a strangely 'prophetic' note where the Flood appears as
a cataclysm to come before that age could emerge.

The poem went too deep for Thompson to be able to take it further than the drafts setting its theme. At the same time the connections with the ideas behind the poems he was writing for 'Sight and Insight' gave the whole group an even greater importance for him, far beyond the contents planned for the rest of the book. Apart from their meaning for him, Thompson knew that these twelve poems formed the most important section of the volume as he was putting it together. The best of the poems composed to add to those he had in reserve were the lyrics for the section of 'Miscellaneous Poems' where he confined himself, as in 'A Question' and 'Field Flower' to 'the simple things that are the wise'. But they did not attempt to equal, let alone surpass, 'The Poppy' or 'Daisy', while 'To a Child' fell far short of the other poems to children included in his first volume. Neither 'A Narrow Vessel' nor the 'Ultima' Sequence, completed at the time of Patmore's departure, could compare with 'Love in Dian's Lap'.

There was one exception, probably due to turning up 'Love Declared' and adding it to the 'Narrow Vessel' Sequence. Otherwise there is no accounting for the appearance of 'Memorat Memoria' among the 'Miscellaneous Poems' — lines addressed to the street girl after an interval of ten years with no lessening of the intensity of his feeling towards her.[33] He had always believed he owed the first promise of his poetic career to her love and now that the promise would remain unfulfilled, her memory is tainted by an acute sense of betrayal. And because the promise has been thwarted by the religious principles he could not evade, the betrayal overlays an even more acute sense of guilt, injecting sin into the pity and tenderness of his remembered feeling for her:

> You are neither two nor one — I would you were one or
>   two,
> For your awful self is embalmed in the fragrant self I
>   knew:
>
> . . .
>
> Naught here but I and my dreams shall know the secret of
>   this thing: —
> For ever the songs I sing are sad with the songs I never
>   sing,
> Sad are sung songs but how more sad the songs we dare
>   not sing!
> Ah, the ill that we do in tenderness, and the hateful horror
>   of love!
> It has sent more souls to the unslaked Pit than it ever will
>   draw above.
> I damned you, girl, with my pity, who had better by far
>   been thwart,

> And drave you hard on the track to hell, because I was
>   gentle of heart.
>
> 5–6
> 9–15

The poem ends with a question which, like the songs he dare not sing,
he dare not answer:

> My child! what was it that I sowed, that I so ill should reap?
> You have done this to me. And I, what I to you? — It lies with
>   sleep.
>
> 21

Then, as the long winter months gave way to spring on the
Pantasaph hills, 'The Cloud's Swan Song' became in effect a requiem
for the unfulfilled promise:

> A lonely man, oppressed with lonely ills,
> And all the glory fallen from my song,
> Here do I walk among the windy hills;
> The wind and I keep both one monotoning tongue.
>
>   . . .
>
> For 'tis an alien tongue, of alien things,
> From all men's care, how miserably apart!
> Even my friends say: 'Of what is this he sings?'
> And barren is my song, and barren is my heart.
>
> For who can work, unwitting his work's worth?
> Better, meseems, to know the work for naught,
> Turn my sick course back to the kindly earth
> And leave to ampler plumes the jetting tops of thought.
>
> 5–8: 13–20

But at the end there is a change, when the otherwise commonplace lines
point significantly towards the future. If he cannot know 'his work's
worth' there still remains the lesson of the passing cloud in fulfilling
its ephemeral destiny. If the poet faces defeat there remains the determination of the man to fight for what life can still mean to him —
to see a pattern behind the battle whatever the outcome. In short

> To make song wait on life, not life on song.
>
> 99

The work on *New Poems* was completed with a sense of relief strong
enough to bring a flash of expectancy, at least for the earlier work. 'I
have great hopes when I look at the poems as a collection' he wrote to
Meynell at the beginning of April. But they had faded by the time he
sent the manuscript the following month:

From the higher standpoint, I have gained, I think, in art and chastity of style; but have greatly lost in fire and glow. It is time that I was silent. This book carries me quite as far as my dwindling strength will allow; and if I wrote further in poetry, I should write down my own fame.[34]

The hopes faded the sooner on account of an event that took place between the writing of the two letters. On 9 April the news reached him that Dr Thompson had contracted pneumonia and was dying. The same day he set off for Ashton, arriving too late to see his father and with more than the distress of the funeral to face. 'My stepmother made it very bitter for me' he wrote afterwards to Wilfrid, apologising, typically, for having lost the return half of his ticket and therefore in need of an additional refund. (In the emergency the fare was presumably supplied by the friars). He had, however, been able to see Mary again at her convent in Manchester, 'looking the merest girl still, and sweeter than ever'. It was ten years since they last met and on her side she had to admit to him she found him 'very changed and worn'. It was the same at Ashton, where, he added: 'Everyone made the same flattering remark'.[35]

Long afterwards Mary wrote to Wilfrid recalling the meeting and the pain which he told her he felt at the reaction from his family and friends:

Poor boy! He said then, he could see his old friends evidently were unable to shake off their former notion of him or believe him changed. God knows all: & it is a mercy, for there is much misunderstanding in this world.[36]

Whatever their 'misunderstanding', he had the consolation of knowing that there was a better understanding between him and his father during the past eighteen months. Since coming to Pantasaph he had wanted a reconciliation and been greatly hurt when, as early as September 1893, he heard that Dr Thompson had been on holiday at Rhyl, a few miles away, without attempting to contact him. Probably the presence of his stepmother on this occasion was the reason, for the next year they did meet with no unwillingness on his father's part. Again it was mainly due to John Carroll. Although since his appointment as Coadjutor Bishop of Shrewsbury he was still living at Stalybridge, he saw Francis on several occasions when he visited Pantasaph. Knowing there was now goodwill on both sides, he invited Francis to stay a few days in order that the two should meet. There are no details of the reconciliation except that it took place. In October 1894 Mrs Thompson's brother, Canon George Richardson, wrote to Wilfrid: 'Frank has been over lately to see his father'. Mary knew of it and years later told Danchin 'my father & brother were reconciled not long before my father's death'.[37]

Since the appearance of *Poems*, several sensational accounts were circulating as to the poet's early career. Rumours reaching the ready ears of journalists resulted in portrayals of Dr Thompson as the cause for his son's sufferings on the streets and drug addiction. Thompson found it hard enough to put up with this on his own account, but he was even more anxious for his father. At least this was put right when they met and more was no doubt said as well. Afterwards, discussing Francis's medical training with a close friend, the doctor exclaimed 'if only the lad had let me know'.[38]

The fact that Dr Thompson's will made no provision for his son may have been because, in his view, it would be no service to Francis to open the way to a return to his addiction. It was more likely due to his wife's influence. In answer to an enquiry on the subject from Wilfrid, Francis commented on it in the letter enclosed with the manuscript of *New Poems*. There was nothing coming to him because, according to Mary, 'There was nothing to leave'. It would have made no difference, for, he added: 'If there had been, my stepmother would have seen that none of it came to me'.[39]

Wilfrid had good reason for asking. Difficulties over the payment of royalties on *Poems* were increasing since the publication of *Sister Songs* last year. It was a delicate situation, for Wilfrid controlled all Francis's financial affairs, and lately there were added complications in the withdrawal of *New Poems* from John Lane. Either during the ghost-watching night or later, Everard Feilding asked Francis what he felt about his work being published by Lane, associated as he now was with 'a certain kind of literature'. Francis quoted his words when sending the manuscript, confirming doubts raised by Wilfrid himself some months before.[40]

Feilding was reminding Francis of the crisis over the *Yellow Book*, published by Lane, that took place only a short time before the appearance of *Sister Songs*. In April 1895 the journal had suddenly achieved doubtful fame in connection with the trial of Oscar Wilde, who at the time of his arrest was said to have had a copy under his arm. Meynell was then partly instrumental in persuading Lane to exclude Beardsley, the chief offender where the journal's reputation was concerned, from any contributions to future issues. How much Thompson knew of all this in far-off Pantasaph is uncertain. But he knew enough to agree to Meynell's proposal to find another publisher.[41]

There were other reasons. In the same letter Thompson stipulated that the new publisher must agree to his own proposals as to the contents and presentation of his next book, implying that Lane had made conditions with which he did not agree. Then there was the continuing vexation over the royalties which Thompson attributed to Lane's negligence — or even dishonesty. Meynell had no difficulty in getting the manuscript of *New Poems* accepted by Constable. Writing to Patmore of his satisfaction with the arrangement, Thompson added:

> I am glad to be out of Lane's hands, because I came to the conclusion two years ago that he was financially unsound. Moreover he was guilty of some sharp practices with me last year, and I vowed to myself I would give him a lesson that not every poet was safe game for that.[42]

According to Thompson, such 'practices' continued after the withdrawal of the manuscript. Soon afterwards he wrote again to Patmore describing Lane as 'most unreliable and dilatory' in the payment of royalties on his previous books. It meant, at the time, that he could not accept an invitation to visit Lymington, 'tied down here to the imperative writing of pot-boilers'.[43] Even so, he did not give full vent to his feelings until much later when, having built up a lasting relationship with Arthur Doubleday, a partner at Constable's, he wrote to him of Lane as 'a scoundrel of the first water' whose 'barefaced rascality' he would not record on paper. 'If Mrs Meynell's books were not at his mercy, I would have insisted on strong measures being taken against him'.[44]

This letter eventually came into the possession of an American collector to whom Meynell, no doubt fearing the consequences for himself as well as for Thompson if the accusations were made known, wrote an explanation. The tone of the letter might reflect badly on Thompson for having written it, but if it was believed it could reflect badly on himself as the poet's 'banker' for having allowed such a situation to develop. Meynell's explanation is worth quoting at length, indicating as it does the way in which he viewed their relationship:

> Of course we, knowing that F. T. had occasional fits of perversion as to the doings & motives of his fellows, placed no importance on such misjudgments. They were for the most part few & far between, — & were, if I may judge by one case, the subject of his speedy regrets & penitences — even to tears. You can easily imagine my invidious position as his banker — receiving, of course by arrangement with him, his royalties, which were only a small contribution to his expenses, & having to become the stern parent when he was in danger of an opium bout if his purse permitted. I write to you thus frankly about things no doubt better forgotten, & *fairest* forgotten, so minute a part were they of his general character & conduct. Personally I could never bear him the faintest grudge for being myself, during a period of perhaps 20 days out of a close friendship of nearly 20 years, the mark of his utterly misjudged resentments.[45]

There was more Meynell could have added if it had suited his purposes. He had been well aware of the situation and of Thompson's anxiety as to the delay in receiving the royalties. In a note to Lane written in September 1897, he urged the payments and the explanation for the delay which he knew Thompson had asked for repeatedly. According to Thompson, money which should have been made over at six-monthly intervals had not been payed for the past year-and-a-half. This was not contradicted by Meynell's note:

> When your clerk goes into the matter in this detail, as promised in the agreement, the Poet believes that he will easily find out a serious error in the amount of sales already requested.
> It is very hard on the Poet to keep him waiting so long or you may be sure I wd. not bother you.[46]

By the time Thompson's letter of accusation against Lane came to light it must have seemed to Meynell to be in the interests of all concerned to excuse it on the grounds which he gave. But in so doing he was withholding information which would have done more justice to Thompson's complaint, however unfortunately it was expressed.

In retrospect the estrangement to which Meynell referred as taking place between himself and Francis is more important. It must have taken place at the start of the trouble with Lane, while Francis was still at Pantasaph and his financial affairs still under Meynell's control.

It was in effect an eruption of the underlying frustration which Francis had felt since his first grateful dependence began to give way to a natural desire to manage his own life. The desire was no less valid because he was often unpractical and remiss on the rare occasions when he did so — as with the loss of the return ticket from Ashton. It could be said that he had too little practice in such matters.

Wilfrid could not see this. To him as to Alice Francis was still the 'child' who, unlike their own family, would always need their 'parental' guidance. At one time it was largely a protection against any damage to the relationship between the three of them due to Francis's feelings towards Alice, and to some extent it continued as a safeguard. But for Wilfrid the overruling consideration now was that, in his view, financial independence would bring a temptation to return to his addiction from which Francis must be protected. In this there was a tendency to dominate the affairs of others that is often latent in personalities who, in their earlier years, possess the genuine desire to help those apparently weaker or less fortunate than themselves. Although it was as yet barely noticeable apart from his dealings with Francis's business arrangements, it meant that Wilfrid also failed to recognise another and even more important need — the need for Francis to be allowed to face the temptation should it arise and come to his own terms with it. Nor could he see the 'occasional fits of perversion' followed by the 'regrets and penitences' as signs of this deeper frustration.

It made no difference to his affection, which was never anything but genuine and generous, while Francis's affection was no less sincere on account of the frustration which made for a more complicated situation on his side. Apart from the affair of the proofs of *Sister Songs* and the break with Lane, there were many lesser occasions when it seethed below the surface of requests for anything extra to the necessities covered by the cheques sent to Cuthbert or Anselm.

At times, even these did not come when expected and then the result could be embarrassing. 'My landlady is urgent with me to remind you about her bill', he wrote in February that year, and again in April: 'My landlady has spoken to me about the bill for my lodgings, which it seems has been running for thirteen weeks'. Owing to Cuthbert's absence he was in 'a very difficult and uncomfortable position' which he was forced to take up himself. Stamps could become a matter of urgency and, when asking for an extra supply, Thompson was careful to list the purposes for which they were to be used.[47] Yet each of these letters, like others of the kind, is full of enquiries after the family and their concerns, ending with 'Always yours affectionately', 'With love and thanks' or 'Always yours, dear Wilfrid'. For the last two years, since the publication of *Poems*, he had used Wilfrid's Christian name. It marked a subtle change in their relationship since the days when, always 'Francis' to both Wilfrid and Alice, he did not feel it proper to address them on such equal terms.

The arrangement with Constable was made in early June and soon afterwards Thompson came to London in order to make himself personally known to his new publisher. The visit was planned to last several weeks, a welcome change from the monotony of recent months at Pantasaph. It was also a gesture on the part of the Meynells in healing the rift that had occurred that spring. In a letter to Patmore begun before he left and finished on arrival, he wrote excitedly of his hopes that they could now meet, while already he had an invitation from George Meredith and another 'from a girl I have met here . . . which is pretty fair for the very first evening one reaches town'.[48]

Thompson was referring to what was to be much more than the chance encounter it seemed then. On reaching Palace Court he was greeted by a young woman who was playing with the children on the stairs. 'Wilfrid, what a charming new nurse you've got' he observed later, knowing that one was expected. Wilfrid remembered the occasion clearly and how he put Francis right. 'An introduction swiftly followed & much else. For they became very close friends . . .'.[49]

The young woman was Katharine, otherwise Katie, Douglas King, who had lately become a frequent visitor on account of her willingness to turn her hand to anything that might be needed from amusing the children to helping out with secretarial duties for their

parents. She knew and admired Francis's poetry and according to
a letter from Wilfrid before he left Wales, was looking forward to
meeting him. He already knew her by name as a writer of short
stories, some of which had appeared in *Merry England* in the past.
They were based on her knowledge of the life of the London poor as
she observed it through her charitable work for children in the East
End. She made no attempt to avoid the sordid details in her direct
portrayals, which were more in line with the 'realist' novelists of the
time than with the cloying sentimentality of most women writers of
her class and background. Her one novel so far, *The Scripture Reader of
Saint Marks* followed the same line and she was now daring enough to
submit a story for the *Yellow Book* — where the effects of a mother
abandoning her children are offset by a defence of the action as due to
the intolerable conditions of the poor.

Such writing on such subjects was calculated to appeal to Thompson. Here was someone who understood those conditions as few did
and who possessed the personal gift of communicating what she
understood. It was the gift that appealed even more than the style and
subject matter, as he wrote in his answer to Wilfrid's letter:

> I read through all her M.E. stories some months ago; and was startled by
> their individual and impressive note. I admired them strongly — not, I
> think, for that which she would desire to be admired in them. I think she
> would claim admiration for their realism. I admire them for their idealism.
> In all the chief characters there is something which never was in any such
> character. And that something is Miss King. This, for which most would
> reprobate her, I admire. It is the light which never was on sea or land.[50]

That is, over and above the actual content of her writing there was, in
his view, a transforming touch of genius.

Even at their first brief meeting he found the author herself more
than equal to the expectations aroused by her writing. Her warm
quick sympathy of manner overlay a strong character that showed
itself in her forthright speech and the openness of her general conduct
and bearing. When she and her mother were in town they occupied a
flat in Cavendish Square and her invitation for Francis to meet her
there was followed by others. Then within a fortnight, Mrs King was
inviting Alice and Wilfrid for a weekend visit to their country home
at Hale End in Essex. They would be 'delighted', she added, to see
Francis as well, 'but I don't know there would be anything he would
care for, except that he seems to take an interest in Katie'.[51]

Mrs King planned the visit, and included Francis, in order that
the Meynells should see how the friendship was developing — easily
missed in the bustle of Palace Court — as well as hear of it from her. It
was certainly deepening, to the extent that Francis persuaded Wilfrid
and Alice to let him prolong his stay in London for several more

weeks. If he sensed any disapproval from Mrs King it did not yet disturb him and there were no grounds for any such disapproval. They shared an interest in literature and Katie showed an insight into the lives and personalities of the London poor such as Thompson had not found in anyone he met since he had left the streets. At this stage there was, for both, no more than the added piquancy which usually exists between friends of the opposite sexes. It was a quality which Mrs King was incapable of understanding and instead she was be-coming seriously worried.

Elizabeth Hamilton King was an imposing woman, past middle age but still proud of the deep red hair of her Scots ancestry. She was related by marriage to both the Hamiltons and Douglases, which accounted for Katie's name differing from her own in retaining the Douglas connection. As a girl she had been infatuated by the Italian patriot Mazzini, with whom she corresponded until his death in 1872. Her marriage to the publisher Henry King meant she could style herself a poetess on the dubious merit of an epic in Mazzini's honour. This was followed by two volumes of verse mainly inspired by the transfer of her loyalties to Cardinal Manning. Through his influence she became a Catholic, and when her husband's death left her with five children to bring up, Manning's support and advice had been her mainstay in practical as well as spiritual matters. His letters to her suggest a complex personality driven in on herself, whereas in another age she might have found satisfaction in public life. As it was, by now she had very little outlet for the energies she expended earlier on Mazzini and then on Manning's behalf. Consequently her frustration turned her into a chronic invalid who demanded the constant atten-tion of her eldest and favourite daughter.

Manning always insisted that the children should not be made to follow their mother into the Church and Katie's determined Angli-canism was a constant cause for regret to Mrs King. Frustrated, too, in the religious upbringing of her family, she became obsessively concerned for their moral character. One son at least had already rebelled and since the previous year she had growing fears for Katie. She could approve of her work for the poor as a socially acceptable occupation and one with which she was genuinely in sympathy. But her daughter's writings, of equal if not more concern to Katie herself, were a social embarrassment and promised to be even worse. The stories in *Merry England* shocked her, yet if the Meynells thought fit to print them that was some reassurance. She had known Wilfrid and Alice since the days when her husband published Alice's first volume of poetry, *Preludes*. But the appearance of Katie's novel in the summer came as a fearful surprise. 'The story is frankly appalling', she wrote to Wilfrid, and 'likely to raise a hornet's nest about her'. Already the reviews were talking about her 'experience' and even her 'virility' —

could not Wilfrid do something to counteract these dreadful insinuations? Wilfrid wisely ignored the appeal, for a few weeks later she
wrote that she was herself trying to persuade Katie to put an end to
the whole disgraceful affair by writing a book 'dealing with the very
highest sphere of life' — although she doubted if Katie had 'the mental capacity' to enter into her idea.[53]

Yet now all these efforts were proving useless and, in Mrs King's
eyes, she was indulging in a relationship more dangerous than
anything else so far. She genuinely admired Thompson as a poet but
his contact with Katie was another matter. This shabby unprepossess-
ing little man, prematurely old and with a more than doubtful
personal history — she could only see him as the most unsuitable
partner imaginable for her beloved Katie. Yet she had no desire to
cause hurt where as yet there was no reason for actual complaint. So
she decided to discuss the whole situation with Wilfrid and Alice who,
she knew, would have Francis's good at heart in whatever suggestion
they made. It was all the more urgent as Katie had arranged to meet
Francis before he left for Wales at the end of July, a dangerous occasion to be avoided if at all possible.

Francis was already outstaying his time in London with some
inconvenience to themselves and whatever they thought of the
'danger' in the meeting with Katie they agreed to ensure his departure
before the date fixed for it. He had spent a few days with Patmore and
his wife in June and was now to make a second visit, returning to
London to see Katie the following week before leaving for Wales. On
the morning he was to travel to Lymington Wilfrid made some excuse
for telling him he would have to return to Pantasaph as soon as he was
back in London.

With his usual reserve Francis said nothing about this at Lymington. Nor did the details of his friendship with Katie come under
discussion. In a letter of thanks to Patmore for the visit and sent from
Pantasaph — where he had no choice but to return as directed — he
wrote he was now 'so completely cut off from the world' that his only
outside contact had been 'very charming and delicate letters of regret
at my sudden departure' from two ladies he met in town. It did, however, provoke him to add:

> That was a very absurd and annoying situation in which I was placed by
> W. M.'s curious method of handling me. He never let me know that my
> visit was about to terminate until the actual morning I was to leave for
> Lymington. The result was that I found myself in the ridiculous position of
> having made a formal engagement by letter for the next week, only two
> days before my final departure from London. Luckily both women knew
> my position, and if anyone suffered in their opinion it was not I.[54]

Francis was well aware that the reason for his enforced departure
was to prevent him from seeing Katie again. At present he attributed

it to some unexpected prejudice on the Meynells' part, so adding to his frustration at Wilfrid's general 'handling' of him. His hurt at the time increased with the loneliness following his return to Pantasaph. Creccas Cottage was about a mile from the Friary and the contact there was not the same as when he was still at the Guest House: and Maggie Brien's company had long since ceased to offer more than the prosaic friendliness of the rest of the family. They took Francis for granted, paying little attention to him beyond seeing to his everyday needs. And grateful as he was for this he knew he could not expect more from them.

Worse than the physical loneliness was the prospect of the months stretching ahead with nothing to give a purpose to the monotony of his daily routine. The preparation and dispatch of the manuscript for his book and the six weeks in London meant it was only now that he began to face a future devoid of hope for his poetry. It had formed the background to all he thought and wrote for as long as he could remember, sustaining him through those 'dark hours' of obscure fears when all other hope seemed dead. The loss was intensified by the sudden cessation of contact with Katie and the suspicion of the reason. As the events of recent weeks merged with those of the past year his sense of an inevitable ending of the friendship became part of the deeper sense of loss. Not long after his return, on a lonely walk over the hills, Francis captured a part of what he felt in a poem to which he gave the significant title 'A Lost Friend', adding the date 'July 27th'. It was the day he left London:

> From height, and cold, and mist I fell,
> > With furléd wing: and on my way
> What waited me, and what befell —
> The silence at Song's heart can only say.
>
> The height and mist again are mine;
> > And all my sad and secret things
> No song can utter, but the fine
> Trembling subsidence of Song's aching strings.
>
> The hill looks with a colder brow;
> > The silence I have made my choice
> Is doubly silent, having now
> The irreparable silence of her voice.

He sent the poem to Katie, who saw in it a degree of pain she longed to alleviate. She wrote a warm appreciation that went a long way to doing so, giving rise to a series of sonnets addressed to her and sent at intervals during the next two months.[55] Much later, when he collected them together as a group he added a note describing them as 'incidental expressions of personal and subjective feeling ... little safety valves through which my momentary self escaped'. He wanted to avoid the impression that they were anything more, comparing them with the 'Narrow Vessel' sequence rather than with the sentiments of 'Love in Dian's Lap'.[56] Yet, while they do not equal the 'Love in Dian's Lap' poems, there is no real resemblance to those addressed to Maggie Brien. The light touch, the tender care to preserve the childlike simplicity of her feelings, are missing. There is a heaviness in their over-strained imagery arising from the heaviness of his heart now in contrast to the early days at Pantasaph. The theme is constant, the sudden beauty of Katie's appearance in his life overshadowed by the fear of coming loss:

> Oh, may that doubted day not come, not come,
> When you shall fail, my heavenly messenger,
> And drift into the distance and the doom
> Of all my impermissible things that were!
> Rather than so, now make the sad farewell,
> While yet may be with not too-painéd pain,
> Lest I again the acquainted tale should tell
> Of sharpest loss that pays for shortest gain.

. . . .

> No, no, it cannot be, it cannot be,
> Because this love of close-affinéd friends
> In its sweet sudden ambush toiléd me
> So swift, that therefore all as swift it ends.
> For swift it was, yet quiet as the birth
> Of smoothest music . . .[57]

Katie understood the poet's homage paid to her in these poems and accepted them as such. She was not deceived by their occasional excesses even if she was quickened to a warmer response by the growing intensity of feeling on his side:

> When that part heavenliest of all-heavenly you
> First at my side did breathe its blosmy air,
> What lovely wilderment alarmed me through!
> On what ambrosial effluence did I fare,
> And comforts Paradisal![58]

It was natural she should be flattered at receiving the sonnets and for her, it went no further than this. But for Francis on his lonely walks and during the lonelier evenings it was even more natural that, before he was aware of it, his feelings should be going beyond those of friendship. He had no companions now that Anselm was more often away than at the Friary and his other friends there had left. The poems and the exchange of letters were his one consolation in his otherwise empty days.

As his feelings deepened, so did the fear of loss. And then, towards the end of October, he received a letter from Mrs King which seemed to confirm the fear into a reality. She had come to know of the poems and something of the correspondence with Katie. At the same time she found their relationship was known and discussed in terms that compelled her to ask him to cease all communication with her daughter. Shocked by such insinuations he answered immediately, denying any grounds for them and, as he had already destroyed all Katie's letters, he requested she should do the same with his, along with the poems.

Both of these letters have disappeared, but a second one from Mrs King makes it clear that the tone of his reply meant she now felt bound to give him a fuller explanation than she had evidently done before:

> I thank you from my heart for your letter, which makes me honour you, and value your friendship more than ever. It was a great pain to me to write and to feel your pain, and yet, I felt it was necessary. Certainly your letters and poems were open to misconstructions, though only of the most honourable kind; and I am thankful for the frank explanation.

She made a point of referring to 'painful misunderstandings in respect of Mrs Meynell' to which he had himself alluded at one time. If a similar situation should arise with Katie, neither he nor she would be 'safeguarded' by her being a married woman. There were grounds for fearing this was already happening, causing Mrs King anxiety and laying Katie 'open to the charge of coquetry'. For, she continued, coming to the real point:

> the matter has been talked over by others, and much more has been pressed upon her in your behalf, than you have pressed yourself. I cannot say more than this: but there seemed no alternative than to speak openly between ourselves.[59]

Presumably the intimacy between the two had been observed by other visitors at Palace Court who, putting their own construction on it, then encouraged Katie towards a direction which she would not have taken seriously but which she may have found difficult to handle with tact. According to Mrs King 'she has all along held your view simply and calmly' and, since her initial 'expostulations' at her mother's letter, was now 'entirely passive'. Katie knew from experience that continued protest would only make matters worse. Outwardly 'passive', she would wait until the storm subsided. It had worked before with the somewhat similar storm following the publication of her novel. She was just completing her second one, where she pursued her own line with no deference to the commands and demands made by Mrs King only a few months ago.

At the end of her letter Mrs King repeated her assurances of friendship and regard, adding that she would return the poems since she had no right to destroy them. She did so a month later, enclosing them with another letter making no mention of what had taken place. Her innocuous description of autumn at Hale End was her way of showing that she bore him no ill will and there is no reason to doubt her sincerity.[60]

It could do nothing to lessen his pain and hurt. Mrs King's regard meant nothing, apart from the fact that it affected his relationship with Katie, to which she was instrumental in putting an end for the foreseeable future. It was made worse because Mrs King's first letter came almost immediately after a brief but memorable respite from what he now felt to be his exile in Wales.

In September Alfred Hayes, a minor poet and friend of the Meynells, asked Thompson to stay with him and his wife at their home outside Birmingham. When they met in London Hayes' unpretentious manner and genuine love of poetry made Thompson welcome the invitation then promised, and he was the more annoyed at its postponement due to Meynell's failure to send the rail fare in time. It was the kind of embarrassment that could so easily arise now from his peculiar financial position.

He went, however, in October. As might be expected he left the train at the wrong station and before arriving at Edgbaston 'performed some other singular feats', according to the letter Hayes wrote to Meynell afterwards. The weather was poor but Thompson was happy to spend most of the day in the library and the evenings in animated talk with his host. His range of literary knowledge stood out in Hayes' recollections of the visit, leaving him with 'a general impression of deep insight and opulent imagination, of many a flash of inspiration and radiant turn of speech'. Clearly Hayes was one of those with whom he could be entirely at ease and therefore at his conversational best.

He felt himself understood and accepted. Hayes' description draws the contrast between these attainments and the personal traits which, to others, were often a source of awkwardness provoking him to further awkwardness on his part. Hayes, on the other hand, saw nothing to criticize in his guest's oddities of manner and appearance:

> At meals he would sit mostly silent, sometimes quitting the table, his food half consumed, as if at some imperious mandate, but somehow without leaving behind him the slightest suspicion of discourtesy. These sudden disappearances, whose cause I never sought to discover, soon came to be expected, and only provoked a smile — it was Thompson's way. But let it not be supposed that he was uncouth or affected; his manner was that of a great child; he was simply incapable of pose or unkindness.

His outward appearance, prematurely aging and bearing the marks of physical and mental suffering, aroused Hayes' pity 'but even greater respect'. More important for Francis, a real affection grew up between them, based on Hayes' unusual insight into the personality behind the appearance:

> I was struck, as were the few intimate friends who once met him at my house, with a strange other-worldliness about him, as if he were conscious of making only a hasty sojourn on earth in the course of an illimitable journey ... I remember how the discoloured face would suddenly light up, and the dazed eyes flash, in such moments of happy excitement, as if a volcanic eruption of delight had broken through the crust of his soul. He gave me the impression of concealing within him two inexhaustible reservoirs of sorrow and joy; ebullitions from each appear in his poetry; but in his long talks with me he rarely drew except from the fountain of joy.[61]

Hayes' description is more perceptive than most. To him the shabby insignificance of his guest was inseparable from a combined dignity and simplicity that accounted for and excused his eccentricities. Hayes knew from the muddled arrival how inconvenient his lack of a normal sense of time could be but behind it he saw an 'otherworldliness' that was not incompatible with his sudden quickness of movement and nervous haste in speech. Thompson gave him the impression of finding life 'an illimitable journey' where its incidental travels were of no real consequence compared with the ranging of time and space possible to the human spirit — and more particularly to the poet's spirit.

What he could not define was the shadow cast over the spirit, the fear of the consequences when the range went too far. Yet he sensed its presence in speaking of the 'crust' from which escape had to be violent and could only be temporary. For him it contributed to the twin capacities for grief and joy that summed up contradictions in Thompson's character which he did not attempt to reconcile.

There were very few who penetrated far enough to find these capacities to be equal. Apart from poetry the opportunities for the joy being given expression depended so largely on the rare occasions when he could respond to another's understanding and acceptance. With Hayes he could do so, during a week that in retrospect seemed like an oasis in the desolate landscape of his last autumn at Pantasaph. A year later he renewed his gratitude in a letter enclosing a poem where he recalled a day the two had spent in and around Stratford upon Avon. The poem is lost but a fragment remains of the draft:

> Do you remember how we walked
> A year ago through S-land,
>
> ...
>
> Where still the reverend homesteads stand,

> The undreamed fulfilment of a dream,
> And breathed about with antique airs,
> Sweet with all childishness and first desire,
> So near our young days and those old days sum?
> Do you remember how we talked,
> Remote a while from modern cares,
> Do you remember how we walked,
> And drew the wild flowers from their lairs?[62]

He reverted to the loneliness of his present life and the arrival of Mrs King's letters, which with the return of his poems seemed to put a seal on any further contact with Katie. Then only a day or two after he received them there came an even more final seal on that other friendship which had touched deeper levels than Katie or even the Meynells could ever reach. Following a short and sudden illness Coventry Patmore died at Lymington on 26 November.

Thompson was not one to allow the extent of his grief to show outwardly. In his notebooks he found some relief in agonized fragments of verse where the pain of this loss took in the farewell to his poetic aspirations over the past year and to Katie only that month. Later he turned one of these fragments into a sensitively simple poem speaking for all who have sensed the vacancy, the void, in surroundings associated with one who will never share them again:

> O how I miss you any casual day!
> And as I walk
> Turn, in the customed way
> Towards you with the talk
> Which who but you should hear?
> And know the intercepting day
> Betwixt me and your listening ear;
> And no man ever more my tongue shall hear,
> And dumb mid an alien folk I stray.[63]

The Friary and surrounding hills were now too full of such memories for him to bear remaining longer. To some extent he had been able to share his grief with Anselm, whose admiration for Patmore's poetry was accompanied by a warm regard for the poet himself. And now, as if the bereavements and losses of the past year were not enough, Anselm was about to leave for good. Having been reinstated in favour with the Order he was to take up his old position as Lector in Philosophy at Crawley.

It was a final blow but it gave Francis the means for release. Anselm was his chief go-between in his financial and personal affairs and with the rest of the original group of friars dispersing elsewhere there was no one to replace him. Even so, Francis said nothing to the

Meynells until the decision was settled, aware that there would be objections. To them his return to London would mean added responsibilities which, until he was there, he could not persuade them were no longer needed. Since the distressing end to his last visit and the incident of the rail fare to Birmingham, his frustration at being prevented from managing his affairs had come to a crisis. Even more than the memories and the isolation at Pantasaph it made him certain that he must leave. He must now lead his own life, take it into his own hands and face whatever might remain in the future.

Anselm supported him in coming to this decision. He knew Francis well enough and enough of the events of the past twelve months to realize there could be no future for him unless he were allowed to make of it what he could for himself. So it was arranged that they should travel to London together, a few days before Francis's thirty-seventh birthday.

As he took his last walks over the hills, his mind went back to the days on the Sussex downs and his hopes then for the future. Nothing seemed left of them now. Yet even then, there was the shadow of the cross cast over the poem of his poetic awakening. And in 'The Hound of Heaven' the final commitment was not made, to clasp the outstreched hand and to find the answer to the question he then asked of the future:

> Is my gloom after all
> Shade of His hand outstretched carressingly?

In what was probably the last poem he wrote before leaving Pantasaph, he took up the theme of 'The Hound of Heaven' as he had concluded it then and gathered into it the losses and failures of the years between. There is nothing of the earlier power in these twenty-three unadorned lines but they carry the theme a stage further in professing a determination that was to sustain him through the future that still lay ahead:

> Till all my life lay round me in great swathes
> Like grass about the mower,
> Then, Lord, then
> The miserable residue, by men
> Cast forth contemptuously beside the ways,
> The sweepings of my days
> (Having, me now bethinketh,
> My whole life long to Him some offering owed)
> 'These will I give to God'.
> And didst Thou bid Thy splendours,
> Keeping their wingéd ward,
> To scourge the mad insulter from thy gate?

No, Thou didst say, O awful King:
'My child, I do accept thy offering.
Only this thing
I ask of thee — not more;
To cleanse it in the fire and with thy tears
Thy few remaining years.
And I will give the tears and give the fire,
And if thou tire
(Although they be few years)
Behold I will be with thee in thy tears,
Behold I will be with thee in the fire'.[64]

9
Silent Lip and Climbing Feet
London again 1897–1903

Yet shall a wiser day
Fulfil more heavenly way
And with appровéd music clear this slip,
I trust in God most sweet.
Meantime the silent lip,
Meantime the climbing feet.

'Retrospect': 40–45

The arrangement for Francis to leave Pantasaph with Anselm had to
be changed when Anselm's departure was delayed at the last minute.
So Francis, his belongings packed and the room at the Briens' no
longer his, travelled to London alone. The separation from the Brien
family was his only real regret. As he watched the familiar scenes from
the railway carriage window he felt an aching sadness for all that the
place once meant to him and all that had happened to change it over
the past six years.

Wilfrid and Alice seem to have been taken by surprise when he
actually arrived, acting on what they probably hoped was another of
his passing whims. As they were either unable or unwilling to give
him a room at Palace Court over Christmas, Wilfrid arranged for him
to stay with Arthur Doubleday until lodgings could be found later.
Doubleday's admiration for the poet whose work he was to publish
had been strengthened by their meeting the previous summer. Neither
he nor his wife were the kind to be put off by his eccentricities and he
was given a warm welcome.

Francis had the freedom of his host's library during the daytime
and in the evenings the three shared a common bond in their love of
music. He wrote appreciatively to Wilfrid, only anxious that as the
Doubledays changed for dinner he must continue to borrow the dress
suit Wilfrid had, with his usual tact, left for him to use on his arrival.[1]
Francis was obviously enjoying the contrast to his recent isolation in
the culture and comfort of the Doubledays' home in Whitehall
Gardens. It gave him time to adjust in one of those interludes in life
that can come when most needed and are of all the more value for
being unexpected.

In the meantime Wilfrid realized he must make some definite plans for Francis's future. With no *Merry England* in the background, his employment must be outside the limited opportunities available through the Meynells' own connections with the Catholic press. Apart from Francis's decided preference for a more independent career there was no practical alternative, and within a day or two Wilfrid contacted the editor of the *Academy*, William Lewis Hind, with a view to Francis joining the journal's staff as one of its regular reviewers. Hind readily agreed and before Christmas Francis collected some back issues from the journal's office, along with a request for an article on De Quincey to be ready early in January. He spent Christmas Day with the Meynells, renewing the custom that had been interrupted by the years in Wales, and directly afterwards he set to work. The article had to be finished before he moved to lodgings in the New Year — to 16 Elgin Avenue, not far from his old haunts along the Harrow Road.

The article convinced Hind that whatever the future held for Thompson as a poet there was one for him as a journalist. An arrangement was made for Francis to submit regular reviews and articles which would at least provide for the essentials of his upkeep. He had no alternative but to accept, although he was toying with other more ambitious ideas. He looked out his earlier attempts at drama and did some further work on a 'Pastoral Play' begun before he left Wales. Then there was the book on Freemasonry for which most of the material he would need was already collected. The draft of his letter on the subject, already referred to, was written out on the reverse pages of 'Venus Fly Trap', one of the plays he revised at the time and which, like the rest, shows he lacked any talent in that direction.[2]

But once he began on the work for the *Academy* he realized there would be no time for anything so extensive or so uncertain. What he must do before all else was to establish himself in the only career that could relieve the Meynells — and himself — from the strain of his financial dependence on them. Nor was he without other more congenial prospects. In March Doubleday suggested he provide the text for a book on London, to be illustrated with engravings by Douglas Hyde. He agreed enthusiastically and a notice on the book appeared in the *Academy* the following month. Doubleday's idea probably arose from conversations when Francis was his guest and his experiences of London life's least known aspects could, Doubleday felt, become the basis for an unusual publication on a subject that never failed to be popular.

Before this, and within a few weeks of each other, two events occurred which together acted as a kind of watershed between Francis's past and present life. Just after he settled into his new lodgings a final break with the past came with the news of John Carroll's death. After his appointment as Bishop of Shrewsbury in 1885, Carroll

19. Katie King

moved from Stalybridge to Birkenhead and Francis visited him there the previous autumn, prompted by rumours of his failing health. It was an added sorrow during the last months at Pantasaph and now the loss was more painful for coming so soon after Patmore's death.

The request from Carroll's old parishioners that the funeral should be at Stalybridge was granted as being in accordance with the Bishop's own wishes. On hearing of this Francis paid the only tribute he could to their friendship by attending the service on what he also knew would be his last visit to his home surroundings. The effort of finding the fare and making the journey was of a kind that probably only Carroll himself could have understood. It has gone unrecorded except for an entry in a local history of the parish. The account of the funeral relates 'that a belated and practically unnoticed mourner at the back of the Church on this occasion was the poet Francis Thompson . . . He slipped out at the end of the ceremonies, one gathers, as unostentatiously as he stole in'.[3]

About a fortnight later Francis received a letter from Katie King. It could not, she wrote, have been sent until some time had elapsed since her mother's letter to him:

I did not want to add (as I fear any words of mine would have done) to the pain & disappointment that letter must have brought you. I say dis-

> appointment because I think you must have been disappointed as well as grieved to find that after all I had apparently not understood & rejoiced in your friendship for me. But indeed I think I did understand it, & it certainly was a great joy & pride to me to know you were my friend. And I should like you to know that I was very sorry indeed that owing to the intervention & as I think misrepresentations of others — even with the best & kindest intents — our friendship has received so severe, unwarrantable & unnecessary a check. My wish was against a letter going to you. It seemed so unnecessary & therefore unjustifiable.

They were strong words but Katie was not going to allow her mother to have the last word now any more than before over the subject-matter of her novels. She knew it would take time and tact to get her way and the time had now come to state the grounds on which she hoped their friendship could continue. The tact was extended to the manner in which she set about this in her letter. Did he want the poems addressed to her returned or could she keep them for the present?

> I am so fond of them, they are so beautiful exquisite [sic], *living*; my mother who alone has seen them thinks they are of all yours the most beautiful. You were *young* when you wrote them, Francis! There is the lovely freshness of all things young & ardent & beautiful. They are yours when you want them, but even then they will always be mine too, will they not?[4]

This is strange, for the poems were returned to Francis by Mrs King the previous autumn. The only explanation is that he had sent them back later to Katie, possibly on leaving Wales. But from the present letter it seems he wrote little or nothing to accompany them. She was now deliberately distancing her own self from the poems, underlined by the careful reference to her mother's present view of them but with just enough personal feeling to avoid it causing him pain. If he had mistaken her reactions before for something more than the friendship she hoped to revive, she was trying to put right any misunderstanding without the harshness of her mother's methods. She ended the letter with an invitation that left the decision as to the future to him. 'I am a great deal at the little children's hospital. Mr Meynell knows the way'. He would have realized already that she had obtained his address from the Meynells and, by involving them, she implied there was nothing secretive in her tentative suggestion — while avoiding a meeting in their company and the company of their friends. Of course he might be too busy — offering him a convenient loophole — 'But if you are able & care to come, you know how glad I should be'.

In his reply Francis must have given the invitation a cautious welcome, hinting that he preferred the Meynells not to know, at this stage, of their renewed contact and expressing some uncertainty as to her mother's attitude. In her next letter, fixing the date for his visit, Katie gave her own directions to the hospital in Leonard Square and suggested they should arrange, when they met, for him to visit Hale End. 'My Mother would so like to see you again. It will give us both such pleasure', she assured him.

Francis went to the hospital and later to her home — when Mrs King showed herself fully confident that all was now in order. After an interval during which she and Katie were ill with influenza she wrote to him with a second invitation to Essex, enclosing some of her own poems for his opinion.

The revival of this friendship was part of the turning point also marked by the death of John Carroll. His death broke the last link with the past, with the background to the poetic career which Carroll had been the only one to encourage, and in which his confidence never failed. That career was now, Francis was sure, likewise dead. Yet the sincerity and warmth Katie was offering him in this other friendship pointed towards a future perhaps less bleak than he expected when he left Wales or which he foresaw in his work for the *Academy*. He clung to the fresh hope, perhaps even now allowing it to grow out of proportion to her intentions. At the same time he knew there was a danger in a close friendship with Katie and on her side she was well aware of the possible outcome and the pain it would cause for them both if they became too intimate. When *New Poems* appeared in May he sent her a copy, for which she wrote to thank him. 'Surely these New Poems will add a fresh lustre to your crown of fame'. But she did not, she added, know if fame mattered to him, 'so little one knows even one's friends'.

Fame in the sense of his reputation as a poet did matter to him very much. He knew that among the earlier poems included in the volume there was some of his best work, and if there was to be nothing more of the kind he did hope and even expect that this at least would be acknowledged.

As a result, his disappointment as the reviews began to appear was acute. Almost without exception they concentrated on the linguistic excesses of the more outstanding poems rather than attending to his work as a whole. They conceded an occasional beauty of expression but there was still too much extravagance and needless obscurity. At times they were roused to errors of exaggeration such as they were condemning. 'A dictionary of obsolete English suffering from a fierce fit of *delirium tremens*' was the verdict of the influential *Literary World*. The *Pall Mall Gazette* selected 'An Anthem of Earth' as typical, 'the work of a medieval and pedantic Walt Whitman'. In the *Athenaeum* Arthur Symons pointed out that 'prodigality is not abundance, nor

profusion taste', taking a simile from the host who overloads his
guests' plates 'under the impression that to do otherwise is to be
lacking in hospitality'.[5]

The reviewers recognized the 'Sight and Insight' poems as being
the most important group but failed to find any linking theme. Too
often they selected 'The Mistress of Vision' for special comment and
neglected the rest. The critic for the *Saturday Review* was representative
in dismissing the poem as 'nonsense verse', regretting that the poet
had been shielded until now from the truth by friends who persuaded
him he was 'a genius'. The accusation that he was being deliberately
put forward by the Catholic intelligentsia was widespread. Only
Quiller Couch, writing in the *Speaker*, recognized that the eulogies
from his Catholic supporters were doing Thompson no long-term service. Yet it would be no less mistaken, he warned, if reaction against
them was to blind future generations to the achievement of a poet who
for all his faults remained 'an extraordinarily fine one'. His selection
of 'monstrance' and 'dove nunceo'd' as examples of needless obscurity
shows how the criticism could often be due to unfamiliarity with the
language of the Church. In quoting from 'The Mistress of Vision' he
went so far as to confuse 'thurible' with 'thimble', a mistake for which
he apologised in the next issue of the journal. Yet unfamiliarity need
not affect appreciation. This poem in particular recalled for him 'the
wonder and delight with which I first read "Kubla Khan"'.[6]

For Thompson, what stood out in the review was the assertion:
'In some of the more ambitious poems, ambitiousness is perilously
near pretentiousness'. It was just this ambition which he had feared
and fought against, and the words cut deeper for containing an element of the truth. Consequently they provoked an angry protest, confided to his current notebook:

> If you, 'tis like, ambition see
>   In yonder rising pine,
> And if your grape ambitions be
>   About its brand new wine
>
> . . .
> Even as their effort, so is mine,
>   And you are clearly right.
> Ambitious stars! how shine
>   Their effort, thinks the night.[7]

Apart from accusations of false pride prompted by the no less
false support of his friends, there were others of weak imitations of
Patmore or inferior renderings of seventeenth century sources. Hurt
and distressed, Thompson was blinded to the occasional more favourable comments. But he could not fail to notice when William Archer
wrote in the *Daily Chronicle* of 'a seer and singer of rare genius'. Archer

was not connected with the Meynells' circle at that time and not yet known to Thompson — who in consequence wrote him an unusually long and revealing letter. Describing *New Poems* as the sinking ship of his poetic career, what has stood out for him in the review is the support from one who admits he does not share the poet's ideas and beliefs. Until now Thompson had not realized, he says, 'how powerfully people's views (theological, philosophical or otherwise) influenced their ideas towards contemporary poetry'. He began to learn this from Patmore, who 'depreciated writers solely or chiefly because he hated their philosophy', whereas for himself:

> Beauty is beauty, though it may be inspired in defence of what I hold to be more or less untrue.

Thompson's view of literature was much wider than that of the majority of his critics and was in fact contributing now to his superiority in their own field. The letter ends with his appreciation of the contrast between them and the breadth he had found in Archer's observations. He put more feeling into his words than was usual with him in writing to strangers:

> I thank you most warmly for an article the insight of which is rendered the more remarkable by your lack of any personal sympathy with my views; and the courage of which, at this juncture, is beyond all praise . . .[8]

In his reply Archer was confident that the poetry would outlive the criticism. Meanwhile, he wrote, 'I assure you no conceivable reactions can wipe out or overlay such work as yours. It is firm based on the rock of absolute beauty'.[9]

At the beginning of June Thompson received another appreciative letter, this time of a more practical kind. H. W. Massingham, editor of the *Daily Chronicle*, wrote in praise of *New Poems* and with a commission for an ode to celebrate the Queen's Diamond Jubilee at the end of the month. This allowed just three weeks for its composition, which together with the *Academy* commitments was a significant challenge to the creative power he felt to be failing him. The result shows that it was not so much the power that was failing him as the motivation behind it. He could no longer write in accordance with his poetic vocation as he had understood it, but the 'Ode for the Diamond Jubilee of Queen Victoria' still rises, in places, well above the average for such poetry. They are mainly concentrated in the first of its two distinct parts, where Thompson allowed his imagination to draw on his habit of nocturnal wanderings in the streets:

> Night; and the street a corpse beneath the moon,
> Upon the threshold of the jubilant day
> That was to follow soon;
> Thickened with inundating dark

> 'Gainst which the drowning lamps kept struggle; pole
> And plank cast rigid shadows; 'twas a stark
> Thing waiting for its soul,
> The bones of the preluded pomp . . .
>
>   1–8

The ghost-like shadows form a procession from the past, of the dead upon whose achievements the coming celebration depends. It is led by the 'holy poets' — the poets consecrated to their high calling — their features captured in condensed lines and phrases such as Thompson was using to effect in the prose of his reviews. After Tennyson, as 'A Strength beside this Beauty' comes Browning, 'meditating still some gnarléd theme': Arnold 'In a fastidious dream': then Elizabeth Browning's 'fervid breathing/Broke on Christina's gentle-taken breath'. So to Rossetti:

> Song's hand was in his hair,
> Lest Art should have withdrawn him from the band,
> Save for her strong command.
>
>   49–51

Coventry Patmore is the last because he was the most recent to join their number. Whereas no other is allotted more than two or three lines, he claims twenty-two, coming as one set apart and with 'his alien eye' disdaining the coming pomp.

Following the other Arts are 'the sabre's children' to whose exploits Thompson gives full reign to his appreciation for the pageantry and pattern of the battle. Yet these conquests, and the conquests of the sea that are their counterparts, are not greater than those of science, whose representatives come next:

> They who pushed back the ocean of the Unknown,
> And fenced some strand of knowledge for our own
> Against the outgoing sea
> Of ebbing mystery;
> And on their banner 'Science' blazoned shone.
>
>   107–111

The procession is completed by the statesmen who have safeguarded the overall course of the past sixty years of English history. The phantom scene has become a commentary on the coming celebration, the procession to which the honour is most truly due:

> And this, O England, is thine All Souls' Day
>
>   132

As the Ode moves into the present, to the occasion itself, it becomes forced, seldom rising above the required patriotic sentiments. Thompson was not unaffected by the prevailing pride in 'The voice of

England's glories girdling in the earth' (97), but he would not indulge in the religious emotionalism common to such poetry. Kipling's 'Recessional', the most widely acclaimed example, announced a kind of Old Testament covenant between the 'Lord of Hosts' and England as a 'chosen people': prosperity would continue as a mark of divine favour provided that it was recognized as such. Kipling, too, looked to the past when stressing the responsibilities that must follow the achievements. But here the similarity ends. Nor is there anything in Thompson's Ode to confuse it with the pseudo-religious claims being made for the occasion by poets of far lesser stature than Kipling.

Instead, notebook drafts for the second part show how differently Thompson would have expressed his reactions had he been free to do so. England may be rightly rejoicing in the display of her imperial glories — but what of the conditions at home? The anticipated pomp and display were reviving his sense of outrage against an indifferent society first aroused by the experiences on the streets and which he would never forget:

> Wilt thou, feasting in thy purple state,
> Police the festering Lazarus from thy gate.
> So, all the inns are full: hast thou for Christ
> No stable: shall the ox be stalled & fed,
> The sea-horse delicately pampered,
> He, in the outer street, bit by the surly wind,
> Not find
> Necessitous bread?
> Shall all thy charity be picked & nice,
> And only then sufficed
> Clean-washed of sin & vermin in thine eyes?
> Alas, this modern Christ,
> Guilty & dirty, stinks against thy sense
> Of wholesome & neat-handed poverty ... [10]

The Ode was the first of the 'public' poems which Thompson regraded as journeyman work and not to be confused with true poetry. He had to undertake them when asked, for they were comparatively well-paid; but in other respects they brought no reward. The frustration at having to comply with a required theme led him to complete his personal memoranda for the Pantasaph years with the uncompromising entry:

> Jubilee Ode. End of the poet. Beginning of the journalist. The years of transition completed. [11]

It was the end of the poet which Thompson believed he had been called upon to be: not, as has been generally asserted, the end of his

poetic life. And it was also a genuine beginning. His determination to
succeed as a journalist in order to keep his independence would never
allow him to overcome his dislike for the work, but he had the confidence of knowing that he possessed the necessary abilities together
with an insight into the world of journalism gained from his years of
collaboration with the Meynells.

Thompson's skills in this direction as he was now developing
them have so far been unfairly neglected. The methodical and painstaking care with which he wrote almost all his reviews and articles is
proved by the many notebook drafts that survive. But as many have
probably not survived, scribbled as they were on odd scraps of
paper to be thrown away when no longer needed. Nor did it make any
difference if an author was well-known or not: all received equal attention. A general description of a book would usually be followed by a
selection from what Thompson found to be its best or most notable
features, ending with an assessment of its merits and faults. Where
possible the merits were stressed and perhaps his main weakness was
a tendency towards undue leniency.

All the same, there were qualities in an author which he never
failed to condemn. Any suspicion of dishonesty, of a desire to write
merely in order to catch the public eye, could arouse an angry protest.
Reviewing a book on the art of the novel, where the prospective writer
was advised to 'feel his public' before starting, Thompson poured
scorn on anyone who wrote from such a standpoint. Again, he had no
use for the term 'average poet', which he maintained was only another
way of describing a 'mental slovenliness' content to rely on 'habitual
phrases, which save him the trouble of finding the true word'. He
could also be severe about his fellow critics 'to whom the monuments
of literature are what other monuments are to the British tourist — an
opportunity for carving his own name on them'.[12] His most considered
observations on the task confronting the critic were made in response
to an over-sensitive poetess who took his unfavourable review as a
personal affront:

> The reviewer has only the book before him. He can only judge it im-
> partially on its internal merits, praising in accordance with its power,
> blaming in proportion to its failure. If the failure be considerable, this may
> be a very painful process to the author; but the reviewer has no choice, and
> the author courted this ordeal, implicitly submitted himself to it, by ven-
> turing authorship. The critic can but register his impressions, coldly
> impartial by his very function ... That an adverse review should give
> pain, is an unhappy necessity. But it *is* a necessity, from which the
> reviewer cannot draw back — though he would gladly shirk the ungra-
> tious and ungrateful task. But the truth, as he sees it, has to be said.[13]

The intergrity that mattered most to him was not always easy to
maintain, particularly when its advisability was questioned even by

Hind himself. According to a notebook comment on his work for the *Academy*:

> The editor demanded naked Truth, yet cried 'Decency!' when I exhibited her. Theoretically, he cared nothing for what people might say; practically, if Mamma protested against the disgraceful attack on Mr Onlyson, he suggested that I had painted the devil with a regrettable neglect of values.[14]

As a reviewer this habit of making sharp, often witty jottings in his notebooks led him to fasten on a telling sentence or phrase that could describe a book better than a whole paragraph. To take a few random examples: in Byron's 'Don Juan', 'The negations and nihilations with which it abounds are uttered as roundly as other men's faiths'. John Wesley is the 'Newman of the plebs and market place' with powers of persuasion arising from convictions no less sincere than Newman's. With Newman himself his admiration did not blind him to certain weaknesses — as on Newman's contribution to the *Lyra Apostolica*: 'The thought of a gravely earnest man forcing on the garment of verse, unheeding if it part a seam or two in the process'.

The same facility applies to many of his more general comments. 'We are still grateful enough for mere beauty in song, as in existence. But we are more grateful for song which has both beauty and conscious significance': 'It is a common mistake of modern artists — poets, painters, musicians and others — to think that they are intense when they are only tense'. He had gained greatly in his critical judgements since his first unfortunate appraisal of Bunyan, whose 'inveterate homeliness of expression' he now sees as 'the main strength of his work in the greater part', giving it the freshness and vigour of the child's view of life with the added perception of maturity. All the same it could weaken 'the higher ranges of perception' and he still cannot accept Giant Despair — 'a schoolboy giant' who even goes to bed at night — 'as if Despair could sleep', Thompson protests.[15]

He always welcomed an opportunity to write on the great names from the past, when his chief aim was to send his readers back to the originals. Here his own love and respect for true literature could make for difficulties. Soon after starting with the *Academy* he was invited to submit three feature articles on Shelley, Browning and Tennyson. Although it was much more congenial work than reviewing he declined: 'Considering the importance — the great importance — of the writers I am asked to treat, I do not feel that I can do justice either to my subject or to my reputation within the limit (of 1,000 words) proposed'. It is to Hind's credit that the articles did appear — each of about twice that length — during April and May.[16]

As editor, Hind would have respected the objection from his own genuine feeling for literature. At one time, on hearing that Hind had been annoyed by a chance remark made by Thompson on his 'taste for letters', Thompson's semi-apology is also an excellent thumb-nail sketch:

> I would be nearer my meaning if I had called you a man of action with a love for letters — and art ... The essential thing is, that *life* occupies the principal place in your regard — not life as it should be lived, the ideal of life in other words — but actual everyday life ...[17]

It was the secret of Hind's success as journalist and editor, enabling him to give a positive welcome to all comers and then seeking out what they had to offer and, with a sure insight, discerning its extent and quality.

To outward appearances Hind and Thompson were exact opposites. Whereas Thompson had come to journalism through necessity and never penetrated far beyond the fringes of the Grub Street scene, Hind was immersed in it from the start of his career and loved it to the end of his life. Even when his active share was over, he relived it in his recollections of the years when, as editor first of the *Pall Mall Gazette* and then of the *Academy*, he rubbed shoulders with the whole literary world of the 'nineties. He could lay claim to having introduced H. G. Wells and Arnold Bennett to that world, to giving it Kipling's *Just So Stories*, even to inventing a form of colour illustration as an innovation in journalism. His enthusiasm for his profession was fed from his conviction of its importance, invigorating whatever he handled. So that when in 1885 he took over the editorship of the somewhat stodgy and backward *Academy* he was determined it should become one of the liveliest and leading journals of the day.

That it did so he believed was largely due to having secured Thompson's services — and having kept them. He was not to be put off by the unusual conditions: 'I forgave him his unpunctualities and evasions for the sake of his magnificent prose'. And again, on their professional relationship: 'Although indifferent to promises and the fulfilling of engagements he never swerved from rectitude in his intellectual performances ... he always gave of his best'.[18]

Fortunately for them both the assistant editor on the *Academy*, Wilfrid Whitten, shared Hind's view of Thompson. The tolerance and patience of these two, along with the easy-going atmosphere at the journal's office, did more towards establishing his success than either probably realized. Later, when ill health and other factors would give rise to constant notes of apology from Thompson for delayed contributions and broken appointments, they were invariably accepted without comment. They were also carefully preserved. It is notable that none survive after Hind was succeeded by Teignmouth Shore in 1903, followed in 1905 by Lord Alfred Douglas. Thompson could look on Hind as a friend as well as count on his professional appreciation.

This was not to be the case with his successors and Thompson's main work for the *Academy* was during the seven years when Hind was still editor.

Their relationship was built up in spite of what must have been, on Thompson's side, a severe test in the first year. One of Hind's devices for invigorating the *Academy* was to select 'Forty Immortals' from the contemporary literary world, and a place in the list was much sought after. When it appeared in November Thompson's name was not among them. Perhaps it was due to his position as a known member of the *Academy* staff but there could be no such reason for a worse disappointment to follow. The journal announced a 'crowning' of the two outstanding literary works of the year, to be accompanied by a generous financial prize for their authors. The awards, published the following January, went to Stephen Phillips for his collection of poetry and W. E. Henley for his life of Burns. An article defending the choices — there had been some fierce arguments on the subject — referred to the three main runners-up as 'Mr Francis Thompson, Mr Watson, and Mr Newbolt'. In Thompson's case *New Poems* was rejected as 'more a collection of magnificent experiments than matured poems'.[19]

It was the more disappointing, since several later more considered reviews were showing a distinct move in his favour, added to which the New Year's Eve edition of the *Morning Post* selected *New Poems* as the best volume of verse published in the past year. Doubleday was optimistic enough to write asking if he could consider a further collection. Thompson replied that he had 'material for a thin volume' which should take about six months to prepare whenever Doubleday might 'desire again to deal in my wares'. There was no suggestion of new work but he knew that, scattered through his notebooks, were finished and unfinished poems on which his private opinion was that 'though not representing an advance' they should not he forgotten. Some, notably the sonnets to Katie King, he regarded as 'urgent of record'.[20]

Then within a week of Doubleday's letter, the *Academy's* verdict on *New Poems* damped whatever interest Thompson might otherwise have taken further. At present he was in any case being urged by Hyde for the text on the book about London. The plan was worked out, based on his habitual absent-minded rambling through the streets and on the memories that had been giving rise to this habit since his return from Wales.

Hyde had already prepared a number of engravings and notes for others, on which Thompson eventually sent him a detailed commentary. Of the book's two sections, provisionally entitled 'Fair' and 'Terrible' London, the second was the one that mattered to him and on which he concentrated:

Since the darker aspect of London is particularly evident to a houseless
wanderer, it is my idea to include in this section a description of the aspect
of London from midnight to early dawn·— for which my own experiences
furnish me with material. I intend to take my wanderer through the
Strand, Covent Garden, Trafalgar Square, perhaps a part of Piccadilly,
the Embankment, Blackfriars Bridge, etc., bringing him round to Fleet
Street opposite St. Paul's at dawn; and to describe the night effects and the
effects of gradual dawn in the streets. And I intend to describe a night
fire; and the effects of vistas of lamps in such a neighbourhood as Pall
Mall. Locality, you will see, is unimportant. It is *effect* I wish to dwell on;
the *character* — of horror, sombreness, wierdness, or beauty — of various
scenes. My own mind turns especially towards the gloomier majesties and
suggestiveness of London, because I have seen it most peculiarly under
those circumstances . . .[21]

It was one of the few occasions when he referred to his habit of reliving
the scenes of the past. But it was not only the past that drew him. On
his night rambles he could join the crowd around the coffee stall or
hot-potato brazier and share something of the fellowship of the streets
that went with the rest of his memories. And, as his words show, he
could feel the haunting beauty of the more deserted parts as he had
felt it even when oppressed by the grim horrors which they also held
for him. But this personal involvement in his subject meant that
Thompson was due for another disappointment. He could not achieve
the detachment required for a book of the kind Doubleday envisaged,
nor was he equipped to deal with the first section, 'Fair' London, even
by way of contrast. Thompson's text was never completed and in 1898
London Impressions appeared under the joint names of William Hyde
and Alice Meynell. Many of Hyde's engravings were, however, still
based on Thompson's notes and suggestions rather than on the text
supplied by Alice.

The emotional strain, together with the demands of his *Academy*
commitments over several months, brought on the signs of overwork
that first became noticeable during that summer of 1897. In less than
a year he had produced at least twenty-five articles and reviews and if
he was to keep his independence there could be no slackening of the
pace. In addition there was another project to which he gave whatever
attention he could spare from the rest. Notebooks in use at the time
contain drafts for a lecture on poetry, probably connected with Alice's
recent election as President of the Society of Women Journalists. In
July the *Academy*'s announcement of the appointment gave notice of a
series of lectures arranged by the Society and among them one 'likely
to be delivered this winter by a distinguished poet who has never
before appeared upon a platform'.[22]

When taken together the drafts follow a line of argument based
on the view that poetry expresses truth by means of beauty and subjective feeling. These must be the means, however, not the end, for

truth as the poet sees it must be his aim. It then gives form and structure to the beauties of language and directs the emotions the language expresses. In this Thompson was choosing a topic close to his earlier attempts at defining the purpose of poetry and the role of the poet. He took the preparation seriously, covering many notebook pages and making constant changes and revisions.[23]

The project was only abandoned when a succession of severe colds that winter meant he fell seriously behind with the *Academy* work. It was essential to keep going despite the effort of concentration at such times — when as often as not he was too late finishing a review to post it and, whatever the weather, he had to deliver it by hand. In March, following an attack of pleurisy when there was no choice but to give in, he wrote to assure Hind of the reason for the recent falling-off of his work: 'It is cutting my own throat for me to neglect it, and you may be sure I would not wilfully keep you waiting'.[24]

Even without these setbacks Thompson could only earn enough to cover his immediate needs. Journalism was notoriously badly paid and most of those who entered the profession did so with a view to promotion to an editorship or a career as an independent writer. The terms and conditions described by Meynell in the 'Career Guide' he published for their benefit in 1880 were very little changed. By working a twelve-hour day and taking no holidays the average yearly earnings then amounted to around £250, which when Thompson was writing for the *Academy* was still not more than £300. Methodical and careful as he was with his actual work his lack of method in most other directions meant that for all his efforts he probably never exceeded the average, and when illness interfered with his normal output, it was considerably less. Nor would he appeal to the Meynells or break his resolve to remain independent. And they for their past treated it with notable tact, well aware of the struggle it often cost him. There was always the open house for him at Palace Court and in 1897, following the success of the Jubilee Ode, Wilfrid appealed — unsuccessfully — on his behalf for a Civil List Pension. But apart from the occasional gift when they knew it was specially needed, the Meynells respected his determination.[25]

In the circumstances Thompson's anxiety about the payment of the royalties due to him is the more understandable. And when Alfred Hayes invited him again for a visit in the autumn his refusal for want of the train fare was as genuine as his regret. A holiday of that kind was in any case now out of the question. The following January, refusing Monica's invitation to accompany her on a day's visit to Wilfrid Blunt, he wrote to her: 'I am simply too unwell and done up to go to Crabbet Park tomorrow, as I should have very much have liked to do'. Having allowed himself a day off last week 'I was up till 6 o'clock this morning, writing'.[26]

Turning night into day was a bad habit for more than the obvious reasons. One night early in the same year his lamp overturned, the curtains caught fire and by the time and he and his landlady had quenched the blaze everything in the room was either burned or unusable. Only the notebooks and papers he always kept in an old tin box were, mercifully, untouched. Badly shaken and with painfully blistered hands he walked the streets for the rest of the night and spent the next day looking for new lodgings — this time at 39 Goldney Road, still in the Harrow Road area.

Nor was this the only mishap to add to Thompson's troubles that winter of 1897–8. The previous November he had been knocked down by a hansom cab in Holborn and was treated for head injuries from which he suffered the after effects for several months. The accident took place when he was on his way to dine with Everard Feilding, who kept up an intermittant contact with him since their ghost-watching night at Pantasaph. That he went in such a condition is a good example of the way he could look forward to social engagements, provided he was sure he would not be expected to abide too closely by the conventions. He knew he could trust his host on this occasion to an unusually severe test. When Feilding wrote to Wilfrid to describe the evening he remembered Francis arriving 'an hour late, and with his head tied up in an appalling bandage'. In the circumstances, Feilding added, his coming at all was 'a complement' he fully appreciated and the evening went well for them both. They dined together again in December 1899 and could have done so more often. Feilding came to regret his failure to continue the friendship on hearing, presumably on account of Francis's later ill health, 'that he had become inaccessible'.[27]

Whoever Feilding's informant was, he was mistaken. Francis never became a self-appointed recluse. The many last-minute cancellations and his notorious unpunctuality arose from his inability to keep to a normal routine, sleeping late and working late in a vicious circle begun years before and now made a habit by the datelines for his *Academy* commitments.

There was, for example, the occasion when W. E. Henley expressed a wish to meet Thompson and asked Hind to arrange it. Henley was by now treated as king of the London literary world, ruling from his remote home at Muswell Hill, and his wishes must be obeyed. Knowing Thompson's ways and, in some fear of the outcome, Hind gained the support of E. V. Lucas and together they agreed with Thompson to meet at the local station. Thompson arrived even later than usual and, also as usual, profuse with apologies. He was ill, he said, and had eaten nothing that day. On the way from the station he was very sick but on recovering 'became suddenly companionable and amusing'. Hind's description continues:

Henley was slightly ruffled when we arrived, as we were (it was, of course, Thompson's fault) two hours and five minutes late. Before entering I had said to the poet, 'Francis, we're dreadfully late. Henley will be mad. You must get him into a good humour by laying the butter on thick — thick, mind you'. Francis, who was as literal as he was unpractical, proceeded to lay it on thick, yet with sincerity, and with the air that Shakespeare must have shown when he killed a calf. The encounter between the two poets was entirely successful. They had, I remember, a rambling bout over Virgil, and courteously compared each other with the Mantuan.[28]

So Hind's fears were ill-founded. Both possessed a sufficiently wide and realistic view of life — and of literature — to enjoy the differences between them.

The three years following his return to London were not only taken up with the weeks when illness or pressure of work or both kept him shut up in his room for days on end. There were other times when he could take an evening off, or perhaps the occasional Sunday afternoon. But his preferences as to how he occupied himself were his own and, knowing they would not be shared by the more conventionally-minded he kept them to himself. They have to be gleaned from the impressions he made on those who remembered the strange shabby frequenter of the local pubs and eating houses — and the even stranger transformation when he began to entertain them with the conversation that could range from imperial politics to the latest cricket scores or which café in north London supplied the best pork pies. But the higher subjects were not generally aired at such times. They were for relaxation and for keeping in touch with the details of everyday life he regarded as no less worthy of his attention.

At his favourite pub, the Skiddaw, on the corner of Elgin Avenue, a place was kept for him by the fire by the order of the landlord, to be vacated as soon as he made an appearance. Sometimes he went further afield. At the George Inn at Southwark, if funds allowed he indulged in a Sunday lunch of roast beef and plum pudding — always his favourite choice for a meal. Or at the Hercules Pillars in Soho he would stay on in the bar to write, being so much warmer and more congenial than his lodgings. Here he made friends with the Manager of the Royalty Theatre, reviving his enthusiasm for the stage in long conversations that led to other meetings at the theatre and the unaccustomed luxury of whisky and cigars in the Manager's private office. There was an unnamed poet, too, whom he counted among his odd assortment of friends, starving in a garret in Brook Street. They read poetry together, sometimes so far into the night that he would find lodgings nearby rather than return to his own. If Thompson was eccentric, it was only a few degrees more than these others. To his theatrical friend he quoted the north-country tag 'There's nowt so queer as folk', adding the less-known corollary, 'All the world's queer

save thee and me, dear, and thee can be tarnation queer other-
whiles'.[29]

If the Meynells had known anything of all this they would have
regarded it as too disreputable to be recorded, and there has been no
reference by his later biographers. The same applies to another group
of friends with whom, for other reasons, Wilfrid and Alice would not
have wished him to be openly associated. His connections with the
Capuchins continued, mainly through the Roger Bacon Society which
was first formed at Pantasaph. The Society was named after the chief
opponent of the medieval Scholasticism from which the friars hoped to
free the 'Church of the Future'. Since Anselm and Cuthbert were now
based at Crawley and Angelo appointed to a small parish in Sussex,
Anselm had re-formed it with meetings either at Crawley or at Holm-
wood, the home of one of its chief supporters, William Gibson. Several
other Capuchins joined and the membership included some of the
leading converts of the day, Mivart being one of the most active.
According to Angelo's carefully veiled references, Wilfrid Meynell
was among those 'especially interested in its affairs'. Angelo's identification of its aims with the ideas of the Modernists is sufficient reason
for the withdrawal of Francis's connection with the Society, after the
Meynells dissociated themselves from any outward connections of
their own with the Modernist movement. But the fact remains that
Cuthbert kept Francis informed of its activities and from January
1898 he attended the meetings fairly regularly. Then, towards the
end of the following year, the crisis created by Mivart's opposition to
the Church led to the withdrawal of several other members and the
Society gradually petered out.[30]

Thompson's friendship with the friars, however, continued. They
still provided the intellectual stimulus he found nowhere else. In
addition they accepted his disagreement with their more extreme
views with the same tolerance of his differences that had always put
him at ease in their company. From opposite ends, so to speak, of his
social life, the friars no less than his friends of the Skiddaw and the
Hercules took him as he was in a way which he needed now more than
ever.

Thompson continued to call at Palace Court several times a
week, when even if it meant working into the early hours next day he
often lingered on through the evening rather than return to his bleak
room in Goldney Road. But as before, the Meynells seldom saw him
at his best on these occasions. There were nearly always other visitors,
members of their circle of literary friends with whom Thompson was
aware that his peculiarities were what they noticed about him. It
made him either become awkwardly garrulous or keep in the background. J. L. Garvin first met him on one such evening. His admiration for Thompson's poetry meant he tried to like the poet himself, 'a

20. Thompson in 1897 from a sketch by R. Ponsonby Staples

middle aged man with rather broad shoulders and rather thin legs' whose flushed countenance and bloodshot eyes he mistook for signs of opium addiction. They were no doubt due to his most recent cold — certainly his frequent heavy colds did not help him to be at his best in 'polite' company. Garvin gave up trying to fit the poet to his expectations. 'A strange, strange creature', he concluded, who 'smiled much but said little'.[31] Lionel Johnson was often at Palace Court and found it equally hard to be on close terms with his fellow poet who, he wrote, 'enchants and exasperates me, both beyond measure, in his work and in himself'. In this he compared Thompson unfavourably with Patmore, whose 'genius' never failed to command respect despite his many eccentricities.[32]

It was much the same with the Meynells' own special friends. When Francis accompanied Alice on the visit to George Meredith in the summer of 1896 he had been awkward and tongue-tied and they did not become any more intimate on further acquaintance. Meredith challenged his views on nature, literature and most other subjects. In

Alice's presence, when confronted by his host's critical eloquence, Thompson was unable to match it as he could otherwise have done without difficulty. He was similarly shy and awkward when, in October 1898, he was taken to spend a day with Wilfrid Blunt in Sussex. Blunt's first impression was shocked surprise that, as they drove from the station, the poet preferred to bury himself in a newspaper rather than join the others in admiring the beauty of the autumn trees. Added to this, when they walked in the woods after lunch he appeared not to know the names of even the most common varieties. As to his appearance:

> He is a little weak-eyed red-nosed young man of the degenerate London type, with a complete lack of virility . . . He is very shy, but was able to talk a little when the general conversation was not too loud, and he seems good natured and quite unpretending.

Blunt was used to the poets of the day who would declaim their work on the slightest provocation — or none. In this instance the difference in Thompson was to his advantage:

> On the whole, however, I liked him, for he was quite simple and straight-forward. Only, it was difficult to think of him as capable of any kind of strength in rhyme or prose.

Significantly it was Wilfrid who left the stronger impression and whose conversation made what could have been an uncomfortable day pleasant for them all.[33]

The reason for Thompson's uncharacteristic withdrawal in the Meynells' company was that with them he could still never be entirely himself. His effort at financial independence could not overcome his sense of obligation towards them or the emotional dependence it had produced. Quite unconsciously, therefore, he attempted to meet the obligation by acting the part of the child he was to them, occasionally 'showing off' but more often reverting to his actual childhood habit of pulling down the drawbridge against the outside world. And the Meynells as well as their friends assessed his social behaviour by the outward signs without understanding the reasons for it.

There was one exception. After the meeting at the children's hospital Katie King sometimes met him at Palace Court, where she continued to be a frequent visitor. But she was not taken in by his manner there. However much or little she realized the reason, she knew him as a very different person when they met either at the hospital or at Hale End. Although none of his letters to her survives, hers to him show that they also kept up a regular correspondence. Following that first meeting at the hospital she wrote:

I count you as an old friend now, but I know now I did not really know you until Saturday when you were by your little genius — Harry's — bed & the baby boy, Percy with the white shoes, was on your knee. That was to me a revelation! I think of you now with that baby boy's serious confiding face upturned to you. It was all so natural. To some people a child is a pretty & ornamental *addition*. Your personality now seems incomplete without the child as the natural & requisite finish to the whole man.

To her, with her genuine love and understanding of children, there was nothing immature in the childlike quality which she did not confuse with his Palace Court manner. She recognized it as a part of his true adult personality, along with the eccentricities she accepted with equal ease. Yet her maternal instincts meant she also saw in him the child whose vulnerability called to her no less than that of the children in her care. Her letters are full of concern for his health and admonitions not to overtax himself or take risks with the weather. She found no difficulty in regarding him as both a poetic genius and a friend, whose childlikeness made him lovable but never childish.

For him the relationship was very different. The 'Ad Amicam' poems had been more than a poetic tribute and the outward change he was bound now to observe could not change the feeling behind them. Katie's letters give no hint that he ever allowed it to appear in his to her. The friendship continued on her terms and if there were times when they were together when she sensed the truth, she never betrayed her suspicions. The only relief for the pain she aroused in him at such times was to turn it into the poetry he could conceal within the safety of his notebooks:

Wake not the still sad years,
Thou canst not cure, if they should wake too sore.
O Sweet! no sweetness withers in my heart,
For none was to impart
What only comes from others fragrancing;
O Sweet! no flowers have withered in my hair,
For none have wreathed them there;
And not to me, as unto others' lots,
Fell flowerful youth, but such the thorns that bare,
Still faithful to my hair.[34]

The poetry is mainly in the form of fragments of unfulfilled longing, but in 'An Arab Love Song' the longing becomes urgent physical desire. It was written after the day spent with Wilfrid Blunt when Blunt's admiration for the love poetry of the East revived Thompson's own feeling for the East — and was unmistakeably, if very privately, addressed to Katie:

The hunchéd camels of the night
Trouble the bright

And silver waters of the moon.
The Maiden of the Morn will soon
Through Heaven stray and sing,
Star gathering.
Now while the dark about our loves is strewn,
Light of my dark, blood of my heart, O come!
And night will catch her breath up, and be dumb.

Leave thy father, leave thy mother
And thy brother;
Leave the black tents of thy tribe apart!
Am I not thy father and thy brother,
And thy mother?
And thou — what needest with thy tribe's black tents
Who hast the red pavilion of my heart?

The real subject was sufficiently veiled to allow for the poem's publication.[35] And if Katie was aware of the source of its inspiration, she knew she had no need to warn him of it and so add to the pain behind it — of which, in the circumstances, she would also have been aware.

Yet at a safer level it was also a genuine friendship. When they met, the exchange of ideas and their shared interests meant much to them both. She was busy with her novels and a collection of short stories, *The Child in the Midst*, for which she had his permission to use a quotation from *Sister Songs* on the title page. She could discuss with him the social issues which she tried to raise through her writing, sharing his view that what was needed was enlightened reform rather than unthinking charity. Then after the outbreak of the Boer War in October 1899 he agreed with her, during its early phases, in supporting 'our soldiers', as she put it, rather than following the lead of the intellectual circles — which included the Meynells — in their support of the Boers. She knew he would not be shocked when she told him 'I am afraid I am a barbarian. I hate the War, I want it to be over, yet war & warfare & fighting appeals to me strongly & I will not hear a word against Cecil Rhodes'.

That same autumn her encouragement was largely responsible for his taking up Doubleday's enquiry about a further volume of poetry, and he began making lists for its contents. He knew there could be nothing ahead once the existing work had appeared, and the proposed title, 'First Fruits and Aftermath', was intended to make this clear. Apart from single poems there would be several groups, among which the 'Sonnets to Katie and 2 lyrics' were the only poems of any real merit in the whole collection.[36] In making these preliminaries he depended on her enthusiasm to override his recurring doubts. To save him the trouble of making additional copies of the sonnets she offered to send him hers. 'They alone would make your name immortal' if it were not already immortalized, she assured him.

Her letters were usually concerned with more practical affairs —
her writing, the children at the hospital, her mother's constant ill
health and, after the outbreak of the War, her frustration at not
being allowed to become an army nurse. The offer to return the poems
was not taken up, for in September she wrote to tell him that she was
re-reading them while on holiday touring the Dutch canals. She was
also writing to reassure him about a misunderstanding that had arisen
which he feared might have caused her offence. A friend, she said, 'is a
poor one indeed unless she can bear and forbear with all her friend's
moods. Dear friend, write to me at all times, whenever you want to,
don't wait for the happy moments'.

Yet that holiday marked the beginning of the end for their relationship. While in Holland she met Godfrey Burr, vicar of Bushall in
Staffordshire, and they were engaged the following spring. She did not
tell Francis directly at the time but the infrequency of her letters
through the winter, and hints from the Meynells, made him aware of
some kind of change on her side. He seems to have attributed it to the
religious differences which had arisen occasionally between them in
the past. They even led him, the year before, to write one of his rare
letters to his sister Mary, asking her to pray for the conversion to
Catholicism of a close friend: and it was probably now that he drafted
a letter on these differences as the reason for his sense of their drawing
apart:

> My ideals are not your ideals, your beliefs and my knowledge (I should
> credit myself with too much if I called it *belief* — to my sore responsibility
> it is more than that) are widths apart. You cannot breathe comfortably
> and humanly in the atmosphere of my intense convictions, even while you
> respect me for holding to them ...[37]

By distinguishing between belief and conviction he was trying to open
up a more candid discussion of their respective religious viewpoints,
but it is unlikely that the letter was sent. There is no reply to it from
Katie, whose next letter was written in April to tell him of her engagement. Although she hoped there would be no change to their future
friendship her concluding words betray the hope as little more than a
formality: 'Goodbye, dear Francis, and may God bless you'.

On his side he knew this was the loss he had anticipated in his
sonnets to her, for which there could now be no restoration. Nothing
could remain but the memories he must keep to himself, and only his
notebooks knew the measure of his grief:

> As morning eyes from sleep awakening
> Upon a shining casement, briefly glimpsed,
> Close back to darkness, but the dazzled gloom
> Still keeps the inward vision; so my heart
> Asleep to love, did open upon thee,

> And took the sudden vision of thy face,
> And from the brief irradiant four year's glimpse
> Closing again to darkness of all love,
> Sees nothing but that face.[38]

Nor could the loss as he now felt it be increased by Katie's tragic death in giving birth to twins within a year of her marriage.

Long afterwards, his reflections on the nature of their relationship gave rise to a number of observations on the wider issue of the relationship between men and women. He had no patience for the emerging 'new woman' whose clamour for her 'rights' could lead to a denial of the differences between the sexes. On the other hand he came to discard the idealization of womanhood which originated from his adolescent dream world and which formed the basis for his poems to Alice Meynell. In his love for Katie he learned that what mattered over and above any poetic ideal was the reality of her independent personality, her openness and the fearless spontaneity of her 'swift sympathy'. Even the 'boyishness' he detected in her and the curious 'bravery' to which it gave rise were entirely compatible with her feminine qualities:

> She was not self-reliant with all her bravery, & I suppose the combination made her real femininity the more piquant. Perhaps it was rather her crystal truth than the courage which I think came from it, not caused it, that won me at sight. Truth — *inlegrity (or one-ness) of nature* — is what calls to me.[39]

But such objectivity came much later. At the time, the shock on hearing of Katie's engagement came as the climax to all the losses and failures that Thompson had experienced before. He did virtually no work for six weeks, but wandered the streets and alleys where he was still the victim of their memories. Those memories had remained with him through the years of his poetic life and now they were all that was left. His poetic life must be finally buried with the friendship — the love — which for a few months gave it a brief flicker of renewal. For the news of Katie's engagement closely followed Doubleday's decision not to publish Thompson's fourth volume of poetry. The reasons are not known. Most probably Thompson's earlier achievements led Doubleday to expect a higher general standard and his doubts were then confirmed by more decided advice from his readers.[40]

In this identification of past with present pain, Thompson could find no will-power to resist the temptation which haunted him as constantly as the rest of his memories. Having failed in all other directions there was no incentive to withstand the final confirmation of failure. So he turned again to the opium which now, as then, offered him the only respite.

As part of this final failure, it was not long before he was forced to appeal to Meynell for the help he had determined never to ask for again. He was hopelessly in debt to his landlady who, on becoming aware of his condition, told him he must leave. He said nothing directly about the opium but Wilfrid knew the symptoms and did not need to be told. As always, he took the immediate problem in hand. He approached the wife of his printer, Barbara Maries, who ran a lodging house in Elgin Avenue. Having told her enough to make her aware of the situation, he persuaded her to accept Francis on account of his poetic reputation and with the assurance of regular financial support from himself. As it turned out, for nearly five years Mrs Maries was to provide Francis with the only semi-permanent home he had known since he left Stamford Street.

For the present, solving this practical problem could do nothing else for him — unless it was to make him more miserably aware of the reversion to his earlier dependence. A few days after Katie's marriage at the end of June he left a letter at Palace Court. He was already in arrears with the rent for his new lodgings and with no work coming in from the *Academy* he had no alternative but to leave. He was going back to the streets and to an end he did not name as suicide but the whole letter gave that impression. He asked Wilfrid 'to take charge of the quantities of MSS. I must leave behind me and make what you can of them'. Those he most valued he preferred to bring with him that evening when he would call to say goodbye. The poems to Katie, returned to him before her marriage, he felt he must send back to her himself, 'disguising the whole truth' for doing so. It was natural that they should assume an undue importance for him, and he enclosed copies, with the request that Wilfrid might find time to read them before he called:

> I want you to be grandfather to these orphaned poems, dear father-brother, now I am gone; and launch them on the world when their time comes. For them a box will be lodgement enough: *they* do not cost £4 a month, and fail wretchedly in the earning of it. I am an expensive taste, the most ruinous taste you ever had, my poor Wilfrid! I should like to know what you think of them before I go.[41]

Yet the arrangement to come to Palace Court first rather than simply disappear back to the streets, and the concluding words: 'My own dear friend, till I see you, Ah, not yet good bye', demonstrated that the letter was a cry for help rather than the farewell he believed it to be at the time.

Wilfrid treated it as such, infusing something of his own abundant vitality into Francis's flagging spirit as only he could. Francis was then reinstalled with Mrs Maries and Hind was informed of the necessity of supplying at least enough work to make Francis feel that his earning capacity was not entirely stifled by his present state. Hind, busy as he was about many other matters, had not realised how a recent fall in book publications was affecting Francis's output, as were the personal factors. With a genuine desire to help where he could he readily agreed to the proposal.

Nothing could do more than relieve the surface symptoms of Thompson's distress and even this was temporary. In July he sent Wilfrid a long letter, still anxious about lack of work and still very much under the influence of his return to opium. He was, he said, sick and unwell, haunted by forebodings of all kinds. In an effort to rid himself of them he had tried to join in a local carnival and been sickened physically and spiritually by the futile attempts at jollification. 'This toil-imbued people knew not how to be gay with humanity or spontaneity' he wrote. Their coarse humour revolted him: but there was still one way to lift his gloom. 'Only the children made amends for their elders, and won me to participation in their play', and for a few lines the letter revives something of his old delight in their company. It makes the contrast more apparent when he added to it a few days later. In a confused opium-oppressed outburst he listed a crescendo of woes trivial in themselves but which, taken together, were enough to break his strength in fighting the urge to return to the streets and abandon the future to them:

> Oh, that I were a *man* again! I must, I cannot help but go if things do not turn soon. Were it not for the power my love of you gives you over me, it is not the fear of consequences would have kept me back. This time, it would be mercifully short. I have neither the latent stubbornness of constitution, nor the latent belief in a destiny, which made it so tough a strife before. The very streets weigh upon me. These horrible streets, with their gangrenous multitudes, blackening ever into lower mortifications of humanity! The brute men; these lads who have almost lost the faculty of human speech, who howl & growl like animals, or use a tongue which is itself a cancerous disintegration of speech: these girls whose practice is a putrid ulceration of love, venting foul and purulent discharge — for their very utterance is hideous blasphemy against the sacrosanctity of lovers' language![42]

The drug was again working on the scenes as they appeared to him, projecting his own inner turmoil on to them in a nightmarish confusion of fact and fantasy. And in the confusion his imagery links his state of mind with the legacy from Owens College as well as that left by the years on the streets.

He was, however, possessed of more strength than he knew. This portion of the letter is almost identical with entries he now began making in his notebooks with a view to a more ambitious piece of writing than he had undertaken since the failure of the text for the 'London book'. When his usual winter colds and other ailments curtailed his outdoor activity he began putting the jottings together for

an autobiographical essay unashamedly based on his street-life experiences. As the winter dragged on it became a self-inflicted torment
which he found himself bound to undergo, its completion bringing on
another compulsive urge to return to the streets, to return to the past
as the only possible future. In February he sent the manuscript to
Meynell with a covering letter addressed to the editor of the *Nineteenth
Century.* The note to Meynell was again intended as a final goodbye,
thanking 'you and yours, dear Wilfrid, for your long and heroic kindness to me'.[43]

Again, too, Wilfrid forestalled him. But this time there was no
relapse. By completing the essay he had at last exorcised his past
memories and in so doing freed himself of the pain from his more recent ones. Yet the manuscript, the most valuable witness to what had
taken place, was not only never printed but was almost certainly destroyed. The Meynells never referred to its existence and Thompson
never mentioned it again. The only possible explanation is that it was
too revealing, too dangerous to his reputation at the time or as it was
to be built up after his death. Whether it was actually destroyed then
or later, Thompson felt himself too indebted to go against Meynell's
advice not to publish the essay, even if he had the will to do so.

The destruction of the essay is probably not as great a loss as it
might appear. In most lives there are areas of mystery, of profound
psychological workings which have to remain part of the essential
secret of another's personality. In psychoanalysis such workings are
brought about though the deliberate reliving of the past, forcing submerged fears and guilt into the conscious mind where they can be
assimilated into an acceptance of the defects and weaknesses of the
true self. For some, a comparable process is generated by circumstances and conditions working on a sufficiently sensitive character.
That Thompson was one of these is shown most clearly by the outcome. By the end of the summer of 1901 he had taken up the work for
the *Academy* with an energy he was to sustain for the next two years
and which, after Hind's withdrawal, was then transferred to the
Athenaeum. But he could not have done so while he was still dominated
by the craving for the drug. The gradual coming to terms with his
addiction is the clearest proof of the change that had taken place. For
he could only have done so through learning a degree of self-acceptance, which is the key to the outcome of such a process. It was to
be otherwise in the future, when physical illness was to overcome
his depleted will-power. But for the present, in an obscure but psychologically understandable sense, Katie's death that same summer
put the final seal on the process. Her engagement took her from him
and her marriage gave her to another. Now her death meant he was
free as he could not be before to remember her as he wanted, as the
woman he had loved, and he need have no fear of guilt in doing so.

Thompson now began to take up his old contacts and to make new ones, of which the most valuable for his remaining years was to be the growing intimacy between himself and Everard Meynell. It developed from Everard's boyish enthusiasm for cricket and Thompson's enthusiasm in encouraging it. His interest in the game revived, and was one which he could also share with several fellow lodgers and the patrons of the Skiddaw. In August he went so far as to arrange a match, which for all its irregularities was successful enough to lead him to invite Everard to a second. It would, he said, be 'only a bit of quiet practice, for amusement's sake' mentioning the names of several mutual cricketing friends. His account of the mishaps of the previous game, 'my first for over eighteen years', included 'a trimmer on the knee-cap (causing it to swell), and a beautiful ball on my left temple, which cannoned off a yard or two behind the wicket'. He had enjoyed it all immensely, however, well worth the aches and pains. 'You will find a very decent ground', he promised Everard, 'with net and all necessaries — including lemonade or Kola if you like to purchase them'.[44]

To the younger girls he remained a part of Palace Court life for whom Olivia remembered having 'no very personal feeling for' and who the adolescent Madeleine tended to despise for 'his peculiar appearance and uncared for dress'.[45] Viola was more affectionate in recalling the oddities of manner, the moustache-pulling, the constant pipe and the habit of hitching his coat over his shoulders that had stayed with him since the Ushaw days.[46] There was a better relationship with his godchild. If the teenage boy sometimes thought him 'rather a joke' it was in the casual manner of youth. The picture left in the memory of the grown man was the more lasting one:

> I . . . remember him with the tolerant-critical memory of a boy of 16 who took his poetry on trust, and with it the untied bootlaces, the overcoat never taken off, the collar much too big — or rather the neck so much too thin; the smoke issuing from a smouldering pipe in the pocket almost as often as from his mouth, a delighted companionship in the Stop Press cricket scores, the elder-brother feeling that even I, 16 years old, could not fail to have for this dear misfit of a man, this absurdly and absorbedly kind comrade; a jack-in-the-box whose comings and goings were always so unexpected because he never knew the time, often not the day, and so was always chasing and never catching the calendar.[47]

Awkward as he was when the Meynells had company, when Thompson was alone with them he displayed the 'natural good spirits' that Alice would insist were much more characteristic of him than the melancholy moods which she was right in attributing mainly to his circumstances during the later years.[48] He shared their latest craze for amateur theatricals and in the tableaux they put on for Christmas, with the *Adeste Fideles* sung by Alice and carols by the children. Whatever their family preferences might have been, he was always invited to spend Christmas Day with them. In 1901 Alice was in America on a lecture tour and her place as hostess was filled by Monica. On Christmas Eve Francis arrived panting at Palace Court, too late for the post as usual, with notes for her and her father. 'I should feel the world had gone off its hinges' he told Wilfrid, if he had been unable to come the next day.[49]

Monica was always his favourite, and he exchanged letters with her during the Pantasaph years. He also preserved the poppy of the Friston holiday episode for her. 'The Poppy', addressed to her, was the best of his poems on children. Now as she grew up he made the episode the subject of another poem. 'To Monica — After nine years' is a tender lyric of regret for himself and hope for her, momentarily reviving his gift for the poetry of childhood. When the following year she became engaged to a young doctor, Caleb Saleeby, he wrote her a letter of singular sincerity and charm:

> I sympathise with you in your happiness, and hope it will be the beginning of a life-long happiness with the lover you have chosen — I say lover, for I hope you will always be lovers, despite dinners and servants and other inevitable, not to say wholesome prose of marriage. Your future husband, of course, I have barely seen, and that but once. But that he is your choice is enough for me, enough to make me regard him as a friend, and extend to him, if he will allow me, the affection which you once — so long since — purchased with a poppy in that Friston field. 'Keep it' you said (though you have doubtless forgotten what you said), 'as long as you live'. I have kept it, and with it I keep you, my dearest. I do not say much or show much, for I am an old man compared with you, and no companion for your young life. But never, my dear, doubt I love you. And if I have the chance to show it, I will do.
>
>   I am ill at saying all I doubtless should say to a young girl on her engagement. I have no experience in it, my Monica. I can only say, I love you; and if there is any kind and tender thing I should have said, believe it is in my heart, though it be not here.[50]

Monica's marriage in June 1903 was remembered by all the family as well as himself as the one occasion when he arrived too early instead of too late. Finding the church empty, he decided he was late as usual, and so missed the ceremony.

The children were beginning to live separate lives and Alice was often away, either on the lecture tours for which she was much in demand or on long holidays, mainly abroad. The wanderlust which she inherited from her mother had for many years been subordinated to the demands of the family, and her one regret now was that Wilfrid was generally either unable or unwilling to accompany her as often as she wished. In all their comings and goings Wilfrid remained constantly at home or in his office. His future position as Director of the

publishing house of Burns and Oates meant that the family's financial position was to improve greatly but just when money was badly
needed to launch the children on their careers, it was short. Alice's
lecturing was as important for this reason as any other. And holidays,
when they nearly always stayed with friends, became essential in coun-
teracting the strain of the lecture tours on her weakening health.

Francis was well aware of the added strain in providing the sub-
sidy for his lodgings. It was by no means the limit of the assistance he
often needed, either when there was a lull in reviews or when his increasingly heavy colds and bouts of influenza forced him to fall back.
The dependence from which he was so determined to escape had
finally overtaken him. Nor was there the compensation he had once
felt in offering his poetry as a return. Among the poems and fragments
of poems which he addressed to the Meynells in these later years 'A
Double Need' is one of the most poignant:

> Ah, gone the days when for undying kindness
> I still could render you undying song!
> You yet can give, but I can give no more;
> Fate, in her extreme blindness,
> Has wrought me so great wrong.
> Gone is my sole and amends-making store,
> And I am needy with a double need.

These poems were not written with any idea of publication. Wilfrid
included 'A Double Need' in his edition of the poetry but forbore from
printing the forty-four lines of another poem which does not even
allow that the poetry had ever been a return offering. Francis owed its
existence to the Meynells as his 'second father, second mother' as
much as he owed his own survival:

> For you were authors of that song indeed
> By you 'twas sheltered from the world's unheed.
> You taught the song; and when I flagged to sing,
> Homeward I flew, and closed my weary wing.[51]

Years before, in his 'Dedication' for *Sister Songs*, he had used the same
image for the refuge that was also an underlying constraint: 'The
golden cage wherein this song bird sings'. The associations remained,
with the vital difference that now the bird was silent.

There was of course far more than material dependence involved.
Wilfrid had made the mistake of over-protection in the past, but increasingly Francis was to need the support and confidence only Wilfrid could now give him. That it was perpetuating the father-child
relationship may be regarded as more damaging than strengthening
from a psychological viewpoint. Yet without it his remaining years
would certainly have been fewer, with no comparable relief from the

21. Wilfrid Meynell in middle age (right)

22. Alice Meynell, 1902 (below)

increasing pain and loneliness that came with them. Nor would such dependence alter the fact that, from the first, they had observed their respect for one another's privacy as a mark of the reticence common to them both. Viola recognised this, taking the opium problem as her example in a key passage in her study of their relationship:

> Only in one thing was there a seeming failure of intimacy; but perhaps it was a deeper intimacy on both sides. Thompson between 1888 and 1907 never told Meynell the painful and paining truth that he had seriously relapsed into Laudanum taking; Meynell never asked what he might have been afraid to hear answered. At this level they spoke to each other with silence.[52]

Apart from dating Thompson's return to the drug too early — there is nothing to suggest it occurred before the summer of Katie's marriage — she attributes his 'silence' only to opium. But undoubtedly there were other reasons. Thompson never spoke of his deeper problems over his poetry, which he knew Meynell would not understand, or about his real feelings for Katie. There may well have been other lesser areas where both remained as silent as Thompson chose to be on his side about his sparetime friends and activities. In addition, Viola's use of the term 'afraid' needs expanding. If Meynell was 'afraid' it was of intruding where he felt he had no right: and, where the drug was concerned, he and Thompson were both aware that there was no need to ask. Each knew that the other understood the truth.

What was important was not so much the return to his addiction but that he did manage, at least until his last months, to maintain a degree of control which was made all the harder by his otherwise disorderly way of life. No one knew the struggle it could mean at the times when illness or pressure of work, or both, intensified the craving. Here again the notebooks provide the only available information. Those in use during the four years following the crisis of 1901 contain scattered lists of the amounts of opium — generally in the form of laudanum — he was taking. They were kept up for a week or two at a time but otherwise undated, the quantities varying from one to three or four bottles a day. Normally the bottles contained about two-and-a-half ounces each, but as the contents could also vary there is no way of assessing with accuracy how much he was taking at any particular time. What does appear is the consistency with which the effort was kept up and any attempt at judging its success or failure has to be based on what is also apparent from his output of work during the same period, together with the deterioration of his general health.[53]

How far the deterioration was increased by the addiction will be open to later questioning. At this time the colds, influenza, rheumatic pains and stomach upsets to which Thompson constantly referred in his letters to Meynell and Hind were largely due to other factors. The

room at his lodgings where he spent much of the day was unheated, a
fire only being allowed in the evenings after normal working hours,
and he frequently complained of the food as unimaginatively stodgy.
Then there was the necessity of being out whatever the weather, either
because he must deliver his work by hand to be on time or because
he must save the postage. In addition there was the mental strain of
keeping up with work which could never be congenial. Week by week
he produced some hundreds of reviews and articles, mostly for the
Academy and *Athenaeum* but also for other journals and all completed
with the same meticulous care. And if this output indicates the extent
of the control he achieved over his addiction there was the constant
psychologically debilitating struggle to maintain it, which also acted
as a drain on his physical stamina. The fact that he had come to terms
with it as part of the self he must learn to accept gave him the strength
to make the effort, but it could not lessen the extent of the effort
itself.[54]

No one knew the details of Thompson's struggle, but for some two
years he did have a friend in whom he could confide his more general
state of mind and whose insight went a good deal further.

    The record of this friendship has been strangely neglected.
Sarath Kumar Ghosh was a fellow lodger at Elgin Avenue, a young
Indian of good family and education now looking for a career in the
London literary world. Soon after Thompson's death Ghosh published his experiences in the form of a rambling, inconclusive novel
where the only chapters of any merit describe the hero's friendship
with Thompson, portrayed as a great poet whose 'mission' had failed
because he was temperamentally closer to the East than to the West.
The hero, Barath, first meets him in a crowded railway carriage. The
description is unmistakeably drawn from life:

> He was of medium height, but very slight of frame, which made him seem
> taller than he really was. His cheeks were so sunken as to give undue pro-
> minence to a little grey beard that was pointed at the end but otherwise
> untrimmed. It was his garb that was against him, and in violant contrast
> with the traditional smartness of City men. His trousers were dark, too
> dark for summer, frayed at the ends, spotted with tallow marks — which
> might have been made from a farthing dip in climbing to a fourth floor up
> rickety steps at midnight. His coat was grey — and did not match the
> trousers — stained with tea at the sleeves. The greatest incongruity, how-
> ever, was that he wore an ulster, though the heat was great. It had been
> originally brown in colour, but was now of several hues in patches . . .
>
> . . . Now Barath had noticed his eyes, which the others had not: in fact,
> struck by them from the first, he had noticed nothing else. Whether they
> were light grey or blue he could not tell; it was their lustre, not their

colour, that arrested his attention. As for his garb, Barath cared little; in
India a Brahmin of Brahmins may trudge along the Grand Trunk Road
in a sixpenny dhoti, and a prince of the House of Rama bathe in the
Ganges among a crowd of beggars. But the lustre of those eyes, intensified
by the contrast of the sunken cheeks and emaciated face, he had never seen
in England before.[55]

When they next meet, in the house of a mutual friend, Barath is fascinated by Thompson's notorious pipe-lighting ritual:

> He took out his pipe, a huge briar, struck a match, gave just one puff, held
> the match over the bowl till his fingers were nearly burnt, threw away the
> match, struck another, also gave a single puff, relapsed into thought —
> and so on, with several matches.[56]

Equally closely observed from life is the light under the poet's door,
briefly extinguished every few minutes as he passes before it in pac-
ing his room far into the night. The friendship grows and the two
exchange views on philosophy, science, mathematics, evolution and,
of course, literature. In real life, Thompson's preoccupation with
Eastern thought was aroused again by Ghosh's wide and well-trained
knowledge of the writers of the East. In the novel it leads to plans for a
great work of translation, probably based on truth. But Barath is most
clearly Ghosh himself when he writes of Thompson's constant pain at
the loss of his poetic powers. '"It is written" says Barath-Ghosh,
"that no true prophet shall be believed in his lifetime, that for his
reward he shall be stoned to death by the roadway outside the city"':

> 'Or be left to starve within its streets', Thompson answered in vague
> agitation. 'It is worse for him to starve to death before he has delivered his
> message, than to be stoned to death after it. There may be one who will
> have both — who will starve first and be stoned afterwards'.[57]

There is an authentic note in the pointed realism of Thompson's rejoinder. So too with the tour of the actual streets on which he takes
Barath, deliberately introducing him to scenes and characters for
which the Indian's admiration for England and English life have not
prepared him. After a day divided between the revelations of a magis-
trate's court and of the slums around Longacre and Kensal New
Town, they end up in Hyde Park. A man lies slumped across a bench,
his face swollen and distorted. A group of onlookers gather as a policeman tries to deal with the seeming drunkard. Barath watches as
Thompson pushes the policeman aside and examines the man with
medical precision. '"Fetch an ambulance at once", he orders, "take
him to the nearest hospital. And the next time you see a man lurching
heavily, do not jump to the conclusion that he is drunk. He may be
merely dying"'. With such 'apparent cynicism' Ghosh, through
Barath, comments, 'Thompson sought to disguise the bitterness in his
heart'.[58]

Soon after this episode, in the novel as probably in reality, the friends part when Barath leaves Lodon. But Ghosh gives his hero his own lifelong love and admiration for the poet whose insights and 'prophecies' had left a deeper impression on him than anything else he encountered during his years in England.

Yet there were aspects of Thompson's character which he could not understand, as when, through Barath, he puzzled over the observation on the dying man. If it was not cynicism, what was it? What the Indian failed to recognise was the twist of paradox Thompson saw shaping, or misshaping, all human life, the slender but unbreakable link between its tragedy and its comedy. His later notebooks are filled with verse and prose fragments based on this sense, often with a sharp edge of bitterness:

> The rich, who with intention pure
> Amuse themselves to help the poor;
> Loving the gospel ordinance,
> All night, to clothe the naked, dance.
> To aid the widow go to balls
> And flirt in aid of hospitals;
> To educate the fatherless
> Array themselves in fancy dress:
> To feed the hungry drink champagne
> And waltz like mad for the insane.

And so on, to the last cutting lines:

> Then feel (if they have not been bored)
> That 'charity's its own reward'.[59]

In another much longer 'Ballad of Charity', only the setting is medieval. The message is of no one age. Friar Peter's appeal for new vestments for the local church is heard with sincere good will by Burgher John. But he has promises to keep: the wine-feast for his friends, Christmas gifts for his children and the new mantle so much desired by his wife. Each time he hears the appeal one or other of these demands gets the better of his intentions. Then he dies and Friar Peter, who has appealed on the basis of 'saving the souls' of the donors, wonders what may be the fate of one who has consistently failed to respond. Meanwhile Burgher John discovers, on arriving in heaven, that the pleasure his gifts have given to his family and friends has caused more joy among the angels than anything he might have given Friar Peter for his church. Such appeals are not infrequent and the poem is a direct attack on the element of spiritual bribery behind them, one still not uncommon today. The aim is the more precise for the seemingly casual humour with which it is driven home.[60]

Poems of this kind and fragments of similar poetry and prose are clustered together, often on the same page, with notes and comments

where the twist in human affairs is applied far more sombrely. It was
the time when the stability of the Empire, hitherto unquestioned,
was beginning to weaken through over-confidence in past achievements, and Thompson was not alone in seeing the Boer War as the
present warning of long term repercussions. Yet the expectations for
the future which were stimulated by the new century were still mainly
directed to an age of future prosperity due to the discoveries bequeathed to it by the one just past. For Thompson its coinciding with
the War brought a revival of his concern for warfare, shorn now of
much of the glamour and appeal the battle once held for him. He saw
the greed giving rise to the ravages in South Africa spreading out to
infect the whole of Western civilization 'till the awful war comes in
which the European nations will finally explode their feuds, their
treacheries, their jealousies — and ultimately themselves'.[61] This
prophetic note is present again when he defines the root cause for such
a cataclysm:

> '. . . the sagaciously selfish millenium to which the nations look is impossi-
> ble . . . the fear of war will never exterminate war . . . While egotism and
> the passions of egotism prevail upon the earth, there will be war. For all
> egotism at root is murder.

It is one of many similar notes, followed here by the typically caustic
comment: 'Nations once went to war for their injured honour; now for
their injured pocket'.[62]

In the light of these notebook entries, the Odes which Thompson
wrote 'to order' during the five years between the Jubilee of 1897 and
the peace treaty with South Africa in 1902 should claim more attention than they have so far been given. In addition, Thompson's gift for
rhetoric lent itself to poetry of this kind. If it had to serve the demands
of a too-facile patriotism, it could at times do so through retrieving
relics from his past store of imagery. In 'To England', commissioned
by Hind a few months after the success of the Jubilee Ode, rhetoric
and imagery were given full rein:

> On other marts than those where the hoarse trader yells,
> There are things bought and sold which not the merchant sells.
> The shares thereon are honour, and the investment blood,
> And honour's shares must rise at length, though all the world
>   withstood.
> A rich estate thou hold'st which thy forefathers got;
> It is not thine to barter, thine to let it rot.

Thompson shared in the sentiments that were not always mere jingo-
ism when accompanied by the fear that England would neglect the
high calling that came with her achievements. But he was more
explicit than most. Of itself, accumulated wealth brings only envy and
envy breeds war:

The merchants of the four-nooked world their chaffer hold;
But what was won by iron, thou shalt not keep by gold.[63]

When Hind asked for an Ode on the passing of the century he advised more caution. 'The Nineteenth Century' draws on the Jubilee Ode for its celebration of the arts and sciences, accompanied by the required allusions to the Empire and it achievements. But the Ode concludes with the warning that, as the nineteenth century began and ended in war, so future warfare could destroy the hopes for the new one as the offspring of the old.[64]

Thompson refused to regard these Odes as poetry in any true sense, commissioned as they were for particular occasions without reference to personal inspiration. Yet they meant more to him than he admitted or perhaps realized, as page after page of notebook drafts show clearly enough. By taking up ideas and themes arising from the subject in hand and exploring them well beyond its requirements, he worked towards a view of the future that was in some respects strangely prophetic. In that view warfare as an evil reality displaced, if it did not entirely replace, the appeal of the idea of battle. At the same time he was coming to see the century ahead as doomed to war. England was leading the way for other nations towards a war of a magnitude only made possible by the discoveries of his own age. When the *Daily Chronicle* commissioned him to write a poem commemorating the peace treaty with the Boers in 1902, he made the warning note too clear and it was discarded as unsuited to the mood of the occasion. He could not celebrate a peace in which he had no confidence, or the treaty for which he felt no elation.[65]

There were two occasions when Thompson's subject allowed for a more genuine response. The death of the Queen the previous year brought a request from Hind for a poem to appear in the next issue of the *Academy*. And the poem he produced two days later celebrated the high motivation that always guided the Queen herself, rather than the future fate of the Empire left in other hands.[66] The second occasion arose, unexpectedly as it might seem, from Hind's commission for an Ode to mark the sudden death of Cecil Rhodes on 26 March 1902. It was on a Monday and the poem had to be ready by Thursday. Hind's record hardly does justice to what was, by any standard, a notable achievement:

> I learnt never to count upon anything by Francis Thompson until it was actually in my hands. His 'Ode on the Death of Cecil Rhodes' which I had urged him to write, was brought to me by a bewildered Thompson when the paper should have been going to press, in various pieces, written upon the backs of envelopes and toilet papers, produced from various pockets. I gave him half a crown to buy food, as in those days 'The Academy' was his banker. I pieced the pieces of the Ode together and had them put into type. When Francis Thompson returned as hour or so later, flushed and

momentarily easy in body, he read the proof swaying (I see him now) and
said in his slow, distinct enunciation, a little blurred, maybe, at that
moment, 'It's all right, Hind'. It was. There was not a word to alter in it.[67]

In fact, Hind recognized in the poem 'a flame of his old poetic fire'
and in this he was right. It had been fanned by a sudden inspiration
where Thompson felt his own dreams of poetic achievement transferred to the dreams that guided Rhodes towards high ideals before
their degeneration into greed for gold:

> But for the dreams,
> For those impossible gleams
> He half made possible; for that he was
> Visioner of visions in a most sordid day:
> This draws
> Back to me Song long alien and astray.
>
> 11–16

And in the line that sets the overall theme: 'So large his dreams, so
little come to act'[53] it comes closer to the truth than Thompson knew,
echoing Rhodes' own words, 'so much to do, so little done'. At the
end, the isolated grave on the Matappo hilltop becomes a symbol for
the failure of the high ideals and the loneliness the failure must bring:

> With, aloof,
> The elements for roof,
> Claiming his mountain kindred, and secure,
> Within that sepulture
> Stern like himself and unadorned,
> From the loud multitude he ruled and scorned,
> There let him cease from breath, —
> Alone in crowded life, not lonelier in death.
>
> 123–130

Thompson's poor opinion of his 'public' poems was fostered
by Everard's dismissal of the 'newspaper odes' as 'pot-boiling journalism: their inspiration by the clock and column'. Even of 'Cecil
Rhodes' he could only say it 'bore the mark of a trumped up emotion's
inspiration'.[68] Nor has the verdict been questioned since. Such poetry
has to be assessed on its own merit and within its definitely limited
scope. In this sense Thompson's contribution is closer to Kipling than
to the clamour of minor voices chasing cheap fame through imitation
of the acknowledged master. Thompson held Kipling in genuine
esteem, recognizing in his work qualities he could not distinguish in
his own. Kipling's didactic poem 'The Islanders' appeared in the
same year, 1902. If he could not entirely approve the famous choice
of metaphor of the complacency Kipling identified there 'With the

flannelled fools at the wicket or the muddied oafs at the goals', he
thoroughly approved of the sentiment behind it as expressing his own
fears for the nation's future. In his review of William Watson's 'Ode
for the Coronation of King Edward VII' Thompson took the opportunity to stress the 'perfunctory dutifulness' of poetry of this kind:
'The whole class of state poems, from cruel experience, is suspect' he
asserted.[69] He found passages to praise, however, and forebore from
drawing attention to several borrowings from his own 'Nineteenth
Century' Ode. But in sending the review to Hind he drew attention
to the fact as a compliment compared with the imitations he must
endure from those lesser self-styled 'bards', whose effusion led him
to stronger protest in some notebook lines:

> Of bards who, feeling half the thing they say,
> Say twice the thing they feel, and in such way
> Pierce out a passion; of all them whose art
> Seeking the scorn inspired and fury fine,
> With 'damn' and 'hell' stuffs out the mouthing line-
> O powers divine!
> How weary is our heart!
> How weary is our heart these many days!
>
> . . .
>
> Of bards indignant in an easy chair
> (Because just so great bards before them were),
> Who yet can only bring,
> With all their toil,
> Their kettle of verse to sing,
> But never boil;
> How weary is our heart these many days.[70]

During these years he did make an attempt to use the ode form as he
had in the past. 'Of Nature: Laud and Plaint' cannot compare with his
earlier achievement and, knowing this, he did not try to publish it.[71]
Yet there are lines where echoes from the past take on a new vigour of
their own, hinting that after all, a revival might still be possible. As
where, after celebrating Nature as the source of childhood's unheeding joys, the poem moves on to the grown man who has learned the
limitations of Nature's gifts:

> once more
> To run and be to the Sun's bosom caught;
> Over life's bended brows prevail
> With laughters of the insolent nightingale,
> Jocund of heart in darkness; to be taught
> Once more the daisy's tale,

And hear each sun-smote buttercup clang bold,
A beaten gong of gold . . .

> . . .

Of all the vain
Words of man's mouth, there are no words so vain
As 'once more' and 'again'!
Hope not of Nature, she nor gives nor teaches;
She suffers thee to take
But what thine own hand reaches,
And can itself make sovereign for thine ache.

78–85
99–105

The impact of Nature as the 'poor stepdame' who 'cannot slake thy drought' in 'the Hound of Heaven' is missing, as it had been since 'An Anthem to Earth'. But in places, the poem witnesses to a possible future.

There is a far more definite witness in the one poem of these later years where Thompson touches on a theme, which in other circumstances could have revived the true poet in him. It is the only way to interpret the sudden appearance of genuine power in the lines that would become almost as well-known as 'The Hound of Heaven', variously called 'The Kingdom of God' and 'In No Strange Land'. In its printed form the poem has been edited from an unfinished draft and a close analysis reveals certain weaknesses in structure and continuity which Thompson would not have allowed in a final text.[72] Recognizing this does not, however, affect the impression of a profound vision of the world born of experience such as only the world can give. He takes the angels as the great traditional symbols of the union of earth and heaven. They are the heralds of the moment of incarnation repeated throughout the Christian centuries in the sacramental and symbolic life of the Church. Is it worth remembering here how Thompson's first poem to show signs of his future as a poet was a celebration of the historical moment, the angel's annunciation to Mary, in the sonnet 'Ecce Ancilla Domine'? According to his present vision this ever-repeating process is cosmic in its application: 'The angels keep their ancient places' as part of the timeless whole of creation: 'Turn but a stone and start a wing' [13–14]. But he does not confuse the two worlds of his vision and so commit the error which he had feared in Patmore's too-ready identification between the natural and the supernatural, carried dangerously further by his Capuchin friends. The mystery remains, 'the many splendoured thing' beyond the confines of 'our clay-shuttered doors'. So he takes another great symbol of the union that contains the essential distinction, the ladder of Jacob's Dream reaching from earth to heaven in a twofold movement of ascent and descent.

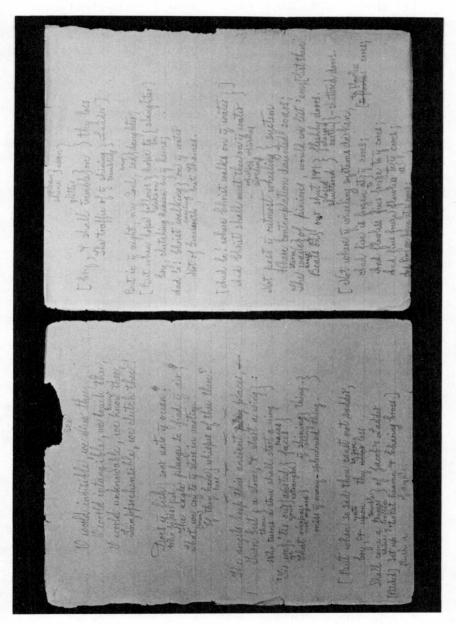

23. Part of the manuscript of 'The Kingdom of God'

For Thompson the ladder had an added meaning. Was the poem
inspired by a sudden memory of the Sussex downs imposed on the
scene of his present life with its other memories of the years on the
streets? So it seems. The 'Ode to the Setting Sun' was completed
'ascending and descending' the 'Jacob's ladder' cut into the downs
above Storrington. Now the shadow cast over the sun from the Cross
in the poem of his poetic awakening had deepened almost to darkness.
But the ladder remained, revived here as a symbol akin to the Cross in
uniting earth with heaven, the two dimensions of his poetic vision, in
a movement which, as a poet, Thompson felt himself unequal to express. Unquestionably, he does so here. The ladder reaches to heaven
because, like the Cross — so significantly recalled at this point in the
poem — it is firmly founded in the earthbound reality of human life.
As such, it leads beyond the shadow to a vision of Christ's presence,
not as symbolised by the sun but as a part of his own life-experience as
man and poet:

O world invisible, we view thee,
O world intangible, we touch thee,
O world unknowable, we know thee,
Inapprehensible, we clutch thee!

Does the fish soar to find the ocean,
The eagle plunge to find the air —
That we ask of the stars in motion
If they have rumour of thee there?

Not where the wheeling systems darken,
And our benumbed conceiving soars! —
The drift of pinions, would we hearken,
Beats at our own clay-shuttered doors.

The angels keep their ancient places; —
Turn but a stone, and start a wing!
'Tis ye, 'tis your estrangéd faces,
That miss the many-splendoured thing.

But (when so sad thou canst not sadder)
Cry; — and upon thy so sore loss
Shall shine the traffic of Jacob's ladder
Pitched between Heaven and Charing Cross.

Yea, in the night, my Soul, my daughter,
Cry, — clinging Heaven by the hems;
And lo, Christ walking on the water
Not of Gennesareth, but Thames!

10
Sight beyond the Smoke
Last Years in London and Sussex
1901–1907

I yet have sight beyond the smoke,
And kiss the gods' feet, though they wreak
Upon me stroke and again stroke;
And this my seeing is not weak.
'From the Night of Forebeing': 333–336

Thompson's personality as it has taken shape and form so far is as different from the etherealised figure presented by his early admirers as from the opium-soaked failure he became to a later generation. Similarly the poetry has revealed itself very differently in its interpretation by either his admirers or directors, while his prose can be said to have acquired a new importance. Throughout, the chief source for these changes has been the notebooks, where Thompson revealed himself as few others have done.

Yet they are unlike even those others — Coleridge being one such example — in that the extent of direct self-revelation is comparatively limited. It is when they are taken as a whole that they reveal the whole man. They are inconsistent, with as little time-sense directing their contents as Thompson himself possessed. He hardly ever dated them and in many the entries can jostle one another from opposite ends of his adult life. The entries themselves are often trivial, whether poetry or prose, and for every page of any particular value there are many apparently with none. But only apparently. It is just because of the trivialities and the banalities that the notebooks are so genuine in portraying the kind of weaknesses which most of us either never record or, if we do, we are careful to destroy. It was part of the child-like quality in Thompson — his lack of sophistication in such matters — that he saw no reason against recording them or for destroying them. Then, very fortunately, they were not considered worth including among the 'unpleasant' features Meynell insisted should be removed.[1] And with regard to the missing pages in many of the note-

books, their absence, however regrettable, hardly damages the portrait as it finally takes shape: taken together they contain more than
enough to compensate for the loss. Again, as with an actual portrait
where one feature can impress more than the rest, so here there is one
which dominates all the inconsistencies and other weaknesses. The
mark of a strong and struggling personality remains stamped on
almost every page, from the schoolboy essays of the 'Ushaw College
Notebook' to the last, the half-filled 'Large Commonplace Book'.

This is particularly true of the last six years and the three factors
which combined to direct them towards the end — the extent of his
opium addiction, the cause of his increasing ill-health and the connection between the two. There are about a dozen notebooks where,
apart from the opium calculations, the contents show they were in use
during that time, with drafts for the odes and for reviews and articles written after Thompson returned to the drug. In none are there
any entries comparable with those made when he was on the streets
or which are even indicative of milder symptoms of the kind. The
only possible exception is a long rambling dialogue he called 'Infera'
where the dreamer relates to the writer the kind of nightmares Thompson had experienced in the past. It could have been stimulated by
his work for the autobiographical essay, which certainly provoked
memories recorded at times in language recalling that of the London
streets notebooks. But it did so as part of his past, not present life, and
'Infera' is more likely to have been the product of his return to opium
before he left London for Pantasaph. It cannot be dated with any certainty and is much closer in style and content to De Quincey than any
of Thompson's later writing.[2]

The notebooks are the best because they are the most intimate
guide; but there is also the continual output of work to which he gave
the same conscientious care right up to the end. Between 1900 and
1904 there was no slackening of the pace, resulting in about 250 contributions for the *Academy* and the *Athenaeum* apart from the Odes and
the many occasional pieces for other journals.[3] It is the attention he
gave them that matters most, something he could not have sustained
if the influence from the drug had been generally more than minimal.
Such as output was certainly largely due to the necessity to earn sufficient for its purchase. From the notebook calculations Thompson
appears to have bought it most often in the form of landanum, usually
sold in bottles containing two to three ounces. Several of his lists
include the cost as well as the number of bottles but, as the prices
varied from year to year and the lists are undated, no accurate esti-
mate of what he spent is possible. What can be said is that, as the
average cost was 1/6d for a bottle which most addicts would need to
replace every third day or so, the drain on Thompson's weekly
earnings was considerable.[4] Even in an average week they seldom
amounted to more than £3, barely enough to cover essentials apart

from the drug. Added to this, the nature of his work as well as his performance of it meant that payments could be erratic — while a few days' illness could set him back for several weeks if he allowed it to interfere with keeping his deadlines. There was never enough to spare for a decent overcoat or winter boots, leaving him no choice but to accept the help which Meynell was always ready to give in the form of discarded clothing of his own. The two were very different in build, resulting in an odd assortment of garments that most regarded as due to choice rather than necessity. On the other hand Thompson's clothes had always been peculiar to himself, picked up in street markets and second-hand shops, and even the Meynells failed to make the distinction between choice and necessity when writing of his appearance during his last years.

They failed to make another and much more important distinction. Influenced by attitudes that developed after Thompson's death, they constantly referred to his sense of guilt where the drug was concerned and its intensification towards the end of his life. It was their way of trying to exonerate him from what was by then regarded as a medical and social evil and the way they interpreted his own silence on the subject. It was also part of their justified effort to distinguish him from the other opium-eaters among the 'decadent' poets who were his contemporaries and with whom he was being too readily identified on account of his addiction.

Undoubtedly Thompson did undergo a form of guilt, but not in the sense put forward by the Meynells and by all who have written on him since without relating it to attitudes prevailing during his actual lifetime. Until well after his death there was still a widely-held view that opium, while more serious than tobacco, was nothing like as damaging as alcoholism. What mattered was the degree of control over its use. A Royal Commission set up in 1895 to investigate the subject concluded that opium addiction had no evil effects comparable to alcohol and its withdrawal could be more harmful than its continuance. Only when alternative pain relievers came on the market at about the same time as the spread of morphine addiction and the use of subcutaneous injections in about 1910, did attitudes harden into those generally held since.[5]

For Thompson the issue was not so much his need for the drug, or even his dependence on it, as the restriction in its use. The accepted view of his last years as being clouded by its oppression and the shame it induced is the product of a later view of the evils of addiction. When physical illness or emotional strain necessitated an increase which he could not afford by any other means than an appeal to the Meynells, it did bring guilt and shame, which accounted for his reticence on the subject and his absolute silence where the Meynells themselves were concerned.

Reticent as he was as it affected himself, his attitude is apparent from his reviews of books by writers known to have been opium eaters. When he drew attention to the fact, which he never failed to do, it was the extent to which the habit had been controlled that interested him most. He had modelled much in his early essays on De Quincey's opium-inspired prose, sensing as he did an affinity which was not broken when he evolved his own more direct and lucid style. It was, he said, by 'a patient tenacity and purpose to which justice has hardly been done' that De Quincey succeeded in assimilating the drug into a life of prodigious hard work. On the sixteen volumes of writings by which he earned 'his journalistic bread' Thompson's comment could be applied to himself: 'It is not a record which merits the charge of sluggishness or a wasted life'.[6]

Coleridge's comparative failure to master the drug blinded Thompson to other aspects of the poet's later years. To him it was inseparable from Coleridge's failure as a poet. The five great poems were his only triumph, 'for which he paid the devil's price of a desolated life and blasted powers'. There was nothing, for Thompson, to compensate in the prose writings that followed or to mitigate 'the saddest and costliest wreck in literary annals'.[7] He was gentler with James Clarence Mangan's lesser genius. 'Pathetically noble in an ignoble setting' Mangan could no more direct his poetic gift than the addiction which too easily dissipated it. On the other hand Baudelaire and Poe, both opium eaters to excess, succeeded in mastering their demon. Each in his own way became 'masters of their destinies and did the thing they willed in the way they willed'. Again, writing of Crabbe and the privations of his London years, Thompson chose to draw special attention to the little-known fact 'that Crabbe was a moderate opium eater, forced by dyspepsia, and throve on it'.[8]

He was exaggerating, but there was also an element of self-identification to account for it. No one ever 'throve' on the drug and Thompson was no exception, however necessary it became to him as his health deteriorated from other causes. The extent to which it did become necessary was perhaps best understood by his Indian friend Ghosh, whose observation that 'to sustain life the drug as stimulant was as essential to his enfeebled body as food or air' seems close to the truth.[9] Everard Meynell, who saw more of him than the rest of the family during his last two or three years, also understood something of the kind. One of his aims in writing the poet's biography was, he said, to show how 'the life that opium conserved in him triumphed over the death that opium dealt out to him'. But in going on to assert that the drug put Thompson in 'constant strife with his own conscience' he was hardly less mistaken than in the claim that at the same time 'it staved off the effects of tuberculosis'.[10] Here he was confirming tuberculosis as the reason for Thompson's chronic ill-health in accordance with the assertions made by the family after his death — for which tuberculosis was also said to have been the cause.

The claim has distorted his portrait ever since. From the time of his illness at Owens College, generally regarded as the first sign of the disease, there is no indication at any stage of his life that he was consumptive. Nor did his own medical knowledge lead him to make any diagnosis of the kind to account for his various ailments. What he did do was to leave a fairly constant record, in his letters, of the progress of these ailments in his later years and of the onset of the more serious symptoms that undoubtedly hastened, if they did not cause, his death.

From Pantasaph he often wrote to Wilfrid Meynell or to Patmore of the rheumatic pains, headaches and stomach disorders he recognised as largely psychosomatic, 'causeless seeming disturbances' to which he was 'intermittently subject'.[11] Then, within a few months of his return to London the damp and fogs gave rise to the frequent colds that could easily turn into influenza and always caused acute anxiety at any falling back with his work. 'I have not been at all well, and it has been all I could do to keep afloat': 'I have been struggling against time and sickness to finish work': 'I could not quite finish the article last night, and find myself ill today with a violent cold'. With the colds came increased rheumatic troubles. 'It is beastly rheumatism which is knocking me up': 'I am upset with a bad cold, and rheumatism in the knees': 'I was very unwell all week ... but had perforce to go out in the bitter weather, catching fresh cold'.

More important are the references to sickness and vomiting. 'I was confined to bed all day, and touched nothing but a cup of tea till eleven tonight': 'I have touched nothing but part of an egg and one piece of toast'. This letter, to Wilfrid Whitten, continues with the only hint, carefully worded, to opium taken on such occasions:

> I never had such continuously acute dyspepsia. The drain on my strength has been going on now for near three weeks, with rarely a day but I vomit up at night whatever I may have taken during the day. And gradually my stomach gets so weak that I cannot eat, without some special stimulus, which I still only use in case of pressing necessity of work, as this morning — since it forfeits its power for good if you make a habit of it.[12]

This was in November 1900, at about the time when Thompson's return to the drug was threatening to become such a habit. From then on a pattern was to develop, with chronic dyspepsia and sickness necessitating the use of opium as a short term stimulus but which at the same time was contributing to the recurrence of the same symptoms.

The letter to Whitten is more detailed in other respects than most. When Thompson wrote of his health it was usually to account for delays in work or broken engagements. Nor can he be accused of exaggerating his physical ills in order to conceal the real reason as being an increase in his use of the drug. This has often been claimed, but the letters are proof enough that the accusation is unfair. They are

as consistently lucid and to the point as the reviews which he somehow succeeded in completing at these times, impossible if an excess of
opium had been the reason.

It was not until 1905 that he first wrote to Everard of an affliction
in his feet causing pain and swelling. Worse, it was preventing him
from taking the amount of exercise to which he was accustomed, the
'one physical pleasure & resource against ill health' on which he had
always been able to depend. The trouble worsened during the next
year and he was persuaded to consult Monica's doctor husband,
Caleb Saleeby, who diagnosed gout. Thompson did not agree. Early
in 1906 he sent Meynell a detailed account of the symptoms as those
associated with beri beri, a disease arising from malnutrition and
more common in the East. Very probably for this reason the diagnosis
had not occurred to Saleeby, but Thompson's description bears out
his own very clearly. The attacks of numbing pain in feet and ankles,
the palpitations and nerve twitchings and the loss of control over the
lower limbs, experienced as if connected with the head and brain, all
are noted with the detached accuracy of the one-time medical student.
The cause of the complaint is equally accurate, a deficiency in the circulation affecting the heart and brain:

> The undoubted fact is that 'twas a deadly disease caused originally by
> mal-nutrition; springing from failure of heart & circulation; presenting the
> symptoms described; & bringing me into imminent danger.[13]

When Thompson wrote this he was recapitulating an earlier description, apparently given to Saleeby and known also to Meynell. It
seemed then that the worst might be over — but this was in fact a
remission characteristic of the disease.

When all the available evidence is taken together Thompson's
own diagnosis is apparently correct.[14] He only began to suffer from
serious illness at the onset of these symptoms within two to three years
of his death. Before this the digestive disorders and vomiting led to the
semi-starved condition often noted by those who knew him. His diet,
even at the best of times after his return to London, was not suited to a
poor digestion and during these attacks there was nothing to tempt
him in the heavy, unimaginative meals at Elgin Avenue. And if he fed
himself, as he often did by choice, it was usually on the cheapest pork
pies provided by the Harrow Road cafés. Equally, if not more important, behind the present conditions there remained a legacy from the
years on the streets, an undermining of his general health that had
gone unnoticed until now.

What place did opium occupy in the process? A fundamental one
if the privations of the London streets period are seen as the outcome
of his addiction, while the digestive disorders of his later years were
undoubtedly bound up with its return. When, shortly before his

death, he broke the long silence on the subject between himself and
Wilfrid with the words 'I am dying from laudanum poisoning' he was,
in essence, right. He was much nearer the truth than Everard who, in
refuting the statement, maintained 'he had but one lung and that
diseased'. In the days before X-rays could determine the nature and
extent of lung damage of this kind, a post-mortem would have been
the only basis for such an assertion and there is no record that one was
performed.[15]

The object in attempting to establish the truth as to Thompson's
medical history is not merely to prove the Meynells and all who have
followed them to be wrong. It also destroys the notion of the sickly
consumptive that fitted in so well with the image of the poet of conventional piety designed to conceal the more awkward aspects of
Thompson's life and work. At both Storrington and Pantasaph, where
he was comparatively well-fed and leading a reasonably regular life
with long walks over the downs or the Welsh hills, he was healthy
enough. Furthermore, these were the two periods of his real poetic
achievement, when his minor physical troubles were of the kind that
are often the price paid for an onset of intense creative energy. It
was before, and again afterwards, that his manner of living and the
dominance of opium eventually brought about the decline and collapse of his last months. And throughout both these periods he displayed a notable physical toughness in withstanding conditions that
would have undermined a weaker constitution much sooner.

Thompson was not afraid of physical pain, but he did fear the grind-
ing unromantic effort his particular afflictions demanded of him. In
this he came to learn a lesson that only pain itself can teach — the
distinction between the idea of pain and the reality. According to his
religious training it was a mark of divine favour, a means for purifying
the soul such as the truly devout might also deliberately seek through
penance and mortification. To seek pain for its own sake and not as
a means to a higher end was always condemned in principle, but in
practice the distinction was often not made at all clear. And life had
taught him another lesson. The medical school introduced him to the
sordid reality of suffering which he made his own on the streets, where
it contained no end that was not as evil as itself. He knew, with the
knowledge of the artist rather than the saint, that as pain is essential
to birth so it is essential to all creative energy. But it was that other,
darker side which threatened to dominate his remaining years, challenging the early teaching on the subject to an extent that his religious
understanding could not match.

This gave rise to a long poem, 'Laus Amara Doloris' which, like
'Of Nature: Land and Plaint', he had no desire to publish.[16] Here,

pain is at first the 'pale Ashtaroth who rul'st my life' but if her presence can be accepted she will reveal another side:

> O great Key-bearer and Keeper
> Of the treasuries of God!
> Wisdom's gifts are buried deeper
> Than the arm of man can go,
> Save thou show
> First the way, and turn the sod.
>
> 64–69

There follows a series of passages where the creative element in pain
arouses echoes from the past rhetoric and relics of past imagery:

> Thou settest thine abode
> A portress in the gateways of all love,
> And tak'st the toll of joys; no maid is wed,
> But thou dost draw the curtains of her bed.
> Yea, on the brow of mother and of wife
> Descends thy confirmation from above,
> A Pentecostal flame; love's holy bread
> Consecrated,
> Not sacramental is, but through thy leaven.
>
> 101–109

But the theme is not sustained when pain becomes the chief presence
on the battlefield:

> Iron Ceres of an earth where, since the Curse,
> Man has had power perverse
> Beside God's good to set his evil seed!
> Those shining acres of the musket-spears —
> Where flame and wither with swift intercease
> Flowers of red sleep that not the corn-field bears —
> Do yield thee minatory harvest . . .
>
> 132–138

The horror of war as Thompson had come to see it can offer no creative outcome. Instead he draws his imagery from his own introduction
to the reality of pain as

> the stagnation
> Of the world's sluggish and putrescent life
>
> 143–144

There is no reminder, at the end, of the pain that leads to birth, to
resurrection. 'Holy and terrible' she remains enthroned as 'Queen of
Calvary'. Thompson was unable to sustain his theme, but at least he
would not descend to the pious hypocrisy too often found in connection with the subject as he had tried, and failed, to treat it.

It was the perennial problem of pain, the solution to which
Thompson was no nearer to finding than any other, no more satisfied
with the idea of pain as a mark of divine favour than with his own
efforts to cope with its reality. But, in another direction, it contributed
to an unexpectedly constructive outcome.

One of Thompson's longer articles for *Merry England* had been
written as a review of a collection of letters by George Porter, Archbishop of Bombay, published in 1891. In them he remembered the suggestion that a new light on the purpose of suffering in the Christian life
was called for. Now, in spite of other demands on his time and energy,
he turned up the review to expand it into a monograph, taking
Porter's views several stages further — further in fact than has so far
been recognized.

Today the view of asceticism put forward in *Health and Holiness* is
so widely accepted that its novelty at the start of the century is easily
overlooked. Even today, a residue from the earlier outlook remains.
The practices prevailing in the Middle Ages are still upheld by some
of the religious orders and the rigours of the saints can still be extolled
as the chief guidelines on the way to sanctity. Against this background
Thompson's eighty-page survey reads like a breath of the invigorating
air he advocated as a better means for some to combat a spiritual
crisis than the Exercises of Saint Ignatius.

Thompson's central argument is that the subduing of the body to
the spirit by deliberate 'mortification' was 'a robust system fitted to a
robust age' which must change in accordance with a changing society;

> We find our austerities ready made. The east wind has replaced the dis-
> cipline, dyspepsia the hair shirt. Either may inflict a more sensitive agony
> than a lusty anchorite suffered from lashing himself to blood.[17]

Perhaps he asserts too much here and a general criticism can be made
of his rather superficial treatment throughout. He does not define
either 'health' or 'holiness' in any precise detail or develop the implications behind his statements far enough. But this is to confuse what
amounts to little more than an extended essay with something it does
not pretend to be. Thompson was not, he knew, equal to an exhaustive study of Christian asceticism or the relation between voluntary
and involuntary suffering in the Christian life. At the time it was a
provocative stimulus, setting tradition against change in a boldly new
direction:

> The modern body hinders perfection after the way of the weakling; it
> scandalises by its feebleness and sloth; it exceeds by luxury and the softer
> forms of vice, not by hot insurgence; it abounds in vanity, frivolity, and
> all the petty sins of the weakling which vitiate the spirit; it pushes to
> pessimism, which is the wail of the weakling turning back from the press;
> to agnosticism, which is sometimes a form of mental sloth — 'It is too much

trouble to have a creed'. It no longer lays forcible hands upon the spirit, but clogs and hangs back from it. And in some sort there was more hope with the old body than with the new one. When the energies of the old body were once yoked to the chariot-pole of God, they went fast. But what shall be made of a body whose energies lie down in the road? ... Can the inertia of the modern body be met by breaking still further the beast already over-feeble for its load?[18]

In spite of his intention to avoid 'the domain of monastic asceticism' some of his severest criticism is directed at the religious orders. Too often their penances have become an official badge of sanctity based on outworn convention: 'Not solely in the kingdoms of this world, but in the kingdom of God, the administration may become infected by the red-tape microbe'.[19]

The change will come. In Thompson's view the Church is always greater than her members make her appear. It is only a matter of time before the signs already present in altered rules on fasting and spiritual direction will lead to a wider and fuller understanding. 'The Church is ever changing to front a changing world' he asserts, even if 'with that insensible gradualness of change, as of Nature's self, which is her secret'.[20] In an age when reform was too easily identified with revolt, it was a bold statement.

He avoids further comment, turning instead to the contribution made by science in discoveries leading to a new understanding of the interactions between mind and body. Already the reactions of the body on the mind are acknowledged as never before and will lead to another truth, 'that sanctity is medicinal, Holiness a Healer'.[21]

It is again deliberately provocative. In the concluding passages Thompson is not only drawing on his medical training but more particularly on his knowledge of homoeopathic medicine, with its central tenet that body, mind and spirit must work together to maintain the health of all three.

The lack of publicity given to *Health and Holiness* when it appeared in 1905 can be accounted for by Meynell's doubts as to its unorthodox trend. His position now as Managing Director of Burns and Oates was confirming his own move towards conservatism. He was in a position to push for notice for the book but in his view there was too much risk. It was therefore due to Thompson's reputation that it received very little attention and Thompson, for his part, lost interest once it was completed. With his poetry it was different but he could never muster anything like the same enthusiasm for the future of his prose.

Meynell had a further reason for his doubts. He could not prevent Thompson from arranging for the Preface provided by George Tyrrell, nor did he entirely disapprove. Tyrrell's serious break with the Church authorities was still to come but he was already in trouble with the Jesuits on account of his writings, which spread more radical views than those of the liberal minded among English Catholics in general. As a friend and admirer of Tyrrell, Meynell was in a difficult position and had been for some time. He had sold the *Weekly Register* in October 1899, largely because of the impossibility of maintaining a Catholic journal independent of the guidelines put forward by the hierarchy. It was the year of the Dreyfus Affair, during which the Catholic as well as the secular press in England protested against the Church's conduct, and there was a disturbing series of exchanges in the *Register* on the methods of government practiced by the Roman Curia. The controversy distressed Meynell, who felt himself unequal as well as unwilling to deal with the more far-reaching issues which he foresaw arising from it. He was soon proved right, for early in 1900 Mivart published his attack on the Church's teachings on hell, to which Tyrrell added the rejoinder 'A Perverted Devotion'. It appeared in the *Weekly Register* in December of that year under the journal's new editor Rooke Ley and less than two weeks before the Joint Pastoral, 'The Church and Liberal Catholicism' issued by Cardinal Vaughan and sixteen of the English bishops. Based on the dangers of relying on private judgement in matters of faith and doctrine, the Pastoral made the mistake, common both then and later, of confusing the steadier liberal outlook with the lengths to which Mivart and his supporters were prepared to go.[22]

Tyrrell did not share Mivert's more extreme views and, as friends, he and Meynell maintained a broadly-based agreement at this time. But in public, while Tyrrell was gaining a reputation for daring innovation, Meynell was withdrawing from the liberalism of his younger years. His position as head of the leading Catholic publishers was partly responsible, but it was not the main reason. He was moving towards the more generally conservative view of life that often comes with middle age.

Thompson would not allow himself to be drawn into these controversies. He had learned a lesson from his Capuchin friends and, in any case, his journalistic career was not to be jeopardised by inviting trouble in that direction. What he did do was to maintain a tacit support for the *Weekly Register* after Meynell had withdrawn. The journal was running a series of articles by well-known writers and poets under the title 'Books that have interested me' and early in 1900 he was invited to submit a contribution.[23]

Thompson's choice of the Bible was a deliberately bold and original one when Catholics were seldom familiar with more than the Gospels and many not even with these. Nor was the study of the Bible by the laity being encouraged, since the rise of historical criticism led to a questioning of its authenticity and to a crisis of faith throughout the Christian world. In this context Thompson's approach was equally bold in appraising the Bible for its literary merits. Reading the psalms as poetry may scandalise some but, he asserts, they possess immense poetic value, while much else in the Old Testament 'may also enter into the category of books which, by their literary greatness, profoundly modify a writer's mind, or style, or both'. Coming to his own experience he admits how, as a child, he read the Scriptures for their narrative and dramatic appeal, drawing a lasting influence from the imagery and language of Books such as *Wisdom* and *Ecclesiastes*. The Bible, he concludes, is for all and has something for all, 'the most elastic of all books'. There is nothing outwardly controversial but there are implications that would have been easily recognized. If the Bible is 'for all' then all should be encouraged to read it. And if at the same time it is so 'elastic', covering the whole range of human interests, its value is wider and deeper than the historical accuracy on which so much was being claimed to depend.

It is worth considering Thompson's position in relation to the controversies that were to intensify during his remaining years. He had no wish to get involved in theological argument but here, as with the later *Health and Holiness*, his attitude shows no sign of following Meynell's lead in a move towards conservatism. It also shows the common ground existing between himself and Tyrrell well before Tyrrell wrote the Preface for his book.

They met on several occasions at Palace Court, on one of which it seems Baron von Hugel was also present. At a later date von Hugel is reported as having spoken of both as 'strange' men and of Thompson, like Tyrrell, as 'a bad subject'.[24] The words suggest he met them together and that Thompson talked freely, sensing a kindred spirit in the Baron as well as in Tyrrell. It could well have been so. What is certain is that he and Tyrrell found definite similarities in their ideas. When Tyrrell described Catholicism in terms of 'Christianised paganism' Thompson responded with an understanding based on his own studies of the origins of Christian symbols. So, too, he could appreciate Tyrrell's constant emphasis in his writings on the presence of God in the world, at once immanent and transcendent. It was very close to the movement of incarnation which he had desired to express in his poetry and now Tyrrell was putting forward something of the aims he had set himself as a poet. If he suspected that the Jesuit's call for a 'new' interpretation came dangerously near the course followed by Angelo and some others among the Capuchins, there was still much with which he could agree.

With regard to the subject matter of *Health and Holiness*, Tyrrell's insistence on the responsibility of the individual in determining his religious life included the purpose of Christian asceticism — which, he was to write, 'unites and co-ordinates body and soul with all their powers and faculties and builds up the personality which consists in perfect self-determination'.[25] In *Health and Holiness* Thompson describes the true ascetic as one who has come to understand the meaning of the 'divine law' for himself, 'whereafter he no longer needs to follow where the flocks have trodden, to keep the beaten tracks of rule'.[26] There were dangerous implications here at a time when the individual conscience was still expected to conform to external authority in almost all religious matters. He made his Preface short and cautious in tone, stressing the exploratory nature of the book and quoting Thompson's own words in his conclusion: 'The mistake of personal speculation is after all merely a mistake, and no one will impute it to authority'.[27]

Another topic discussed between them at Palace Court was the need for a new approach to the writing of lives of the saints. Most hagiographies concentrated on their austerities, usually in morbid detail, and the miracles attributed to them. Anything suggestive of human weakness was considered a distraction from the sanctity to which, as a result, they appeared to have been more or less born into. Both Tyrrell and Thompson therefore welcomed the appearance, in 1897, of Henri Joli's *Psychologie des Saints*, translated into English the following year as an introduction to a series of saints' lives that was to extend to twenty-four volumes. In his review of the French original, Tyrrell gave full support to Joli's presentation of the saints as normal men and women with the characteristics and problems common to human nature. Then, in a Preface to the English translation, he drew attention to the writer's psychological knowledge applied to the 'psychology of sanctity' as embracing other religions besides Christianity. Tyrrell also stressed the interpretation of mysticism adopted from Abbé Huvelin, von Hugel's mentor. 'All mystics are not saints', while on the other hand mysticism based on the love of God forms an essential part of the psychological processes at work in the saints. Joli's aim was to distinguish pseudo-mystical states induced by physical causes from the true mysticism with which they were too often identified.[28]

Thompson was in full agreement with these views, as he was with the similar views expressed by Tyrrell in the prefaces which he supplied for the first nine volumes in the series. When the tenth appeared in 1901 it was accompanied by a note from the publishers, Duckworth, declaring that 'Circumstances have made it necessary' to find another editor. The 'circumstances' were by then Tyrrell's other writings and the reputation he was acquiring through them. In the meantime Thompson had allied himself with Tyrrell in his review of the English translation of Joli's book and Tyrrell's Preface to it. He was much more outspoken than Tyrell on the need for a new approach:

The regulation hagiography has been a compost of tedious moralities and platitudinous reflections, served up in miraculous jam to get it down the light and worldly reader's recalcitrant throat.

In what was to be one of his longest reviews Thompson traced the reaction among those who would deny all supernatural elements in sanctity and the more balanced approach found in the writings of William James and W. H. Stead. Following his own inclinations to an extent unusual for him in a review, he took up Joli's examination of 'the psychology of genius' to compare the processes at work in the saint and the poet. 'The insight of the poet springs from intuition, which is the highest reason' and like the sanctity of the saint, 'is acquired through contemplation, which is the highest effort'. This illustrates the link between the poet and the saint, for whom 'the foundation is the same, the edifice more marvellous'.[29]

Thompson could be equally daring in other reviews of books on mysticism. In a study of the subject by A. Thorold he claims that the average reader is not prepared for the shock in store for the excesses said to be the signs of both mysticism and sancitity. 'He steps into them as from a bathing machine — and I can fancy may gasp'.[30] Again, on the confusion between mysticism and the spread of spiritualism: 'If a man turns a table or keeps a private spook he is a mystic; if he writes about people who were considered mystics he is himself a mystic'. Here Thompson was reviewing W. R. Inge's *Studies of English Mystics* and of the author's own views he adds: 'Dr. Inge (we say it without offence) is something of a half-baked mystic', content with the 'half way chalets' on the mountain side of mysticism. The summit is not for him. 'For Dr. Inge is rootedly Britannic. He likes an airing among the heights, but always provides for his return to the safe domestic hearth'.[31]

Thompson would have been ready to admit that he preferred this attitude to other notions of mysticism current at the time. There are several notebook entries where he defines the popular idea of a mystic as, among much else, 'a person who said his prayers and believed in saints and angels' or equally 'a person who did not say his prayers and believed in medicine-men and devils'.[32] In spite of his denials, the suggestion was often made of mystical qualities in himself on account of his poetry and the same has been asserted since his death. His own reaction was either mild irritation or to dismiss the motion as laughable. The 'Sight and Insight' poems were first called 'Poems Partly Mystical', but in a cancelled Preface to *New Poems* he denied aspiring to any mystical heights in his poetry and subsequently changed the title of the group most likely to invite such a view.[33]

It depends on how the term is understood. As applied to the recognized mystics he was right. But he himself recognized similarities between the mystic and the poet and, in this sense, he would have allowed a mystical element in his poetry. For what is certain is his interest in the subject and its connection with the religious and the creative impulses in human nature.

This interest was also largely responsible for his next project, in which Tyrrell may well have had a share when Meynell, knowing Thompson's interest, first put it forward. As part of his training Tyrrell was familiar with the life of Saint Ignatius Loyola, the founder of the Jesuits, and from the number of references to Ignatius in *Health and Holiness* the proposal was probably being discussed between the three of them before that book was finished. This next one was to be much more ambitious in length and the time it would need — a biography of the Saint based on an earlier work by Stewart Rose, *Saint Ignatius and the Early Jesuits*. A magnificent illustrated edition of Rose's book, first published in 1870, had appeared in 1891. For all its impressive format and the engravings on almost every page, it amounted to no more than the usual hagiography padded out by historical detail which was often of doubtful accuracy.

According to Wilfrid's idea, Francis was to produce an updated and mildly revised version. Francis welcomed the suggestion as an opportunity to apply his theories in *Health and Holiness* to a saint made notorious by his austerities and the miracles accredited to him. It was also a release from the strain of reviewing, which to Wilfrid was the chief reason for encouraging it. Wilfrid was well aware of Thompson's increasing struggle to maintain the required number, mainly for health reasons but also since Hind's resignation from the *Academy*. He and Everard arranged that Francis should be paid one pound for every three pages delivered to the bookshop Everard had recently opened in Westbourne Grove. It was much nearer to Francis's lodgings and it also meant that Wilfrid was relieved of the practical problems likely to arise, with which Everard was well able to cope through his growing understanding of Francis and his ways. There were not as many problems as they expected. 'He delivered every few pages as he finished them' Everard remembered, 'and, so final was his method of composition, he neither desired nor needed to see a single page of the manuscript again'.[34]

Everard added no comment to change the impression that the result was virtually a rewrite of the earlier book. At the start, Rose's account of Ignatius's preparatory withdrawal to Manresa concentrates on his mortifications and miracles. Their proof of sanctity is taken for granted, whereas Thompson cuts out much of the detail and summarises the rest with the comment:

> Throughout his long Manresan preparation his interior sufferings were so mingled with the bodily breakdown induced by his iron self maceration, that it is not possible to say how far they were sharpened by the very weapons he used to combat them ... That he learned to condemn the indiscretion of his young and inexpert ardour we also know.[35]

Throughout the three hundred-odd pages that follow there are

cuttings and alterations from the original to form what can be claimed
to be a biography in its own right. Rose's book ends with a lengthy
series of reports by Ignatius's contemporaries on the miracles and
other supernatural occurrences connected with his life. In place of
this Thompson writes:

> He did not need the trappings of Saintship, which the Saints themselves
> have ever condemned as undeserving of note. The whole tenor of his life,
> both in what he did and in what he refrained from doing, a character of so
> singular dignity and recollection maintained through the heat and weari-
> ness of a long warfare with the world and its circumstances, wherein some
> error, some lapse and stumbling would seem, and is, inevadible by our un-
> sustained humanity — in these is manifest that indwelling of the spirit of
> God which is sanctity; in these more than in a long bede role of formal
> virtues such as were easy enough to compile from the records of his
> followers.[36]

The book was not finished until a few months before Thompson's
death. Its publication two years later by Burns and Oates — and so
under Meynell's direct auspices — was followed by the same neglect
accorded to *Health and Holiness* and for similar reasons. Its treatment of
the Saint was too unconventional for the time and its reputation as a
rewriting of Rose, as then put forward, has gone unquestioned since.
This is not only unfair to the book but means that the research involved has also gone unrecognized. And this during the last years
when Thompson has been represented as incapable of the creative
effort demanded by serious writing.

When Thompson began on *Saint Ignatius* in 1905 the research was a
passport to long hours at the British Library. And, if his studies were
not always strictly confined to the subject in hand, he was only one of
many others before and after him who have found in the Reading
Room the warmth and quiet that made an evening lingering there
preferable to his lodgings. But unlike most of those others he had
achieved a certain fame, his presence recorded by more than an
admission card and application slips. To have met him was to remember him and there were many who had come across him either at
Palace Court or at the *Academy* office. He would have been more surprised than gratified to know that the popular thriller writer Harold
Evans recognized him as a 'famous poet' too exalted above his own
pedestrian level to be approachable. And he would have regretted the
similar reluctance preventing Roger Ingpen, Shelley's biographer,
from making contact with him.[37]

Thompson was quick to sense a meeting ground even with those
who, when they addressed him, were by now strangers to him on his
side. When a young Catholic writer, John Stuart Young, claimed an

earlier acquaintance it led to an afternoon's discussion on the nature of true poetry — huddled under Young's umbrella on a bench near Temple Bar. Young was sensitive to the curious contradictions in Francis's manner and appearance. The conversation went with the brilliant intensity of his eyes and the artistic hands, 'long and white and plastic'. Yet the 'frowsy Inverness cape' and the fish basket strapped to his shoulder as the most convenient receptacle for his books and papers gave him the appearance of a street pedlar rather than a poet.[38]

Young was surprised but not in any way put off, and so Francis was at ease. The seat in the rain was more congenial to him than the West End restaurant to which he was invited on another occasion. Daniel O'Connor, then an ambitious young literary agent, met him on leaving the Reading Room late one evening and, undeterred by the poet's strange garb, asked him to join his supper party. Francis was not prepared for the glamour of the scene or the exotic menu. Embarrassed and confused he announced slowly in a tone his host would not forget: 'I — want — some PORRIDGE', followed after a pause by '— and — some — BEER'. O'Connor realised he was not just being uncouth. His awkwardness in such surroundings and company made him react in a way that exaggerated his discomfort further.[39] It was very different when Wilfrid Whitten invited him to dine at the cosmopolitan Vienna Café in New Oxford Street. Whitten compared the experience with those evenings when Boswell found dinners with Johnson 'impossible to report' — due to Francis's eloquent command of the conversation and his flawless quoting from 'the masters of poetry'.[40]

Incidents of either kind were rare. In the mind's eye of most of those who knew or came across him, Thompson was a part of the London street scene, most often a scene shrouded in rain or fog from which he emerged as an essentially lonely figure. To St John Adcock, who understood more than the rest about the London society of the time, he seemed as cut off from the superficialities and fashions of his own day as Blake had been from his a century before. He was no more a part of 'the squalid London which the best of contemporary realist novelists were putting into their books' than of 'the tawdrily or haggardly gay London of those resolutely unconventional poets who revelled irresponsibly at the Café Royal or took themselves too seriously at the Cheshire Cheese'.[41]

In contemporary terms he was neither a realist nor an idealist. Yet in himself there coexisted a realism and an idealism that puzzled those who knew him and which some have attempted to reconcile. The attempt has been as mistaken as any notion of a split personality would be. His north country background followed by the years at Owens and on the streets gave him a tough uncompromising view of life which meant that, as a poet, he never lost hold on life's realities however far above them he could sometimes rise. It meant that for him Christ could indeed be encountered walking the waters of the Thames and the Incarnation was re-enacted in every creative act from the moment of consecration in the Mass to the birth of a child or a poem.

If in this Thompson found a source of spiritual strength for himself, he left no direct record. He showed no interest now in the outward observances of his religion and although he went to Church it was by no means according to the rule of regular attendance. Nor did he seek out the services where the liturgy he loved was best presented. For him the liturgy was something wider and deeper than any particular celebration could make it, and he was content with the makeshift and often crude forms he found in the churches nearest to his lodgings.

It was wider and deeper because it was also inseparable from his religious outlook as a whole. He had come to accept the fact that he must stand apart from the religious as well as the cultural norms of his day. So, too, the many letters he continued to receive from Catholic admirers of his poetry went unanswered as meaning nothing to him. If his poetry was to live it would be for more far-reaching considerations than they could comprehend. After his death and the sorting of his papers, his dilatoriness in this direction was attributed by the Meynells to a general carelessness in dealing with his correspondence. Up to a point they were right. He disliked letter-writing unless he could expand on a subject of mutual interest, as in his letters to Alice and to Coventry Patmore. In any case there was very little time now for more than the notes sent or delivered to Palace Court and offices of the *Academy* or, increasingly, the *Athenaeum*.

On the other hand he could answer a genuine enquiry. When Gustav Holst wrote for permission to use part of *Sister Songs* for a musical setting his reply led to a similar request for 'Dream Tryst'. Quiller Couch's letter asking to include an example of his poetry in the first edition of the *Oxford Book of English Verse* prompted a long and careful answer. 'Q' had been responsible for the only worthwhile review of *New Poems* and Thompson wrote openly as to a fellow poet. He was doubtful about the choice of 'The Mistress of Vision' as differing from his more characteristic work — though, remembering 'Q''s praise for the poem, he was careful to attribute the view to others. The example eventually chosen was the much better one of 'The Poppy'.[42]

So, too, he valued the continued appreciation shown by E. V. Lucas. They met occasionally at the Meynells' Sunday gatherings and between them there was the added bond of two cricket enthusiasts. After his death Lucas paid a valuable tribute to a side of Thompson's life which has since been either deliberately neglected or not considered worthy of more than passing notice. From the later notebooks Lucas extracted a series of poems on the games and the players Thompson had watched in his youth. Lucas only printed extracts, but unlike most of the notebook poems, several were completed and corrected as if meant for publication at some future and improbable date.[43] Thompson remained a firm supporter of the Lancashire teams and the poems are not without humour in the allusions known to those conversant with the history of the game. Almost all are treated in such a way that the game is also a battle, transforming the art of war into one of peace. For behind them there is not only his lifelong preoccupation with the battle and the game but the way he had come to regard warfare in more recent years, legitimate only in the cause of peace.

Lucas did not see as far as this. What he did recognize was the technical knowledge behind the poems which was also displayed in occasional prose pieces. Above all he was impressed by the elegiac tone, the remembered games and the past players whose ghosts haunted the cricket grounds of the present. As in this verse from 'At Lords':

It is little I repair to the matches of the Southron folk,
    Though my own red roses there may blow;
It is little I repair to the matches of the Southron folk,
    Though the red roses crest the caps I know.
For the field is full of shades as I near the shadowy coast,
And a ghostly batsman plays to the bowling of a ghost,
And I look through my tears on a soundless clapping host.
    As the run-stealers flicker to and fro,
        To and fro,
O my Hornby and my Barlow long ago!

Taking the poem as representative of the rest Lucas commented:

Such a mood imports a new note into cricket poetry. Cricket poetry hitherto has been descriptive, reflective, gay, humorous. It has never before to my knowledge been made a vehicle for a lament for the past of profoundest melancholy.

Lucas remembered Thompson's technical understanding of the game as that of a connoisseur rather than a player. His appearance was hardly suggestive of either, but then it was even less in keeping with the popular idea of a poet. Unlike most, Lucas was content to accept the anomaly with the brief truth that 'Thompson was born to baffle the glib inference'.

It would be another 'glib inference' if all Thompson's affairs during these years were seen as dominated either by loneliness or increasing ill-health. He still possessed the child's ability to enter into and enjoy the small everyday pleasures so often missed in the pursuit of the larger ones he knew were beyond his reach. He might have to find excuses to avoid accompanying Everard to Lords for fear of the ghosts from the past. But he could thoroughly enjoy a game arranged among his fellow lodgers and their friends. The invitation to Everard to join them was repeated on at least one occasion, and remembered by Everard chiefly on account of the mingled excitement and gravity with which Francis prepared for it. The excitement was such that at the last minute he had to return to his lodgings for the pads he forgot to bring.[44]

His sister Mary kept her interest in the game, which for the enclosed nun was as improbable in its way as his own. She also wrote to him of other interests and pleasures from the past, of the countryside and the sea she might never again visit and of the sunsets she sometimes watched, reminding her of his first Ode. There was occasional news of their sister Maggie, now settled for many years in Canada, and of their half-brother Norbert. On his side, apart from sending her copies of his books, Francis hardly ever wrote. She made the excuse later to Meynell 'that writing to me would bring up painful memories'.[45] She was right, but probably not in quite the way she meant. He would not want her to guess from his letters how far short his present life fell from the promise of a few years ago. And for all her special feeling for him he knew she shared the family's attitude and that, to her, his brief poetic fame was no compensation for the distress he had caused them.

Cricket was of course a frequent talking-point at the Skiddaw. So it was at Elgin Avenue. Although, after the departure of Ghosh, there was no one with whom he could be on close terms, he was at ease with the rest of his fellow lodgers. Arriving back in the evening often long after the usual suppertime he would call in at the kitchen for the porridge and beer that really were his preferred choice. Then for an hour or so he entertained the others with talk about anything from cricket to politics or the latest subject of national interest or local gossip. They were a seedy rundown company, the drabness of their daily struggle to retain self-respect temporarily lifted by the wit and often caustic humour of the one among them who, as a member of the group expressed it, managed to live where the rest only existed.

Then he would go to his room to work far into the night, either at the table or tramping round it, wearing out the carpet in the circle that puzzled his landlady until she surprised him at one time in his perambulations. It was, she decided, only another of his harmlessly eccentric habits — like the distinct enunciation of his prayers, 'as if he was preaching'. It did not occur to her that he might be reciting poetry. To Mrs Maries, as to his other landladies, he was an enigma. They knew they would not have tolerated such disregard for time and carelessness as to his room and his clothes from their other lodgers, yet with him they took it in good part. They were won over in spite of themselves by his courtesy and that childlike quality of seeming help-lessness in practical matters which, for them, held a special appeal.

They accepted him, for which he was grateful. But they gave him no special treatment, nor did he expect it. When he could not eat Mrs Maries' hefty meals, porridge and beer became the simplest alterna-tive and he never asked for anything more suited to his digestive trou-bles. He had other preferences if an extra shilling or two could buy him a meal in an eating house. There was one near the bookshop in Westbourne Grove where, he told Everard, 'I get what I like', adding by way of explanation, 'The beef is always excellent'. The same could not be said of the Sunday lunches he often shared with the Meynells. 'Wilfrid', he once exclaimed, 'the Palace Court food is *shocking*'. Perhaps there was too much mutton in their menus. 'I hate mutton' he was heard to say on an occasion when it was being served as the main dish.[46]

After lunch one of the family's amusements was the game of listing 'likes' and 'dislikes' and someone thought of preserving a list of 'likes' contributed by Francis. For food, beef was his predictable choice, with mosel being his preferred drink. His favourite pastime he gave as music, with Beethoven, Berlioz and Chopin as his somewhat eclectic choice of composers. As to books, his favourite was 'Any great one I am reading'. Where would he choose to live? Unquestionably Sussex. He who never left the shores of England saw no attraction in a foreign resort. Even an escape from the English climate which he so abhorred could not tempt him from the Sussex downs where he had spent his most hopeful months and where he would return if he could. The list ends with the question 'What is your favourite adage or motto?' His reply is marked by the ironical twist he saw behind so much in life: 'Every scope, by the immoderate use, turns to restraint'.[47]

The choice is typical of Coventry Patmore's use of the aphorism in his last books. Patmore certainly encouraged, but equally certainly did not originate, Thompson's fascination for the aphoristic phrase or sentence. For it is part of the language of paradox, the language which in its various forms recurs throughout the notebooks as constantly as in his poetry and prose writings. The purpose of paradox can be defined as an apparent contradiction leading to a deeper understand-ing of the meaning in what is being said. As such it played an essential part in the formation of his poetic language and of his later prose style, expressing as it did the seeming contradictions in man and nature that so often provided the stimulus for his initial inspiration. And the aphoristic phrase, like the irony that is indispensible to it, is one of the readiest forms of paradox.

So too is wit. The caustic humour that marked Thompson's conversation led him, when no conversation was possible, to note down observations such as they occurred to him. 'A man who can never reach a conclusion without a proof is a man who can never cross a gap without a bridge'. So he wrote on the draft of 'Form and Formalism' and the notebooks, especially those of his later years, are filled with similar entries. 'Man cannot worsen without ruin also to Nature, to the land' is perhaps better appreciated by the present day than it would have been by his. 'When I find nothing done by me much may have been done in me' is no more an excuse for idleness than the corollary: 'For the thing today done in you, will be done by you to-morrow many things'. The medical imagery on which he relied as a poet often reappears in his writing on poetry: 'Poetry, it may be said, is truth in peptonized tabloids. A very few are enough for a meal and will last you for some hours . . . when they are digested you find you have full nourishment'. He had used medical images in many of his more intense poetic moments. 'In the first shock of disillusion the soul seems to suffer a kind of moral haemorrhage' in potential poetry of this kind as well as a sharply defined truth in its own right.[48]

Among the longer entries in the later notebooks, by far the greatest number concern the function of poetry. Thompson's failure to meet the demands he had set himself led him to explore again and again what these demands involve and how they affect the poet. To him, all art was a personal expression of a process of incarnation taking on the form best suited to the gift of the particular individual. It followed, for him, that fidelity to the gift meant incarnating some facet of the truths about life which was poetry's highest aim to express. As far as he evolved a poetic theory, it was based on this idea of incarnation that had been central to his own poetic development:

> I know that art goes to the very vitals of life: art aloof from life is not even spirit without body, for art takes its body from life, being nothing else than the spiritual incarnated in terms of life. But it may, according to its aims, remove from the sordid materialities of life, the husks & chaff of life it has the right to eschew these as nothing to its purpose, if they be not to its purpose. For there are many arts, not one art- or rather the many are modes of the one, and all depends on the purpose.[49]

The purpose itself he saw in the same terms, when the creative power of poetic 'incarnation' raises the aim above the level of mere imitation of life:

> The poet does not invent a new order of things. He sees the real order. To see it as it really is, to interpret it, & represent it to us who cannot see so clearly or so well — This is the highest aim of poetry . . . (But) in seeing & revealing them he brings them, as it were, to the birth: he produces rather than reproduces, he creates rather than imitates.[50]

Many of these entries deal with the poet in relation to his time as one blind to truths that will have to await the recognition of a future age. The truly great poet is therefore

> ... a prophet because he is too soon for his day: rather, his day comes after him. None the less it is not true that he gives no utterance to his time. He could not be conscious of the things he speaks, did he not find them about him. He brings up treasure from the deep sea of his time, impenetrable by those who look only on the surface-levels; but the deep waters of his time are the surface waters of a time to come. The many do not know what is breeding in their time — listening to the cries of the street, they hear not what the time is pondering in its heart.[51]

It was the means he had found to accept his sense of failure. His time, too, would come.

Thompson's more exalted ideas are constantly tempered by his realism. A grounding in 'common sense' is, he insists in several places, as essential to the highest poetry as its inspiration:

> Common sense is so far from being the sense common to the many, that it is really a rare and priviledged possession. It is nothing else than the intuition whereby a well-balanced mind judges at a glance of truth or wisdom in common affairs (that is, affairs falling within ordinary experience). If few possess common sense, still fewer possess the power of applying this intuitive faculty we call common sense to extraordinary affairs ... There is something wanting in genius when it does not show a clear & strong vein of common sense, such as is visible in the genius of Shakespeare, Milton, Wordsworth, and again in the mystic Dante. Dante, indeed, is a perfect rebuke to those who suppose that mystical genius, at any rate, must be dissociated from common sense. On the contrary, the higher the poet soars, the more ballast he needs. the kite is nothing without its tail, and the stronger the kite, the greater its tail.

Towards those of his own day who call themselves 'mystical' poets he is predictably stern:

> A 'mystic' poet who is all vaporous fancy will not go far. Every such poet should be able to give a clear & logical resume of his teaching, as terse as a page of scholastic philosophy.[52]

Common sense being one of the features of the Anglo Saxon temperament has, in his view, done much towards giving English poetry the reputation it has rightly achieved. Yet there is another side. If the poet benefits from the asset, his readers often do not. Too often they react with an obtuseness that is not common sense but 'no sense'. As a result

> ... we have the extraordinary spectacle of a race of poets, singularly delicate & at the same time majestic in their melody & harmony, produced by

a nation too dull & obtuse of ear to apprehend their harmony, & but im-
perfectly capable of understanding their melody.[53]

So again he finds and notes a paradox.

The 'public' Odes had led him to reflect on the English character
and his notebooks are full of observations where the qualities he was
called on to praise are shown in another light. It was a relief to react
against the required solemnity by poking fun, as in a mock sermon on
the text 'Be good and you will be respectable'.

> It is not very difficult to keep from serious lies if you are a healthy Anglo
> Saxon. With a decent income, it requires only a firm self-command to
> abstain from pocket-picking, shop-lifting, or even coveting your neigh-
> bour's umbrella. A married person, with a little practice, can really keep
> from adultery in a way quite surprising to the frequenter of 'problem
> plays' ... With assiduous cultivation you can, I affirm, arrive at praying
> to your Maker as much as twice a day without serious inconvenience; and
> an hour or two at Church on Sunday, by means of a prudent selection of
> attire and preachers, will not pass unpleasantly. Whence we must needs
> conclude that for a well-disposed person, and on about eight hundred or a
> thousand a year, the Kingdom of God is an amazing bargain.

By poking fun he was also attacking the self-complacency that can
become the reverse side to the coin of success and which, in a different
context, he allied to the blindness to social problems which he so
much abhorred.

At other times Thompson simply enjoyed seeing the comic side
for its own sake. The mischievous irony in 'The Heretic's Tragedy'
would have shocked many of his readers then and later. Taking a
pretended medieval source in the record of a 'Canon Regular of Saint
Godocus', the tale of the heretic convicted for so-called 'blasphemy' is
a good example of Catholic humour at its own expense.[55]

But it was writing doggerel verses that became a real pastime.
These could turn into poems of considerable length and were
obviously written with great facility, since hardly any corrections were
made or needed. They could be on any topic from 'A Ballad of the
Boer-ing War' to the history of Doris Biggs the 'sell-fish maid' whose
amorous exploits are recounted entirely in terms of her fishmongering
trade:

> 'O Doris Biggs, how can you thus
>   Pursue your finny sales?
> The time has been, alas! you weighed
>   Me in quite other scales'.
>
> Said she, 'They say I fished for you',
>   (She gave a bitter look),

'And hooked you; but if so, you now
          Can go — and take your hook'.[56]

And so on, for several pages. As humour, the verses are feeble enough
but they show Thompson still fascinated by words and their many-
sided meanings. Probably the best example is the more caustic skit on
evolutionary theory in 'A Retrograde Fancy':

'Beasts' said Mr Swift
          In his haste, 'now and then
(It is a complement to humankind)
          Degenerate into men'.
The birds and beasts, I've heard of late
          To put this past dubiety,
Have betook themselves to Science
          And a Royal Society.

. . .

Mr Worm read a paper
          On *The Structure of our Earth*,
And a little Koch's Bacillus
          Gave them *Man: His Death and Birth:*
Mr Curlew, *Deep Sea Fishing*,
          And *The Habitants of Ocean*,
Mr Swallow talked of Ether
          And *The Planetary Motion*.
They had scientific certainties
          Of the latest new variety
'Twould have made you think of Pentecost
          To have heard that Royal Society.[57]

It may be mere 'schoolboy' humour, yet it cannot be dismissed
on that account. Given the conditions in which the limericks and fragments of doggerel were written, there is something of genuine courage
in Thompson's effort to lighten the burden life had become. And in
spite of the burden the variety and vitality of the notebooks in use
during his last five or six years are hard to convey in selected extracts.
Drafts for reviews and constant memo notes jostle for space with ideas
for poems and, of course, the recurring opium records. Along with the
observations on poetry are many on art, a subject which always held a
special appeal for his essentially visual imagination. They range from
the evils of French influences and the notion of 'art for art's sake' to
the problems he saw in portrait painting and the need for art to be
functional as well as beautiful. Here he has harsh words for the mock
gothic style of Tower Bridge as a meaningless imitation. There are
drawings of his own, not without some ability. His knowledge of

anatomy gives his sylphs and 'spirits of poetry' correct if somewhat sexless proportions. But his best effort is a group of birettared priests in consultation, caricatured in a few deft lines.[58]

Many of his more casual notes begin with phrases such as 'you may feel', 'have you ever considered', 'it has often occurred to me', as if conversing with some unseen companion. The notebooks were substituting for the audience he so much desired, the only outlet for his need to communicate at a level other than that of the journalist. It is in this sense, as much as any other, that their importance towards the end of his life can be best understood. When nothing could ease the burden there was some relief in confiding to them the extent of his sheer physical misery. In 'Earth Plains' he tried to incorporate it into a vision of suffering shared by earth and man. But the attempt remained only a 'Fragment from a designed poem'. The design, like the execution, was beyond him, and both petered out into broken lines on his own pain:

> Lo, behold me sick,
> Fevered, unhealéd,
> Dying!
> My flesh grows old, my flesh grows old in pain,
> There is no rest at all from ills,
> There is no space from sorrow,
> There is no pause from pain![59]

There were days when he felt close to death. He was still haunted then by the idea that he would have to die on the streets where he had come close to death before. His life as far as it held any meaning for him began with the reprieve that led to the birth of his poetry: and after all, it was only a reprieve. He did not now try to anticipate the end by making a return, but was prepared to wait for some kind of call when the time came:

> Out of the depth I came into the world of literature, & back into the depths must I go. God only grant that the final act in the London streets, to which I incessantly look forward, may be brief in its consummatory agony.[60]

He was dramatizing his situation, like many sufferers who can only face reality by treating it as drama. So, too, he would compose letters describing his afflictions, the self-addressed letters that are one of the last resorts of the lonely spirit:

> The other night after work against time which belated my dinner till past eleven I went to bed foredone, dripping with cold, quivering at the icy sheets, mashed & riven with cramp, so that I had to get up every quarter of an hour & walk about, to rid myself of the gnarled & wringing pain. I could have cried with Caliban: 'I am not Thompson but a cramp!' Sleep

was impossible till towards six or seven of the morning, when I subsided
into broken & uneasy slumber. I felt as if I could hold on the struggle no
more, but must give way through sheer outspent body.[61]

Along with the self-dramatization the entry indicates the kind of
conditions in which many of the others were written.

Thompson tried to keep the letters he did send to matters of fact,
but his worsening health was one of them. They were mostly notes to
Everard apologising for delayed deliveries of the remaining chapters
of *Saint Ignatius*, with the pain and swelling in his feet as the constant
reason. Their tone shows a marked deterioration in his general health
between April and August. At first he could still comment on the
latest cricket scores, and in one he gave a vivid account of his efforts to
rid his room of a persistent rat by throwing his boots at it. Everard
was taking over much of his personal affairs from Wilfrid, and there
were times when he failed to realize how dependent Francis now was
on extra help towards expenses which the payments for the book
would not cover: it took several letters and some doggerel verses
before Everard agreed to assist in the purchase of some much-needed
shirts. They both knew, though neither spoke of it, that the main reason was the increasing amount of opium which Francis now needed,
leaving him barely enough for subsistence from his earnings. By
August the cheerful tone was almost stifled. 'This ignominious life
cannot, I think, go on many days further' he wrote at the start of the
month. But within a week he was apologising for writing 'so gloomily'
and regretting that the trouble in his feet prevented him from accompanying Everard on a walking tour, the exercise being 'the one thing
which has ever been life-giving to me'.[62]

Thompsons's closer contact with Everard was largely due to a
major change in the family's affairs. There was no longer a focal point
for either the Meynells or Thompson at Palace Court. As the children
grew up and left home, a house of that size and expense became unpractical. Furthermore Alice was so often away, either on lecture
tours or visits abroad, that the management proved virtually impossible for Wilfrid alone and with his commitments at Burns and
Oates. In the spring of 1905 they let the house and moved to a flat
over the publishers' office in Granville Place, just off Oxford Street. It
was an hour's further walk from Francis's lodgings whereas Everard's
Serendipity Bookshop in Westbourne Grove was comparatively near.
Even that distance, which before Francis would have taken literally in
his stride, he found increasingly hard to cover.

He still managed visits to Granville Place but it was not the
same. There was not that sense of refuge and security which he had
never failed to find at Palace Court since his return to London.
Family recollections of these visits give the impression of a folorn lost-

seeming figure disappearing into the fog or rain after an evening divided between silence and small talk. He could not resume his readily assured place in the family in their new surroundings and, although the welcome was the same, it could not alter his sense of change, causing him to become more gauche and awkward than ever in their company. Sometimes he arrived too exhausted for conversation, or suffering from the too-obvious effects of the drug. To their friends he could then appear positively 'repellent', as one of them put it, 'with his ragged sandy beard, blotched skin and watery eyes, his blurred consciousness unaware of us or anything that was going on'. Yet there was still something in his presence suggesting a 'dignity of sorrow', the impression that remained behind after Alice tactfully led him off to another room to rest.[63] On one occasion the walk took him so long that he arrived well after bedtime. The maid who tried to dismiss him was terrified as if by a burglar when he pushed past her, demanding paper and pen to leave an explanation. It was a minor incident that amused Alice in the telling, but it was not so to Francis. As he faced the long walk back to his lodgings he must have felt himself lonelier than ever, a stranger to the one place he had been able to think of as home.[64]

Not that either Wilfrid or Alice was less concerned on his account and they watched his obvious decline with growing anxiety. Perhaps the same solution would serve now as it had done in the past and so an approach was made to Father Cuthbert at Crawley. Cuthbert, also still concerned for Francis's welfare, arranged for him to stay in the village for a so-called holiday of indeterminate length. Mrs Blackburn now had rooms near the Friary and she and the friars could keep an eye on him, reporting back to the Meynells and at least preventing, if possible, any further increase in his drug taking.

Francis raised objections on account of the Ignatius biography but they were waived aside. There was no time limit for its completion and the change of air and rest would, he was assured, benefit the work in the long run. He did not try any further. Twice before he had felt bound to agree to similar plans made for him for what he knew were for the same reasons. But he felt no more enthusiasm now than when he had left for either Storrington or Pantasaph. Since he could not walk a few yards without pain there was nothing to look forward to in the prospect of being confined in lodgings which were otherwise within easy reach of the downs he loved.

There was, however, an incentive in a recent commission from the *Dublin Review* to write an ode in honour of the English Martyrs. Much as he disliked these public odes the subject was very different, and one he felt might result in a better testimony to his remaining poetic powers than the rest could have been. But he knew he stood more chance of achieving something nearer success at Crawley than by remaining in London.

From his arrival there in August it took Thompson five months to write the Ode 'To the English Martyrs'. Considering his state of health and the fact that he wrote at least ten reviews during the same period, this is at least a tribute to his determination to complete what he realized would be his last serious poetic effort. The result is more than the 'journeyman work' it has too often been referred to, along with his own view of the other commissioned Odes. Beyond the required eulogistic tone and the formal framework, it makes a gallant, if barely successful attempt to place the subject of religious persecution in the wider and fuller context of the meaning of true freedom.

Some three hundred Catholics are known to have been martyred during the English Reformation, of whom about a hundred died on the famous Tyburn gallows. Francis had passed the site almost daily on his way from his lodgings to Palace Court, when the paradox of a scene of shame and infamy which had now become a hallowed spot must have often occurred to him. Then, when he began on the poem, the Tyburn 'cross' took on other associations. The shadow cast from it became an extension of the shadow cast from the Calvary at Storrington, reaching from the vision of his own future as he saw it then towards a future he would not live to see:

> Rain, rain on Tyburn tree,
> Red rain a-falling;
> Dew, dew on Tyburn tree,
> Red dew on Tyburn tree,
> And the swart bird a-calling.
>
> The shadow lies on England now
> Of the deathly-fruited bough,
> Cold and black with malison
> Lies between the land and sun;
> Putting out the sun, the bough
> Shades England now![65]

1–11

The shadow of an ominous future covers the country that claims to be the home of freedom but which has failed to honour those who once died at her hands in its cause.

In the Ode as Thompson completed it this is his chief concern, but in the text as edited by Meynell it only reappears at the end. What remains is the secondary and supporting theme, the manner in which the martyrs died. The wit that was a common feature in their last words and actions represents their independence of spirit, the inner freedom which no persecution can destroy. In this Thomas More is his special hero. Twenty-eight lines are given to the 'Dear Jester in the Courts of God' which, even if they stress only one side of More's character, remain among the best tributes to the 'holy ease' of his

sanctity, the quality that makes him perhaps the best loved saint of
the English Calendar.

More was, too, one of those 'who thought as Shakespeare wrote',
who would surely have appreciated passages in the Ode such as:

> You did, with thrift of holy gain,
> Unvenoming the sting of pain,
> Hive its sharp heather-honey.

51–53

For with the right stimulus, there was still a rich store of imagery at
his command.

Throughout, the contrast between the physical effects of torture
and imprisonment and the freedom of the inner spirit reflect Thompson's own present sense of the imprisonment of pain. Perhaps, too,
there is something equally intimate in his appreciation of the wit,
of the way a witty remark can relieve the tension of acute physical
suffering. But the poem as he intended it to be read can only be understood in his own final text, which differs from the various printed
versions as much as they all differ from his preparatory draft. The
draft covers twenty-four notebook pages, worked over with cancellations and variations, all proof of the effort which the composition cost
him.[66] It does much more, taking over and expanding the vision of the
future contained in the drafts for his earlier Odes. There, the vision
arose from the corruption of the country in its pursuit of war for evil
ends. Now the corruption spreads out as a moral evil infecting the
nations of the world and threatening them with a future warfare not to
be measured by any known standards. Medical images of disease and
death are set against the life-bringing image of the sun in a conflict
where the pollution of that life, arising from 'the unlawful heart of
man', will infect the human and natural worlds alike:

> So to red doom sinks down the western world,
> The sun with fiercelier tormented heart
> Compressed, outspirts urgent & malignant energy
> Vibrant & urgent through each artery
> Cranny & channel of the infected world,
> Maddening the nations — That which was their mettle
> And Nature's life-blood, by man's villainy
> Disnatured & envenomed to his hurt[67]

The tortured notebook pages eventually resulted in forty-seven lines
at the start of the poem, appearing only in the text as Thompson completed it:

> We watch the avenging wrath
> Drawn downward on its unavoided path
> Of the malignant Sun.

Our world is venomed at the flaming heart,
That from its burning systole
Spirts a poisoned life-blood. See
The gathering contagion thence
Sick influence
Shed on the seasons, and on men
Madness of nations, plague, and famine stern,
Earthquake, and flood, and all disastrous birth
Change, war, and steaming pestilence.

                                                              6–17

How is it that England holds a key position in this terrible course?

Whence is the scourge come on us? Why
O land, hast thou calamity?
England, England, what the root
That yields thee now so ill a fruit?

                                                              43–46

The penalty she must pay for the deaths of the martyrs is part of the
penalty to be paid for the denial of freedom to nations who have
looked to her as their model and guide. The martyrs' triumph will
therefore be completed in the overthrow of England's misused powers
and the acknowledgement instead of the true freedom for which they
died:

Till she shall know
This lesson in her overthrow:
Hardest servitude has he
That's gaoled in arrogant liberty;
And freedom, spacious and unflawed,
Who is walled about with God.

                                                              174–179

This idea was allowed to survive in the published poem as referring
back to its opening lines. But the wider vision, where England's fate
forms a part of the worldwide scene of approaching terror, can only be
found in the draft and in the text which Thompson sent to Meynell
that autumn. Today the text and the draft can be said to present a
prophetic view of a world dominated by the fear of nuclear warfare.
Nor is the impression lessened by the probable influence of opium on
his heightened awareness. But for Meynell the theme was inexplicable
except as suggestive of opium delirium and must therefore be either
drastically revised or suppressed. For Thompson, having completed
the poem was enough and in refusing to revise the opening lines he
wrote:

The last reserve of power I could husband was discharged into
them, & I can summon up no more, Any attempted change

would but make bad worse. Such as they are, they must suffice. One quite certain thing is, the *Dublin* might go further & fare a great deal worse. Even in my ashes, I think there little more fire than in any other Catholic versifier of whom I know.[68]

He was more right than in his half apology: 'God knows I have little indeed left to brag about'. Meynell, however, was insistent and Thompson remained adamant, with the result that the Ode appeared shorn of its opening passages and with minor deletions and alterations to the rest.

Thompson submitted the Ode in two instalments. With the second he wrote Wilfrid a letter saying he could now go out a little, was reasonably warm and comfortable and better fed than he had been since he was at Storrington. As usual and in spite of an attack of influenza, he was reacting to improved conditions which, given that beri beri was the basic cause for his worsening health, were those best suited to its treatment.

The only problem was his landlady's annoyance at his habit of late rising. It blew up into a real crisis during January and February, largely due to Mrs Blackburn's interference. Her lodgings were close by and as the two landladies knew each other she came to hear of it by roundabout means. Both she and Francis were ill with influenza at the time so could not meet. Instead she wrote to him accusing him of increasing the opium and so causing the whole trouble. He answered with a dignified but definite denial, regretting she should rely on hearsay as to his present illness rather than waiting for the full facts either from himself or from Father Anselm.[69]

He did in fact come to an arrangement with Mrs Gravely, his landlady, who agreed to enter his room each morning to make sure he had heard her call — the whole cause for the upset and for which this proved a satisfactory solution. But it took place after 'Madam' had sent his letter on to Wilfrid, enclosed with one from her repeating her fears as to the increase in opium and the likelihood that Francis would have to leave. Hearing of this — he did not say how — Francis was understandably angry. In sending an explanation and the proposed solution, still with no direct reference to the drug, he added:

> I think the difficulty will be overcome; — practically, I am *sure* it will. But the worry I have had with Madam's sporadic outbreaks into sudden & groundless letters or action, whenever some unforeseen & unforeseeable thing makes her boil over! — it is like living at the foot of Vesuvius.
>
> As for any new cause for anxiety about my health, it is baseless moonshine — apparently caused by the notion that late rising means serious illness.[70]

He was, he assured Wilfrid, better than he could ever expect to be after a winter in London. Yet Wilfrid was not entirely convinced, for

Francis's next letter contained the detailed account of the symptoms he attributed to beri beri, to which reference has been made.* He wrote by way of a further explanation but as if he expected continued improvement.

His anger soon cooled and the friendship with 'Madam' was renewed. It had stood similar tests before and went deeper on both sides than the surface storminess provoked by her bossy but well meant ways. Her lodgings were within Francis's present walking distance and with the spring weather he often called there. Her landlady, Mrs Payne, had two boys aged seven and five who he took to entertaining with the stories he could always invent on demand. The younger, Richard, was to join the Capuchins and, as a member of the community at Pantasaph, he can still recall the affection he and his brother had for 'the poet'. With the clear memory of age for the more distant past he has a vivid recollection of Francis's strange appearance, the pocket of his overcoat always stuffed with papers from 'penny exercise books'. Francis would sometimes stay on for a meal and had a special liking for Mrs Payne's griddle cakes.[71]

Pleasant as the visits were, they could not satisfy the need for the companionship he expected to find again at the Friary. His two closest friends there, Cuthbert and Anselm, were in Crawley off and on through the winter when they did their best for him by inviting him for an occasional meal and keeping in touch with notes and letters. But both were now fully committed to their new duties. Cuthbert was starting his mission to the Kent hop-pickers and, when at the Friary, was occupied with writing on social issues — an outlet for his more radical ideas which did not involve him in direct theological controversy. Anselm, as Guardian, had little free time, and in any case he was due to leave soon after Easter. With the approach of spring Francis became restless, unable as he still was to take the walks which the proximity of the downs made him miss all the more. The lack of physical stimulus together with a lack of its intellectual equivalent meant that by May he was asking to be allowed to return to London. Nor could the Meynells, reluctant as they were to end an arrangement that had worked well so far, find an adequate reason to prevent him.

Yet the short train journey exhausted Francis to the extent that when he set out the next day to see them he was forced to give up half way. Even on that occasion he would not spare his pennies for public transport, for which he developed an almost obsessional dislike. He would force himself to walk as the one achievement left to him — it was in fact one where he would not have to admit failure.

He agreed to return to Elgin Avenue on condition that he found his own meals. Boarding with a London landlady, he told Wilfrid, 'is

* See Chapter 9, p. 314, and note 13.

a semi-starvation, especially for a dyspeptic'. Like the rest of Mrs Maries' lodgers he used to bring in most of his own food and eating out would, he calculated, be cheaper in the end and meant he would be better fed.[71]

Another problem was not so easily solved. When Wilfrid and Alice insisted he should not be out of doors in all weathers, Francis pointed out that no landlady would allow him to remain in his room through the day, and certainly not with a fire, except for a consideration well beyond his means.[12] Mainly for this reason, before the next winter he moved to cheaper accommodation at 128 Brondesbury Road. There the extra charge could be met — even if, as usual, with Wilfrid's help.

Unlike most of his lodgings the house remains much the same today, drab and dull in the equally drab and dull environs of Kilburn Underground Station. The attic window of his room still looks out over a dismal garden behind the house towards the District Railway that runs parallel with the road in front. A few lines of verse hint at the complaints he was in no position to make except to his notebook:

> The very demon of the scene,
> The screaming horror of the train,
> Rushes its iron and ruthless way amain,
> A pauseless black Necessity,
> Along its iron and predestined path.[73]

His landlady would certainly not have understood. 'It's very nice for Mr Thompson', she told Everard, 'he's got the trains at the back every hour and more, when he's in his bedroom'. Even so, she did not like to feel that he was dependent on their company all day. 'Many a time I've asked him to have his bit of lunch with me and the other "mental"' — referring to a fellow lodger. Francis had no objection to being so classified, occasionally accepting her well-meant invitations.[74]

He was no hermit and the days when he was confined to his room could be intolerably lonely. The way to get through them was to keep up with as much work as was still possible. The biography of Saint Ignatius was finished during the summer, after which he maintained a steady though much reduced number of reviews. None shows any sign of a falling off in his usual critical acumen or in the conscientious care he had always given to the work. The one he found most challenging to his depleted energies was also the most successful. He wrote to Meynell that reviewing Henry James's *The American Scene* 'has been a series of perpetual abortive efforts ... a beast of a book to get through — I didn't know what I was undertaking so light-heartedly'.[75] In spite of this the review contains some penetrating comments. 'Distinctly it is the process rather than the result that fascinates Mr

James, and you must let it fascinate you'. The book under discussion
he regards as a by-product 'of the most fastidiously probing mind in
present literature'.[76]

Although reviewing had never been satisfying to Thompson,
he knew his prose was well thought of where his poetry was almost
forgotten. So he set about listing all that would have to be done to
produce a volume of his prose writings. He made out a long and
complicated series of possible locations for them, goaded by self
admonitions:

> There may be money in it: there must be posterity, if I close up
> the rivets. And there, at any rate, is a congenial yet practical
> labour for me — at last; if not on too late a day ... Now all is un-
> certainty and labour immense, with failure too, too possible! On
> every side, in every way, failure threatens. Yet try, ere the night
> close utterly in and my prose be lost to posterity after a lifetime of
> toil not less than set De Quincey at the front of English prose.
> Pull yourself together at this last, and try it.[77]

If Thompson had made the right enquiries he would have found that
most of the work he envisaged could be undertaken by any publisher
prepared to accept his proposal and many besides Constable, his first
choice, were likely to welcome it. But perhaps even then it was 'too
late a day'. As it was he bought a new exercise book to make a start
but got no further than a few titles and references to remembered
articles.

Instead, this last notebook has another and greater value. Because it can be dated entirely to the last year of his life it shows how
little his mental energies were affected by his physical decline. Its
pages retain the range and variety of the notebooks in general, gathered here within the space of a few months. He started it with some lines
he worked into a finished poem, intended as the Preface for his prose
volume. They amount to nothing much more than a litany of the
saints whose aid he must invoke in undertaking the task. But if they
have no other value they make it clear that, whatever the shortcomings in his religious observances, the essential sincerity and simplicity of his faith was unchanged. They end with an appeal to the
saint he had come to love as well as revere above the rest:

Thomas More
Teach (thereof my need is sore)
What thou showedst well on earth —
Good writ, good wit, make goodly mirth![78]

The pages that follow include notes for unwritten poems along
with comments on metre and symbolism. There are prose reflections
or brief remarks ranging from Shakespeare to cricket and from the

English character ('The Englishman in general will take anything you don't give him if only you give him his grumble') to the character of woman ('Woman is the explanation of man, would man but understand her rightly'). And on another page, 'God has shut up no man, assuredly, but by God's aid will open' is a commentary on the reticence he could so seldom set aside except in his notebooks. Perhaps the most revealing entry is where he tries to account for his altered attitude to time in recent years, suggestive of the sense of the future in the drafts of his Odes:

> The future is grown so near that it seems I might almost touch it by the reaching forth of my hand, And I do not know but, by myself, I live pretty well as much in the past & future as in the present, which seems a very little patch between the two.

He has, he continues, always been aware of this sense but during the last few years 'it has come to dominate my mental outlook'. Apart from the prophetic element in his later poetry, it could have contributed to that lifelong inability to keep to a normal timetable which proved so damaging to his health and so irritating to others where practical matters were concerned.

The pages include many scattered lines of doggerel but there is one attempt at a serious poem, intended to describe the dismal scene around his lodgings. Even in its unfinished state it conveys something of his intention and even at this late stage can be taken as an example of his meticulous method of composition:

```
     The dreary scream of crowing cocks
          Comes ghastly through the dark,
     The slaty blue of day
          Slant on the dreary      ⎫
                    wretched  ⎬      park;
          [A slate-blue slant of day⎫
           A slant of slate-blue day⎭
                    Adown the dreary park;]
     [Slate-blue slants the day⎫
      Slants the slate-blue day⎭
               Adown the dreary park;]
     The houses ⎰hardened fume[s] [piléd fume|s|
                ⎱sooty
          Against the heartless light,
                         smoke  ⎫
     [The houses smeared fume|s|⎭
                         smears   ⎫
                    sooty blears ⎬
                         stains ⎭
```

24. The last notebook entries: pages 45–46 of the 'Large Commonplace Book'

Against the heartless light;]
       that soak in ⎫   and weightily ⎫
         sucked in ⎬   ⎬
They have soaked in ⎭   heavily ⎭
That soak in and most

Retain   ⎫
          ⎬ the ebbing night, ⎫
That hold ⎭   ⎬
Hold the   ⎧ retreating night.
           ⎨ thick-oozing ⎫   night.
           ⎩ thick ooze of ⎭
Hold the black ooze of night.
That hold the oozing ⎫   night.
         oozy   ⎬
         ooze of ⎭

The final entry is in its own way no less characteristic: 'Mem. Buttons top coat tomorrow if at all possible'.

The winter of 1906 brought a series of chest colds and attacks of influenza which caused a return of Thompson's foot condition and reduced him to an alarmingly weak state. Nor did the spring promise the customary improvement and he could seldom muster the energy for even a weekly visit to the Meynells. Wilfrid realised that more than financial help was needed but Francis refused to ask for any medical advice after the — to him — mistaken report from Caleb Saleeby. He may also have feared the verdict on the opium he was certainly increasing now well beyond the amount any doctor would consider acceptable.

The problem was raised in the course of a conversation with Wilfrid Blunt, whose liking for Francis had grown with their occasional meetings at Palace Court since that unfortunate visit to Newbuildings ten years ago. Even then, in spite of Blunt's criticisms, he approved of the poet's simplicity and lack of affectation. Now, as a temporary measure he suggested that Francis should spend a few weeks of rest and possible recuperation on his Sussex estate. It would put him to no inconvenience and so the offer was welcomed. At Newbuildings, Blunt's own residence as distinct from the family home at Crabbet Park, a summer house in the grounds was fitted out so that Everard could stay with Francis for the first week to see how the experiment worked. They all realised that constant care was becoming essential. 'The poor poet seemed to be in the last stages of consumption', Blunt noted in his diary for 24 August, the date of their arrival: 'He is

emaciated beyond credibility, his poor little body a mere skeleton'.[79]
It was the obvious inference to draw from his appearance, and one
Blunt never saw the need to question. It should be remembered that
Blunt had seen his mother, brother and sister die of the disease and
outwardly Francis had all the appearance of a consumptive.

At first there seemed hope for an improvement. Francis and
Everard were attended by an old retainer of Blunt's, David Roberts,
who agreed to taking the poet into his own cottage when the prescribed week was over. Roberts and his wife soon developed a liking
for their strange charge and Francis, as usual, responded well to their
easy friendliness. Blunt would collect him for a midday meal, after
which he dosed or read either indoors or in the garden until the
evening. They also had several long conversations, Blunt not having
suspected his protégé of holding views in some respects similar to his
own:

> We first got in touch with each other over a common hatred of European
> civilization and the destruction wrought by it on all that was beautiful in
> the world, the destruction of happiness, of the happier races by the less
> happy, and so gradually to the despair of the intellectual part of mankind
> with what life gave and the craving for a life after death. I gave him some-
> thing of my view and asked him abruptly what his own view was.
> He said, 'Oh, about that I am entirely orthodox: indeed, it is my only
> consolation'.

Blunt was impressed that Francis should so combine radical social
and political views with the unquestioning Catholic faith which he
had himself felt bound to give up and never ceased to regret. Further
questions resulted in Francis recalling his religious upbringing and
early years, leading on to their mutual connections with the Capuchins.* Clearly he had kept in touch with Angelo as well as with the
others. In giving Blunt news of their present activities he told him how
Angelo had gone to America at the time of the Dreyfus affair, where
within a year he joined the Episcopalian Church. Francis showed no
sign of shock or special disapproval. 'On the whole I find Thompson
much saner and more sensible than I expected', Blunt commented in
his diary:

> Of his poetry he talked reasonably and said that he took a soberer view of
> his talents now than he had done as a boy ... 'If I have at all succeeded it
> is because I have tried to do my best'.[80]

There is no record that Tyrrell joined them during these weeks,
although Blunt made several references to him and he was staying in
nearby Storrington at the time. The only hint is an entry in the diary
for the following year when in October he and Tyrrell picnicked on

---

* For Thompson's recollections of his early years see Chapter 2, p. 41.

the downs above the Priory there. Tyrrell then 'read us out a part of Thompson's "Ode to the Setting Sun" which was very appropriate to the time and place'.[81] Perhaps they would not have found much to discuss. Thompson was never willing to be drawn into the kind of controversies with which Tyrrell was by now deeply embroiled.

When Francis was not at Newbuildings, Roberts and his wife reported that he spent most of his time, and much of the night, in prayer. He was also reading his well-loved Sir Thomas Browne again, the subject of his last review. One passage in particular he copied out as if it held a special meaning for him:

> 'Be substantially great in thyself, & more than thou appearest unto others; and let the world be deceived in thee, as they are in the lights of heaven'.[82]

The review was finished by the end of September. It shows no more sign of his condition than does his last surviving letter written a week or so before to Alice, on the Latin and Gaelic origins of the word 'sallow' as it appears in Keats's 'Ode to Autumn'.[83]

His condition might not show in his writing but his appearance betrayed it very clearly. During the first few weeks the artist Neville Lytton was staying at Newbuildings, and the sketch he made of Thompson is unrecognizable as one of a man in his prime, still two years short of fifty. Yet, with the sunken cheeks and greying hair, there remains a piercing intensity in the eyes to indicate another reason than age for his appearance.[84]

Soon afterwards Thompson's health began to deteriorate more rapidly. The brief improvement was not maintained and, although Blunt persuaded him to see a doctor, he seems to have so evaded the main issue as to make any detailed diagnosis impossible. The doctor could do no more than confirm the generally accepted belief that he was suffering from consumption, the commonest cause for such a decline.

The main issue was, as Thompson himself knew, the effect of the amount of laudanum he now needed to gain any relief on his weakening condition. It was sent regularly from London and Blunt believed he was taking up to six ounces a day, often mixed with alcohol for stronger and more immediate results. His most distressing symptom was the diarrhoea that was part of his digestive troubles and for which opium was in fact a common treatment. The Roberts did their best for him, but by the autumn and with the prospect of the winter ahead, Blunt had to ask Meynell to find more expert care than they could provide.[85]

So in mid-October Francis returned to London, insisting on making a final effort before he would submit to hospital treatment. Within a fortnight he knew, with the instinct of the dying, that there

25. Thompson in his last months from a pencil sketch by Neville Lytton, 1907

was no alternative and he agreed to enter the Catholic Hospital of Saint John and Saint Elizabeth as soon as arrangements could be made. Then at last he told Wilfrid what they both believed to be the basic cause of his illness: 'I am dying from laudanum poisoning'.[86]

His name appears in the hospital register as admitted for 'morphomania' and the nurse who admitted him remembered finding opium powder concealed in his shoes. He told the house doctor who examined him that he had been accustomed to taking up to seven ounces of the drug daily.[87] The attempted smuggling shows his anxiety at having it reduced and he may well have stated an amount in excess of the truth. He need not have worried. It soon became clear that withdrawal was out of the question at this stage, and the decreased dose that was ordered did in fact serve to satisfy him, given as it was at regular intervals during the ten days he remained in the hospital's care. Blunt may or may not have been mistaken in his assessment. If he was correct it is probable that the change on entering hospital and the relief from all personal responsibility was sufficient to allow for the reduction without causing the distress that might be expected. Furthermore, on admission he weighed only seventy pounds and the effect of opium, as with other drugs, has to be calculated according to the body weight of the patient. If he told the house doctor he was taking a quantity in excess of what he had done in the past, far less would have the same result now on his weakened constitution — less even than he may have needed while at New-buildings and still struggling with the demands of life outside hospital. All the same, towards the time when the dose was due he would become restless, on one occasion exclaiming 'Thank God' when the nurse brought it. Her reply shows singular lack of tact: 'You don't mean that. You mean "thank God" for having sent me here where I may learn to give it up'. As reported, his answer, 'Yes, that is what I mean' was taken as agreement. Rather, it was impatience at her obtuse refusal to face the truth.

The incident was retold in a letter to Alice from a priest friend, the Dominican Vincent McNabb.[88] His duties included visiting the hospital so it is likely he saw Francis there. But as he gave no details of any conversation it was probably at a time when Francis was only semi-conscious, repeating to himself the phrase from 'The Poppy', 'My withered dreams, my withered dreams'. Later McNabb bitterly regretted his refusal when asked to administer the Last Rites to him. The patient's name was not given, another priest was available and he was in a hurry — and so he lost what he was sure would have been a great privilege.[89]

During these last days Francis had no special pain and he could still read. The book he chose, *Light Freights* by W. W. Jacobs, was more in keeping than might appear. The toughness and resilience, the humour and the pathos of the London poor come through this novel as in most of Jacobs' books. Francis's sense that he would die on the streets was mistaken but the book absorbed him into the atmosphere and ethos where he had always felt that he and his eccentricities best belonged.

Although Alice and Everard called occasionally, Wilfrid was his one constant visitor. They said very little, Francis with his hand in Wilfrid's and both content to be silent. The reticence as to the deeper side of their friendship remained to the end: each, by unspoken common consent, wished it so. Wilfrid could not put his mind to more practical matters at this time and it was his son-in-law Caleb Saleeby who ensured that Francis made a will, something which neither Wilfrid nor Francis had apparently thought of before. His poetry was as much a part of the Meynell family life as he was himself, and they never considered the complications which could arise if the fact was not recorded in legal terms. As he had nothing to leave beyond his writings, the will, drawn up by Saleeby and witnessed by one of the patients, is probably the simplest in literary history:

> I leave absolutely my literary copyrights and papers, including my manuscripts of published and unpublished poems, to Wilfrid Meynell, of 4 Granville Place Mans. W.[90]

At the end he was, fittingly, alone. The most solitary moment in a human life comes at its close and for Francis who had so often known loneliness it brought no fear. In the early morning of 13 November the sunset shadow cast by the Calvary in the Field of the Cross at Storrington deepened at last into night. But he knew, as he had told Blunt, that this night was not the end. As he watched the grey dawn filter through the windows of the ward, his sun's setting was also leading to sunrise.

Conclusion

Like his death, Thompson's funeral was in keeping with his life. There were less than a dozen mourners gathered in the Catholic portion of the Kensal Green cemetery when he was buried on 16 November. But they came from a genuine love and regard which meant so much to him. There was no publicity, none of the hypocrisy of attending as a duty he would have wanted least of all. And it would have meant much to him that Meredith, whose ideas were so opposed to his own, paid a tribute that went beyond the differences: 'A true poet: one of the small band'.[1]

There were reasons for keeping the funeral as quiet as possible. When Wilfrid realized there could be no hope for a recovery he wondered whether hospitalization had been the right decision or if the reduction of the drug was hastening the end. He confided his doubts in a letter to Caleb Saleeby whose reply, written on the day of Francis's death, was not as reassuring as he presumably intended it to be:

> Though he undoubtedly died from the drastic deprivation of his necessary drug the tuberculosis would shortly have killed him and his life would have been worth nothing to him or to the world. There is therefore no cause for regret that you put him in hospital. Not otherwise would his last days have been so peaceful and free from distress.[2]

Obviously Saleeby was sure the immediate cause of death was due to an enforced withdrawal of the drug. Yet Wilfrid may have noticed the inconsistency in referring to the effect of its 'drastic deprivation' while at the same time describing his condition as 'peaceful and free from distress'.

Where the administration of the drug was concerned, the house doctor's assurances sent a few days later were closer to the truth. Dr Williams attended Francis regularly and was of the opinion that he had exaggerated the amount he was taking before, considering the much smaller doses that satisfied him in hospital:

> However this may have been, the pulmonary disease was so far advanced, that he could not have lived 6 months at the outside, whether he was an opium drinker or not.

Then, as if this still left too much room for doubt:

It is some consolation to know that his death was mainly due to natural and entirely unpreventable causes rather than to any acts of his own.[3]

Yet there remained the significant insertion 'mainly'. Williams was bound to uphold the verdict of the death certificate which gave tuberculosis as the cause of death, but clearly there was room for doubt as to the extent to which the drug had hastened it. No one, however, considered the possibility of an alternative to tuberculosis as the disease he was suffering from. Nor, apparently, did it occur to Wilfrid to recall Francis's own diagnosis as first given to himself and Saleeby and repeated in the letter written from Crawley.

What mattered now to Wilfrid was his determination that the support he had been giving for over twenty years must be continued in another form. No hint of anything other than 'unpreventable causes' for death must be allowed to appear in the obituaries that were planned as a means for reviving the poet's fame.

Wilfrid's first act was to contact Blunt, who knew more than anyone outside the hospital about Francis's condition. Blunt agreed to write an obituary for the *Academy* to appear simultaneously with notices in the London papers submitted by the Meynells' circle of friends. On 22 November almost all the papers carried eulogistic paragraphs on the poet's career, giving special prominence to consumption as the cause for his silence in recent years as well as for his death. They were followed by longer accounts in the weeklies and monthlies, with just the result Meynell desired. There was an upsurge of interest in Thompson and his work which, largely due to the constant vigilance of both Wilfrid and Alice, was maintained for over a decade.[4]

There was a further outcome to which neither had given any serious consideration. As the royalties from Thompson's poetry mounted they were, for the first time, becoming free from financial anxiety. At last he was repaying the debt he always felt he owed them, and in a way that went far beyond the financial benefits. Between 1909 and 1910 the sale of his poetry went up to 18 000 volumes[5] and the following year the Meynells were able to purchase the seventeenth-century Sussex farmhouse that still remains the family home.

From then onwards Humphreys Homestead became the centre of the Meynells' lives and those of their children. After Alice died in 1922 Monica took over its management and, since Wilfrid's death in 1948 at the age of ninety-six, it has been in the care of their grandchildren and great grandchildren. It has also remained as it was from the first, a literary centre. Many writers have found there a period of quiet for their work or come to consult the books and manuscripts in the library which Wilfrid built on to the main house. There could be no better memorial to the relationship where, for once claiming Francis to have been wrong, Wilfrid always insisted he was the debtor — in words which he might have borrowed from Francis himself: 'The rusty pipe which bore to the world his wine of song'.[6]

Neither Wilfrid nor Alice, nor later Everard, could foresee that the reputation they built up on his behalf could not last. In the first place it was false to both his life and work to an extent which they were unable to recognise. In addition there have been changes in outlook such as no one could have foreseen in the years before the First World War or even those immediately afterwards. Just two months before Francis's death the Encyclical *Pascendi Gregis* systematized the teachings of Catholic Modernism and drew no distinctions in condemning any tendency that threatened a compromise with the changes of the modern world. The presence of such tendencies in Thompson's life and writings had therefore to be suppressed if the Meynells were to perform their service to his fame as they saw it at the time. But change had to come, in the religious sphere as in all other areas of life during the present century, and the carefully constructed image of Thompson as the poet of orthodox Catholic piety finally collapsed among the ashes of the Second World War.

Thompson believed that his poetry contained a message that must wait for a future age to be understood. He was also aware of some great cataclysm ahead and he even seems to have had a prophetic sense of the fears consequent on a nuclear age. What he could not see, as is now apparent, was the connection between the two. Because of the upheavals separating his day and ours we can understand how vital the link must be between tradition and change, the link that formed the basis for his poetic inspiration and which stemmed from his religious background combined with the outlook he derived from the experiences of his earlier adult years. Today there is no need to question his 'orthodoxy'. To use a metaphor he would himself have favoured, the infusion of new blood into the tired body of the Christianity of his own day meant that, rather than destroying the past, it should be restored to flesh life and vigour. And the means, the revival of a new emphasis on the presence of God in His creation, has become one of the central messages of Christianity to the contemporary world.

Therefore his poetry did not, as he sometimes feared, end in the prophetic sense of an impending holocaust such as the nuclear threat now makes a part of present day reality. He was aware, too, of a time to come when to reach out beyond the limits of time and space would no longer be an ambition beyond the legitimate range of the human spirit. In this sense Thompson will find his true role as the poet of the space age, presenting in poetic form the necessary counterpart to the scientific achievements he would have welcomed with genuine enthusiasm, at the same time convinced of their ultimate place in God's plan for the future and survival of mankind.

He was not a great poet according to the standards set by English poetry. But he had a great vision, even if necessarily blurred by the limitations his day imposed upon it. He saw the essential values in Christianity as common to all human experience, reaching back to man's earliest symbolic acts and utterances where they express the union between divine, natural and human life. And the way to communicate this vision to the future is through the still-living language of symbolism shared by religion and poetry.

If he was unable to do so in an age not ready for it, he refused to compromise. For him the angels would always keep their ancient places in the cosmic world of man and nature, a world where renewal, not revolution, remains the source for its continuing life:

> Wherefore should the singer sing,
> So his song be true?
> Truth is ever old, old,
> Song ever new.
>
> Ere the world was, was the lie,
> And the truth too:
> But the old lie still is old,
> The old truth new.[7]

Notes

Abbreviations

WM   Wilfrid Meynell.
EM   Everard Meynell.
TLC   Terence L. Connolly, S. J.
NB   Francis Thompson's notebooks.
BC   Francis Thompson Collection, Boston College.
G   Manuscript and letters in the possession of the Meynell family at Greatham, Sussex.
Poems   *Poems of Francis Thompson*, edited with Biographical and Textual Notes by Terence L. Connolly S. J., Ph.D. Revised edition (1941, reprinted Westport, Connecticut, 1979).
Works   *The Works of Francis Thompson*, edited by Wilfrid Meynell, 3 vols. (1913).
MHW   *The Man has Wings: New Poems and Plays by Francis Thompson*, edited by Terence L. Connolly S. J. (New York, 1957).
Lit. Crit   *Literary Criticisms of Francis Thompson*, edited by Terence L. Connolly S. J. (New York, 1948).
Real RLS   *The Real Robert Louis Stevenson and Other Critical Essays by Francis Thompson*, edited by Terence L. Connolly S. J. (New York, 1959).
Letters   *The Letters of Francis Thompson*, edited by John Evangelist Walsh (New York, 1969).
Life   Everard Meynell, *The Life of Francis Thompson* (1912). All references are to this first edition, not the second shortened edition published in 1926.
La Vie   Piérre Danchin, *La Vie et l'Oeuvre d'un Poéte* (Paris, 1959).
SHSS   John Evangelist Walsh, *Strange Harp, Strange Symphony: The Life of Francis Thompson* (1968).
FT & WM   Viola Meynell, *Francis Thompson and Wilfrid Meynell: A Memoir* (1952).
IHP   Terence L. Connolly S. J., *Francis Thompson: In His Paths* (Milwaukee, 1944).
Diaries   Wilfrid Scawan Blunt, *My Diaries*, 2 vols. (1919).
ME   *Merry England*.
DR   *Dublin Review* (*Wiseman Review* since 1961).
Ac.   The *Academy*.

Manuscripts
Unless otherwise stated, all Thompson's manuscripts and notebooks referred to in the notes are in the Francis Thompson Collection at Boston College, Massachusetts.

Secondary Works
The place of publication is London, unless otherwise stated. The date of the edition refers to the one used, but if the first edition appeared more than ten years earlier this date is also given. In some cases, if the edition used is a paperback reprint the first is given within a shorter period.

Introduction

1 N.B. 24
2 *MHW*, pp. 7–8.
3 Alice Meynell, '*Selected Poems of Francis Thompson*', review in *DR* (Jan–April, 1909), 184–187.
4 *IHP*, p. 190.
5 J. C. Reid, *Francis Thompson: Man and Poet* (1959), pp. 135: 217.
6 *The Times Literary Supplement* (8 Jan. 1960), 20.
7 Geoffrey Grigson, 'Rags and Rubbish', *Catholic Transcript* (31 March, 1960).
8 Professor B. Ifor Evans, *English Poetry in the Later Nineteenth Century* (1966), p. 175.
9 *SHSS* (See List of Abbreviations).

Chapter One

1 Details for the Thompson family background are taken from Percival Lucas, 'The Pedigree of Francis Thompson the Poet', *Pedigree Register* (March, 1913), 354–357: *Life*, pp. 1–3; *SHSS*, p. 246.
2 For Catholicism in nineteenth century England see Edward R. Norman, *The English Catholic Church in the Nineteenth Century* (Oxford, 1984); John Bossy, *The English Catholic Community 1570–1850* (1979): J. Derek Holmes, *More Roman than Rome: English Catholicism in the Nineteenth Century* (1978); Alec R. Vidler, 'The Pontificate of Pius IX', in *The Church in an Age of Revolution*, ed. Vidler (Harmondsworth, 1968); Frederick Heyer, *The Catholic Church 1648–1870* (1969): M. D. R. Leys, *Catholicism in England 1539–1829: A Social History* (1961); E. I. Watkin, *Roman Catholicism in England from the Reformation to 1950* (Oxford, 1957). Several earlier studies have not been supplanted, among which the most important are Denis Gwynn, *The Second Spring 1818–1852: A Study of the Catholic Revival in England* (1942); Maisie Ward, *The Wilfrid Wards and the Transition, I. The Nineteenth Century* (1934); Bernard Ward, *The Eve of Catholic Emancipation*, 3 vols. (1911–1912): also his *Sequal to Catholic Emancipation* 2 vols (1915).

For the groups within the Church see, in addition to references in the above works, G. A. Beck (ed.) *The English Catholics 1850–1950* (1950), especially David Mathew, 'Old Catholics and converts': Denis Gwynn, 'The Irish Immigration'; John Hickey, *Urban Catholicism in England and Wales from 1829 to the present day* (1969); Roger Swift and Sheridan Gilley (eds.) *The Irish in the Victorian City* (1985), especially M. A. G. O'Tuathaigh, 'The Irish in nineteenth century Britain: Problems of Integration': Gerard Connolly, 'Irish and Catholic: Myth or Reality?'; J. C. H. Aveling, *The Handle and the Axe* (1976), pp. 284ff; David Mathew, *Catholicism in England 1535–1935: Portrait of a Minority its Culture and Traditions* (1936); Jean Alain Lesourd, *Les Catholiques dans la Societé Anglaise*, 2 vols. (Lille, 1978), I, pp. 347–379.

For the special character of English Catholicism see Joseph P. Chinnici, *The English Catholic Enlightenment: John Lingard and the Cisalpine Movement 1780–1850* (Shepherdstown, Virginia, 1980): Martin Hale and Edwin Bonney, *The Life and Letters of John Lingard 1771–1851* (1910); Peter Doyle, 'Bishop Goss of Liverpool (1856–1872) and the importance of being English', in *Religion and National Identity*, ed. Stuart Mews, *Studies in Church History*, 18 (Oxford, 1982): Marion Norman, 'John Gother and the English Way of Spirituality', *Recusant History*, 2 (1972), 306–319. The special flavour of northern Catholicism comes through very clearly in Barbara Charlton, *Recollections of a Northumbrian Lady*, ed. L. E. O. Charlton (1949).

3 W. E. Gladstone, *The Vatican Decrees and their Bearing on Civic Allegiance: A Political Expostulation* (1874). For anti-Catholic prejudice see Edward R. Norman, *Anti-Catholicism in Victorian England* (1968): also his *English Catholic Church*, pp. 310–312. For the reactions to the pronouncement on infallibility among English Catholics see also James Hennessy, 'National Traditions and the First Vatican Council', *Archivum Historiae Pontificiae*, 7 (1969), 491–512. For the more general reaction see Cuthbert Butler, *The Life and Times of Bishop Ullathorne 1806–1889*, 2 vols (1926), 2, pp. 88–94.

4 Owen Chadwick, *The Victorian Church: Part Two* (1970), pp. 401–423: 462–465; Raymond Chapman, *The Victorian Debate: English Literature and Society 1832–1901* (1968); L. E. Elliott Binns, *English Thought 1860–1900: The Theological Aspect* (1956), pp. 293–308 'The influence of Literature'; Aveling, *Handle and Axe*, pp. 297–298.

5 The correspondence between Cardinal Newman and E. H. Thompson has been put together from several sources, chiefly *The Letters and Diaries of John Henry Newman*, ed. C. S. Dessain, 19 (1969), pp. 37–38: 70: 78–79: 148–151: 173–174; Wilfrid Ward, *The Life of John Henry Cardinal Newman*, 2 vols. (1912), I, pp. 489–490: 501. Letters from E. H. Thompson to Newman and others form part of the Newman Collections in the archives at the Oratory, Birmingham, and the Downside Abbey Library. For the *Rambler* controversies with references to Thompson see also W. Ward, *W. G. Ward*, pp. 196–204; Cuthbert Butler, *The Life and Times of Bishop Ullathorne*, 2 vols. (1926), I, pp. 308–333; Joseph L. Altholtz, *The Liberal Catholic Movement in England: The RAMBLER and its Contributors 1848–1864* (Montreal, 1962), pp. 94–95: 103–104. See also John Coulson's Introduction to J. H. Newman, *On Consulting the Faithful in Matters of Doctrine* (1961, reprinted from the *Rambler*, July 1859).

It is worth adding that E. H. Thompson's wife Harriet corresponded for several years on spiritual matters with F. W. Faber. See *Selected Letters by F. W. Faber*, ed. R. Addington (1974), pp. 230–231.

E. H. Thompson died in Cheltenham in 1891, having been an invalid for many years. There were no children.

6 Herbert A. Smith, letter to *The Church Times*, 21 April 1911.

7 For the principles of homoeopathic medicine see Samuel Hahnemann, *Organon of Medicine* (Kothen, 1810: 6th. edn. 1842, reprinted 1983). The best recent study of the subject is Anthony Campbell, *The Two Faces of Homoeopathy* (1984). For the history of its spread and influence see G. Ruthven Mitchell, *Homoeopathy* (1975); M. G. Blackie, *The Patient not the Cure* (1978); John V. Pickstone, 'Establishment and Dissent in Nineteenth Century Medicine', in *The Church and Healing*, ed. W. J. Sheils, *Studies in Church History*, 19 (Oxford, 1982); D. Lesser, *The Contribution of Homoeopathy to the Development of Medicine* (High Wycombe, 1945), pp. 5–15; Sir John Weir, 'British Homoeopathy during the last Hundred Years', *British Medical Journal*, 2 (1932), 603–605.

8 'An Address to Medical Students', *Lancet*, 7 Sept. 1895. For the same outlook earlier in the century see S. W. F. Holloway, 'Medical Education in England 1830–1858: A Sociological Analysis', *History*, 49 (1964), 299–324.

9 Charles J. G. Saunders, *A History of the United Bristol Hospitals* (1965), p. 58.

10 Sir Charles Brown, *Sixty Four Years a Doctor* (Preston, 1922), especially pp. 53–55.

11 Quoted in *Vanished Preston*, Catalogue for an exhibition of the same title held at the Harris Museum and Art Gallery, Preston, March 1983.

12 Charles Dickens, *Hard Times* (1854: Oxford, 1974), p. 22. For Preston and its background see P. Whittle, *The History of the Borough of Preston*, 2 vols. (Preston, 1883); Henry Fishwick, *The History of the Parish of Preston in Amoundeness in the*

County of Lancaster (1900), especially pp. 160–165; William Savage, The Making of our Towns (1952), p. 146.

13 References to homoeopathy in Manchester at the time are taken from the Annual Reports of the Manchester Homoeopathic Institution and its predecessors, from the tracts by William Sharp and the pamphlets by William Roberts printed in response to them. All are in the archives of the Central Library, Manchester. For medical botany and the widespread use of herbal remedies in Ashton and elsewhere see John V. Pickstone (ed.) Health Disease and Medicine in Lancashire 1750–1950 (Manchester, 1980): also his 'Medical Botany and self-help Medicine in Victorian England', Memoirs of the Manchester Literary and Philosophical Society 119, (1976–1977), 85–95.

14 W. H. Henderson, The Lancashire Cotton Famine 1861–1865 (Manchester, 1978), pp. 72–92.

15 J. Saxon Mills, 'Francis Thompson: Some Personal Recollections of the Poet', Cassell's Weekly, (26 May 1928).

16 IHHP, p. 246.

17 M. Bowman, England in Ashton-under-Lyne (Altrincham, 1960): William Glover and John Andrew, A History of Ashton-under-Lyne (Ashton, 1884); Edward Baines, The History of the County Palatine and Duchy of Lancaster, 2 vols. (1868), I, pp. 423–425; P. J. Gooderson, A History of Lancashire (1980), p. 51.

18 W. E. A. Axon, Lancashire Gleanings (1883), pp. 186–187; Henry Fishwick, A History of Lancashire (1894), p. 289; Bowman, England in Ashton, pp. 282–289.

19 Robert Smith, Ye Old Catholic Community of Ashton-under-Lyne (Ashton, 1920), p. 33.

20 Charles A. Bolton, Salford Diocese and its Catholic Past (Manchester, 1950), pp. 165–166. For the Murphy Riots see John O'Dea, The Story of the Old Faith in Manchester (1910), pp. 190–192; Glover and Andrew, Ashton, pp. 332–339; Bowman, England in Ashton, pp. 234–235; Walter Arnstein, 'The Murphy Riots: A Victorian Dilemma', Victorian Studies, 9, No. 1 (1975), 51–71.

21 Margaret's recollection is from a letter to TLC, 12 Jan. 1939 (BC). Mary's are from La Vie, p. 19: IHP, p. 108.

22 Letter to TLC, 27 Nov. 1937 (BC).

23 Life, pp. 7–8: SHSS, p. 246. (Walsh corrects EM, who attributes the note to the death of Mrs. Thompson). Mary's observation was made in a letter to WM, 25 Nov. 1907 (G).

24 Letter to William Archer, 31 May 1897, Letters, p. 192.

25 Letter to TLC, 11 May 1931 (BC).

26 MS 'Miscellany of FT Fragments'.

27 La Vie, p. 36, note 17. M. Danchin has kindly allowed me to quote from the complete letter from which this extract is taken and which is in his possession, written to him by Mary Thompson, 20 Jan. 1947.

28 NB BC29.

29 Ibid.

30 Letter to Danchin, 20 Jan. 1947 (See note 27).

31 There is no biography of John Carroll. Details of his career have been obtained from the Shrewsbury Diocesan archives, from obituaries and an account of his consecration as Coadjutor Bishop of Shrewsbury in the Harvest (Nov. 1893). Specific references to his literary interests are included in an article by WM, 'The Coadjutor Bishop of Shrewsbury', ME (Nov. 1893).

32 La Vie, p. 36, note 35.

33 C. S. Spencer, speech recorded in the Ashton Reporter, (27 March 1926).

34 Letter to Danchin, 20 Jan. 1947 (See note 27).

35 Life, p. 9.

36 Letter to EM, 19 June 1908 (G).

37 SHSS, pp. 8–9, quoted from E. Byrne, 'Boyhood Days in Ashton: Francis

Thompson', the *Ashton Reporter*, (Dec. 1930). The quotation is from a clipping at (BC) for which the exact date cannot be traced in local sources.

[38] The holidays in Wales are described by Mary in a letter to TLC, 2 April 1945 (BC). Other details appear in a letter from her to EM, 10 June 1908 (G).

[39] *Life*, pp. 6–7.

[40] NB 28.

[41] NB 21.

[42] 'The Fourth Order of Humanity', *ME* (Dec. 1891). The passages quoted here were deleted from the text printed in *Works*, 3.

[43] *La Vie*, pp. 35–36. Danchin quotes from a notebook then in the possession of Francis Meynell which cannot now be traced.

[44] *Works*, 3, p. 7.

Chapter Two

[1] David Milburn, *A History of Ushaw College* (Durham, 1964); *Records and Recollections of St Cuthbert's College, Ushaw, by an Old Alumnus* (Preston, 1889); Vincent Allen Mclelland, *English Roman Catholics and Higher Education 1830–1903* (Oxford, 1973); Maisie Ward, *The Wilfrid Wards and the Transition: 2: Insurrection versus Resurrection* (1938), pp. 47ff: see also *I: The Nineteenth Century*, pp. 68–73.

[2] Milburn, *History of Ushaw*, pp. 267–282. Tate's correspondence with Lingard is in the Ushaw College archives. For quotations see Chinnici, *English Catholic Enlightenment*, pp. 139 and *passim*.

[3] Henry Gillow wrote a number of articles in leading journals on Catholic education. His main contributions to the argument concerning London University degrees appeared in *DR* (April and October, 1869). See also H. Tristram, 'London University and Catholic Education', *ibid.* (Oct. 1936), 269–282; H. O. Evennett, 'Catholics and the Universities', in Beck, *English Catholics*; W. J. Battenbury, 'Secondary Education for boys', *ibid.*; McLelland, *English Roman Catholics and Higher Education*, pp. 46–55.

[4] Wilfrid P. Ward, 'The Ushaw Centenary and English Catholicism', *DR* (Oct. 1908), 217–243.

[5] For the buildings and general appearance of the College at the time I am grateful for information from Dr J. Derek Holmes and from the College Librarian, Dr. Michael Sharratt. Further details are from Robert C. Laing (ed.) *Ushaw College: A Centenary Memorial* (Newcastle, 1895).

[6] L. C. Casartelli, letter to WM, 28 Nov. 1907 (G); *Life*, p. 15. Louis Casartelli was to oppose the taking of London degrees as, in his view, substituting 'cramming' for genuine learning. He was Bishop of Salford from 1903 to 1925 and well known as an orientalist. See Milburn, *History of Ushaw*, p. 277.

[7] MS 'Personal Data'.

[8] MSS fragments, mainly detached notebook pages (G).

[9] Recollection by Adam Wilkinson, quoted in *IHP*, p. 175.

[10] F. J. Hall, A. Wilkinson and H. K. Mann, 'Francis Thompson: A Tribute from his Schoolfellows', *Ushaw Magazine* (March, 1908), 61–95; Joseph Scott, 'The game of Cat', *ibid.* (March, 1893), 19–32.

[11] Recollection by George Phillips, quoted in *Life*, p. 16.

[12] Father Nowlan, letter to Dr Thompson, Easter 1872, quoted in *Life*, p. 26. EM adds details of Thompson's position in class obtained from another member of staff. This was decided by the results of the 'Compositions' held each term, where in Latin he was first six times and in English, sixteen times. In Greek his position

ran from second to tenth and in French his average place was about eighth. But 'of his Arithmetic, Algebra and Geometry the less said the better'. The letter and these details are confirmed by the College records, where Thompson's name appears consistently towards the top of the lists of names for his classes. The records also show that, unknown to him, his literary tastes were shared by two of his contemporaries. Lafcardio Hearn's later career led him away from England and from the Church but at this time he was being educated at Ushaw with the priesthood in view. The other, Coventry Patmore's son Henry, attended the same art classes as Francis but otherwise there seems to have been no contact between them. Through his later friendship with Patmore Francis would certainly have heard then of Henry's poetical gifts and of his tragic early death soon after his ordination.

[13] The accusation that Thompson was 'persecuted' by his schoolfellows is well refuted by one of them, Adam Wilkinson, in a letter to the *Tablet* (13 Dec. 1913). See also 'Francis Thompson: A Tribute': *Life*, p. 19.

[14] *Works*, 3, p. 10.

[15] The earlier version appears in the poem as first printed in *ME* (Jan. 1892).

[16] Recollection by Harriet Patmore, letter to WM, 25 Nov. 1907 (G). She was Patmore's third wife and apparently quoting from a description by her stepson Henry Patmore.

[17] J. B. Milburn, 'Francis Thompson's Poems', *Ushaw Magazine* (March, 1894).

[18] Alfred McDonagh's Commonplace Book is in the Ushaw College archives, bequeathed by his brother Austin. In an accompanying letter Austin maintains that the Latin poem was written out and signed by Thompson. A comparison with the handwriting in the 'Ushaw College Notebook' (see note 19) suggests that this is unlikely, although it is possible as Thompson adopted several different styles when copying out his earlier poems. Alfred seems to have had a high regard for their friendship. He pasted three photographs of Thompson on the second and third pages of the Commonplace Book, two from childhood and one of the youth he himself knew. There is also a pasted-in page of 'drawings by Francis Thompson' with sketches of hands and facial features.

[19] The 'Ushaw College Notebook' is said to have been given by Thompson to a schoolfriend, Alfred Walmesley, who later sold it to a priest, Father Richmond, in Lancaster. From him it came into the Meynells' possession and so to (BC). It is worth adding that according to an undated letter from WM to Seymour Adelman, probably written during the nineteen thirties:

> Francis, when he heard that his old schoolfellow had the little book & said it was a gift from Francis, used to shake his head in a manner full of suggestion to the contrary!!
> (Seymour Adelman Collection, Bryn Mawr College Library)

The contents of the Notebook remain largely unpublished but some prose passages and a few poetry extracts are quoted in *SHSS* and in 'Francis Thompson: A Tribute'.

[20] Untraced NB, quoted in *La Vie*, p. 489, note 11.

[21] MS 'Shelley', draft in the Harris Library, Preston.

[22] Letter to Quiller Couch, undated. The letter is not included in *Letters* but was printed by F. G. Atkinson in 'Q. and Francis Thompson', *Times Literary Supplement* (5 Feb. 1970), 140.

[23] Mary Thompson confided this detail in her later years to Sister Francis, a member of the Presentation Community in Manchester, who repeated it to me in a telephone interview, June 1984. According to Sister Francis's own recollections Mary seems to have been well aware of her brother's dilatoriness and of his unsuitability for the priesthood. 'You see, he had another gift' was a phrase she used as from Mary herself.

24 MS note for *Life* but not in the published text. Quoted in *SHSS*, p. 17. These notes
    made by EM which do not appear in *Life* cannot now be traced at (G) or
    elsewhere. Nor is there any manuscript of the complete book now in existence.
25 Anonymous writer to the *Ushaw Magazine* (March 1900),
26 Anselm Kenealy, O.S.F.C. 'Francis Thompson', *Franciscan Annals* (May, 1922),
    151–155.
27 MS note for Life, quoted in *SHSS*, p. 18 (see note 24).
28 Letter to Dr Thompson, June 1877, quoted in *Life*, p. 32.
29 E. M. Brockbank, *The Foundation of Provincial Medical Training in England* (Man-
    chester, 1936); R. M. Walker, *Medical Education in Britain* (1965), especially
    pp. 13–26; Charles Norman, *The Evolution of Medical Training in the Nineteenth
    Century* (Oxford, 1967); Victoria University, *The Victoria University of Manchester
    Medical School* (Manchester, 1908); Parliament, House of Commons, *Report of
    the Select Committee on Medical Education* (1834); W. Brockbank, *The Early History of
    the Manchester Medical School* (Manchester, 1968): also his *Manchester's place in the
    History of Medicine* (reprinted from the British Association, *Manchester and its
    Region*, 1962).
30 Robert H. Kargon, *Science in Victorian Manchester* (Manchester, 1977); Trevor H.
    Levine, 'The Rich Economy of Nature: Chemistry in the Nineteenth Century', in
    Nature and the Victorian Imagination, ed. U. C. Knoepfmacher and G. B. Tennyson
    (Berkeley and Los Angeles, 1978).
31 W. Brockbank, *Portrait of a Hospital* (1952): also his summary account, *The M.R.I.
    Story* (Manchester, 1969).
32 References to the courses of study at the Owens College Medical School are based
    on the College Prospectuses for the years 1878–1883, now in the Manchester
    University Library archives.
33 *Diaries*, 2, pp. 187–188.
34 Thompson recalled his visits to the Art Gallery in 'The Fourth Order of Hu-
    manity', *Works*, 3, pp. 68–70. For the Manchester libraries and Art Gallery see
    T.H.G. Stevens, *Manchester of Yesterday* (Altrincham, 1958), pp. 99–100: 132–138.
35 The 'Notebook of Early Poems' contains some thirty pieces. Most are written
    down from memory but some seem to have been copied from other early note-
    books now lost. The extracts that follow here are all from this Notebook, unpub-
    lished except for the lines on Rossetti's death, for which see *SHSS*, pp. 28–29.
36 *Life*, p. 39; John Thompson, *Francis Thompson: Poet and Mystic* (1912: second
    rev. edn. 1923), pp. 26–27; J. S. Mills, 'Francis Thompson: Some Personal
    Recollections'.
37 *Life*, p. 46.
38 The assertion that Thompson had read De Quincey's *Confessions* before asking for
    the book as a present was made by his half brother Norbert Thompson. *See SHSS*,
    p. 22.
39 De Quincey's *Confessions of an English Opium Eater* first appeared in the *London
    Magazine* in 1821 and in book form the following year. Its appeal increased later
    in the century when concern for the effects of opium caused it to be cited both for
    and against the non-medical use of the drug. There were at least 13 editions and
    reprints between 1880 and 1910. In all these later editions De Quincey's efforts to
    clarify his prevaricating attitude are based on his chief aim — to explore the effect
    of opium on dreams in order to find out more about the dreams themselves. See
    The Collected Works of Thomas De Quiney, ed. D. Masson, 14 vols. (Edinburgh,
    1889), 13, p. 335. It is worth noting that the first biography of De Quincey
    appeared in 1877, the year Thompson began his medical training, and aroused
    fresh interest in the *Confessions*. For the influence of the book and De Quincey's
    views see E. Sackville West, *A Flame in Sunlight: The Life and Work of Thomas De
    Quincey* (1936, new edn. 1974); Grevell Lindop, *The Opium Eater: A Life of Thomas*

De Quincey (1981). De Quincey was born in Manchester in 1785 and died the year Thompson was born. Many writers have commented on De Quincey having frequented the same Public Library in Manchester as Thompson but in his time it was still housed on its original site at Campfield.

40   Terry M. Parssinen, *Secret Drugs, Secret Remedies: Narcotic Drugs in British Society 1820–1930* (Manchester, 1983); Virginia Berridge and Griffith Edwards, *Opium and the People: Opiate Use in Nineteenth-Century England* (1981), especially pp. 49–61; Margaret Goldsmith, *The Trail of Opium* (1939), pp. 134–145; Elizabeth Lomax, 'The Uses and Abuses of Opiates in Nineteenth-Century England', *Bulletin of the History of Medicine*, 47 (1973), 167–176; M. H. Abrams, *The Milk of Paradise* (1934), p. xii.

41   MS 'This is my beloved son'. The poem is quoted in *La Vie*, p. 34: *SHSS*, p. 25.

42   WM (ed.) *Who Goes There* (Toronto, 1916), p. 112. For his notes on the poem see pp. 27–29. The version he printed also appears, with other minor alterations, in a collection of Thompson's early poems, *Uncollected Verses*, privately printed the following year.

43   *Life*, p. 46; Reid, *Francis Thompson*, p. 21; *SHSS*, pp. 20: 248–249, note 1.

44   Thompson, *Francis Thompson*, p. 35.

45   Unpublished passage in letter to Danchin, 20 Jan. 1947. (See Chapter One, note 27).

46   Letter to WH, 25 Nov. 1907 (G).

47   Letter to WH, 15 Nov. 1907 (G).

48   The harsh picture of Thompson at this time is reported as coming from 'an informant' by Robert McKenna in an essay in *As Shadows Lengthen* (1932). Other accounts quoted here are by Mills, 'Francis Thompson: Some Personal Recollections' and from an anonymous article in the *Ashton Reporter* (20 Feb. 1909). Mary Thompson's denials appear in an unpublished passage in her letter to Danchin, 20 Jan. 1947 (see note 45) where she confirms an earlier conversation with him, for which see *La Vie*, pp. 31–32.

49   Letter to EM, 24 Nov. 1913 (G).

50   *Diaries*, 2, p. 188.

51   Mary made this observation to TLC, quoted in *IHP*, p. 10. Her comment on her mother's love for her brother appears in her letter to WM, 25 Nov. 1907 (see note 46).

52   NB BC20. Blunt, in *Diaries*, refers to Blake and the Bible as the books Thompson took to London but all other sources follow the information from Thompson as it appears in *Life*, p. 58. Blunt is at times inaccurate on details of this kind.

Chapter Three

1   Mills, 'Francis Thompson: Some Personal Recollections'.

2   London street life and the conditions of the London poor had not appreciably altered since the reports by Henry Mayhew, *London Labour and the London Poor*, 4 vols. (1861–1864, reprinted 1967). See especially I, pp. 2–137. His findings were confirmed by Charles Booth, *Life and Labour of the People of London*, 16 vols. (1892–1902). See especially First Series, Parts 3 and 4. See also George Sim, *How the Poor Live* (1889); Jack London, *The People of the Abyss* (1903); George Orwell, *Down and Out in Paris and London* (1933). These last two writers spent several weeks living as, and with, the very poor. Although it was by choice, not necessity, their descriptions are among the most moving of the accounts of the conditions. For recent surveys of these conditions and the efforts to overcome them see Gareth Stedman

Jones, *Outcast London: A Study in Relationships between Classes in Victorian Society* (1971, new edn. Harmondsworth, 1984); Peter Keating, *Into Unknown England* (Glasgow, 1957); Kellow Chesney, *The Victorian Underworld* (Harmondsworth, 1972). Both writers take London as the example for the wider national scene and draw largely on Mayhew and Booth.

3 'Railway stations: Liverpool Street Station', *The Poems of John Davidson*, ed. Andrew Turnbull, 2 vols. (Edinburgh, 1973), 2, pp. 441–442.

4 David C. Lamb, letter to *The Times* (24 May, 1938).

5 Andrew Mearns, *The Bitter Cry of Outcast London: An Enquiry into the Conditions of the Abject Poor* (1883), quoted in Keating, *Into Unknown England*, pp. 96–97.

6 William Kent, *Encyclopaedia of London* (1951), p. 358. For the Guildhall Library that Thompson knew see Walter Thornby and Edward Walford, *Old and New London*, 6 vols. (1873–1878), 1, pp. 392–393.

7 The incident is recorded in a lecture by Agnes Tobin, a friend of the Meynells, where she says it was told to her by Thompson himself. The manuscript of the lecture is at (BC). For the probable identity of the painting see *SHSS*, p. 272, note 4.

8 Fair copy in the 'Notebook of Early Poems'. Rossetti's painting is now at the Tate Gallery.

9 De Quincey, *Confessions*, *Works*, 13, pp. 441–443. For the opium nightmares of Coleridge and De Quincey see Grevell, *Opium Eater*, pp. 233–234: 370–373.

10 The 'Notebook of Early Poems' contains the finished poem. It has only been printed in *SHSS*, pp. 47–48.

11 NB BC45 contains the complete poem, from which stanzas 2, 5, 6, 8 and 10 are quoted here. It is printed in full in *SHSS*, pp. 57–60. Walsh attributes it to a later period of Thompson's life on the streets but Thompson's own note cannot be disregarded.

12 Much has been written on the forms assumed by the 'Archetypal Feminine'. The two chief works available in English are C. G. Jung, *The Archetypes and the Collective Unconscious: Collected Works*, 9, Part 1 (1954, 2nd. edn. 1969); Erich Neumann, *The Great Mother: An Analysis of the Archetype* (1955), especially pp. 5–13. See also Jung, *Symbols of Transformation: Works*, 5, Part 2, especially pp. 295–301.

13 *Wit and Drollery: Jovial Poems* (1632), pp. 149–153.

14 'Tom o' Bedlam's Song', stanzas 5, 6 and 8. The poem was printed in the *Dome* (May, 1898), but not elsewhere. Part of stanza 8 is printed in *Life*, p. 65.

15 The fullest report of the churches' work for the poor and of the Catholic Church in particular is Booth, *Life and Labour*, 7, Third Series: *Religious Influences* (1902), especially pp. 250–268. See also Hugh McLeod, *Class and Religion in the late Victorian City* (1974); Richard Mudie Smith (ed.) *The Religious Life of London* (1904). For the specific 'solutions' referred to here see Francis Peek, 'The Workless, the Thriftless and the Worthless', *Contemporary Review* (Jan–Feb. 1888), 39–52: 276–285; Arnold White, *The Problems of a Great City* (1886), especially pp. 228–239. These and other responses, notably the schemes put forward by the Charity Organization Society, are well summarized in Stedman Jones, *Outcast London*, pp. 286–287.

16 'Degraded Poor', NB IO and NB BC21. The poem is printed as a footnote in *Life*, pp. 77–78.

17 *Life*, pp. 70–72; *SHSS*, p. 41. McMaster's denial of EM's description of the first meeting was made to C. Lewis Hind, who recorded it in an article, 'Poets Happy and Unhappy', *Daily Chronicle* (1 April, 1925). Other details are from McMaster's own account in the topographical study he wrote in his later years, *A Short History of the Royal Parish of St. Martins-in-the-Fields* (1916), pp. 116–117. It is elaborated by R. Thurston Hopkins in *This London: Its Taverns Haunts and Memories* (1927), p. 197.

18   *Life*, p. 73.

19   *Works*, 3, p. 50.

20   McMaster, *A Short History*, p. 117. Mary is not identified by name as the sister who accompanied Dr Thompson but it is more probable that it was she rather than Margaret. Her special feeling for her brother would have been all the stronger owing to her prospective departure for the convent.

21   The 'Ballad of Fair Weather' is copied into the 'Notebook of Early Poems', with drafts in NB's BC24 and 46B. It has only been printed — unexpectedly, considering its subject matter — in *MHW*, p. 74. But there is no editorial comment.

22   In addition to sources given in note 12 for the Mother Archetype, see Barbara A. Schapiro, *The Romantic Mother: Narcissistic Patterns in Romantic Poetry* (Baltimore, 1983). The narcissistic element in Thompson's poetry is very similar to the narcissism which Schapiro finds characteristic of Romantic poetry as a whole. Shelley's 'Alastor' is taken as a representative example, where the poet's self-absorption in his unfulfilled longing for an ideal woman is the symptom of an incomplete break with the mother image. It is therefore significant that Walsh, the only writer on Thompson who has made more than passing use of the notebooks, has seen a connection between Thompson's career and the course of the poet in 'Alastor' (*SHSS*, pp. 1–4). But he does not take the analogy beyond the surface pattern of the poem and so misses most of the psychological content as examined by Schapiro — who in turn makes no reference to Thompson among the poets discussed.

    For the severed head and the associations mentioned here see Erich Neumann, *The Origins and History of Consciousness* (1954); Gertrude Rachel Levy, *The Gates of Horn* (1948); Otto Rank, *Art and Artist: Creative Urge and Personality Development* (New York, 1957), pp. 180–181: 199–293: Arthur Wormhaudt, *The Demon Lover: A Psychoanalytical Approach to Literature* (New York, 1949), especially pp. 1–10. For the symbolism of the forest, the fair weather and the feathers see J. C. Cooper, *Fairy Tales: Allegories of the Inner Life* (Wellingsborough, Northants. 1983), pp. 18–26: 39: 83: 140–145; Marie Louise von Franz, *The Interpretation of Fairy Tales* (Zurich, 1970, 3rd. ed. Zurich and New York, 1975): also her *The Feminine in Fairy Tales* (1976). For the stepmother as witch see also Rosemary Haughton, *Tales from Eternity: The World of Faerie and the Spiritual Search* (1973), p. 95.

23   Letter to EM, 19 Jan. 1908 (G).

24   *Life*, p. 14.

25   WH repeated the words as coming from Thompson when telling Blunt the story of the poet's background. See *Diaries*, 2, p. 192. Dr Thompson's visit to McMaster's is based on a recollection by Mary Gertrude Richardson, a niece of the second Mrs Thompson. In an interview with Walsh in April 1964 she told him she had often heard her aunt speak of it and of having accompanied Dr Thompson (*SHSS*, p. 55). From the information obtained by Thurston Hopkins (see note 17) McMaster seems to have given the first visit a later date without making it clear whether there were two. Mary's denial appears in her letter to Danchin, 20 Jan. 1947 (see Chapter 1, note 27). In an unpublished passage she answers a question from Danchin on the subject: 'My father and sister did not go to London nor have any communication with McMaster at all. None of that is true. If Mr McMaster wrote that he must have been dreaming'. This still allows for Mary having accompanied her father on a first visit, if there were two, although one might expect a reference to it from her. In addition, a second visit would have taken place after Mary had left home and she may not have been told of it since the outcome would have distressed her. If Dr Thompson did make the second visit with his new wife it strengthens the view that it was she who was

largely responsible for any subsequent 'rejection' on the ground given by Thompson to WM and reported by WM to Blunt.

26 MS fragment (BC)
27 *Life*, p. 78.
28 NB BC29.
29 NB BC20.
30 Mayhew, *London Labour*, 3, pp. 428–429. For the conditions in the dosshouses see descriptions in most of the works cited in note 2. See especially Sims, *How the Poor Live*, pp. 43: 83: 148. Sims is more penetrating than most in noting the amount of mutual help often exchanged among the destitute. Jack London in *The People of the Abyss* describes his own experience of a single night in a dosshouse. The conditions and the lack of serious social concern are stressed by Gustav Doré and Blanchard Jarrold, *London: A Pilgrimage* (1872), pp. 141–160: 171–191. See also Eric de Maré, *The London Doré saw: A Victorian Evocation* (Harmondsworth, 1973).
31 NB BC29.
32 NB 10.
33 References, in order, are to: unnumbered notebook (G): *Life*, pp. 64–65: NB BC29.
34 NB 5. Thompson made use of the incident years later in a light-hearted apology to C. L. Hind for one of his frequent financial muddles. (See *Letters*, p. 202).
35 *Life*, p. 67.
36 'Francis Thompson: A Tribute'.
37 The source for the story is Osbert Sitwell's Introduction to Davies's *Collected Poems*, quoted (as being without foundation) in *FT & WM*, pp. 16–17. The letter from Davies to WM is at (G). It should be noted that the story appears and is accepted, in Richard J. Stanifer, *W. H. Davies: A Critical Biography* (1963), p. 55.
38 NB 45. Some similar lines also appear in NB 46B.
39 *Diaries*, 1, p. 180. The question 'did Francis Thompson attempt suicide?' was first raised publicly by W. D. Hennessy in an article of the same title in the *Catholic World* (Feb. 1950). He had corresponded with WM on the subject in 1938, when WM, then aged eighty-five, admitted to blurred memories of the details but still held by the main outline. He also added words that show something of his own attitude. Thompson would have known the Church's view of suicide, 'but there may have been occasions in his life in the streets when he lost his Catholic consciousness'. (Letter to Hennessy in the Francis Meynell Collection at the University Library, Cambridge). Hennessy did not write his article until after WM's death. In 1949 he opened the subject again in a correspondence with Francis Meynell, who regarded the story as improbable and due to the 'misrepresentation of an opium fantasy'. Hennessy based his article on this argument, but it does not account for WM's acceptance of Blunt's record of Thompson's words, despite his corrections of many other entries in the *Diaries*, made before their publication. (See *FT & WM*, p. 76). It should be added tht the two earliest biographies of Thompson, written before the pulication of *Life*, both refer to the suicide attempt. Both authors obtained their information from WM: Thompson, *Francis Thompson* (1st. edn. 1912. The title of this edn. *Francis Thompson: The Preston born Poet*); Kingsley Rooker, *Francis Thompson* (1913, based on an earlier thesis). See also *La Vie*, p. 47: *SHSS*, p. 354. Viola Meynell should perhaps have the last word. In a letter to Hennessy, 27 April 1953, she gives her reasons for disagreeing with Hennessy's article and with her brother's argument, adding 'that my own feeling is that if in his plight he thought of suicide, that is neither surprising nor shocking. The fact that he did not take his own life, however supported by Chatterton's influence, was his own triumph'. (Letter in the Francis Meynell Collection).
40 *Diaries*, 1, p. 180.
41 *Ac.* (23 Nov. 1907).

[42] MS note for *Life*, quoted in *SHSS*, pp. 253–254.

[43] *Sister Songs*, 'Part the First', 275–295.

[44] For prostitution in London at the time see William Acton, *Prostitution considered in its Moral, Social and Sanitary Aspects* (1857, rev. edn. 1970); Mayhew, *London Labour*, 4. The section on the subject is reprinted in Chesney, *Victorian Underworld*, pp. 363–433.

[45] *Life*, pp. 81–82.

[46] WM, 'Mr Francis Thompson', *Athenaeum* (23 Nov. 1907).

[47] *Diaries*, 1, p. 148, 2, p. 184.

[48] NB BC22.

[49] 'Sad Semele' has only been printed in *MHW*, p. 42.

[50] 'After Love's End' is copied into the 'Notebook of Early Poems' from drafts in NB's 43B and BC24. There may be a connection between this poem and lines in 'Orizon-Tryst':

> I was then
> Like one who, dreaming solitude, awakes
> In sobbing from his dream; and, straining arms
> That ache for their own void, with sudden shock
> Takes a dear form beside him.
>
> 13–17

Walsh sees these lines as proof of a sexual relationship with the street girl. (*SHSS*, p. 53). In his view Dr Thompson's rejection took place on finding his son with the girl on the second visit to London (see note 25). The visit, if it occurred, was some eighteen months before the earliest possible date for Thompson's meeting with the girl and Mary Richardson made no reference to any such confrontation in her interview with Walsh. There is no factual basis for it or even a hint from any of those concerned.

[51] The fair copy of 'Une Fille de Joie' in the 'Notebook of Early Poems' is printed in *MHW*, p. 43. The first six lines and the last appear in *Life*, p. 81.

[52] NB 45 and 'Notebook of Early Poems'. The last four stanzas are quoted here.

[53] NB BC47.

Chapter Four

[1] The description of the meeting as given by WM appears in *Diaries*, 2, p. 190.

[2] *Letters*, pp. 23–24. The letter is dated 14 April 1888.

[3] *Ibid.* p. 23.

[4] There has been some confusion as to the length of time that elapsed after the arrival of Thompson's manuscripts. WM sometimes referred to it as two or three months and it is given as six months in *Life*, p. 87. But the dates of Thompson's two letters confirm it as just over a year. Of the poems sent with the essay 'The Passion of Mary' and 'Dream Tryst' are the only two known for certain. It is probable that 'The Owl' was included, and others of a similar kind. One of EM's manuscript notes for *Life* refers to his mother having read 'The dirty manuscripts of Paganism and along with them some witch opium poems which she detested'. (*SHSS*, p. 69). If Thompson had sent poems such as 'The Nightmare of the Witch Babies' it indicates the unbalanced state of his mind at the time. But it also does credit to WM's critical sense that despite Alice Meynell's reaction he could distinguish between these poems and the rest.

[5] *Life*, pp. 89–90.

6 Letter to WM, 25 May 1888 (G).

7 *FT & WM*, p. 130.

8 The similarities between north country Catholics and Quakers are discussed by Bossey, *English Catholic Community*, pp. 392–394.

9 *The Cousins: A Medley of Modes among our People* was published anonymously in 1895. It caused some offence and appears to have been withdrawn, a reaction in keeping with WM's character. The only known copy, apart from one in the British Library, is at (G). Except for some short tracts printed during the First World War his only other effort at imaginative writing was *Come and See: Faith found in London*, published in 1902. Like the earlier book it is very short, this time based on a 'tour' of places in London connected with the city's Catholic past. Also like the other it has a strong moral content. The 'tour' ends with the foreign visitor's deeper appreciation of the truths of his religion, which he had not gained from continental forms. But there are wider implications as well, bearing in mind the reactions of English Catholics to foreign influences as discussed in Chapter One.

10 WM's high regard for Newman appears in his editing of a collection of letters which Newman authorized for publication. *The Catholic Life and some Letters of Cardinal Newman with Notes on the Oxford Movement and its Men* appeared in 1885. Newman died in August 1890 and the whole issue of *ME* for the following October was devoted to a monograph under WM's pseudonym John Oldcastle. It constitutes, in fact, the first biographical study of the Cardinal.

WM published a monograph on Manning in 1886 and in 1890, edited a collection of Manning's essays, *Pastime Papers*, aimed at showing the range and depth of his interests. It was in keeping with WM's character that biographical writing came easiest to him and when his journalistic work lessened he devoted several years to his two-volume *Life of Disraeli*, published in 1903. The concentration on his subject's personality and private life is also typical, tending to weaken the result as a rounded portrait.

11 Viola Meynell's monograph on her mother remains the best biographical and critical study, *Alice Meynell: A Memoir* (1929, reprinted in *Life and Letters* series, 1933. Quotations are from this later edition). June Badini, *The Slender Tree: A Life of Alice Meynell* (Padstow, 1981) makes extensive use of letters and some unpublished sources. For a bibliography of Alice's writings see *Alice Meynell: Prose and Poetry, Centenary Volume* (1947), pp. 393–394. Most of her major works are listed and described in the Catalogue compiled by G. Krishnamurti for an exhibition of the same name, *The Eighteen Nineties: A Literary Exhibition*, held at the National Book League, September 1973.

12 Pseudonyms were often shared between the Meynells and their staff, sometimes causing difficulty in identifying individual contributions. WM retained the name John Oldcastle for himself but both he and Thompson wrote under the pseudonym Francis Phillimore, and Thompson occasionally appeared as Philip Hemans.

13 For *ME* and the English Catholic press see J. J. Dwyer, 'The Catholic Press' in Beck, *English Catholics*. For the *Weekly Register* see J. R. Fletcher, 'Early Catholic Periodicals in England', *DR* (April, 1936), 284–310. For contemporary journalism see Joanne Shattock and Michael Wolff (eds.), *The Victorian Periodical Press* (Leicester and Toronto, 1982), especially Walter E. Houghton, 'Periodical Literature and the Articulate Classes', pp. 3–28, Alvin Sullivan (ed.) *British Literary Magazines, 3: The Victorian and Edwardian Age 1837–1913* (1984)

14 For the Meynell circle see Calvert Alexander, *The Catholic Literary Revival* (Milwaukee, 1935). References to the weekly meetings at the Meynells' home and to those who attended appear in C. Lewis Hind, *Authors and I* (1921), p. 217: Francis Meynell, *My Lives* (New York, 1971), p. 24: *FT & WM*, pp. 43–65. See also James G. Nelson, *The Early Nineties: A View from the Bodley Head* (Camb. Mass. 1971), pp. 36–77.

[15] WM to F. H. Day, 9 Nov. 1895 (G).

[16] *FT & WM*, pp. 83–84.

[17] Katherine Tynan (Mrs. Hinkson), *The Middle Years* (1916), p. 294.

[18] Richard Le Gallienne, *The Romantic Nineties* (1926), pp. 99–100.

[19] 'Bunyan in the Light of Modern Criticism' appeared in *ME* (Nov. 1888), re-printed in *A Renegade Poet and Other Critical Essays by Francis Thompson*, ed. Edward J. O'Brien (Boston, 1920).

[20] *Life*, pp. 99–100. See also p. 107, note 2, which appears to refer to the same meeting. The essay first requested by Vaughan was not 'Shelley' as EM states but 'The *Macbeth* Controversy', which appeared in *DR* the following July, 1889. Based on a recent study of *Macbeth* by C. Comyn Carr, it deals ably and with some humour with the misplaced efforts of Shakespeare critics at 'improving' on the plays. See *Letters of Herbert Cardinal Vaughan to Lady Herbert of Lea 1867–1903*, ed. Shane Leslie (1942), p. 391. In a letter dated 12 April 1889 Vaughan refers to the article as overdue.

[21] 'Not even in Dream' appeared in *ME* (Dec. 1888). It has not been reprinted.

Chapter Five

1 There is a good description of Storrington and the Praemonstratensian Priory in *IHP*, pp. 32–34. See also Thomson, *Francis Thompson*, p. 51; Hilaire Belloc, *The County of Sussex* (1936), pp. 19–20. I am grateful to the present community at the Priory for information on the White Canons and their history. Also to Mrs Joan Ham for local history in addition to her published studies of the village and its environs, *Storrington in Pictures* (Chichester, 1979): *Victorian and Edwardian Storrington* (Chichester, 1983).

2 *Letters*, pp. 25–26.

3 *Ibid*, p. 27.

4 'The Error of the Extreme Realists', *ME* (June, 1889). Reprinted in *Renegade Poet*.

5 *Works*, 3, pp. 103–104. 'The Way of Imperfection' first appeared in *ME* (Nov. 1889), reprinted in *Renegade Poet*. The essay is examined as part of Thompson's later literary theory by I. H. Buchen, 'Francis Thompson and the Aesthetics of the Incarnation', *Victorian Poetry* (Autumn, 1965), 235–244. (See also Chapter 8, note 15).

6 'Richard Crashaw', *ME* (May, 1889), reprinted in *Renegade Poet*. Thompson's special interest in Crashaw led to three later studies of the poet, two in *Ac.* (20 Nov. 1897 and 21 Dec. 1901), and the third in the *Athenaeum* (24 Sept. 1904). Reprinted in *Works*, 3, *Lit. Crit.* and *Real RLS* respectively.

7 W. S. Blunt, 'Mr Francis Thompson died at dawn', *Ac.* (23 Nov. 1907): Alice Meynell, 'Some Memories of Francis Thompson', *DR* (Jan–April. 1908), 160–172.

8 Unnumbered notebook at the State University of New York, Buffalo. It was probably at this time that he composed three poems for *ME* which were not used but which show a marked influence from the Storrington background. 'Fair Niente', 'Above and Below' and 'A garden scene' bear the marks of his early work, similar in this respect to the poetry composed at Owens, but the subject matter in each concerns nature and the countryside. The proof sheets for the three poems are at the Harris Library Preston.

9 NB BC31. The lines are printed in *MHW*, p. 51, with the title 'All things are Joy' taken from the opening words.

10 *Life*, p. 95.

11 'Ode to the Setting Sun', Prelude, 1–12. This is the text as printed in *ME* (Sept. 1889). The Prelude was considerably altered when the poem was revised for *New Poems* (see Chapter 8, p. 242). Quotations from the Ode itself and from the After Strain are from passages in the original text, which apart from a few minor changes were left unaltered in the revised version.

12 There is an unexpected recent reference to the 'Ode to the Setting Sun' as an example of the English poetic tradition in J. A. W. Bennett, *Poetry of the Passion: Studies in Twelve Centuries of English Verse* (Oxford, 1982), pp. 187–188.

13 Many of Thompson's liturgical and similar images and allusions are explained by TLC in his notes to the poems. For this particular reference see *Poems*, p. 376.

14 For the worship of the sun-god and dismemberment rites see Otto Rank, *The Trauma of Birth* (1929, reprinted New York, 1973), pp. 150–153; Mircea Eliade, *Myth and Reality* (1964), pp. 168–172; Neumann, *Origins and History of Consciousness*, pp. 220–256; C. G. Jung, *Alchemical Studies*, Collected Works, 13 (1973), pp. 70–72; also his *Symbols of Transformation*, pp. 208–251.

15 NB BC27. The other entries appear in NB's 3 and 23A.

16 'Daphne' first appeared in *ME* (May, 1890). The poem owes much of its rhythm and mood to Shelley, with possible overtones from Swinburne. But Swinburne could not have been a strong influence at the time: 'don't know much about him', Thompson wrote to WM when referring to some comments on his essay on Shelley (*Letters*, p. 31).
What he may have known was the belief that inhaling smoke from burning laurel leaves could inspire dreams and prophecies. It was widespread in the ancient world and as late as the seventeenth century, according to John Evelyn, the smoke induced 'poetical fury'. (*Encyclopaedia of World Mythology*, 1975, p. 240). The connection would have given the subject of the poem an added significance for him after his recent experience of opium withdrawal.

17 'Non Pax — Expectatio' appeared in *ME* (July, 1889). The draft in NB 25 contains several fragments from the 'Ode to the Setting Sun'.

18 See *The Tempest*, 11 (i), 152: 163.

19 *Letters*, p. 32. Thompson was writing to WM after Browning's letter had been printed, without referring to himself by name, in ME (June, 1890). Browning had died the previous December.

20 Edward Healy Thompson's letter is dated 14 Nov. 1889 (G).

21 *Letters*, p. 28.

22 Daisy Stanford recalled the incident that gave rise to the poem in a letter to EM, 17 Oct. 1913 (G). Before he left Storrington Thompson also knew her family. In a letter to WM he refers to her nine brothers and sisters and the pets and animals they raised — only, he then discovered, for the family table. His reaction, neither shocked nor surprised, shows his appreciation of the realism induced by poverty in a child's mental outlook. (See *Letters*, p. 31).

23 *Works*, pp. 133–134. 'Finis Coronat Opus' was printed in *ME* (June, 1890). Finished portions of the story appear on several pages of the MS of the essay on Shelley at (BC), showing that it was nearing completion by the time Thompson was working on the Shelley essay in the autumn of 1889.

24 *Letters*, pp. 28: 36.

25 *Works*, 3, p. 18. There is a MS of the finished essay at (BC) and another, with many additions at the start, at the Harris Library, Preston. A third, now lost, was given by WM to W. S. Blunt soon after the essay first appeared in 1908. A letter from WM to Blunt at (G) refers to the gift and to a draft of 'Daisy' on the reverse of one of the pages. The main drafts for the essay are in NB 7. Here and in several other notebooks Thompson's difficulty in achieving the result he wanted is clear. Page after page is scrawled over with sometimes as many as half a dozen alternative words in a single sentence: and the sentence itself can be altered, deleted or

placed in another version of the particular passage.

26 *Works*, 3, p. 34.

27 *Ibid*, pp. 1–3.

28 This passage, like others addressed directly to the Catholics of the time, is omitted (without editorial comment) from *Works*, 3. It is included in the essay as first printed in *DR* (July, 1908).

29 These lines form part of the long introductory section in the MS at the Harris Library.

30 *Letters*, p. 31.

31 'Shelley' was published as a posthumous essay 'recently discovered', with no reference to its earlier history. The introductory comments are worth quoting in full, the editor having gained his information from WM:

> The editor thinks that his readers will welcome this very remarkable posthumous essay in the precise form in which it was found among the papers of its author, the late Francis Thompson. It lacks of course the author's final revision, and may contain a sentence here or there which Mr Thompson would not finally have endorsed without those omissions or qualifying phrases which a writer makes or adds before passing his work for publication. Such modifications cannot, however, be satisfactorily made by another hand, and only obvious corrections necessary for literary reasons have been made by the author's literary executor, Mr Wilfrid Meynell, to whose kindness the *Dublin Review* is indebted for the offer of the article.

WM had no hesitation in altering Thompson's other manuscripts but in this case he could not have done so without it becoming obvious to the editor of *DR*. In offering the essay the impression he desired to convey is clear. He knew that Thompson had in fact revised it with special care and that he never changed in the views it expresses. But by this time WM had become far more cautious in his own outlook. His editorial comment is a good example of the way this affected his efforts to avoid presenting Thompson as critical of Catholic attitudes and conventions.

32 Psalm 138, 7–10. Quotations from the Bible here and elsewhere are from the Douai translation of 1609, the version most widely used by Catholics until recent years.

33 Saint Augustine of Hippo, *The Confessions of Saint Augustine* translated by F. J. Sheed (1943), p. 225.

34 References to the main religious sources for 'The Hound of Heaven' are included in the notes on the poem by TLC, (*Poems*, pp. 350–371). There is a good summary of these and some other sources in *SHSS*, pp. 259–261. Considering the highly visual content of the poem, as of Thompson's poetry as a whole, one source suggested by Walsh is of special interest. While working on the Shelley essay Thompson put together a short piece, 'Stray thoughts on Shelley' for *ME*, although it did not appear until September 1892. (It is reprinted in *Renegade Poet*). In it he refers to the impression made on Shelley by the ruins of the Baths of Caracalla at Rome and maintains they provided much of the scenic background for *Prometheus Unbound*. Shelley's own description of the Baths had recently been printed in Edward Dowden's *Life of Percy Bysshe Shelley*, 2 vols. (1886), 2, pp. 260–263. As Thompson almost certainly read the book while writing the Shelley essay the scene probably also contributed to the opening stanza of 'The Hound of Heaven'. Shelley describes the wonder and awe inspired by the vast chambers, the 'towers and labyrinthine recesses, hidden and woven over by the wild growth of weeds and ivy. Never was any desolation more sublime and lovely'. He continues with an account of paths which 'wind on, threading the preplexed windings, other labyrinths, other lawns, and deep dells of wood and lofty rocks and terrific chasms'.

Although 'The Hound of Heaven' has generally been regarded as a religious poem in the specifically Catholic tradition it has also been studied for its psychological content. In some cases this has led to a concentration on the workings of the mind behind the poem at the expense of the poem itself. Examples occur in Thomas Vernor Moore, 'The Hound of Heaven', *Psychoanalytical Review*, 5(1918), 345–363: Ella Freeman Sharpe, 'Francis Thompson: A Psychoanalytical Study', *British Journal of Medical Psychology*, 5 (1925), 329–344. But an outstanding synthesis of the religious, mythical and psychological content of the poem has been achieved by the American artist, Robert Hale Ives Gammell. Taking its visual content as their basis, his twenty-three paintings incorporate imagery and symbolism drawn from a wide range of sources, many of which would have been unknown to Thompson. The series, which is of mural size, demonstrates the universality of the poem's fundamental theme while retaining an intensely personal application to the artist's own spiritual and mental outlook. He has outlined his view of the poem and the relation of the paintings to it in the Catalogue, *A Pictorial Sequence painted by R. H. Ives Gammell based on 'The Hound of Heaven' by Francis Thompson* (Camb.Mass. 1956).

It has not so far been recognized that a striking comparison can be made between Thompson's poem and 'The Wreck of the Deutschland'. Like Thompson, G. M. Hopkins universalises a personal experience of Christ's pursuit of the soul and like Thompson he ranges far beyond their common Christian and Catholic heritage. Hopkins may be the more daring in his treatment but the similarities are sufficient to show both poets reaching out in two directions — to the distant Christian and pre-Christian past, and towards a future where their cosmic vision must assume a new immediacy today.

There are no extent drafts for 'The Hound of Heaven' in the notebooks, which is surprising considering the number that exist for other poems and for poetry from this period in particular. But Walsh has discovered one reason in deciphering erased lines from the poem beneath later drafts for *Sister Songs* (*SHSS*, p. 262). Thompson was short of paper and saw no special reason for preserving the drafts, once the poem was written. As printed in *ME* (July, 1890) there is only one significant variation from the text as it appeared in his first volume of poetry. Following the lines:

> Even the linked fantasies, in whose blossomy twist
> I swung the earth a trinket at my wrist,
> Are yielding;

126–128

the *ME* text continued:

> I grazed
> Too closely Thy blue window as I gazed,
> Jutted a careless elbow through clear Heaven
> And gashed me with the splinters. See, I bleed.

These were later deleted, replaced by:

> cords of all too weak account
> For earth with heavy griefs so overplussed.

128–129

The alteration shows Thompson's growing awareness, by then, of his besetting fault of excess.

The two extant MSS of the poem are at (BC). The first is the text as sent to WM on its completion, the second was copied from it by Thompson when preparing the contents for *Poems*. The only other alteration appears in the last line where 'dravest' becomes 'drivest': although in the text as printed in *ME* it is already changed to 'drovest'. At the start of the original MS Thompson's signature appears in WM's handwriting, with the date of the issue of *ME* far which it was intended. Thompson hardly ever remembered to sign his poems and Meynell, in a hurry to get it to the printers, had no alternative but to 'forge' the poet's name, as he himself explained later. (See *IHP*, p. 11).

³⁵ Thompson's wide knowledge of sixteenth and seventeenth century poetry means that he probably knew the lines from Robert Southwell's 'Saint Peter's Complaint':

> Did Christ manure thy heart to breed him briars?
> Or doth it need this unaccustomed soyle
> With hellish dung to fertile heaven's desires?

(*Poems of Robert Southwell*, ed. J. H. McDonald, Oxford, 1967, p. 79).

³⁶ *Ecclesiastes*, 12: v.6; *Isaiah*, 30: v.14.

³⁷ Unnumbered notebook (G).

³⁸ *Letters*, p. 30.

³⁹ *Works*, 3, p. 80.

⁴⁰ *Ibid*, p. 87.

⁴¹ NB 21.

Chapter Six

¹ Letters, pp. 33–47. The Journal Letter appears to have been left to Mary Thompson on the death of Canon (then Bishop) Carroll in 1897. Copies of it were made by the Meynells after Thompson's death but Mary withheld parts which apparently contained unfavourable criticisms of Katherine Tynan's poetry — she being a close friend of the Meynell family. Soon after this Mary sent the Letter to her sister Margaret in Canada who, at her request, destroyed it in about 1825. From the only remaining copy, now in the possession of John Walsh, it is not possible to tell where the withheld sections occurred or what they may have contained — or what further deletions may have been made in the copies. References to the Journal letter appear in letters from Margaret Richardson to WM, 12 Nov. 1910, and from Mary Thompson to WM, 11 and 26 June 1911 (G). There is also a letter from Margaret to TLC referring to the destruction of the original, 23 Nov. 1938 (BC). But none adds anything to the few known facts. There is a typescript of the remaining copy at (G).

² 'Our Literary Life' is printed with deletions in *Lit.Crit*. These include the passages on the limitations of 'religious' writing, which form three separate MS pages of the draft. Thompson revised a section on Alice Meynell as the basis for an estimation of her poetry which appeared in *The Tablet* (21 Jan. 1893). It is reprinted in *Lit.Crit*. as a separate essay. For comments on Wiseman's 'schoolboy' attitudes see Norman, *English Catholic Church*, p. 117.

³ 'John Henry Newman', the *Weekly Register* (16 Aug. 1890). The lines are reprinted in *SHSS*, p. 263. They have been used to illustrate Catholic attitudes of the time by Holmes, *More Roman than Rome*. See also my article, 'Francis Thompson: Towards a Revaluation', *Clergy Review*, 61 (1976), 253–256. Thompson's later use of the theme appears in the poem 'From the Night of Forebeing', 255–260. (See Chapter 7, p. 218).

⁴ As editor of *Memorials of Cardinal Manning* (1892) WM included many references to his work for the poor and his insight into the radical nature of the reforms needed. Manning's criticism of the lack of concern among Catholics is well illustrated in a letter to Bishop Vaughan quoted in Vincent Alan McLelland, *Cardinal*

Manning: His Public Life and Influence (Oxford, 1962), pp. 20–21. In spite of faulty statements in other respects there is a good account of his charitable activities and of the dockers' strike in E. S. Purcell, *The Life of Cardinal Manning, Archbishop of Westminster*, 2 vols. (1895), 2, pp. 587–671. These are also well-documented in the fullest recent biography, Robert Grey, *Cardinal Manning* (1985). For his ecumenical attitude in joining non-Catholic organizations see also Paul Thureau, *The English Catholic Revival in the Nineteenth Century* (1914). Perhaps the best summary of this aspect of Manning's career is found in the opening lines of a poem written by WM at the time of the dockers' strike and printed in *ME* (Oct. 1889):

> He heard the hungry crowd outside the gate:
> Some were the Church's sons, and some not hers —
> Yet all his hundred thousand worshippers.
> He did not stop to reckon up the rate
> With pedants in the sum of toll and freight.

5   William Booth, *In Darkest England and the Way Out* (1890), especially pp. 91–93. The idea of Labour Colonies had been first put forward by Samuel Barnett in 'A Scheme for the Unemployed', *Nineteenth Century* (24 Nov. 1888). It was taken up by Booth, *Life and Labours*, First Series, vol. 1. See also John Brown, 'Charles Booth and Labour Colonies', *Economic History Review*, Second Series, 21, no. 2 (1968), 349–361.

6   For T. H. Huxley's criticism of the Salvation Army and contemporary charity see his *Social Dilemmas and Worse Remedies* (1891). In the same year at least fifteen books and many more articles appeared, mainly condemmning Booth's methods without recognising his far-sighted intentions. Of the books the most influential were Bernard Bosanquet, *In Darkest England: On the Wrong Track*; A. O. Lovejoy, *Life in Darkest London*; Phillip Dwyer, *General Booth's Submerged Tenth: or The Wrong Way to do the Right Thing*. A series of articles had appeared in *The Contemporary Review* in August and September 1882, drawing attention to the 'cheapening of Christian worship' which was one of the chief points made by Booth's critics. In the September issue Manning had contributed a summary where he argued that for all the truth in their views the facts of the conditions and what was being achieved by the Salvation Army must be given priority. For later appraisals of the extent and limitations of the Army's success see Richard Mudie Smith, *The Religious Life of London* (1904); Booth, *Life and Labours: Religious Influences*, pp. 322–329; David E. H. Mole, 'Challenge to the Church', in *The Victorian City: Images and Realities*, ed. H. J. Dyos and M. Wolff, 2 vols. (1973), 2, pp. 815–836; Hugh McLeod, *Class and Religion in the late Victorian City* (1974), especially pp. 25–28.

7   'Catholics in Darkest London', *ME* (Jan. 1891). Quotations are from the *ME* text. The essay in *Works*, 3, 'In Darkest England', is based on the original but no comment is made on the adaptation with its many deletions and the addition, at the end, of a conclusion taken from another essay, 'The Life and Labours of John Baptist dela Salle'. (See note 38).

8   J. G. Snead Cox, *The Life of Cardinal Vaughan*, 2 vols. (1911), 1, p. 82. For Manning's activities on behalf of the London poor see John Fitzsimmons, *Manning: Anglican and Catholic* (1951), p. 138ff. Conditions among the Catholics have been studied mainly as they affected the Irish immigrants. The subject has been examined in a series of articles by Sheridan Gilley, the most representative being 'Heretic London — Holy Poverty and the Irish Poor', *Downside Review*, 69 (Jan. 1971), 64–89: 'English Catholic Charity and the Irish Poor in London 1840–1870', *Recusant History*, 11 (April 1972), 253–269: 'Catholic Faith and the Irish Slums', in Dyos and Wolff, *The Victorian City*, 2, pp. 837–854.

9   McLelland, *Cardinal Manning*, p. 207.

10   *Life*, pp. 106–107.
11   References in this passage, in order, are to Alfred Hayes, letter to WM, 30 Oct. 1911 (BC); W. E. Henley, letter to WM, 31 Oct. 1911 (G); Katherine Tynan, 'Francis Thompson', *Fortnightly Review* (1 Feb. 1910), 349–360: also 'Francis Thompson', *The Bookman* (June, 1918), 87–88; *Life*, p. 12.
12   Le Gallienne, *Romantic Nineties*, p. 101.
13   Edgar Jepson, *Memories of a Victorian*, quoted in Nelson, *Early Nineties*, p. 161. For the Rhymers' Club see also P. Kitchen, *Poets' London* (1980), pp. 80–81. The reference to Thompson's 'scorn' appears in a MS note for *Life*, quoted in *SHSS*, p. 264.
14   C. L. Hind, *Napthali* (New York, 1926), pp. 96–97.
15   *Letters*, pp. 50–51.
16   *FT & WM*, p. 183; F. Meynell, *My Lives*, pp. 18–19.
17   *Letters*, p. 211. An example of this poetic idealizing of womanhood in 'The Sere of the Leaf' shows that Thompson did not confine it to Alice Meynell only. The poem was addressed to Katherine Tynan and written about a year before he first met her.
18   *FT & WM*, p. 183. In the MS of her book Viola Meynell is more emphatic on Thompson's dependence and the problems it caused. Thompson was 'in love' with Alice but 'out of duty, or gratitude'. The poems addressed to her are 'lovely formalities' to be read at the 'face value' which here also 'represents the inmost heart'. The words suggest some confusion on the subject and a consequent difficulty in clarifying them. The MS is at (G).
19   WM, 'A New Poet', *ME* (Nov. 1893).
20   The poems in the original Sequence of 'Love in Dian's Lap', written between 1890 and 1892, were:
I   'Before Her Portrait in Youth'
II   'To a Poet Breaking Silence
III   'Manus Animam Pinxit'
IV   'A Carrier Song'
V   'Scala Jacobi Portaque Eburnea'
VI   'Gilded Gold'
VII 'Her Portrait'
The Sequence, as printed in *Works* I and elsewhere since, contains poems added later, although apart from 'Promium' and the 'Epilogue' it is not clear if all were intended by Thompson for the Sequence:
    'Promium'
VIII 'Domus Tua'
IX   'In Her Paths'
X   'After Her Going'
XI   'Beneath a Photograph'
    'Epilogue to the Poet's Sitter'
21   *Letters*, p. 43. Alice's poem 'Veni Creator' was printed in the *Scots Observer* (2 Aug. 1890).
22   *Letters*, pp. 57: 54.
23   At first the poem was to be called 'Amphicypellon', then 'Songs Wing to Wing: An Offering to Two Sisters'. It was privately printed under this title in 1895 by the Westminster Press and later the same year was published by John Lane as *Sister Songs: An Offering to Two Sisters*. The final corrected MS with the title 'Amphicypellon' is at the Harris Library, Preston. This, and the proof sheets at (BC), contain passages Thompson deleted before the poem was published as *Sister Songs*. The passages concern a 'Burmese Doll' as his rival for the younger sister's affection and were printed in a (BC) publication, *Stylus* (1934).
24   *Letters*, p. 61.

25 The Journal Letter, *ibid*, p. 41.
26 F. Meynell, *My Lives*, pp. 23–24.
27 *Letters*, pp. 62–63.
28 *Life*, p. 104.
29 *Letters*, pp. 51–52.
30 Katherine Tynan, 'Francis Thompson', *Bookman op cit*. For recollections by Olivia and Madeleine see *SHSS*, pp. 112–113. For Viola's see *FT & WM*, p. 119.
31 *Life*, p. 119.
32 Unnumbered notebook (G). The poppy is preserved in the same notebook. See also *SHSS*, p. 341.
33 *Letters*, pp. 66–67.
34 The signed MS of 'A Threnody of Birth' has been printed in *Real RLS*, but quotations are from the MS.
35 *Letters*, pp. 65–66. The text is taken from a draft in the MSS 'Personal Data'. In an editorial note on the letter Walsh suggests it may not have been sent in the form in which it survives in the draft — where at the end Thompson implies that if the enclosed essay is not acceptable to the *National Observer* it is only fit for the waste-paper basket.
36 The signed MS of 'Modern Men: The Devil' has been printed in *Real RLS* but quotations are from the MS.
37 *Letters*, p. 69.
38 Quotations from 'The Life and Labours of Blessed John Baptist de la Salle' are from the text in *ME* (April, 1891). Some passages from it were added by WM to form the conclusion to 'In Darkest England' in *Works*, 3. (See note 7). The *ME* text was published as a separate monograph in 1891.
39 Thompson's review of *The Letters of the late Father George Porter SJ, Archbishop of Bombay* appeared in *ME* (Aug. 1891).
40 Father Cuthbert OSFC, 'A Wayside Essay', *ME* (Nov. 1892). In adopting the term 'rationalistic' he has in mind the pronouncement of the First Vatican Council, that if anyone should deny the proof of the existence of God 'with the natural light of human reason by means of the things that have been made: let him be anathema' (*The Church Teaches*, translated by J.F. Clarkson SJ *et al*. St Louis, 1954, p. 28). The teaching here is based on the principles of Scholasticism, which in the essay are identified with 'rationalism'. Information on the Capuchin friars and their 'System' has been drawn from a variety of sources but mainly from the thinly veiled reference in Father Angelo's autobiography of his early years, *Franciscan Days of Vigil* (1910), written under the name he resumed on leaving the Order, Richard de Bary. Many of the references were elucidated for me by Father Cassian Reel OSFC in an interview in Oxford, September 1976. I was also helped by Father Stephen Innes OSFC at Pantasaph in June 1984. De Bary's book gives the only available account of the ideas and expectations of the group. The observations by Blunt in *Diaries* provide some useful sidelights but cannot be regarded as reliable for facts. (See note 52.)
41 Father Anselm Kenealy OSFC, 'Francis Thompson', *Franciscan Annals* (May 1922), 151–155. Father Anselm was later appointed Archbishop of Simla in India. In giving his name as he was known during the years of his contact with Thompson I am following the custom adopted by other writers on Thompson who have quoted from his recollection and letters.
42 Letters from Father Anselm to Alice Meynell, quoted in *FT & WM*, p. 41.
43 *Letters*, pp. 69–71.
44 *Ibid*, p. 72.
45 Mivart's main article, 'Happiness in Hell', appeared in the *Nineteenth Century* in December 1892. The argument that progress towards ultimate redemption is possible in hell had been put forward by Newman in *The Grammar of Assent* and

summarized by him in a letter to Nevins in June 1842. It was included in a collection of Newman's letters published shortly after Mivart's article and reviewed by Thompson in *ME* in July 1893. Thompson selected the letter for special comment, though without explicit reference to Mivart, stressing the point made by Newman that the early teachings of the Church had not precluded such a view. He also called attention to the fact noted by Newman, that a number of early Missals contain Masses for the souls in hell. Thompson was anticipating an important link between the thinking of Newman and Mivart, for which see J. Derek Holmes, 'Newman and Mivart: Two attitudes to a Nineteenth Century Problem', *Clergy Review*, 50 (1965), 852–867. On attitudes towards hell among Catholics and others at the time see D. Geoffrey Rowell, *Hell and the Victorians: A Study of Nineteenth Century Controversies concerning Eternal Punishment and the Future Life* (Oxford, 1974), especially pp. 161–162: 176–179. For Mivart's part in the controversies see Jacob W. Gruber, *A Conscience in Conflict: The Life of St. George Jackson Mivart* (New York, 1960). For Mivart's connections with the Meynell family see also *FT & WM*, pp. 70–74.

46 Unnumbered notebook at the State University of New York, Buffalo. It is worth nothing that at this time Thompson was preparing a spirited defence of Mivart in an article 'Catholic and Scientist' for the *Weekly Register* (9 July, 1892).

47 *Letters*, p. 81.

48 Unnumbered notebook (G). The metre of 'A Judgement in Heaven' is based on the rhythm of Anglo-Saxon poetry. According to Thompson's explanatory note: 'I have throughout this poem used an asterisk to indicate the caesura in the middle of the line, after the manner of the old Saxon section-point'. The note does not, of course, apply to the Epilogue. Thompson's familiarity with the form of Anglo-Saxon poetry, if not with the language itself, is unusual for the time.

49 *Letters*, p. 77. Vaughan was not, in fact, 'satisfied'. He wrote to the Pope in 1892 on his sense of inadequacy for the Westminster appointment compared with his predecessors. In referring to the qualities expected, 'in none am I above a poor mediocrity'. (See Snead Cox, *Bishop Vaughan*, 2, p. 3).

50 *Letters*, p. 74.

51 *Ibid*, pp. 80–82.

52 *Diaries*, 1, p. 93. For Blunt's meeting with Father Cuthbert and his observations on the Modernist tendencies of the group see p. 102. Blunt's reports of WM's conversations at this time became a source of embarrassment to Meynell when the diaries were published in 1919. By then the repercussions following the Modernist crisis meant that his support for the Capuchins' 'System' could cast doubts on his own orthodoxy. In any case his ideas were by then very different from his earlier outlook. According to Viola Meynell, when Blunt sent him the published *Diaries* he was so 'dismayed' by the entries on the subject that it was agreed to insert a slip 'to qualify or rectify' his statements. The slip was to read:

> 'Mr Meynell tells me that I unintentionally misrepresent the views held by Father Cuthbert and his friends. "Not one", he says in particular, "Of that fervent group of young Franciscans but fixed all his hope and all his faith on the doctrine, fundamental and final, of the divinity of Christ"'.

(*FT & WM*, pp. 77–78). It is curious that when Blunt asked WM to check the text of the diaries before publication he seems to have missed out this section. The slip does not appear to have been inserted. It is not included in any copies of *Diaries* I have seen, nor is it preserved in the British Library copy or at (G). It is worth noting how WM is as much concerned for the reputation of the group as for his own. Father Cuthbert was by then a prominent member of the Order and Father Anselm had been appointed Archbishop of Simla. According to E. B. Poland, *The Friars in Sussex: 1228–1928* (Hove, 1928), pp. 184–185, Francis Blunt,

Wilfrid's younger brother, endowed the Crawley Friary. This is probably due to the effigy of Francis which Wilfrid himself carved for the Friary Church after Francis's death in 1892.

[53] *Letters*, pp. 84–90.

[54] The incident is only recorded as told by WM to Blunt. See *Diaries*, 2, p. 183.

[55] 'How the Singer's Singing wailed for the Singer' appeared in *ME* (Nov. 1892). It has not been reprinted.

Chapter Seven

[1] H. A. Hinkson, 'Francis Thompson: A Reminiscence', *Pall Mall Gazette* (15 Oct. 1908). There is an account of the journey by Katherine Tynan (Mrs Hinkson) in *The Middle Years, op.cit.* pp. 17–19, reprinted from the *Fortnightly Review* (Feb. 1910). She describes the contrast between Thompson's reaction to the Irishmen and the feelings of the other passagers, but not the episodes of the bandaged hand or the canary recalled by her husband. EM gives the date of Thompson's arrival at Pantasaph as early in 1892 (*Life*, pp. 128: 180). In an entry made by Thompson for his autobiographical notes he gives November as the month (MS 'Personal Data'). But the notes were made much later and he put a question mark against this entry. There are too many references to his being in London until the date given by Hinkson to doubt its being correct. This is further confirmed by letters Thompson wrote early in January 1893, clearly very soon after his arrival.

[2] Father Sebastian OSFC, *The Capuchins* (Glasgow, 1963), pp. 52–55. For the convert families' introduction of religious communities on their lands see Mathew, *Catholicism in England, op.cit.* pp. 217–219.

[3] *Letters*, p. 91, quoted from a draft in NB BCIO.

[4] *Ibid*, p. 92. Only extracts from this letter survive, quoted by Mrs Blackburn in one to WM dated 9 Jan. 1908 (G).

[5] The 18-line poem as first written formed the basis for 'Little Jesus' as published in *ME* (May, 1893). It was reprinted in *Franciscan Annals* (Dec. 1896) but did not first appear there as has sometimes been stated (see *IHP*, p. 121). The poem occasionally appears under Thompson's alternative title 'Ex Ore Infantium'.

[6] *Letters*, pp. 93–94.

[7] Quoted in *Life*, p. 180.

[8] Anselm Kenealy, 'Francis Thompson', *op.cit.*

[9] NB BCIO.

[10] NB 16A. For the reinterpretation of Thomist philosophy in the present century and its earlier anticipation in the last one a good summary is provided by David Tracey, *The Analogical Imagination: Christian Theology and the Culture of Pluralism* (1981), pp. 414–421. See also references in his notes 14 & 15, p. 441.

[11] The recollections here and to follow are from Anselm Kenealy, 'Francis Thompson: The Man and his Poetry', *Capuchin Annual* (1933), 39–59.

[12] Anselm Kenealy, 'Francis Thompson: Some Personal Reflections', *Carmina* (1931), 1–6.

[13] The MS is a fair copy written out and signed as if intended for publication. Fourteen verses are printed in *SHSS*, pp. 129–131.

[14] NB 20A. There is also a separate MS of the poem with a different order of verses but the notebook version is the more finished and corrected text.

[15] Letter to WM, dated 10 Nov. 1911 (G).

[16] Thompson wrote a humorous account of the removal of the photograph from his

room in a letter to Monica Meynell some months afterwards. Maggie had asked for one and then, apparently, appropriated his remaining copy. He was explaining the reason he could not therefore send one to Monica (*Letters*, p. 116). His other references to the family are from the letter quoted by Mrs Blackburn in hers to WM, 9 Jan. 1908 (see note 4). Her own observations are from this letter. The family's recollections are quoted in *SHSS*, pp. 134: 267; also *La Vie*, p. 96, note 79.

17 NB 101. The notion of simplicity as co-ordination or harmony of spirit, which underlies this passage, is the subject of a complete essay, 'Anima Simplicitas', which Thompson also chose not to publish. It has been printed in *Real RLS*.

18 'Form and Formalism' has been heavily edited as it appears in *Works*, 3. The MS of the original text is marked with WM's alterations and deletions.

19 'The Image of God', *Franciscan Annals* (July, 1893). Reprinted in *Lit.Crit.*

20 Detached notebook page in MS 'Miscellany of FT fragments'.

21 *IHP*, p. 97. See also Anselm Kenealy, 'Francis Thompson', *op.cit.*

22 *Franciscan Annals* (Jan. 1908). 'Form and Formalism' appeared in the *Annals* in March 1893, 'The Image of God' in July and 'Franciscus Christificatus' in October. 'Sanctity and Song' was divided between December the same year and January 1894. Thereafter Thompson's only contributions were translations — of a poem by Pope Leo XIII in February 1894 and in September, of lines on Saint Francis by the medieval author of the *Dies Iriae*. Significantly, Thompson only wrote for *Franciscan Annals* when Anselm was in charge. He was away for several months in 1895 and nothing was submitted until after his return, when a translation of Saint Bonaventure's 'Hymn to Saint Anthony' appeared in the August issue. In September the following year another translation was based on lines describing the presentation of a sword fish to the Pope by the fishermen of Calabria. It was reprinted in Anselm's article 'Francis Thompson: Man and Poet', *op.cit.*, as an example of Thompson's skill as a translator and also of the lighter side to his poetry. 'Little Jesus' was reprinted in the December issue of the *Annals* in 1896, the month Anselm left Pantasaph and Thompson returned to London. Anselm then gave up the editorship, resuming it again at the beginning of 1901. In January that year Thompson sent him a poem, 'Bethlehem'. His only later contributions were two reviews written in 1906.

23 Father William OSFC, 'Francis Thompson and Ourselves', *Franciscan Annals* (Jan. 1908), 1–14.

24 *Works*, 3, p. 75.

25 MS 'An Enemy hath done this'. Printed in *Real RLS*.

26 MS 'Miscellany of FT fragments'.

27 Kenealy, 'Francis Thompson: Some Personal Recollections', *op.cit.*

28 *FT & WM*, p. 186.

29 Le Gallienne's report to John Lane on Thompson's poetry is at (BC).

30 The quotation is taken from the text in *New Poems*. The poem first appeared in *ME* (Dec. 1893), after which Thompson made some slight alterations and deleted one stanza before its publication in *New Poems*. But the version in *Works*, 2 and elsewhere since is a patchwork taken from both his texts, with stanzas altered from their intended order and others deleted. The many notebook drafts indicate the amount of work that went into its composition, the fullest being in NB 30.

31 *Letters*, pp. 108–109.

32 The main entries on symbolism in the notebooks appear in BC21 (Sun and Moon symbols): 12 (Rod and Branch as related to Reed, Staff and Sceptre): 14A (animal symbolism): BC18 (interpretations of the planets): BC30 (symbolic meaning of the four points of the compass): 46 (the Sacred Tree. Herodotus's interpretation of spawning of fish, flower symbolism and Easter as derived from the festival of the goddess Ishtar). There are in addition over 30 single notebook pages collected under the title 'Notes on Symbolism'. Over half concern symbols

connected with Freemasonry (see note 48). But they also refer to the planets, the Jewish Kabbala, the Anima Mundi, bird and animal imagery, Hindu and Egyptian gods and the symbolic meaning of gases, jewels and precious stones. The Tau Cross, recurring in these pages and in the notebooks, was to be the subject of one of Thompson's last contribution to *Franciscan Annals*, in January 1906. 'The Seraphic Keepsake', a review of a book on Saint Francis by Reginald Balfour, includes a detailed discussion of the symbol as the one used by the Saint in the Blessing he gave to Brother Leo. Thompson's account of the origin of the Tau Cross in the ancient world and its adoption into Christianity is one of the few instances when he made use of his private studies in published form.

[33] The notes from d'Alviella's *Migration of Symbols* appear in NB 46. The separate MS of the review, entitled 'Symbolism', has been mistakenly listed as an essay draft in the Collection at (BC).

[34] In NB BC21 Thompson listed the pocket edition of Swedenborg's *Heaven and Hell* at 1/- with other cheap editions of *Divine Love and Divine Wisdom* and *Divine Providence* at 1/6 and 2/-. There follows a note 'Swedenborg Society, Bloomsbury Street'.

[35] *Letters*, pp. 95–96. For the parable of the ewe lamb see 2 *Kings*, XII, vv. 1–5 (Douai text. In other versions see the same chapter and verses in 2 *Samuel*).

[36] *Letters*, pp. 97–98. The letter is dated 15 June 1893, indicating that the second 'letter conciliatory' was probably written a few weeks later. The 'proposed article' is drafted on separate notebook pages, put together and printed in *Real RLS* under the title 'A prose Fragment on the Analogies between God, Nature, Man and the Poet'.

[37] Coventry Patmore, *Religio Poetae* (1893), p. 3.

[38] 'A Poet's Religion', *ME* (Sept. 1893).

[39] The Meynells were mainly responsible for initiating the view that Thompson depended on Patmore as model and guide. To them, one of the surest ways to further Thompson's fame after his death was to align him with Patmore, whose reputation in Catholic circles was unquestioned and for whom their own admiration was almost equal to their regard for Thompson. The connections they put forward have been maintained since, culminating in J. C. Reid's assertions that the only value in Thompson's later writing is derived from Patmore. His previous study of Patmore is an added influence on his viewpoint.

[40] The letter from Father Clarke, written from London and dated 20 June 1893, is in the possession of EM's grandson Vivian Meynell, who has kindly allowed me to use it here. It is worth noting that a series of articles under the same pseudonym XYZ had appeared in the *Rambler* in 1859–1860, at the time of Edward Healy Thompson's connection with the journal. The articles, advocating a liberal outlook in Catholic education, were fiercely contested by W. G. Ward — in whose view any literature other than orthodix religious writings was only legitimate as a carefully regulated recreation. Although there is no direct evidence Francis may well have met Father Clark through the Meynells, when the earlier controversy and his uncle's connection with the *Rambler* would have given the articles in *ME* an added interest for him, For a summary of the *Rambler* controversy see Wilfrid Ward, W. G. Ward and the Catholic Revival (1893, reprinted 1912), pp. 147–149.

[41] The first of these essay drafts appears in NB's BC18 and BC10. The second is in BC18. It has been printed, with additions from other entries, in *Real RLS* as 'A Preface and Essay on Symbolism'. Patmore's interpretation of East and West occurs in an essay 'Love and Poetry' in *Religio Poetae*.

[42] MS 'Personal Data'.

[43] *Life*, p. 193, note 1. Father Anselm's comment was made in a letter to Revd. J. Austin Richmond, written from Rome and dated 31 Dec. 1910 (Ushaw College archives).

[44] Elizabeth Blackburn's letter to WM, written from Crawley and dated 15 Dec. 1909, is at (G).

[45] Between the years 1870 and 1890 at least forty books on Freemasonry were published in England, all of which were available to Thompson at the British Library. The most notable as source books were A.F.A. Woodford, *Masonic Encyclopaedia* (1878) and R. F. Gould, *History of Freemasonry*, 3 vols. (1882–1887). Thompson's notes suggest a special interest in the Rosicrucians, for which the two main studies were Hargrave Jennings, *The Rosicrucians: Their Rites and Mysteries* (2nd. edn. 1879) and A. E. Waite, *The Real History of the Rosicrucians* (1887). For recent works on Freemasonry see Stephen Knight, *the Brotherhood: The Secret World of Freemasons* (Granada and London, 1984); W. Preston, *Illustrations of Freemasonry*, ed. C. F. W. Dyer (1985).

[46] The draft of the letter was probably overlooked when other references to Freemasonry were destroyed because it was written on the reverse side of a page from Thompson's play 'Venus Fly Trap' (see ahead, Chapter 9, note 2).

[47] The only surviving notebook entries on Freemasonry are in BC25, 20A and 14A.

[48] The 'Notes on symbolism' from a separate packet of MS pages, including those referred to in note 32 above.

[49] The full 'Order of the Day' is quoted in *La Vie*, p. 97 from a notebook then at (G) but not now traceable. Part is quoted in *FT & WM*, pp. 154–155, where Viola Meynell dates it to the year at Storrington. But references to regular meetings with 'Madam' mean it must have been made out during the summer or autumn of 1893 while Mrs Blackburn was at Pantasaph.

[50] *Letters*, p. 99.

[51] *Ibid.* p. 97.

[52] *Ibid.* p. 107.

[53] Ibid. p. 106. When published the Dedication was addressed 'To Wilfrid and Alice Meynell'.

[54] *Ibid.* pp. 110: 103.

[55] Derek Patmore, *The Life and Times of Coventry Patmore* (1949), pp. 223–224.

[56] *Ibid.* p. 224.

[57] WM, 'Francis Thompson: A New Poet', ME (Nov. 1893); Katherine Tynan, 'A New and Great Poet', *Illustrated London News* (16 Dec. 1893).

[58] Father Alphonsus's letter to WM, dated 8 Jan. 1894, is at (G).

[59] Coventry Patmore, 'Mr Francis Thompson: A New Poet', *Fortnightly Review* (Jan. 1894).

[60] *Letters*, pp. 112–113.

[61] *Ibid.* p. 115.

[62] References in this passage, in order, are to Arthur Symons, '*Poems* by Francis Thompson', *Athenaeum* (3 Feb. 1894); H. D. Traill, 'Mr Francis Thompson's *Poems*', *Nineteenth Century* (18 Feb. 1894); 'A. Fogey' [Andrew Lang], 'The Young Men', *Contemporary Review* (Feb. 1894); J. L. Garvin, 'The New Planet: Francis Thompson', *Newcastle Chronicle* (15 Feb. 1894).

[63] Mrs Blackburn's letter to WM, dated 23 Feb. 1894, is at (G). It has been quoted as the one to which Thompson referred when contradicting her report on his finding Pantasaph 'dull' (*Letters*, p. 114). Thompson's letter is, as usual, undated, but he mentions 'Any Saint' as appearing in 'this month's *ME*'. As the poem was printed in the January issue his letter to Alice Meynell was written before Mrs Blackburn's to Wilfrid and refers to an earlier one from her to Alice that has not survived.

[64] The letter is quoted in *Life*, p. 183. EM attributes it to 'an observer', but although the letter itself cannot be traced it could not have been written by anyone except Mrs Black-burn.

[65] Alice Meynell quoted this passage from her own draft of the essay in a letter to Thompson dated 22 April 1894 (G). The essay 'At Monastery Gates' appeared in

the *Pall Mall Gazette* (26 July 1895). In her letter she comments on the editor's alteration of the passage, which in the printed form reads: 'Homeward, over the verge, from other valleys, his light figure flits at nightfall, like a moth'.

66   *Letters*, p. 101.
67   *Ibid*, p. 117.
68   *Letters*, p. 120.

Chapter Eight

1   *Diaries*, 1, p. 102; De Bary, *Franciscan Days of Vigil, op. cit.* pp. 151–152.
2   *Ibid*. pp. 167–168.
3   NB 101.
4   Basil Champneys, *The Memoirs and Correspondence of Coventry Patmore*, 2 vols. (1900), 2, p. 133.
5   *Letters*, p. 119.
6   G. M. Hopkins' poem 'Heaven-haven' was printed in *A Little Book* of *Life and Death*, an anthology collected by Elizabeth Waterhouse and reviewed in *Ac.* 19 July, 1902. For Thompson's authorship of the review see *La Vie*, p. 96, note 67. For the friendship between Hopkins and Patmore see C. C. Abbot (ed.) *Further Letters of G. M. Hopkins including his correspondence with Coventry Patmore* (1949), pp. 118–199.
7   David Bearne SJ, quoted from the *Irish Monthly* (Nov. 1908) in *Life*, p. 185. For Anselm's account of the visit to St. Beuno see *IHP*, p. 199. A more moderated version is included in his article 'Francis Thompson', *op. cit.* See also *La Vie*, p. 82.
8   NB 21.
9   Coventry Patmore, *The Rod the Root and the Flower* (1895), p. 40, 'Homo', XXXIV: p. 201, 'Magna Moralia', XLIX.
10 The letter from Angelo to Patmore is quoted in full in Champneys, *Memoris and Correspondence*, 2, pp. 378–379. A draft of Angelo's essay forms part of a collection of papers connected with his later career (G). There is a vast literature on the subject of Catholic Modernism in England but for a concise and accurate summary see Bernard M. G. Reardon, 'Roman Catholic Modernism' in *Nineteenth Century Religious Thought in the West*, ed. N. Smart, J. Clayton, S. T. Katz and P. Shery, 3 vols. (Cambridge, 1985), 2, pp. 141–177.
11 MS 'An Enemy hath done this' Printed in *Real RLS*.
12 The presence of some degree of conflict in Thompson's mind at this time has been noted by his three chief biographers but not its nature or extent. To EM the visionary element in his poetry began to give way to the true vision of the mystic which poetry cannot express, largely through Patmore's influence (*Life*, p. 201). According to Walsh there was a change due to 'a return to the professed religious attitudes of his youth' (*SHSS*, p. 142). Reid sees the same process as the outcome of the contact with Patmore, prompting him 'to discard his poetry as an adequate substitute for religious truth' (*Francis Thompson: Man and Poet*, p. 110). The only attempt at taking the source of the conflict further is by I. H. Buchen in 'Francis Thompson and the Aesthetics of the Imagination', *Victorian Poetry, op.cit.* (see Chapter 5, note 5). Basing his argument on Thompson's published prose writings he sees the poetry as 'verbal icons — incomplete verbal sacraments poised for fulfilment'. In this sense he maintains they illustrate Thompson's concept of incarnation by means of the symbolic language shared by religion and poetry. The poet can move towards a moment of fulfilment, of union between matter and spirit, but cannot achieve it for himself. That must await a movement from God,

incarnating Himself in the created world in a process for which the symbol can only be an incomplete witness. According to Buchen: 'In these terms all Thompson's poems are incomplete. They move towards a point of final mystery but never unmask it'.

[13] Patmore's letters to Thompson on Alice Meynell at this time are quoted extensively in Badini, *Slender Tree*, op. cit. pp. 120–122. For Thompson's replies see *Letters*, pp. 142–143: 179.

[14] The entry is on a single notebook page at (G).

[15] Quotations from 'Love divided against itself' are from a copy of the original text at (G) made by myself. The MS has since been lost.

[16] *Letters*, p. 135.

[17] *Ibid.* p. 129.

[18] *Ibid.* p. 131.

[19] Patmore's letter, dated 28 August 1895, is quoted by Walsh in a note in *Letters*, p. 132.

[20] In *Franciscan Days of Vigil*, p. 140, Angelo confuses this visit to London in 1894 with Thompson's final departure from Pantasaph.

[21] The reason for the privately printed edition, in order to supply Lane with type and proof sheets, has not so far been known. It is explained by WM in an undated letter to Seymour Adelman, now in the Adelman Collection at Bryn Mawr College Library.

[22] *Letters*, p. 123.

[23] J. Lewis May, *John Lane and the Nineties* (1936), pp. 68–69. Houseman's illustration appeared later with the rather dubious title 'Barren Life' in the *Yellow Book* (July, 1896).

[24] *Letters*, p. 125.

[25] *Ibid.* p. 130. In the letter from Storrington Thompson only refers to medicine sent down from London by WM. But as his symptoms were much the same there can be no doubt that it was the homoeopathic medicine which he now asks to be repeated. The earlier letter is the same one where he describes his reactions to the stress of composing 'The Hound of Heaven' (see Chapter 5, p. 140).

[26] In his review of *Sister Songs* E. M. Dowden found 'hardly a page that is unmarred by faults which it is in no one's power to pardon': but at the same time he had to admit on every page 'beauties which are at the command of no other living poet' (*Illustrated London News*, 10 August, 1895). The reactions are probably best expressed by E. K. Chambers: 'After all, Mr Thompson is the only one of the young poets of the day who persistently tempt one, page after page, to waive one's critic right, and contentedly to stand and admire' (*Ac.* 14 Sept. 1895). The sales were, as Thompson expected, disappointing. Only 349 copies were sold during the first six months. A further 250 sold in America, where Thompson's reputation had begun and would be retained long after it faded in England. For the sales see *SHSS*, p. 269, note 37.

[27] Everard Feilding recalled the ghost watching night and the conversation with Thompson in a letter to WM written after Thompson's death and quoted in *Life*, pp. 186–188.

[28] *Letters*, pp. 139–140.

[29] *Ibid.* p. 156. The reference to 'night and day work' is from the MS 'Personal Data'.

[30] All subsequent editions of Thompson's poetry have followed WM's lead and included 'Carmen Genesis' and 'Ad Castitatem' in the 'Sight and Insight' group. Both poems were first printed by WM in *DR* (July, 1910). It is worth noting that when Thompson was preparing the poems for 'Sight and Insight' he placed the 'Ode to the Setting Sun' with them: it appears in the MS of the completed final texts for the group. His reason for the alteration was probably because he rightly

decided it should stand alone as too powerful to be incorporated with the rest, which it would then dominate to too great an extent.

[31] The 'mystical' interpretation was at first the most widespread. It forms the basis for the commentary by TLC in his notes (*Poems*, pp. 429–443). It has also been made the subject of a separate commentary, *The Mistress of Vision by Francis Thompson with a Commentary by John O'Connor STP and a Forword by Father Vincent McNabb OP* (1918, reprinted with Introduction by Joseph Jerome and an essay by Henry Williamson, 1966). EM admits the wider mystical context influencing both Thompson and Patmore but sees close connections between the two poets here. He also makes no attempt to account for what he sees as the 'Shelleyan' influence, beyond marvelling 'that Thompson's teaching comes from those illusive lips' (*Life*, p. 165). Predictably, Patmore's influence dominates Reid's interpretation, who sees it leading Thompson 'to the centre of true vision' where 'he receives the message of a new life and responsibility' (*Francis Thompson: Man and Poet*, p. 143). For Walsh it is 'the most Patmorean' of the 'Sight and Insight' poems, which he maintains are the direct outcome of the contact with Patmore and constitute a pseudo-mystical failure with 'little left but cleverness for a second reading' (*SHSS*, p. 147). In the psychological view of the poem taken by Ella Freeman Sharp the Lady in the Garden represents an infantile regression to the womb due to an inability to come to terms with adult experience (Francis Thompson: Λ Psychoanalytical Study', *op. cit.*) But in concentrating on one possible aspect of the poem's earlier stanzas far too much is ignored in the rest.

[32] The first draft for 'Incipit Canticum Novum' is at (BC). The second forms the main part of the Thompson Collection at the State University of New York, Buffalo. It is remarkable that no writer on Thompson has seen the importance of these drafts or made any reference to them.

[33] 'Memorat Memoria' appears to have caused WM some misgivings. In his own copy of *New Poems* he wrote on the fly leaf, referring to the poem: 'This was written, I think, less in autobiography than in an imitative Swinburnian mood. At the time of its composition he was often quoting Swinburne's *Triumph of Fame*, some lines of which he left in his own writing

> I shall never be friends again with roses;
> > I shall loathe sweet tunes, where a note grows strong
> Relents and recoils, and climbs and closes,
> > As a wave of the sea turned back by song.
> There are sounds where soul's delight takes fires,
> > Face to face with its own desire;
> Λ delight that rebels, a desire that reposes;
> > I shall hate sweet music my whole life long.

There is some similarity here with Thompson's lines:

> I shall have no comfort now in scent, no ease in dew, for this;
> I shall be afraid of daffodils, and rose-buds are amiss;

It is possible that the poem was written earlier, to account for WM's assertion that Thompson was 'often quoting' Swinburne at the time, something WM would not have known during the Pantasaph period. The similarity is not as marked as WM maintains, apart from the rhythm, and does not affect the very different message of Thompson's poem or diminish the intensity of its feeling. Nor is this altered by a draft for the concluding lines WM added to his note as a further illustration to his argument. He was quoting from a source now apparently lost:

> Λ girl's kiss through my soul strikes echoes of ominous sin;
> I shall never feel a girl's soft arms without horror of the skin;

At the breath of her hair, as a phantom, mine shall creep;
You have done this to me — and I to you? It lies with sleep.

WM's copy of *New Poems* is at (G).
34 *Letters*, pp. 145: 150.
35 *Ibid.* p. 147.
36 Letter to WM, 18 Nov. 1907 (G).
37 Dr Thompson's failure to contact his son while on holiday at Rhyl is referred to in a letter from Thompson to WM dated 14 Sept. 1893 (*Letters*, p. 107). His earlier desire for a reconciliation is clear from a notebook entry that must have been made before he knew of the visit: 'Dear Father, Francis Thompson. I am earnest in this request. Put me in communication with anyone who may shortly be seeing you; unless (which I can scarcely hope) yourself should be able soon to see me' (NB BC27). Bishop Carroll's invitation is mentioned by Mrs Blackburn in a letter to WM dated 28 Feb. 1894, where she adds: 'Francis wants so much to see his people again' (G). Canon Richardson's letter to WM is also at (G). Mary's references to the meeting appear in an unpublished portion of her letter to Danchin dated 20 Jan. 1947 (see Chapter 1, note 27).
38 J. Saxon Mills, 'Francis Thompson: Some Personal Memories', *op.cit.* Dr Thompson had reason to be disturbed at the stories put about as to his son's early life. According to Edward Bok, writing in the *Dispatch* (22 April 1894), the poet's father had forced him to choose between literature and the medical profession and when he chose the former, 'cut off all personal assistance'. Thereafter, Bok continues, the young man wandered the streets of central London with his only food 'a fish caught by him in a rural brook, and fried over a few pieces of wood on the shore'. The ridiculous picture should have called the rest in question but the fact that Bok claimed he actually met Thompson on one occasion gave credence to the account as a whole and to his reflection on 'the feelings of a father who had caused so much suffering to come into the life of that son who may yet never fully overcome its terrible inroads upon his health'. Dr Thompson could have grounds for believing much of this was instigated by Thompson himself through the encounter referred to by Bok. Thompson's anxiety as to his father's reaction to this and similar articles was a strong reason for his wish to see him. According to a fragment of a letter quoted in the MS of *Life*: 'To say the truth I feared he would be hurt'. The observation, and the report by Bok, are quoted in *SHSS*, p. 139.
39 *Letters*, p. 150.
40 In a reply to a letter from WH written in March 1896 Thompson refers to 'intelligence' WM had given him concerning Lane 'which confirms my worst fears' (*ibid.* p. 141).
41 The crisis over the *Yellow Book* is fully described in J. L. May, *John Lane and the Nineties*, pp. 80–86. See also M. L. Mix, *A Study in Yellow* (1960), pp. 143ff; Jean Moorcroft Wilson, *I was an English Poet: A Critical Biography of William Watson 1858–1936* (1981). Watson was the other chief influence on Lane in excluding Beardsley from the *Yellow Book* after Wilde's arrest.
42 *Letters*, pp. 179–180.
43 *Ibid.* pp. 145–146. Walsh places this letter earlier than the preceding one. Neither is dated but it is clear from the arrangement with Constable that the references to Lane here follow the account Thompson had given in what must be the previous letter.
44 *Ibid.* p. 199. Thompson's letter to Doubleday is dated 10 Jan. 1898.
45 WM's letter was addressed to Seymour Adelman. There is no date but as he refers to his age as seventy-eight it was written during 1940. The letter is now in the Adelman Collection at Bryn Mawr College Library. It is worth nothing a curious sidelight on the affair in an obscure and incomplete draft by Thompson for a reply to what appears to have been an accusation from Lane concerning the

withdrawal of *New Poems*. Thompson defends his action solely on the grounds of Lane's association with what he again describes as 'a certain kind of literature'. The draft appears in NB 20. But Lane's accusation which called forth the reply (probably never sent) suggests there were more reasons for anxiety about the royalties than WM may have known.

[46] WM's note to John Lane, dated 7 Sept. 1897, is at (BC).

[47] *Letters*, pp. 140: 144–145: 154.
According to a receipt for payments made in March 1896 at (G) the rent for Thompson's lodgings was 15/- a week for board with an extra charge for laundry amounting to about 2/-.

[48] *Letters*, p. 177.

[49] WM's recollection of the first meeting between Thompson and Katie King was added by him in a note to the 'Ad Amicam' sequence of poems (see note 56 below).

[50] *Letters*, pp. 173–174. Between 1893 and 1894 about half a dozen short stories by Katie King were published in *ME*. Her first novel, *The Scripture Reader of Saint Marks* (1895) was followed by three others: *Father Hilarian* (1897), *A Bitter Vintage* (1899) and *Ursula* (1900). In addition she wrote a collection of short stories, *The Child who will never grow old* (1898). The story for the *Yellow Book*, 'Lucretia', appeared in the issue for July 1896. This is the only one of her writings to have been reprinted, included in a representative selection of contribution to the journal collected by Fraser Harriton under the title *The Yellow Book* (1914, Wood-bridge, 1984).

[51] Mrs King's letter, addressed to Alice Meynell and dated 22 June 1896, is at (G).

[52] Cardinal Manning's letters to Mrs King start in October 1889 and continue at regular intervals until January 1892, the month of his death (Ushaw College archives).

[53] Mrs King's letters to WM on Katie's novel, dated 12 and 14 Nov. and 11 Dec. are at (G).

[54] *Letters*, p. 179. That the visit to Patmore in July was the second of two made during Thompson's stay in London is shown by a note of thanks to Mrs Patmore for a visit that was followed by an invitation to dine with Meredith. In it Thompson mentions the second one as having been suggested before he left. As usual the note is undated (*ibid.* p. 178).

[55] 'A Lost Friend' is the opening poem for the sonnet sequence 'De Amicitia' which later formed part of a collection of twenty four poems addressed to Katie King under the title 'Ad Amicam'. They remained unpublished until five sonnets called, as a group, 'Ad Amicam', were included in *Works*, 2. Thirteen sonnets and other mainly fragmentary poems to Katie were printed in *MHW*. The remaining six poems are still in manuscript, including 'A Lost Friend'. Verses from the longest, 'Nocturns for my Friend', were published in *Life* and *Works*, 2. Others appear in SHSS, with four lines from 'A Lost Friend'.
The MSS for the 'Ad Amicam' poems are at the Lilly Library, Indiana University and the Harris Library, Preston. There are facsimiles at (BC) in the 'Ad Amicam Notebook' which also contains facsimiles of poems not addressed to Katie: 'Body and Sprite', 'Earth Plains', 'Marriage in Two Moods' and 'Eleverunt Flumina'. A further poem, 'The Singer Saith of his Song', may have been intended by Thompson as a prologue to the sonnet sequence: three stanzas are printed in *Works*, 2.

[56] Note added by Thompson to the 'De Amicitia' sequence and included in the 'Ad Amicam Notebook'. It is accompanied by WM's note on the start of the friendship (see note 49 above).

[57] Quotations from the fourth and the first sonnets in the 'De Amicitia' sequence. Both appear in *Works*, 2.

58 Quotation from the fifth sonnet in the sequence, to which Thompson gave the title 'Of her Aura'. Included in *Works*, 2, without the title.

59 Mrs King's letter to Thompson, dated 31 October 1896, is at (BC) Walsh is the only writer on Thompson who has treated the friendship with Katie in detail. He recognizes its importance but his account is conditioned by his certainty that they had marriage seriously in mind at this time. He sees the Meynells as encouraging this and having been the source of Mrs King's fears for Katie's 'reputation' — and Thompson's dismissal from London on his return from Lymington as merely meeting her 'demands'. But if they were encouraging Katie so soon afterwards to think of Thompson as a future husband, they would hardly have agreed so readily then with her mother's attitude and wishes. (See *SHSS*, pp. 157: 162–163). In addition, Mrs King wrote to him on 30 August to reassure him about some he had equvalled following an unrecorded discussion of the matter: 'Do not please be uneasy that you have in any way *betrayed* Francis Thompson to me. You have told one very little I did not know and for Katic's sake, ought to know'. Her words make the Meynells' attitude clear and exonerate them from any encouragement of the relationship. The letter is at (G).

60 Mrs King's letter to Thompson, dated 23 Nov. 1896, is at (BC).

61 Alfred Hayes's recollection of the visit and his letter to WM at the time are quoted in *Life*, pp. 248– 249.

62 NB BC20. (For the letter enclosing the poems see Chapter 9, p. 281).

63 Separate MS, quoted *IHP*, p. 98.

64 The lines were printed by EM in 'The Notebooks of Francis Thompson', *DR* (Jan. 1913). They were reprinted in *Uncollected Verses*, an anonymously edited collection of Thompson's poems based on those quoted in the article by EM and privately printed in Preston the same year.

Chapter Nine

1 *Letters*, p. 188.

2 Thompson made five attempts, at different times, at drama. The longest is the 'Pastoral Play', mainly in blank verse, which he began before leaving Wales and was based on the scenery around Pantasaph together with ideas arising from the loss of poetic inspiration. 'Venus Fly Trap', in prose, was probably first drafted as a reaction to his encounter with the aesthetes of the Cheshire Cheese since its main purpose was to satirize that group of contemporary writers. Like the 'Pastoral Play' it remained in unfinished draft form, though taken further than the fragmentary verses for a tragedy based on the life of King Saul. Two short closet plays, 'Napoleon Judges' and 'Man Proposes, Woman Disposes', were completed and later printed in *MHW*. The first concerns an imaginary incident in one of Napoleon's campaigns, the second is a caustic commentary on the changing place of women in the society of the time. Neither suggests any more promise than the unfinished drafts. But Thompson continued to have intermittant hopes, probably encouraged by his interest in the theatre. In December 1900 he sent 'Napoleon Judges' to William Archer for advice, when Archer's reply was cautiously but distinctly negative. Then in 1903 he sent the play to the editor of *T.P.'s Weekly*, again receiving an unfavourable response. (See *Letters*, p. 215: *Life*, p. 337). The MSS of all five plays are at (BC).

3 F. Duckett, *The Hundred Years: A Short Sketch of St. Peter's Catholic Church Stalybridge 1839–1946* (Stalybridge, 1946), pp. 24–25. Other information on Bishop Carroll's death has been supplied by the Secretary to the present Bishop of Shrewsbury, July 1984.

4 Katie King's letter, dated 8 Feb. 1897, is at (BC). As all her surviving letters to Thompson are now at (BC) references will not be given to future quotations from them.

5 Arthur Symons, 'New Poems', Athenaeum (12 June, 1897). There is a representative selection of other critical views in Life, pp. 239–241.

6 Quiller Couch, 'A Literary Causerie', Speaker (29 May and 5 June, 1897).

7 The lines are printed in MHW, edited from a rought draft in NB BC9 and given the title 'On a Reviewer calling my poetry "ambitious"'.

8 Letters, p. 192.

9 William Archer's letter to Thompson is quoted in Life, p. 242.

10 NB 20. The longest section runs to 28 lines, with others of varying length scattered through the remainder of the notebook.

11 MS, 'Personal Data'.

12 Quotations in this passage, in order, are from reviews for The Responsibilities of the Novelist and other Literary Essays by Frank Morris (Ac. 7 Nov. 1903), The Poetry of George Withers, ed. Frank Sidgwich (ibid. 31 Jan. 1903) and an article, 'Macaulay' (ibid. 23 Jan. 1897).

13 Letters, p. 205.

14 NB BC39.

15 Quotations in this passage, in order, are from 'A Poet's Table Talk' (Ac. 2 May, 1903): 'Wesley and his Preachers' (ibid. 6 June, 1903): 'White-hot earnest verse' (ibid. 20 April, 1901): 'The City of the Soul' (ibid. 15 July, 1899): 'The Pilgrim's Progress after two centuries (ibid. 27 Aug. 1898).

16 Letters, pp. 189–190. Walsh dates the letter 'April 1897' but as the first of the three articles, on Tennyson, appeared on 17 April, the arrangement and the correspondence concerning it, is more likely to have taken place in March.

17 Ibid. p. 204.

18 C. L. Hind, Naphtali (1926), p. 110; Authors and I (1921), p. 276. For the Academy see A. Sullivan, British Literary Magazines, op.cit. pp. 3–6.

19 The list of the 'Forty Immortals' and the 'crowning' of the writers chosen by the Academy are described by Hind in the Introduction to his edition of Stephen Phillips Christ in Hades (1917).

20 Notes made on a detached page not now traceable but quoted in SHSS, pp. 178–179. The letter to Doubleday is the one where Thompson confided the dishonest dealings for which held John Lane responsible (Letters, p. 198. See Chapter 8, p. 253).

21 Letters, pp. 196–198. There are three pages of notes on the plan for the book and the section on 'Terrible London' in the MS, 'Miscellany of F. T. fragments'.

22 Ac. (10 July, 1897).

23 The main drafts for the poetry lecture are in NB BC20. Related topics are tried out, either as alternatives or to be included, in NB 46A.

24 Letters, p. 201.

25 For the earnings of the average journalist at the time see Nigel Cross, The Common Writer: Life in Nineteenth Century Grub Street (Cambridge, 1985), pp. 226–228. For Thompson's name put forward for a Civil Pension see p. 87.

26 Letters, pp. 194: 200.

27 Feilding's letter describing the dinner and Thompson's accident is quoted in Life, pp. 187–188. He refers to it as the second of the two invitations but one dated 11 Dec. 1899 shows that this would have been the first (BC).

28 Hind, Introduction to Christ in Hades, pp. 42–43: Authors and I, pp. 130–131. See also Life, pp. 262–265.

29 References in this passage are from recollections quoted in R. Thurston Hopkins, This London, op.cit. pp. 189–192.

30 The only direct reference to the Roger Bacon Society and the Capuchins' connec-

tion with it is in *Diaries*, 2, p. 283. Blunt does not mention Thompson in the context but there are four letters from Father Cuthbert to him concerning the Society's activities and with dates and details of meetings. There is also an invitation from William Gibson for Thompson to dine with himself and his wife before a meeting in July 1898. A letter from Cuthbert sent at the same time has a pencilled note added: 'F. T. went'. A brief mention of another meeting he attended in January that year is made in *Life*, p. 183. The letters and the invitation are at (BC).

[31] Letter from J. L. Garvin to his wife, quoted in David Ayers, *Garvin of the Observer* (1985), p. 30. There is no evidence that Thompson was taking opium in 1897, the year Garvin first met him at Palace Court.

[32] *FT & WM*, p. 39.

[33] *Diaries*, 1, pp. 366–367. For the meetings with Meredith see *Life*, pp. 246–247.

[34] These lines are from a rough draft of the poem in NB 20A. Another separate MS sheet contains other lines intended for it. Some selected lines from both are printed in *MHW* as a complete poem and extracts appear in *Life*, p. 293 and *SHSS*, p. 160. Walsh finds an echo here from Shelley's 'Alastor', where the poet in fruitless pursuit of love longs to wreath 'his withered hair' with flowers no one else has bestowed on his fading youth. For Walsh's identification between Thompson and the poet of this poem see *SHSS*, Chapter 3, note 22, p. 616.

[35] 'An Arab Love song' first appeared in the *Dome* (Jan. 1899). It was reprinted in *Eyes of Youth* (1910), *op.cit*. In his note for the poem TLC is wrong in giving this as its first appearance. In the Introduction to *Eyes of Youth* G. K. Chesterton said of Thompson that 'he could write separate lines that were separate poems in themselves', quoting from 'An Arab Love Song' as an example.

[36] The contents of the proposed fourth volume of poetry were scribbled on a detached notebook cover not now traceable but quoted in *SHSS*, p. 275, note 2. The title, 'First Fruits and Aftermath' appears on a separate MS page where Thompson listed the poems on children to be included. (BC)

[37] The draft was written on detached notebook pages quoted in in *SHSS*, p. 274, note 33. The pages were then in the possession of Mrs Sowerby (Olivia Meynell) but have since been lost. Thompson's letter to Mary asking her to pray for Katie's conversion has not survived but in a letter to him, dated 18 Feb. 1898, she wrote: 'I have not forgotten your request for prayers for the conversion of your friend'. (G).

[38] The lines are printed in MHW, p. 28, edited from a separate MS draft.

[39] NB 23.

[40] Walsh suggests that the reason for the rejection was a request from Katie King that the poems addressed to her be withdrawn, on account of her engagement (*SHSS*, pp. 179: 275, note 4). But there is no reference to such a request in any of her surviving letters to Thompson and in his letter referred to in note 41 below he appears certain of her permission for their publication. The fact that Walsh was not aware of the existence of the letter in its entirety accounts for the mistake.

[41] The original of the complete letter is now at the Harris Library, Preston, Extracts from it are included in *Letters*, pp. 206–207, quoted from *La Vie*, pp. 103–104.

[42] *Letters*, p. 210. For other extracts from this letter see pp. 207–210.

[43] *Ibid*. p. 221.

[44] *Ibid*. p. 222. In his note to this letter Walsh identifies the occasions with a game described in *Life*, p. 44. But the reference there dates it to 1904, too late for the eighteen years since he last played as given by Thompson in this letter. It would make the last time in 1886, when he was living on the streets. But eighteen years from 1901, the date for the game referred to in the letter, goes back to 1883 and his years at Owens College, a much more likely period for his last game.

[45] Personal recollections, quoted in *SHSS*, p. 196.

[46] *FT & WM*, p. 86.

[47] Francis Meynell papers, Cambridge University Library. For a similar but shorter description see *My Lives, op.cit.* p. 26.

[48] Alice Meynell, 'Some Memories of Francis Thompson', *DR.* (Jan. 1908), 160–162.

[49] *Letters*, p. 227. The tableaux are described in a letter from Father Anselm recalling a Christmas spent at Palace Court at time and quoted in *FT & WM*, p. 41.

[50] *Letters*, p. 230.

[51] The lines form a rough draft with many variants in NB 15. From it an apparently finished poem is printed in *MHW*, pp. 94–95.

[52] *FT & WM*, p. 184.

[53] There are nine notebooks containing opium lists: 23: 30: 37: 47: 47A: 1: BC7: BC31: BC26. In addition there are lists on several detached notebook pages and covers at (G).

[54] According to the bibliographical lists compiled by TLC in *Lit.Crit.* and *Real RLS.* the number of Thompson's reviews so far identified amounts to 484, the majority written during the years after he left Pantasaph. The full number may never be known, as identification often depends on internal evidence, many of his reviews and articles being unsigned.

[55] Sarath Kumar Ghosh, *The Prince of Destiny* (1909), p. 181. The only previous use made of the novel in connection with Thompson is a short extract and comment in *SHSS*, p. 188.

[56] *Prince of Destiny*, p. 190.

[57] *Ibid.* p. 215.

[58] *Ibid.* p. 249.

[59] NB 47A. The lines are in draft with many variants but the sense and mood remain the same.

[60] There is a fair copy of 'A Ballad of Charity' at (G).

[61] NB BC32.

[62] NB 16. For the historical context for these extracts and for the public Odes the best survey of the course of the Empire is the trilogy by J. F. Morris: *Pax Britanica — The Climax of Empire* (1968) covers its rise: *Heavéns Command — An Imperial Progress* (1973) deals with the later developments and the period covered by the Diamond Jubilee: *Farewell the Trumpets — An Imperial Retreat* (1978) follows the decline. The main events and features in the trilogy are summarized in *Spectacle of Empire* (1982).

[63] 'To England' appeared in *Ac.* (19 March, 1898). It has not been reprinted.

[64] 'The Nineteenth Century' appeared in *Ac.* (29 Dec. 1900). It is reprinted in *Works*, 2.

[65] The Ode 'Peace' as printed in *Works*, 2 is edited from an autograph draft with many variants. But the poem as submitted to the *Daily Chronicle* no longer exists. It was based on drafts contained in NB's 43A, BC21, 12, 41 and 122. Lines from several different drafts have been edited and printed as separate poems in *MHW* with the titles 'Fuit', 'Victoria Regina: In Memoriam', 'England Old and New'. The first seven lines of the last named were included in the article by EM, 'the Notebooks of Francis Thompson', *op.cit.* and in *Uncollected Verses, op.cit.* — where they were given the title 'Written at the time of the Spanish American War'. It is worth adding that Thompson composed another 'public poem', probably as a commission he decided not to carry out. 'On the threat of the French Invision' can be dated to the time of the Fashoda Incident in 1898 when a threat of this kind was widely feared. The lines bear the mark of much patriotic poetry of the period and are of interest mainly for their similarity in metre and rhythm to an earlier 'Ecclesiantical Ballad'. In 'The Veteran of Heaven' the theme of Christ as Defender of the Church owes much to Macaulay's metrical style and the same

therefore applies to the later poem. A fair copy is preserved at the Humanities Research Centre, Texas.

66 Queen Victoria died on 22 January 1901 and 'Victoria' appeared in *Ac.* four days later. In has not been reprinted.

67 C. L. Hind, *Christ in Hades, op.cit.* p. 42. See also his *Authors and 1, op.cit.* p. 276; *Life*, p. 255. The draft of the Ode as taken to Hind for printing fills eight notebook pages at the Harris Library, Preston.

68 *Life*, pp. 311: 334.

69 *Ac.* (28 June, 1902). For Watson's Ode and its composition see Wilson, *I was an English Poet, op.cit.* pp. 63–89. For Kipling's 'The Islanders' and other public poetry see Charles Carrington, *Rydyard Kipling: His Life and Work* (1955, 3rd. edn. 1978), pp. 81–82: 380–381; Angus Wilson, *The Strange Ride of Rudyard Kipling* (1977), pp. 202–204: 238–239.

70 The fragment consists of 24 lines on a detached notebook page. The first 11 were printed in *Life*, p. 270. For the comment to Hind see *Letters*, p. 229.

71 'Of Nature, Laud and Plaint' first appeared in *Works*, 2.

72 Thompson's title for the poem was 'The Kingdom of God' with a subtitle 'In No Strange Land', possibly derived from the opening lines of Patmore's 'The Three Witnesses':

> Musing, I met, in no strange land
> What meet thou must to understand:
> An Angel.

'The Kingdom of God' first appeared in the *Athenaeum* (8 Aug. 1908), edited from a draft. The only surviving draft, very rough and with many variants including an additional stanza, has been printed in *SHSS*, pp. 191–195. Stanzas 2 and 4 were also printed in *FT & WM*, p. 156. At the time of its publication in 1908 another draft was in existence and seems to have been a fair copy. In 1904 the poem was apparently dictated by Thompson to the brother of a family friend of the Meynells, Maitland Dodd. Dodd kept it in his possession until February 1966 when he sent it to Mrs Sowerby (Olivia Meynell), who never received it. There is an element of mystery about the affair, which is recorded in correspondence between Dodd and the Meynells at (G), but no trace remains of the draft.

Chapter Ten

1 See Introduction, p. xiii and note 4.

2 'Infera' occupies some 40 pages of NB BC21, together with numerous drafts and fragments on dreams and dream states.

3 The number of Thompson's reviews and articles in his last years is based on the bibliographical lists by TLC in *Real RLS.* and *Lit.Crit.* For his probable earnings during these years see *SHSS*, p. 277, note 20.

4 For the amount of laudanum purchased by the average addict and the retail prices of opium and laudanum between the years 1885 and 1909 see Parssinen, *Secret Drugs, Secret Remedies, op.cit.* pp. 99: 229 (Table 3).

5 The fullest account of the views on opium and other forms of addiction at the time is Norman Kerr, *Inebriety or Narcomania: Its Etiology, Pathology, Treatment and Jurisprudence* (1888, 3rd. edn. 1894). For opium in particular see pp. 100–117: 312–355: 526. Kerr's main object was to show that addiction is a definite disease requiring careful medical treatment. The limited extent to which his view was held is shown in the reaction to a paper read for the Society for the Study of Inebriety

and published in the Society's *Proceedings* for November 1896. William Huntley's 'Opium Addiction: Is it a Disease?' was followed by a discussion where the majority regarded the drug as far less harmful in its effects than alcoholism.

[6] 'Thomas de Quincey', *Ac.* (9 Jan. 1897), reprinted in *Works*, 3. Thompson adopted very similar views when writing of De Quincey's *Confessions* in 'A Monument of Personality' (*ibid.* 29 April 1899).

[7] Thompson's two later articles on Coleridge appeared in *Ac.* in February 1897 and October 1903. The first of these is reprinted in *Works*, 3, and the second in *Lit.crit.*

[8] References in this passage, in order, are to 'A Bewildered Poet' (*Ac.* 16 May, 1903): 'Mangan the Unhappy' (*ibid.* 15 August, 1903): 'A Dreamer of Things Impossible' (*ibid.* 28 Sept. 1901): 'Concise but Adequate' (*ibid.* 10 Oct. 1903).

[9] Ghosh, *Prince of Destiny, op.cit.* p. 360.

[10] *Life*, p. 49. For EM's view of Thompson's sense of guilt in later years and his general manner and appearance see pp. 342–343.

[11] *Letters*, p. 113.

[12] *Ibid.* p. 215. For references to other letters quoted in the preceding paragraph see pp. 194: 199: 203: 225: 227: 212.

[13] *Ibid.* p. 257.

[14] That the disease from which Thompson was suffering in his last years was beri beri has been corroborated by a medical expert in retrospective diagnosis. In his view Thompson's letter gives an accurate description of the symptoms, which are confirmed by his deprivation during the years on the streets and his erratic eating habits since leaving Wales. Having examined all the available evidence nothing could be found to suggest that Thompson was ever consumptive. The summary that follows is based on this professional interpretation of his medical history.

[15] *Life*, p. 349. For further details of the cause of Thompson's death see ahead, pp. 395.

[16] 'Laus Amara Doloris' first appeared in *Works*, 2.

[17] *Health and Holiness* (1905), p. 21. Reprinted in *Works*, 3.

[18] *Ibid.* pp. 44–46.

[19] *Ibid.* pp. 48–49.

[20] *Ibid.* p. 59.

[21] *Ibid.* pp. 79–80.

[22] For Tyrrell's connection with the *Weekly Register* and the effects of the Joint Pastoral see J. M. Weaver (ed.) *Letters from a Modernist: The Letters of George Tyrrell to Wilfrid Ward 1893–1908* (1981), pp. 56–60; M. D. Petre, *Autobiography and Life of George Tyrrell*, 2 vols. (1912), 2, pp. 146–148. For his position at the time and the liberal Catholic movement in relation to Modernism in England see William J. Schoenl, 'George Tyrrell and the English Liberal Catholic Crisis 1900–1901', *Downside Review*, 92 (1974), 171–184.

[23] Thompson's article for the series 'Books that have influenced me' appeared in the *Weekly Register* (26 Jan. 1900).

[24] Thomas M. Loome, 'George Tyrrell: Revelation as Experience', *Heythrop Journal* (April, 1971), 117–150.

[25] George Tyrrell, *Lex Credendi* (1906), pp. 231–232. It is worth noting that, according to Basil Champneys, Tyrrell and Patmore showed 'great similarities of religious thought' and in the Preface to his biography acknowledged help provided by both Tyrrell and von Hugel (*Memoirs and Correspondence of Coventry Patmore, op.cit.* 2, p. 24: 1, p. viii.

[26] *Health and Holiness*, p. 37.

[27] *Ibid.* p. x. Tyrrell's Preface is reprinted as part of the Notes in *Works*, 3.

[28] Henri Joli, *The Psychology of the Saints* (1898), pp. 37–38. Tyrrell's review of the French original appeared in the *Month* (Dec. 1897) and was reprinted in *The Faith of the Millions* (2nd Series, 1902).

29 'A Modern Study of Sanctity', *Ac.* (13 August, 1898). The review is reprinted in *Lit.Crit.* where TLC adds an uneasy note on the reference to intuition as the highest form of reason as 'a touch of modernism' weakening the overall argument.

30 'Some Mysticisms and a Mystics', *Ac.* (14 April, 1900).

31 'Studies of English Mystic', *Atheneaum* (14 July, 1906), Reprinted in *Lit.Crit.*

32 Detached notebook page, one of several pages and fragments collected under the title 'Mysticism Jottings'

33 The MS of the 'Cancelled Preface' to *New Poems* is at BC.

34 *Life*, p. 336. When Thompson's *Saint Ignatius Loyola* was published in 1909 it was accompanied by the same engravings by H. W. and H. C. Brewer used to illustrate Rose's book. Though considerably shorter it compared favourably with the other in general presentation. It has been reprinted in the Universe Books series (1962) with an Introduction by James Broderick, SJ. He points out historical inaccuracies taken over from Rose but does not find they detract from the biography as presented by Thompson.

35 *Saint Ignatius Loyola*, p. 21.

36 *Ibid.* p. 315.

37 R. L. Mégroz, 'Portraits of Francis Thompson', the *Bookman* (April, 1927), 17–18.

38 M. Stuart Young's recollection of his meeting with Thompson appeared in the *Catholic World* (August, 1927) and is quoted in *SHSS*, p. 189.

39 Megroz, 'Portraits of Fracis Thompson'.

40 Wilfrid Whitten, 'Francis Thompson as I knew him', *John o' London's Weekly* (10 July, 1926), 437–438.

41 St. John Adcock, *London Memories* (1931), pp. 230–231.

42 F. G. Atkinson, 'Q and Francis Thompson', *op.cit.* Thompson's letter to Quiller Couch is undated but Atkinson attributes it to the period between April and October 1900 as the time when Q wrote most of the letters connected with the Oxford Book of English Verse. Other letters referred to from Thompson's correspondence are at (BC).

43 E. V. Lucas, 'Francis Thompson's Cricket Verses', *Cornhill Magazine* (July–Dec. 1908), 58–66. The article was reprinted in his *One Day and Another* (1909). A few verses from cricket poems were quoted by EM in 'The Notebooks of Francis Thompson', *op.cit.* and reprinted in *Uncollected Verses*, *op.cit.* Some other extracts appear in *Life*, pp. 41–43. Most of the drafts for these poems are in the Harris Library, Preston, in an unnumbered notebook and some 15 detached notebook pages.

44 *Life*, p. 44. For the confusing of this game with the one played in 1901 see Chapter 9 note 44. EM is also mistaken, as a result, in giving this game as the first time Thompson had played since childhood. A similar mistake was made by WM in his obituary notice: 'He who had never handled a bat since he left Ushaw College knew every famous score of the last quarter of a century' ('Mr Francis Thompson', *Athenaeum*, 23 Nov. 1907, 654–656). But WM was right in the sense that Thompson was a connoisseur rather than a player, a distinction noted also by E. V. Lucas. One of the notebook entries on cricket contains a passage on the advantages of being a connoisseur, giving the game an added range of meaning through knowledge of the skills it demands (NB 35).

45 Mary Thompson's letter to WM on her correspondence with her brother, dated 15 Nov. 1907, is at (G). Her surviving letters to Thompson are at (BC). One contains a description of a sunset that merits the observation of a member of her community, Sister Veronica, who knew her in her last years. By then it seems 'she had something of a poet in her herself'. Mary died on 29 December 1954, aged ninety-three.

46 *Life*, pp. 279–284.

47   The list of 'Preferences' is at (G).
48   References in this passage, in order, are to NB's BCIO: BC29: 12: BC5.
49   NB 16.
50   NB BC21.
51   NB 2.
52   NB 50.
53   NB 8Λ.
54   NB BC8.
55   The MS of 'The Heretic's Tragedy' is at the Harris Library, Preston.
56   The poem forms part of a collection of MS and notebook pages with the title 'Light Verses'.
57   NB BC18,
58   MS 'Francis Thompson's Drawings'. This is a folder containing 10 drawings, mostly extracted from the notebooks.
59   There is a draft for 'Earth Plains' in NB 103 from which the quotation is taken. Thompson seems to have hoped to take the 'Fragment' further as he made a fair copy. The MS of this copy is at the Lilly Library, Indiana University.
60   Single MS sheet.
61   NB BC39.
62   There are 14 surviving letters to EM written between January and August 1905 (*Letters*, pp. 236–249). The doggerel verses on the need for a shirt appear in *Life*, p. 331.
63   Harriet Monroe, *A Poet's Life*, pp. 148–149, quoted in *SHSS*, p. 196. Walsh points out the mistake in the date given for this description as 1897. As the meeting was at Granville Place it must have been after the Meynells moved there in 1905 (see *SHSS*, p. 279, note 33).
64   Alice Meynell's letter describing the incident is at (G). It is quoted in Badini, *Slender Tree*, *op. cit.* p.175. For other family recollections of Thompson at Granville Place see *Life*, p. 314.
65   The lines are quoted from the text as it appears in *Works*, 3 and subsequent editions of Thompson's poetry. There are six further lines to the passage in the final text as sent to WM, which are included in the first published version in *DR* (April, 1906). The MS of Thompson's final text is in the Ushaw College archives.
66   The drafts are mainly divided between NB's 50 and 53.
67   NB 50. Twenty one lines, taken almost at random from this draft and edited as a poem with the title 'The Time is Now', were printed by EM in 'The Notebooks of Francis Thompson', *op.cit.* (Reprinted in *Uncollected Verses, op.cit.*)
68   *Letters*, p. 257.
69   *Ibid.* pp. 252–253.
70   *Ibid.* p. 255. Mrs Blackburn's letter to WM on Thompson's health, dated 30 Jan. 1906, is at (G).
71   Recollections by Father Richard Pagne OSFC, at an interview with the author, June 1985.
72   *Letters*, p. 261.
73   Quoted in *Life*, p. 280.
74   *Ibid.* p. 279.
75   *Letters*, p. 265.
76   'Henry James, The American Scene', *Athenaeum* (9 March, 1907). Reprinted in *Lit.Crit.*
77   Quoted in *SHSS*, p. 206, from a notebook then in the possession of Mrs Lucas (Madeleine Meynell) but not located since.
78   The last notebook is known as the 'Large Commonplace Book'. The lines intended as a Preface for the collection of prose were first printed by Alice Meynell in 'Some Memories of Francis Thompson', *op.cit.* (Reprinted in *Uncollected Verses*,

op.cit.) They were placed by WM at the start of *Works*, 3, the first collection of Thompson's prose to be published.
79 *Diaries*, 2, p. 180.
80 *Ibid.* p. 181.
81 *Ibid.* p. 222.
82 The extract is copied into the 'Large Commonplace Book'. Thompson's review of the third volume of the *Works of Sir Thomas Browne*, ed. Charles Sayle, appeared in the *Athenaeum* (19 Oct. 1907).
83 *Letters*, p. 266.
84 *Life*, p. 327. EM says this was the only portrait made of Thompson. He avoids referring to the pencil drawing by himself made during Thompson's last years and apparently did not know of the portrait by Ponsonby Staples made in 1897. Staples was known to the Meynells and was in London that year when he was exhibiting at the Royal Academy. See Algernon Graves, *The Royal Academy of Arts: A Complete Dictionary of the Contributors 1769–1904*, 7 (1906). It is worth adding that another well known artist of the time, William Rothenstein, was also a visitor at Palace Court. He liked Thompson for his individuality and as a portrait painter was attracted by his 'sad, brooding eyes'. For Rothenstein's observations see his *Men and Memories: 1872–1900* (1931), p. 282.
85 *Diaries*, 2, p. 187.
86 *Life*, p. 349.
87 The information on Thompson's admission to the Hospital of Saints John and Elizabeth was given to Walsh by a member of the staff. See *SHSS*, p. 213. Thompson's assertion as to the amount of opium he had been taking was reported by Dr E. V. Williams to WM in a letter dated 22 Nov. 1907 (G).
88 Father Vincent McNabb's letter, dated 11 Jan. 1908, is at (G).
89 McNabb's recollection of Thompson repeating the lines from 'The Poppy' appears in his article 'Francis Thompson', the *Universe* (2 Oct. 1908). For his refusal to administer the Last Rites see also K. Tynan, *Middle Years*, *op.cit.* pp. 348–349.
90 There is a copy of Thompson's will, dated 12 November 1907, at (G).

Conclusion

1 Letter to WM, dated 14 Nov. 1907, quoted in *Life*, pp. 81–82.
2 Caleb Saleeby's letter to WM, postmarked 13 Nov. 1907, is at (G).
3 Dr Williams' letter to WM, dated 22 Nov. 1907, is quoted in *SHSS*, p. 220. Walsh saw the original, then in the possession of Olivia Sowerby but since her death it has not been located. Of the writers on Thompson Walsh is the only one who has raised doubts as to the cause of his death but has allowed tuberculosis to be at least a contributing factor. It is necessary, however, to call the death certificate in more serious question than he has done, it now being clear that Thompson did not suffer from tuberculosis at any earlier period and showed no symptoms of the disease during his last months other than loss of weight. It should be added that Viola Meynell did in fact comment on this as an unexplained aspect of his condition (*FT & WM*, p. 190).
4 Blunt recorded WM's request for the obituary and the reason for it in a diary entry for 14 Nov. 1907 (*Diaries*, 2, p. 189). A separate folder at (G) contains well over fifty obituary notices and later accounts of Thompson's career cut from newspapers and journals. A survey of the main ones immediately following his death appeared in the *Tablet* (30 Nov. 1907).

5　*Diaries*, 2, p. 315.
6　WM's phrase occurs in an undated letter to TLC, probably written between 1932 and 1937 (BC). For descriptions of the Meynells' home in Sussex and for their later lives see Badini, *Slender Tree, op.cit.* p. 204; *FT & WM*, pp. 194–196: 205; *SHSS*, pp. 221–223. A whole chapter in *IHP* is devoted to the family's home in WM's extreme old age by TLC in 1946. For a summary of the later lives of the Meynell children see Pamela Hinkson, 'Clan Meynell', the *Tablet* (1 Feb. 1975).
7　The lines form a separate MS draft, printed in *MHW* with the title 'A Question'.

Select Bibliography

For manuscript sources see Introduction.
The place of publication is London unless otherwise stated.

1. THOMPSON'S WRITINGS

Poetry: Collections and Selections

The list does not include individual poems, such as the many editions of 'The Hound of Heaven' during the decade following Thompson's death.

Poems (London and Boston, 1893)
New Poems (1897)
Selected Poems, edited by Wilfrid Meynell (1908)
Works of Francis Thompson, edited by Wilfrid Meynell, 3 vols. (1913). Poetry:
vols. 1 & 2
Collected Poetry of Francis Thompson (1913)
Uncollected Verses by Francis Thompson (privately printed, 1917)
Complete Poetical Works of Francis Thompson (New York, n.d., c. 1920)
Youthful Verses by Francis Thompson (privately printed, Preston, 1928)
Selected Poems, revised edition (New York, 1930)
The Poems of Francis Thompson, edited by Francis Meynell (n.d., c. 1930)
The Poems of Francis Thompson, edited by Terence L. Connolly, S. J. (New York, 1932, revised edition, Westport, Connecticut, 1979)
The Poems of Francis Thompson, edited by Wilfrid Meynell (Oxford, 1937)
Selected Poems of Francis Thompson, edited by Paul Beard (1938)
Collected Poems of Francis Thompson (1946)
The Man has Wings: New Poems and Plays by Francis Thompson, edited by Terence L. Connolly, S. J. (Garden City, 1932)

Prose

Life of Blessed John Baptist de la Salle (1891, reprinted from *ME* April, 1891)
Health and Holiness (1905)
Shelley (1909)
Saint Ignatius Loyola, edited by John H. Pollen, S. J., (1909)
Works of Francis Thompson, edited by Wilfrid Meynell, 3 vols. (1913). Prose:

vol. 3
Sir Leslie Stephen as a Biographer (privately printed, 1915)
Selected Essays (1917)
A Renegade Poet and Other Essays, with Introduction by Edward J. O'Brien (Boston, 1920)
Literary Criticisms of Francis Thompson, newly discovered and edited by Terence L. Connolly, S. J., (New York, 1948)
Minor Poets: Criticisms by Francis Thompson, newly discovered and edited by Terence L. Connolly, S. J., (Los Angeles, 1949)
The Letters of Francis Thompson, edited by John Evangelist Walsh (New York, 1969)

2. BOOKS ABOUT THOMPSON: BIOGRAPHICAL AND CRITICAL

Connolly, Terence L., S. J., *Francis Thompson, In His Paths* (Milwaukee, 1944)
Danchin, Piérre, *Francis Thompson: La Vie et l'Oeuvre d'un Poéte* (Paris, 1959)
de la Gorce, Alice, *Francis Thompson*, translated from the French by H. F. Kynaston Snell (1933)
Megroz, R. L. *Francis Thompson: The Poet of Earth in Heaven* (1927)
Meynell, Everard, *The Life of Francis Thompson* (1913, revised and condensed, 1926)
Meynell, Viola, *Francis Thompson and Wilfrid Meynell* (1952)
Owlett, F. T. *Francis Thompson* (1936)
Reid, J. C. *Francis Thompson: Man and Poet* (1959)
Rooker, J. K. *Francis Thompson*, reprinted from a thesis written in French (1913)
Thomson, John, *Francis Thompson, the Preston born Poet* (1912, third revised edition, *Francis Thompson, Poet and Mystic*, 1933)
Thomson, Paul van K. *Francis Thompson: A Critical Biography* (New York, 1961)
Walsh, John Evangelist, *Strange Harp, Strange Symphony: The Life of Francis Thompson* (1968)
Wright, F. C. *Francis Thompson* (1936)

3. BOOKS ON THE RELIGIOUS, LITERARY, HISTORICAL & SOCIAL BACKGROUND

Abrams, M. H. *The Milk of Paradise* (New York, 1934)
Alexander, Calvert, *The Catholic Literary Revival* (Milwaukee, 1922)
Aveling, J. C. H. *The Handle and the Axe* (1976)
Badeni, Jane, *The Slender Tree: A Life of Alice Meynell* (Padstow, 1981)
de Bary, Richard, *Franciscan Days of Vigil* (1910)
Beck, Bishop G. A., (editor), *The English Catholics, 1850–1950* (1950)
Blunt, Wilfrid Scawen, *My Diaries*, 2 vols. (1919)
Booth, Charles, *Life and Labours of the People in London*, 16 vols. (1892–1902)
Bossy, John, *The English Catholic Community, 1570–1850* (1975)

Bowman, Winifred M. *England in Ashton-under-Lyne* (Altrincham, 1960)

Campbell, Anthony, *The Two Faces of Homoeopathy* (1984)

Chadwick, Owen, *The Victorian Church*, 2 vols. (1970)

Champneys, Basil, *Memoirs and Correspondence of Coventry Patmore*, 2 vols. (1900)

Chesney, Kellow, *The Victorian Underworld* (1970)

Cooper, J. C. *Fairy Tales: Allegories of the Inner Life* (Wellingborough, 1983)

Cross, Nigel, *The Common Writer. Life in Nineteenth Century Grub Street* (Cambridge, 1985)

Dyos, H. J. & M. Wolff (editors), *The Victorian City: Images and Realities*, 2 vols. (1973)

Eliade, Mircea, *Myths, Dreams and Mysteries* (1960)

Evans, B. Ifor, *English Poetry in the later Nineteenth Century* (1933, second revised edition, 1966)

Fiddes, Edward, *Chapters in the History of Owens College and of Manchester University, 1851–1914* (Manchester, 1937)

Fraser, Hilary, *Beauty and Belief. Aesthetics and Religion in Victorian Literature* (Cambridge, 1986)

le Gallienne, Richard, *The Romantic Nineties* (1926, new edition, 1951)

Ghosh, Sarath Kumar, *The Prince of Destiny: The New Krishna* (1909)

Gray, Robert, *Cardinal Manning: A Biography* (1985)

Gwynn, Denis, *The Second Spring, 1818–1852* (1942)

Hahnemann, Samuel, *Organon of Medicine* (Köthen, 1810, sixth edition reprinted 1983)

Hastings, Adrian (editor), *Bishops and Writers. Aspects of Modern English Catholicism* (Wheathampsted, 1977)

Haytor, Alethea, *Opium and the Romantic Imagination* (1968)

Hickey, John, *Urban Catholics. Urban Catholicism in England and Wales from 1829 to the present day* (1967)

Holmes, J. Derek, *More Roman than Rome: English Catholicism in the Nineteenth Century* (1978)

Jackson, Holbrook, *The Eighteen Nineties* (1913)

Jerrold, Blanchard, & Gustave Doré, *London: A Pilgrimage* (1872, reprinted New York, 1970)

Jung, C. G. *Symbols of Transformation* (1911–1912, reprinted in *Collected Works* 5 (ii), 1952)

Jung, C. G. *Symbols of Transformation* (1911–1912, reprinted in *Collected Works* 5 (ii), 1952)

Jung, C. G. *The Archetypes and the Collective Unconscious* (1934, second edition reprinted to *Collected works* 9 (1), 1969)

Keating, Peter (editor), *Into Unknown England, Selections from the Social Explorers* (Glasgow and Manchester, 1976)

King, Katharine Douglas, *The Scripture Reader of St. Mark's* (1895)

King, Katharine Douglas, *Father Hilarion* (1897)

King, Katharine Douglas, *The Child who will never grow old* (1898)

King, Katharine Douglas, *A Bitter Vintage* (1899)

King, Katharine Douglas, *Ursula* (1900)

Knight, Stephen, *The Brotherhood. The Secret World of Freemasonry* (1984)

Leys, M. D. R. *Catholicism in England* (1961)

Lomax, Elizabeth, 'The Uses and Abuses of Opiates in Nineteenth Century England', *Bulletin of the History of Medicine*, 47 (1933), 167–176

Longford, Elizabeth, *A Pilgrimage of Passion. The Life of Wilfrid Scawen Blunt* (1979)

Mathew, David, *Catholicism in England 1598–1935: Portrait of a Minority, its Culture and Traditions* (1936, second revised edition, 1948)

May, John Lewis, *John Lane and the Nineties* (1936)

Mayhew, Henry, *London Labour and the London Poor*, 4 vols. (1861–1864, reprinted 1967)

Meynell, Francis, *My Lives* (New York, 1971)

Meynell, Viola, *Alice Meynell: A Memoir* (1929, reprinted in the *Life and Letters* series, 1933)

Meynell, Viola, *Francis Thompson and Wilfrid Meynell: A Memoir* (1952)

Milbourn, David, *A History of Ushaw College* (Durham, 1964)

Morris, J. *The Spectacle of Empire* (1982)

Nelson, James G. *The Early Nineties. A View from his Bodley Head* (Cambridge, Mass. 1971)

Neuman, Charles, *The Evolution of Medical Education in the Nineteenth Century* (Oxford, 1957)

Neumann, Erich, *The Origin and History of Consciousness* (1954)

Neumann, Erich, *The Great Mother. An Analysis of the Archetype* (1955)

Norman, Edward R. *Anti Catholicism in Victorian England* (1968)

Norman, Edward R. *The English Catholic Church in the Nineteenth Century* (Oxford 1984)

Parssinen, Terry M. *Secret Passions, Secret Remedies: Narcotic Drugs in British Society 1820–1930* (Manchester, 1983)

Patmore, Coventry, *Religio Poetae* (1893)

Patmore, Coventry, *The Rod, the Root and the Flower* (1895)

Patmore, Coventry, *Poems of Coventry Patmore*, edited by F. Page (Oxford 1949)

Patmore, Derek, *The Life and Times of Coventry Patmore* (1949)

Purcell, E. S. *Life of Cardinal Manning, Archbishop of Westminster*, 2 vols. (1895)

Reid, J. C. *The Mind and Art of Coventry Patmore* (1957)

Rowell, D. Geoffrey, *Hell and the Victorians. A Study of Nineteenth Century Theological Controversies concerning Eternal Punishment and the Future Life* (Oxford, 1974)

Schiefen, Richard J. *Nicholas Wiseman and the Transformation of English Catholicism* (Shepherdstown, 1984)

Secker, Martin, *The Eighteen Nineties* (1948)

Stanford, Derek, *Critics of the Nineties* (1970)

Stedman, James Gareth, *Outcast London. A Study in the Relationship between Classes in Victorian Society* (1971, new edition, Harmondsworth, 1984)

Symondson, J. A., (editor), *The Victorian Crisis of Faith* (1970)

Tuell, Anne Kimball, *Mrs. Meynell and her Literary Generation* (New York, 1925)

Ward, Bernard, *The Sequel to Catholic Emancipation, 2 vols.* (1915)

Ward, Maisie, *The Wilfrid Wards and the Transition*, 2 vols. (1934)

Weir, John, 'British Homeopathy during the last Hundred Years', *British Medical Journal*, 2 (1932), 603–605

Index